Advanced Techniques in AutoCAD

Advanced Techniques in
AutoCAD®

Robert M. Thomas

San Francisco • Paris • Düsseldorf • London

Cover art by Thomas Ingalls + Associates
Cover photography by Michael Lamotte
Book design by Jeffrey James Giese

Library of Congress Card Number: 87-62724
ISBN 0-89588-437-2
Manufactured in the United States of America
10 9 8 7 6 5 4 3 2 1

To my wife,
Krista Diane Thomas,
with love.

ACKNOWLEDGMENTS

This book was a team effort. I am very grateful to many people who gave a great deal to help create this book: Valerie Robbins, developmental editor at SYBEX, who led the way in organizing and unifying the original manuscript; Michael Wolk and Kay Luthin, copy editors, for making it readable and consistent with itself; Fran Grimble, developmental editor, for her additional editorial support and advice; Jeff Giese and Dan Tauber for technical review; Greg Hooten for technical advice and support early on; Paul Erickson and Scott Campbell for word processing; Jonathan Rinzler for proofreading; Jeff Giese and Amparo del Rio for design and pasteup; Michelle Hoffman for producing the screen shots; and Cheryl Vega for typesetting.

Special thanks to Francia Friendlich and Rich Teich of the Aquarian Age Computer Center in San Francisco, for getting the ball rolling in 1985 and for backing up this project ever since with considerable expertise and support.

Special thanks to the architectural firm David Baker + Associates of Berkeley, California, for the use of the sample drawings.

Thanks to my students and seminar attendees, who were generous in their suggestions and never hesitated to tell me what they needed to know.

And finally, thanks to Roscoe and Elaine for their spirit of adventure, and for being there when they were needed.

Table of Contents

Chapter 3: Custom Line Types and Hatch Patterns

Chapter 4: Shape Files and Text-Font Files

Chapter 7: Introduction to AutoLISP

Chapter 8: Fundamental AutoLISP Functions

Chapter 9: Enhanced Macros with AutoLISP

Chapter 10: Writing LISP Files

INTRODUCTION

If you have mastered the basics of AutoCAD and are looking for ways to increase your drawing productivity, as well as for ways to make the CAD process faster and easier, then this book was written for you. It will show you how to use your own drawing style to create a unique, customized version of AutoCAD that is built around your needs.

WHO SHOULD READ THIS BOOK

You can use this book even if you are not an AutoCAD expert; the only requirements are that you understand the basic command structure and have a little practice in using the program. This book refers to many AutoCAD commands, but it does not explain their fundamental use. If you are completely new to the program, you should come back to this book a little later.

You do not need to be a computer expert or programmer to use this book. Some computer programming concepts are touched upon in these pages, but they are mentioned only when they are necessary for teaching you AutoCAD customization skills. This book assumes that you are a drawing professional, more interested in maximizing your use of AutoCAD than in becoming a professional computer programmer. Thus, you should not think of this book as a programming tutorial. If it inspires you to learn more about computer programming and the LISP language in particular, so much the better. Many good books that deal with this subject in depth are available to you in your local library or computer bookstore.

Customization is worthwhile. To use AutoCAD only in its off-the-shelf version is to waste this product, because AutoCAD is expressly written to be customized. The off-the-shelf product is only a foundation for the elegant product you can create.

Learning to customize an AutoCAD program is no more difficult than learning basic AutoCAD. You must learn some new terminology, study the examples, and above all, practice and experiment. Customization is really an investment in time and patience. The investment is well worth it, because customization can offer you significant profit. You will make AutoCAD easier for yourself and for those who use the systems you develop. If you persist, you might even develop a third-party AutoCAD application you can market to other users.

HOW TO USE THIS BOOK

The best way to use this book is to read it while you have AutoCAD up and running close by. You can then run through the examples for yourself and assimilate the underlying concepts as fully and quickly as possible.

This book should be read from front to back. The chapters build upon each other, moving from simpler material to the more complex. Everyone should read Chapter 1, "Overview." After that, you may skim ahead to material that is of particular interest to you. However, be prepared to back up to previous chapters if you suddenly find yourself too far ahead.

Although the examples in this book will stand alone and you may be able to put several of them to use right away, that is not all they are intended to do. The examples are intended to spark your imagination and to get you thinking about your needs and the steps necessary to create completely original features, commands, and routines. You may get your money's worth just typing in the examples, but taking the time to read and understand the commentary and explanations will pay the biggest dividends.

WHAT THIS BOOK IS ABOUT

This book serves as a bridge between the customization concepts presented in the AutoCAD/AutoLISP documentation and the user who is apt to skim over those concepts because of limited background in what the documentation is presenting. You cannot successfully use this book as a replacement for AutoCAD's documentation. You will want to return to the AutoCAD/AutoLISP documentation after you complete this book; you will then find that the documentation is easier to understand.

The contents of the book include the following:

- Chapter 1 presents an overview of AutoCAD.

- Chapter 2 discusses AutoCAD's relationship to the computer's disk operating system and illustrates techniques for maximizing its performance.

- Chapters 3 and 4 show you how to expand and modify some AutoCAD features: line types, hatch patterns, shapes, and text fonts.

- Chapters 5 and 6 present techniques for reconfiguring the AutoCAD screen and digitizer menus, and for creating new menus from scratch.

- Chapters 7 through 12 introduce you to AutoCAD's internal instruction language, AutoLISP. These chapters show you how to create new commands, features, and utilities that can improve performance and increase AutoCAD's power to serve you.

The book has three appendices. Appendix A includes a few lengthy LISP routines for you to study, modify, improve upon, or just copy and use if you so desire. Appendix B presents third-party products and vendors, which will be of interest to AutoCAD customizers. Appendix C discusses customization techniques that can be used with the latest version of the program, AutoCAD Release 9. Features of the new version include fully customizable pull-down menus and pop-up icon menus, as well as the ability to redefine standard AutoCAD commands.

WHICH VERSION OF AUTOCAD SHOULD YOU USE?

I recommend that, if possible, you use AutoCAD Version 2.6 or later. Much of the material will work if you have Version 2.18 with ADE-3, including the hatch patterns, line types, shape files (without bulge arcs), and many of the macros and AutoLISP functions. Almost everything will work with Version 2.5. Where Version 2.6 is required, it is so noted. This version is preferred because it contains powerful new features and new AutoLISP functions that will save you the trouble of defining additional complex functions of your own, making your customization process easier. AutoCAD Release 9 is the most recent version at the time of this writing.

OBTAINING THE EXAMPLES ON DISK

If you do not wish to type the examples and AutoLISP programs yourself, you can obtain them on disk. Use the order form at the end of this book, and specify your version number when ordering. If your version of AutoCAD is 2.5 or later, the disk also contains a bold outline font in a style similar to Helvetica (both SHP and SHX). (You must specify that your version number is 2.5 or later to receive this font file.)

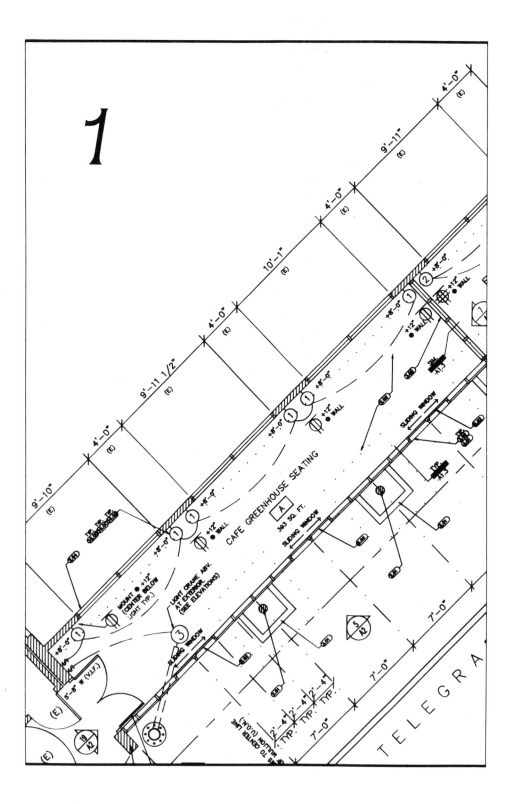

Chapter 1
Overview

ONE OF THE MAJOR REASONS for AutoCAD's position as the standard for PC-based CAD is its adaptability. AutoCAD can be modified to meet the needs of drafters and designers of virtually any discipline. Learning to modify the program is, of course, up to AutoCAD users, who, for the most part, are drawing professionals under strict deadlines with little time to master the skills needed to customize and reconfigure computer programs. However, the basic concepts related to the customization of AutoCAD are actually far simpler to learn than they may first appear, and the results easily justify the investment of time taken to learn them.

This book shows you what parts of the program can be customized. It demonstrates the techniques necessary to design and develop a version of AutoCAD containing specialized features to make your drawing process as efficient as possible.

To benefit from this book, you must have at least a working knowledge of the fundamentals of AutoCAD. If you are able to create and make changes to drawing entities in AutoCAD, you should be able to understand the material presented here.

WHAT DOES CUSTOMIZATION INVOLVE?

Customizing AutoCAD can take a variety of forms, from creating simple custom drawing entities, through the creation of custom screen menus and command macros, to the development of unique AutoCAD commands based on AutoCAD's internal programming language, AutoLISP.

As you will see in Chapter 2, customizing AutoCAD for your requirements can also involve reorganizing your files into subdirectories, which will give you the ability to choose easily between multiple configurations of the same program; setting up AutoCAD to work from a RAM disk to increase processing speed; and configuring AutoCAD to run other programs (for example, your word processor) while inside the Drawing Editor.

Chapter 3 shows you how to develop libraries of your own custom line types and hatch patterns. Chapter 4 shows you how to create and compile shape files that contain your basic drawing entities and symbols. These resources save you from having to recreate the same patterns and symbols repeatedly and from maintaining a large number of external block-drawing files. Chapter 4 also introduces you to the technique for creating your own text fonts, so that your text insertions can give your drawings a unique appearance.

Chapters 5 and 6 demonstrate how the AutoCAD screen menu works and how it can be changed to suit your drawing preferences. You will also learn how to incorporate AutoCAD commands into macros that accomplish a series of tasks with a single-screen menu selection.

Chapters 7 and 8 examine AutoLISP, AutoCAD's internal programming language. AutoLISP can be used to create your own AutoCAD commands for performing calculations and analysis, and for producing drawing entities. It can also be used to develop special utility commands to simplify and speed up the drawing process. Subsequent chapters present these techniques in more detail.

Chapter 9 shows you how to incorporate AutoLISP syntax into macros. Chapter 10 demonstrates LISP *routines*—LISP functions that work together in series to accomplish complex tasks. Chapter 11 provides example LISP routines that demonstrate different approaches to various drawing problems. Chapter 12 examines *entity-access* functions, used for direct manipulation of AutoCAD's drawing-entity database.

WHY BOTHER CUSTOMIZING?

Is it really worth spending the time necessary to customize and reconfigure AutoCAD? Even though I know that hundreds of AutoCAD users are satisfied with the product as it was supplied from Autodesk, I believe the answer is yes.

Most of the time spent producing and editing drawings in AutoCAD is spent in selecting and/or typing commands in a precise order, and then selecting the correct options within those commands. For the experienced AutoCAD user, customization can make the process of drawing more efficient by allowing you to combine long series of keystrokes into just a few. In addition, if the process of creating a drawing involves calculations, customization can build these calculations right into the drawing commands.

Some part of the AutoCAD drawing process undoubtedly will be spent managing the program—changing layers, turning them on and off, adjusting the grid, setting drawing parameters, and so on. A customized version of AutoCAD will reduce the amount of time spent on these management tasks and allow the user to focus on the actual drawing and design.

A customized AutoCAD, once developed, can also benefit the inexperienced user by presenting a more compact, familiar interface that reduces learning time and offers the opportunity to produce usable drawings as soon as possible.

Why didn't AutoCAD provide these things in the first place? In a way, it did provide them. AutoCAD is not just a drawing program. It is also a large, comprehensive toolbox containing a vast array of drawing tools. These tools are the basis for a program that can be used by many different kinds of drafters. Undoubtedly some tools will be more useful to you than others. The process of customizing AutoCAD, therefore, is the process of arranging the tools in a way that is most efficient for you, bringing the more frequently used tools together, and using the existing tools to create new drawing tools of your own.

INTRODUCTION TO ASCII FILES

Most word processors add special codes to your document as you produce it. These embedded codes handle printing and formatting tasks such as underlining, boldfacing, word wrapping, and paragraph reforming. An *ASCII file* is simply a file that does not contain any of these special printing and formatting codes. ASCII files contain only letters of the alphabet, numerals, and standard punctuation marks.

Customizing AutoCAD involves creating and editing ASCII files, which are read and used by the AutoCAD program at various times during its processing. The DOS text editor, EDLIN, can be used to produce and edit an ASCII file, but the most efficient way to do this is to use a word processor.

Computer instructions are referred to as *source code;* thus ASCII files that contain computer instructions are known as *source-code files.* AutoCAD handles source-code files in one of two ways: it either reads the source code directly, interpreting each line in the file in sequence, or it compiles the source code into a different, machine-readable format. Each treatment has its advantages, but in either case the result is the same: AutoCAD carries out the instructions that it finds in the source-code file.

When AutoCAD is given a command that causes it to read one of its source-code files, it may do one of two things:

- Locate the appropriate file and copy the entire contents of that file into an area of memory reserved for that purpose. This process of placing the contents of the file into memory is called *loading* the file. Once the file is loaded, AutoCAD can respond to its contents more efficiently. AutoLISP files and AutoCAD shape files, for instance, are loaded in this fashion.

- Locate the appropriate file and copy only that part of the file into memory that it has been instructed to find. In the case of long ASCII files, such as the file containing the standard AutoCAD hatch patterns or a file containing line-type definitions, this approach is more efficient.

AUTOCAD'S MODIFIABLE SOURCE-CODE FILES

AutoCAD recognizes source-code files by their file-name extensions, a group of three letters placed after the file's unique name and separated from the file's name by a period. The source-code file-name extensions recognized by AutoCAD are LIN, LSP, MNU, PAT, PGP, and SHP. The following are brief descriptions of each of these types of files. In cases where a file type may have several different names, an asterisk is used to represent the file name.

*.LIN

An ASCII file with this extension contains information required by AutoCAD to draw different line types. AutoCAD's standard line types are contained in the file ACAD.LIN. You can add line types of your own creation to this file or build up a library of line types in different files, provided they are each given a unique name and the extension LIN.

Individual line types are also given unique names to identify them within the LIN file. When you wish to use a new line type, the new line-type information must be retrieved from the LIN file and stored within the drawing database. The AutoCAD command for loading a new line type is LINETYPE. When you issue this command, AutoCAD first prompts for the name of the line type, and then for the name of the file to search in order to find the line-type information. When the line-type information is located, AutoCAD displays a message to that effect.

New line-type definitions can be added to LIN files from within Auto-CAD's Drawing Editor, giving you the capability of creating new line types "on the fly" as drawing progresses.

*.LSP

An ASCII file with this extension contains source code written in Auto-LISP, AutoCAD's internal programming language. It is common for customized AutoCAD to use many different AutoLISP files. Files containing AutoLISP source code can have any of a number of names, but they are required to have the extension LSP for AutoCAD to recognize them and properly interpret their contents. Currently, AutoCAD does not compile these files. Instead, it loads them into memory and executes their instructions in sequence.

*.MNU

This file extension identifies an AutoCAD screen-menu file, which contains screen-menu prompts as well as the commands that are executed when you choose from displayed options using your pointing device. You can create any number of AutoCAD menus; each one must have its own unique name and the extension MNU.

Earlier versions of AutoCAD treat this file differently than later versions. Versions 2.18 and earlier read the file directly and display it on the screen. Versions 2.5 and later compile the menu file and display the compiled version. This process of compiling the menu takes place automatically the first time the MNU file is loaded into AutoCAD's Drawing Editor and whenever the file is edited. By compiling the menu file (which is often quite large) AutoCAD saves time both in the loading process and the menu display during drawing sessions.

Once compiled, the machine-readable version of the menu file is contained in a separate file. This separate file has the same file name but a new extension, MNX. Thereafter, only this compiled version of the menu is loaded and displayed. The source-code version remains available, in case you want to make additional changes to it.

The compiled version of AutoCAD's standard menu is contained in the file ACAD.MNX. The source code for the standard menu is contained in the file ACAD.MNU. ACAD.MNU is not automatically installed on your hard disk with the other AutoCAD files. Therefore, before you can modify it, you must copy it onto your AutoCAD subdirectory.

It is wise to change the name of ACAD.MNU when copying it onto your AutoCAD subdirectory. This prevents AutoCAD from overwriting its standard menu with any unwanted changes you happen to make.

ADVANCED TECHNIQUES IN AUTOCAD

You will find ACAD.MNU on the AutoCAD Support Files disk in a separate subdirectory called SOURCE. To copy it onto your AutoCAD subdirectory, follow these steps:

1. Place your AutoCAD Support Files disk in drive A. (Substitute the letter of your floppy drive if it is different.)

2. Log onto your AutoCAD subdirectory.

3. Enter this command:

COPY A:\SOURCE\ACAD.MNU CUSTOM.MNU

In a moment or so, DOS will respond with the message

1 file(s) copied

This places a copy of ACAD.MNU on your AutoCAD subdirectory and gives it the name CUSTOM.MNU. You may modify CUSTOM.MNU without fear of harming AutoCAD's standard menu or its original source code.

*.SHP

An ASCII file with this extension contains definitions of drawing symbols, shapes, or objects that can be inserted into a drawing in ways similar to a block. AutoCAD compiles this file into another file, which is given the file extension SHX. These files are referred to as *shape files*. Shape files are loaded into the drawing database using the AutoCAD LOAD command. After the shape file is loaded, the shapes may be inserted into the drawing using the AutoCAD SHAPE command. Shape insertion is faster than block insertion, but it is intended to be used with relatively simple drawing symbols. For complex symbols or one-time insertions, block insertion is the preferred method.

A *text font file* is a special type of SHP file, which contains shapes that correspond to text fonts as well as special shape definitions that indicate the overall scale and orientation of those characters. The source code for AutoCAD's standard text fonts is stored in these files: TXT.SHP, SIMPLEX.SHP, COMPLEX.SHP, ITALIC.SHP, MONOTXT.SHP, and VERTICAL.SHP. These files can also be found on the SOURCE subdirectory of the AutoCAD Support Files disk. Copy them onto your AutoCAD system subdirectory if you plan to edit them.

ACAD.PAT

This file contains AutoCAD hatch patterns. Unlike the previous files, you cannot use several files with the extension PAT—AutoCAD recognizes only ACAD.PAT. You can add hatch pattern definitions of your own to the list of standard patterns contained in this file, using your word processor.

ACAD.PGP

ACAD.PGP contains nonAutoCAD commands that can be accessed from within the Drawing Editor. This file is the only one that can use the file-name extension PGP. We will begin customizing AutoCAD by making a modification to this file. Once it is modified, you will be able to move back and forth quickly between AutoCAD and your word processor.

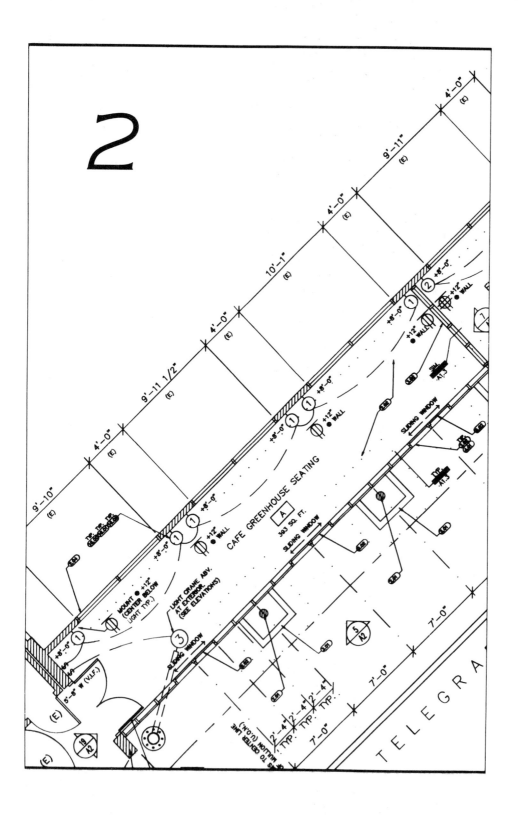

Chapter 2
Customizing the DOS Environment

MUCH CAN BE DONE to customize AutoCAD without major alterations to its accompanying ASCII files. This is accomplished by executing certain DOS commands prior to executing the AutoCAD program itself. Although these commands do not modify the performance of AutoCAD directly, they have a significant effect on the DOS environment in which AutoCAD works and can thereby make your CAD work much faster and easier.

In this chapter we will look at ways of setting up AutoCAD to work with multiple drawing subdirectories and multiple hardware configurations. We will discuss using AutoCAD on a RAM disk and examine techniques for creating batch files that quickly establish a customized AutoCAD-DOS environment.

Finally, we will make a small modification to an ASCII file supplied with AutoCAD, ACAD.PGP, so that we can use a word processor while inside AutoCAD's Drawing Editor. This modification will greatly enhance our ability to further customize AutoCAD.

ACCESSING MULTIPLE DRAWING DIRECTORIES

For many users, maintaining different drawings in separate hard-disk subdirectories is a necessity of drawing life. For example, by organizing related drawings in their own subdirectories, users can simplify the process of locating them or backing them up.

There are two ways to use a single copy of the AutoCAD program with multiple drawing-file subdirectories. One way uses the DOS PATH command; the other makes use of the AutoCAD SHELL command.

Using the DOS PATH Command

The following example assumes that your AutoCAD program files are located on a subdirectory called ACAD. If your subdirectory is different, substitute its name when appropriate. We are also assuming that drawing files are located in two subdirectories called DRAW1 and DRAW2.

To use AutoCAD with the drawings on DRAW2, type the following command at the DOS prompt:

PATH = C:\ACAD

and press Return. You will see another DOS prompt.

Next, log onto the DRAW2 subdirectory by typing this command and pressing Return:

CD\DRAW2

Finally, invoke AutoCAD, which will execute normally because you have issued the DOS PATH command and told DOS where to search for command files that aren't on the currently logged drive. Since we were logged onto the DRAW2 subdirectory when we issued the ACAD command, DOS didn't find the AutoCAD program files at first. The PATH command instructed DOS to check the ACAD subdirectory next, where it found the AutoCAD program files.

With AutoCAD now up and running, drawing files will be accessed from the DRAW2 subdirectory. It is not necessary to type the subdirectory name when accessing its files. DRAW2 is therefore referred to as the *default* subdirectory.

You can still access drawing files on nondefault subdirectories by typing the full path name of the desired drawing. For example, if the current default subdirectory is DRAW2, you could ask for a file in DRAW1 by typing the name of the file this way:

C:\DRAW1*drawing file name*

Alternatively, you could wait until you leave the AutoCAD program and return to DOS. At the DOS prompt, you could change to the DRAW1 subdirectory by typing the following command and pressing Return:

CD\DRAW1

At this point, invoking ACAD again would return you to the AutoCAD program with DRAW1 as the new default drawing-file subdirectory.

Using the AutoCAD SHELL Command

It is possible to change the default subdirectory without leaving the Drawing Editor. I recommend that you use this method only when you first enter the Drawing Editor, but not after you have begun editing a drawing, because it may lead to confusion.

The AutoCAD command used to accomplish this is the SHELL command. At the AutoCAD command prompt, type

SHELL

and press Return. AutoCAD responds with the prompt, "DOS Command:" Type the following command and press Return:

CD\DRAW1

AutoCAD will then return to the Drawing Editor with the new subdirectory as the default. You may have to press the Flip Screen key (F1) to see the Drawing Editor. Your current drawing is still understood to be on the old logged subdirectory and will be saved there when you invoke AutoCAD's END command. This method should not be used as a way to move drawing files around. It can lead to confusion regarding which subdirectory is the current default; therefore, use it carefully.

SETTING UP MULTIPLE AUTOCAD CONFIGURATIONS

Some AutoCAD users have more than one peripheral hardware device to use with AutoCAD. For example, you may have more than one plotter. It is possible to use a single copy of AutoCAD with more than one hardware configuration and to switch from one configuration to the other without having to reconfigure AutoCAD each time.

The first time AutoCAD is run, you are required to select various hardware devices from the AutoCAD configuration menus. AutoCAD saves this information in a special file called ACAD.CFG. When AutoCAD starts up, it finds the information in this file and thus sets itself up for use with your hardware.

This information can be located only in a file called ACAD.CFG. No other names or extensions will work. In addition, AutoCAD normally expects to find ACAD.CFG on the same subdirectory as its other system files. Therefore, only one configuration at a time can be accessed.

You can, however, establish multiple hardware configurations by setting up different versions of the ACAD.CFG file, each in its own subdirectory. In the next example, we will do that; then, we will use a special DOS command to tell AutoCAD where to find the particular version of ACAD.CFG we want AutoCAD to use.

This example, which again assumes that the AutoCAD system files are located in the subdirectory ACAD, configures AutoCAD for use with two different plotters: one that does only C-size check plots (we'll call this one the check plotter) and a big behemoth that cranks out our final product (we'll refer to this one as the final plotter). Two special subdirectories, named CHECK and FINAL, are used to keep our configurations separate.

First, we must have copies of the AutoCAD driver-file disks handy. We will use them in drive A. If your floppy-drive letter is different, substitute that letter in the commands used in this example.

To begin the process, create the two subdirectories on the hard disk. These subdirectories will exist for the sole purpose of holding our two versions of ACAD.CFG and will contain no other files. At the DOS prompt, type

MD\CHECK

and press Return. Next type

MD\FINAL

and press Return.

With the two subdirectories created, the next step is to use the DOS SET command, which will cause AutoCAD to place the different versions of the ACAD.CFG file in their appropriate subdirectories.

The DOS SET command directly establishes certain variable conditions within your computer's operating system. AutoCAD can take advantage of this by means of a variation on this command, SET ACADCFG = .

At the DOS prompt, type

SET ACADCFG = C:\CHECK

This command tells AutoCAD that the ACAD.CFG file will be found in the CHECK subdirectory on the hard-disk drive. If your hard disk is not C or if you are using a different subdirectory name, substitute your drive letter and subdirectory name for C:\CHECK.

You are now ready to configure AutoCAD for your check plotter. Start AutoCAD as you normally would. (But don't reboot your computer. If you normally start AutoCAD by rebooting, log onto your Auto-CAD system subdirectory and type **ACAD** instead.)

AutoCAD begins, but responds with a message that AutoCAD is not configured. You may then be asked to supply the name of the disk drive or subdirectory containing the AutoCAD device drivers. Place the Auto-CAD disk containing the display device drivers in the A drive and respond to this question by typing

A:

and pressing Return.

Select the appropriate display device from the menu and place the second driver disk in the A drive, again responding as before. Answer all the hardware-device prompts as is appropriate for your particular configuration and save the configuration changes when finished.

Next, exit AutoCAD and return to the DOS prompt. Type the following command and press Return:

SET ACADCFG = C:\FINAL

Start AutoCAD as you did before. Once again, you will be called upon to configure ACAD. Answer the configuration prompts, inserting the proper driver disks when asked to do so. In this case, select the final plotter. Save the changes, exit AutoCAD, and you are finished.

From here on, if you wish to use the check plotter before you begin AutoCAD, type the following at the DOS prompt and press Return:

SET ACADCFG = C:\CHECK

Then start AutoCAD normally. AutoCAD will use the correct check-plotter configuration file.

If you wish to use the final plotter, at the DOS prompt, type

SET ACADCFG = C:\FINAL

and press Return. Then start AutoCAD normally. AutoCAD will use the correct final-plotter configuration file.

You can use any subdirectory names you choose, and you can have as many different configurations as you need, but each ACAD.CFG file must be on its own subdirectory.

CREATING, EDITING, AND USING BATCH FILES

All this typing of DOS commands does not have to be done each time you enter AutoCAD. You can create another type of ASCII file called a *batch file*, which contains DOS commands in sequence, one to a line. Once this file is created, you can simply type its name, and all the DOS commands therein will be issued automatically. This is a convenient alternative to remembering which set of DOS commands goes with which version of AutoCAD. Batch files require a special file extension, BAT.

Single-Purpose Batch Files

The simplest batch file is one that contains the exact commands necessary to accomplish a single task. In the following example, you will create a batch file that will log you onto the DRAW2 drawing-file subdirectory and also call up AutoCAD in the check-plotter configuration.

To create the batch file, use your word processor to create an ASCII file. Give the file a unique name that you will easily remember. In this example, I chose the name CHECK-2.BAT, a short name that stands for "check plotter—drawing directory number 2."

Enter your word processor, follow its instructions for starting a new ASCII file, and name the batch file CHECK-2.BAT. When your word processor is ready, type the following commands as you see them below, substituting your own drive letters and subdirectories as necessary:

```
PATH = C:\ACAD
SET ACADCFG = C:\CHECK
CD\DRAW2
ACAD
```

When you are satisfied that your batch commands are correct, save the ASCII file and return to DOS. To be certain that you have created a valid ASCII file, log onto the subdirectory containing CHECK-2.BAT (if necessary), type

TYPE CHECK-2.BAT

and press Return. This will cause the contents of the new batch file to appear on the screen.

If there are any extra characters, peculiar symbols, or typing errors, the chances are that the batch file won't work. In such a case, you will have to go back to your word processor and edit the file.

If the batch file looks correct, try it. At the DOS prompt, type

CHECK-2

and press Return. You will now see the commands in the batch file being typed on the screen. You will automatically enter AutoCAD, with the DRAW2 subdirectory as the default subdirectory, using the check-plotter configuration file.

You can have as many batch files as you need to handle your various combinations of drawing-file subdirectories and hardware configurations. Simply note which DOS commands are required, copy them into a batch file with a unique name and the extension BAT, type the file name at the DOS prompt, and you are up and running.

You may want to copy your batch files to your system's root directory; this is usually the handiest place for them. On the other hand, if you wind up with a lot of different batch files, or your root directory is too crowded, you may want to place them on their own hard-disk sub-directory.

Be sure to make backup copies of all the files you create to save time in the event your originals are inadvertantly lost.

Multipurpose Batch Files

If you choose, you can write a single batch file that can call several different AutoCAD configurations. For example, you could create the following batch file named CAD.BAT, located on your system's root directory, which would call a specific AutoCAD configuration based on information you type at the DOS prompt. Using this file, for example, you could type the following at the DOS prompt:

CAD DRAW2 CHECK

AutoCAD would then execute with the DRAW2 subdirectory as its default, configured for the check plotter. Alternatively, you could type

CAD DRAW1 FINAL

and AutoCAD would execute with the DRAW1 subdirectory as its default, configured for the final plotter.

These are the lines contained in CAD.BAT:

```
PATH = C:\ACAD
CD\%1
SET ACADCFG = C:\%2
ACAD
CD\
```

The first line in this batch file establishes the search path DOS will use to locate the AutoCAD system files.

In the second line, the %1 will be replaced by the first word you type after CAD. If, for instance, you typed DRAW2, this line would appear on the screen as

CD\DRAW2

thus establishing the default drawing subdirectory.

The third line uses %2 to pick up the second word you type after CAD. If, for example, the second word were CHECK, this line would appear on the screen as

SET ACADCFG = C:\CHECK

thus establishing the subdirectory where AutoCAD could find the configuration file.

The fourth line invokes AutoCAD, and the final line logs back onto the root directory upon exiting AutoCAD.

Error Trapping in Batch Files

If you use CAD.BAT exactly as it is written above, you will be required to supply all the necessary extra information at the DOS prompt in order to get the results you intended. If you accidentally leave out or misspell the second word, for example, you may get the message, "AutoCAD is not yet configured."

To safeguard against this, you can add some extra lines to the same batch file that will cause it to cease if errors are detected:

```
ECHO OFF
IF "%1%2" = = "" GOTO NONE
IF "%1" = = "" GOTO NODWG
IF "%2" = = "" GOTO NOCFG
IF NOT EXIST C:\%1\*.DWG GOTO NODWG
IF NOT EXIST C:\%2\ACAD.CFG GOTO NOCFG
ECHO Now loading ACAD - Drawings on C:\%1, Configuration C:\%2
PATH = C:\ACAD
CD\%1
SET ACADCFG = C:\%2
ACAD
CD\
GOTO END
:NONE
CLS
ECHO CAD—Please enter drawing subdirectory and configuration file.
GOTO END
:NOCFG
CLS
ECHO CAD %1 %2—Configuration file not found. Please try again.
GOTO END
:NODWG
CLS
ECHO CAD %1 %2 – Drawing Subdirectory not found. Please try again.
:END
```

In this fancier version of CAD.BAT, the first line, ECHO OFF, will suppress the screen display of the subsequent lines while the batch file is running.

The second, third, and fourth lines determine if one or both of the key words were left out of the initial typed command. If so, the batch file will display an error message and quit.

The fifth and sixth lines determine if the drawing-file subdirectory and the configuration file exist. This helps to trap typing errors or misspellings. If the batch file cannot find the correct files, it will display a message and quit.

As a convenience to the user, the seventh line displays a message indicating which configuration of AutoCAD is being loaded. The next five lines are the same as the simpler version of the batch file.

The thirteenth line will be read by DOS if no errors have occurred. It causes the batch file to bypass the error-message commands and go immediately to the last line of the file.

The fourteenth through the twenty-fourth lines contain commands that execute only if a previous error condition has been detected. In that case, they display the appropriate messages.

The twenty-fifth line is the end of the file. Each previous section of the file ends with the line

GOTO END

Thus, no matter what section of the batch file is processed, DOS will bypass the following sections and skip to this last line in the file.

Using AUTOEXEC.BAT

As you settle on the appropriate DOS environment for AutoCAD, you may find that some DOS commands (for example, PATH) remain consistent, regardless of any specific configuration. You can, if you wish, add such commands to the AUTOEXEC.BAT file instead of your system batch files. DOS looks for AUTOEXEC.BAT when booting; if found, AUTOEXEC.BAT will then execute automatically. This can save a little time and disk space.

USING AUTOCAD ON A RAM DISK

Because AutoCAD is a large program with several overlay files, it is possible to improve its performance by copying the program's files onto a RAM disk and running AutoCAD from there.

A RAM disk is an area of the computer's random-access memory which, by means of special software, has been set aside and configured to appear to the computer's operating system as an additional disk drive. Because this disk drive is not a physical device, but is instead located entirely in memory, running programs from it will result in a noticeable increase in processing speed. This is especially true when using AutoCAD, which frequently accesses the disk.

You must be careful when storing data on a RAM disk, however. Because the data is located within memory and not on a physical device, any interruption of power, even for a fraction of a second, will cause the RAM-disk data to be irretrievably lost. If you are considering using a RAM disk with AutoCAD, keep the following in mind:

- You should back up your drawing files to the hard disk as often as you reasonably can. The more critical the potential damage from accidental data loss, the more frequently you should save drawings to your hard disk or other physical data-storage device.

- For all practical purposes, and especially when using a customized version of AutoCAD, the program will require the full 640K of DOS-addressable RAM for its processing. Therefore, in order to use AutoCAD on a RAM disk, you will need to install expansion memory in your computer and place the RAM disk there.

- A working minimum size for this expansion memory is about two megabytes. This size will accommodate the AutoCAD system files plus allow enough space to work on drawings about 150K in size. Your RAM disk may need to be bigger if you intend to work on several drawings, if your drawings are large, or if you intend to use many shape files, menu files, LISP files, and so on.

- Use of a RAM disk will increase the time spent starting up Auto-CAD, while the RAM disk is created and all necessary files are copied onto it.

- The relative increase in processing speed you can expect from a RAM disk depends on the current speed of your host hardware, especially your hard-disk drive. If your hard disk is relatively slow (40 milliseconds or more), a RAM disk will help you achieve a noticeable increase in processing speed.

Required Files

Here is a list of the AutoCAD program files that must be copied onto the RAM disk in order to run AutoCAD from there:

File Name	Description
ACAD.EXE	Executes the AutoCAD program from DOS
ACAD.OVL	AutoCAD main program overlay file
ACAD0.OVL	Supplementary overlay file
ACAD1.OVL	ADE-1 overlay file
ACAD2.OVL	ADE-2 overlay file
ACAD3.OVL	ADE-3 overlay file
ACADL.OVL	AutoLISP overlay file
ACADM.OVL	An additional supplementary overlay file
ACADPL.OVL	Plot commands overlay file
ACADPP.OVL	Printer-plot commands overlay file
ACADVS.OVL	Prompts and messages file

Optional Files

There are several files that aren't absolutely required on the RAM disk in order to run the program; however, you will probably want most of them on your RAM disk as well. They are described in the following sections.

ACAD.CFG (1K) As previously noted, this file contains the hardware-configuration information required by AutoCAD. This file can be located elsewhere than on the RAM disk and accessed via the DOS SET ACADCFG= command, as previously described. However, it is small and it will not take up much space on your RAM disk. If you are not using the SET ACADCFG= command, this file must be present on the RAM disk.

ACAD.DWG (?K) This file is the AutoCAD prototype drawing file, which contains default settings for layers, colors, line types, and so on. Most users modify this drawing sooner or later to contain their own default settings. If you have made changes to this drawing and it is not too large, you may decide simply to include it on your RAM disk. However, if you have made considerable changes, and the drawing has become very large, or if you use several different prototype drawings, you can use them without copying them to your RAM disk. To do this, specify the full path name of the prototype drawing when giving a name to a new drawing on the RAM disk, such as

NEW = C:\ACAD\ACAD

For example, suppose that you wished to create a drawing named NEW.DWG using the defaults found in ACAD.DWG, which was not copied onto the RAM disk. After you picked Task #1 from the main menu, you would respond to the "Drawing Name:" prompt with

NEW = C:\ACAD\ACAD

In this case, AutoCAD would use the settings found in C:\ACAD\ ACAD.DWG as defaults for NEW.DWG, but the prototype drawing would not take up space on the RAM disk.

If you are conserving RAM disk space and have never modified ACAD.DWG, you can easily access its default settings without copying it onto the RAM disk. To do this, type an equal sign after a new drawing name. For example

NEW =

In this case, drawing NEW would contain the standard ACAD.DWG defaults set by Autodesk.

ACAD.HLP (83K)   The Help file is quite large. If you are an experienced user and do not access AutoCAD's HELP command, you can save space by not copying this file onto the RAM disk.

ACAD.LIN (600 bytes)   This file contains AutoCAD's standard line types. If you use any line type other than continuous, you will want to include it. Note that in its standard version, it is extremely small.

ACAD.MNX (46K)   This file is the compiled version of AutoCAD's standard screen menu. It is not needed if you choose to type all commands or enter them by means of a digitizing tablet, or if you substitute a custom menu of your own. AutoCAD will prompt you for the name of a menu file if it cannot find any menu files when it begins, but you may choose None as a menu option if you wish.

ACAD.PAT (5K)   This file contains descriptions of AutoCAD hatch patterns and can be omitted if your drawing is not hatched. Even without this file, you can continue to use simple user-defined hatch patterns in your drawing.

ACAD.PGP (200 bytes)   This file is necessary if you wish to access external DOS commands from within AutoCAD. It is an important file for customizers. Note that it is extremely small.

*.SHX   Files with this extension are shape and text-font description files. They are required only if you plan to include shapes or text in your drawing. If this is the case, only those specific shape or font files that are needed should be copied to the RAM disk.

   If you wish, you can copy none of these files to the RAM disk, and AutoCAD will prompt you for the full path name of font- and shape-description files it expects to find. If your drawing requires many of these files and RAM disk space is at a premium, you can use this method and supply the necessary full path names by typing them out, or by means of a script file.

Other Miscellaneous Files   Depending on your needs, you may want to include on your RAM disk optional files, such as LISP files, menu files, script files, slide files, and special drawing files that contain blocks.

   AutoCAD hardware-driver files (files with the extension DRV) are needed only when AutoCAD is being configured for your hardware setup. Once you have configured AutoCAD for your hardware, copies of these driver files are no longer needed and may be safely erased from your hard disk.

   You may find a RAM disk most useful when developing your custom AutoCAD applications. You will move between AutoCAD and your word processor fairly frequently during the development process, and a RAM disk will save you significant loading and reloading time as you do.

   Again, the most critical thing to remember is to save your important drawing and data files frequently to the hard disk.

USING A WORD PROCESSOR INSIDE AUTOCAD

   Customizing AutoCAD involves switching back and forth between your word processor and AutoCAD in order to modify the ASCII files and to test the results in AutoCAD. Since you will probably want to switch back and forth fairly frequently, it is useful to access your word processor without actually leaving AutoCAD's Drawing Editor. Doing this will save you a lot of time, because you will not have to wait for AutoCAD to reload each time you make a change to an ASCII file.

You can access most word processors from inside the drawing editor by making a modification to ACAD.PGP.

Before you begin modifying this file, you will want to know how Auto-CAD and your chosen word processor work together. To begin, you will need to determine the best means to activate your word processor when you are logged onto the AutoCAD system subdirectory.

If your word processor is small and can reside comfortably on the same subdirectory as AutoCAD, the simplest approach is to place a copy of it there. This is acceptable and efficient, and by doing so, you ensure that all your word processor commands will work.

However, if your word processor is large, or if, for any reason, you don't want it on the same subdirectory as AutoCAD, you may be able to place it on its own subdirectory. (Some word processors will allow you to start from a subdirectory other than their own, while others have trouble with this.) If you choose to place your word processor on a different subdirectory than the one AutoCAD is on, it is worthwhile to test your ability to access it from AutoCAD's subdirectory.

For example, suppose that the command to access your word processor is normally WP, that the word processor is on a subdirectory named WORD, and that AutoCAD is installed on the subdirectory ACAD. Begin by typing

    PATH = C:\ACAD;C:\WORD

and press Return. This DOS command will ensure that both AutoCAD and your word processor files can be accessed from anywhere on your hard disk.

Now log onto AutoCAD's subdirectory. Try calling your word processor with the command WP. Check for the following:

- Does your word processor's opening screen appear, perhaps after only a few seconds longer than usual?

- If you can access a list of files on the default subdirectory, are they the ACAD files? If not, can you change the subdirectory to the AutoCAD subdirectory while inside your word processor?

- While inside your word processor, open up a test file, type some characters, and save the file. Leave the word processor program, enter it again and edit the same test file. Did everything work?

- Exit the word processor. Are you in the ACAD subdirectory? If not, can you set up your word processor so that it will exit to the ACAD subdirectory?

If you can configure your word processor to function fully while logged onto the AutoCAD subdirectory, and if it will place you in the AutoCAD subdirectory when you exit, you will be able to use it while inside the Drawing Editor.

There is one other thing you will need to know: the amount of computer memory required by your word processor. This information can be found in your word processor's documentation. Word processors usually require between 128K and 256K. Look it up to be sure and make a note of it. The maximum amount of memory you will be able to use is 512K. If your word processor needs more than this (which is unusual), you will have to use a different one or use it outside of AutoCAD.

Check your word processor's documentation to determine if it requires increasing amounts of memory for editing files as they become larger. If this is the case with your word processor, plan on using the maximum amount of memory, 512K.

Modifying ACAD.PGP

You are now ready to modify ACAD.PGP. To begin, log onto the Auto-CAD subdirectory. Enter the word processor, using the commands you noted earlier.

Now edit the file ACAD.PGP. Remember to edit it as an ASCII file (or nondocument file, or whatever name your word processor uses for ASCII files). When your word processor locates the file, something like this should appear on the screen:

```
CATALOG,DIR /W,24000,*Files: ,0
DEL,DEL,24000,File to delete: ,0
DIR,DIR,24000,File specification: ,0
SH,,24000,*DOS Command: ,0
SHELL,,125000,*DOS Command: ,0
TYPE,TYPE,24000,File to list: ,0
```

If the file is not found, be sure you are accessing files from the AutoCAD subdirectory. Check the AutoCAD subdirectory for the existence of the file.

ACAD.PGP contains a list of DOS commands. Each command occupies its own line in the file. Each line contains five elements of information, separated by commas, as follows:

1. The command to be issued while within the Drawing Editor

2. The actual command AutoCAD passes to DOS when the Drawing Editor command is issued

3. The amount of memory required to execute the command

4. A prompt offered to the user for any additional needed information

5. A special number code used by AutoCAD when it returns to the Drawing Editor

Move the cursor down to just below the bottom line in the file and type the new AutoCAD command you wish to use in order to access your word processor when inside the Drawing Editor. This command can be the same as your word processor command, or it can be an abbreviation. Any brief combination of letters will work, but do not use an AutoCAD command, such as TEXT, for instance, or your modification will not work. Type the command in capital letters. This example uses the command WP. Type a comma after the command.

Here's how the last line of ACAD.PGP looks so far:

WP,

Next, type the command that will access your word processor. This is followed by another comma. In this example, the command is the same, WP, so the line now looks like this:

WP,WP,

Next, add the memory requirement of your word processor (from the word processor's documentation or your notes), followed by another comma. In this example, the memory requirement is 128K. Notice how it is added to the example line in the ACAD.PGP file:

WP,WP,128000,

As you see, the memory requirement is typed out fully. An abbreviation, such as 128K, will not work. If your word processor has the expandable memory feature mentioned earlier, you may wish to type in the maximum allowable amount, which is 512000.

Next comes an optional prompt that will display from within AutoCAD whenever you type the command WP at the AutoCAD command prompt. If you don't intend to supply additional information (such as the name of the file you intend to edit) you can simply type another comma.

The example line would now look like this:

WP,WP,128000,,

However, some word processors allow you to type a file name at the DOS level before you actually enter the word processor. This can save a little time. If your word processor has this feature and you wish to take advantage of it, you may do so here by entering a prompt for AutoCAD to display. For example, you might want to include the prompt, "File to Edit? ," so that you can type a file name before entering your word processor. Here is how the example line looks with this prompt included:

WP,WP,128000,File to Edit? ,

Notice the space after the question mark in the prompt. This will cause a space to appear between the prompt and the name of the file on the screen, which improves readability.

Lastly, we need a single-digit *response code* that AutoCAD will use when it returns from the word processor to the Drawing Editor. If this code is zero, AutoCAD will remain in Text mode when it returns. If this code is 4, AutoCAD will flip back to Graphics mode upon its return. Other numbers are possible but they execute specific technical functions beyond the scope of this book. If you are curious about their meaning, you will find an explanation in the AutoCAD documentation.

In this example, the return code used is 4, so that AutoCAD will flip back to Graphics mode automatically. This time press Return instead of typing a comma. This is how the entire new line looks:

WP,WP,128000,File to Edit? ,4

The cursor should be just below the first character in the line. This completes the necessary modifications.

Take a moment to study the other lines in the file. Notice how they all use the same basic structure. Using the technique described here, you can make additional modifications to ACAD.PGP, calling other programs, such as a spreadsheet or database, from within the Drawing Editor.

Double-check your work and save the file onto the AutoCAD system subdirectory. You can test the results of your work by starting Auto-CAD, beginning a new drawing, and typing the word processor command from inside the Drawing Editor.

Additional Tips

Here are some extra tips that all users will find helpful to bear in mind, although the tips may not all be relevant to your particular needs and circumstances.

Spaces in Response to Prompts AutoCAD normally responds in the same way to either a press of the Space bar or the Return. This feature also applies to responses to the optional prompts in ACAD.PGP. If you choose to make further edits to ACAD.PGP, and a response to an optional prompt may require spaces, you can precede the optional prompt with an asterisk (*). When you do this, only a Return will work as a finish to the user's response, so spaces can be used within the response. Refer back to the printed example of ACAD.PGP to see illustrations of this feature.

A Last-Resort Batch File If you find that your word processor simply will not work from within the Drawing Editor, here is a batch file named SWING.BAT that will allow you to *swing* back and forth between Auto-CAD and a word processor located on another subdirectory. It will save you keystrokes, but you will have to wait for AutoCAD to load each time you wish to test a change you have made.

This batch file should be located on the same subdirectory as the AutoCAD system files. The file is invoked by typing the SWING command followed by the name of the ASCII file you wish to edit.

In the lines that follow, substitute your word processor's subdirectory for WORD and your word processor's startup command for WP. Likewise, if your AutoCAD subdirectory is not ACAD, substitute that as well.

SWING.BAT contains the following lines:

```
IF "%1" = ="" GOTO END
CD\WORD
WP
COPY %1 C:\ACAD
PAUSE
CD\ACAD
ACAD
PAUSE
SWING %1
:END
```

The first line of the file tests to be certain that a file name was used when SWING.BAT was invoked. If not, the line instructs DOS to skip to the last line of the file, which causes the batch process to end.

The second and third lines log onto the WORD subdirectory and invoke the word processor. Upon exiting the word processor, the fourth line copies the named file onto the AutoCAD subdirectory.

The fifth line, the PAUSE command, causes DOS to pause execution of the batch file and issue the prompt

Press any key to continue...

When you no longer wish to swing back and forth between AutoCAD and your word processor, simply press Ctrl-C (hold down the Ctrl key and press C) in response to this prompt. You will then see this message:

Terminate Batch Job (Y/N)?

Answer Y to return to the DOS prompt. If you press any other key, the batch file will continue.

The sixth and seventh lines log onto the AutoCAD subdirectory and invoke AutoCAD. When you exit AutoCAD, the eighth line repeats the PAUSE command, and you again have the opportunity either to continue or to terminate the batch job. If you choose to continue, the ninth line of the batch file calls itself, and the whole process is repeated.

The tenth line marks the end of the file. The batch file skips to this line if no file was named when it was invoked.

This batch file is an example of an *endless loop*, a series of commands that repeat indefinitely until it is interrupted by the user.

A Word About Experimenting You may have to experiment a bit with AutoCAD and your word processor to determine the best possible configuration and subdirectory organization. For example, you may decide to create a single subdirectory for use as your development subdirectory, placing your word processor files on that directory and logging there before calling AutoCAD for customizing and development work.

This experimentation is not harmful to your hardware. At worst, your system may *lock*, offering you no response and forcing you to reboot. Nor will it damage your software. You should, however, always use copies and not your master disks.

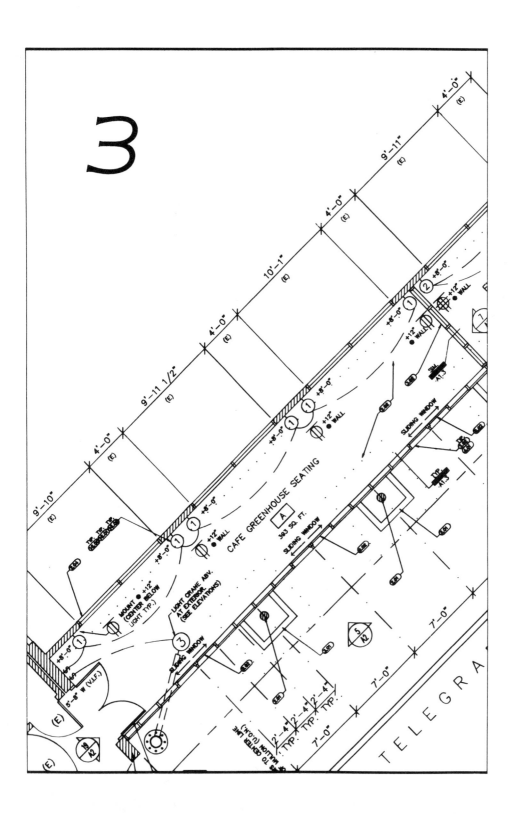

Chapter 3
Custom Line Types
and Hatch Patterns

AUTOCAD COMES EQUIPPED with 8 standard line types and 41 standard hatch patterns. This is a generous number, but you are not limited to these. If your drawing requires a unique line type or hatch pattern, AutoCAD has the tools to create line types and hatch patterns that are distinctly your own. This chapter introduces you to these tools and provides examples of their use.

CUSTOM LINE TYPES

In addition to a standard continuous line type, AutoCAD can construct a wide variety of other line types composed of various combinations of dashes and dots. AutoCAD creates these dashes and dots by applying mathematical precision to up and down movements of an imaginary *pen* that draws a line between two points. The dashes, dots, and the spaces between them are the *elements* of the line type. The relative lengths of the elements in a line type are translated into a series of numbers that express these lengths as *drawing units*. Regardless of the drawing units selected using AutoCAD'S UNITS command, their expression in line-type descriptions is always in decimals.

AutoCAD requires some information in addition to these numbers: a unique name for the line type and an approximation of the line type's appearance using periods and underline characters. When grouped together according to a specific format, the line-type information is called the *line-type description*.

By supplying AutoCAD with various line-type descriptions, you can create a wide variety of custom line types. You can store these descriptions in an ASCII file, giving the file a name of your own choosing and the extension LIN. Descriptions for AutoCAD's standard line types are stored in the file ACAD.LIN. It is a short file and can easily accommodate additional line-type descriptions of your own. In this section, we will focus on adding new line-type descriptions to this file, emphasizing the

ADVANCED TECHNIQUES IN AUTOCAD

principles involved so that you can then create whatever line types suit your fancy.

There are two ways to add line-type descriptions to the file ACAD.LIN. One way is to enter the line-type information from within AutoCAD's Drawing Editor. The other way is to edit the file ACAD.LIN directly with your word processor. Both methods have their advantages.

Before attempting to create a new line type, it is useful to sketch it out on a piece of paper or draw it using AutoCAD. The goal is to have a clear idea of the relationships between the lengths of the dots, dashes, and spaces that make up the new line type.

As an example, Figure 3.1 illustrates a new line type consisting of dashes alternating with groups of three dots each. It looks somewhat like the boundary lines used on highway maps, so we will call this line type Boundary.

While analyzing this line type, you can make some reasonable assumptions about the relationships between its elements. Begin by assigning the line's dash element a length of one drawing unit. (This is a good arbitrary value for the average dash.)

Having assigned this value to the dash, you can surmise that the spaces in the line type are about ¼ drawing unit long. It may be odd to

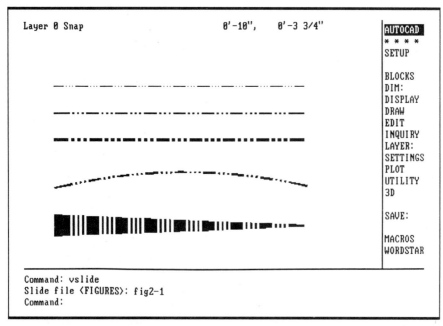

Figure 3.1   The Boundary Line Type, Drawn as Various AutoCAD Polylines

think of a space as having a length, but in fact the space is simply another element of the line.

When writing line type descriptions, fractions are converted to their decimal equivalents. AutoCAD reads spaces as negative numbers, to differentiate them from dashes. A space that is 1/4 drawing unit long, therefore, is expressed as – .25.

Dots have no significant length at all. They are always assigned a length of zero.

A list of such numbers in a line-type description will create the Boundary line type in AutoCAD, as you'll see next.

Using the Drawing Editor

To add this line-type description to AutoCAD, enter AutoCAD, start a new drawing, and enter the LINETYPE command. AutoCAD responds with this prompt:

?/Load/Create:

Select the Create option by typing **C**. AutoCAD prompts

Name of linetype to create:

Respond by typing the name of the new line type, in this example, **Boundary**. AutoCAD then responds with this prompt:

File for storage of linetype <ACAD>:

If you respond to this prompt by pressing Return, AutoCAD will store the line-type description in the file ACAD.LIN. If you want to create or use a new file of line-type descriptions, type the name of the file you wish to create or use at this point. The extension LIN is always assumed when using this method.

AutoCAD checks to see if a line type with the name Boundary already exists in the named file. Since it does not, AutoCAD prompts

Descriptive text:

In response to this prompt, type a rough approximation of the line by entering periods and underline characters in the same pattern as the dots and dashes of the new line, until the pattern repeats enough to look like the line type. The periods and underline characters used in this rough approximation need not line up with each other as precisely as the actual dots and dashes in the line type that AutoCAD draws. AutoCAD uses these periods and underline characters to display a visualization of the line type's elements in response to the LINETYPE command.

In the case of the Boundary line type, type three underlines, a space, three periods, and a space. Repeat this pattern two or three times, and then press Return.

Next, AutoCAD supplies an A,. This A, is required in all line-type descriptions. Therefore, leave it and begin entering numbers to represent the Boundary line type. Separate each of the numbers with a comma.

First, enter the number representing the dash, which is one drawing unit long. This is expressed with a positive number, 1. The numerical description line will look like:

A,1,

Next, describe a space, ¼ drawing unit long:

A,1,-.25,

Next, a dot

A,1,-.25,0,

Next, another space

A,1,-.25,0,-.25,

Next, another dot

A,1,-.25,0,-.25,0,

Next, another space

A,1,-.25,0,-.25,0,-.25,

Next, the last dot in the pattern

A,1,-.25,0,-.25,0,-.25,0,

Finally, we end the pattern with another space. The finished line description now looks like this:

A,1,-.25,0,-.25,0,-.25,0,-.25

Press Return, and AutoCAD will store the description in the file and return to the Drawing Editor.

At this point, you may wish to load the Boundary line type, create a layer for it, and draw some lines to see how it looks. The first thing you may notice is that the scaling of the line type needs to be changed. Using the AutoCAD LTSCALE command, you can establish whatever scale is necessary to achieve a pleasing line in the Drawing Editor.

If you decide to change the line type description, you can reissue the LINETYPE command, select the Create option, use the name Boundary again, and AutoCAD will ask you if you wish to overwrite the previous line description. If you respond **Y**, AutoCAD will allow you to recreate the line-type description from scratch, including the descriptive text.

The major advantage of creating line-type descriptions in the Drawing Editor is the ability to create such descriptions "on the fly," test their appearance, and make any adjustments that seem appropriate while in the midst of editing a drawing.

You can use any combination of dashes, dots, and spaces, but a few hard-and-fast rules apply:

- Do not begin a line type with a space. Begin it with either a dash or a dot.

- You must have at least two line elements, but no more than twelve. Otherwise, the description won't work.

- The line-type text description, including the name, should be no more than 47 characters long.

- The numerical line-type description should fit on a single 80-character line.

Using the Word Processor

Once you have gained experience creating line types, you may want to edit them using your word processor. Using your word processor to edit line types is often faster than using the Drawing Editor, especially if the intended change is small—for example, if you only intend to change a single element, update the descriptive text, or change the line type's name.

To see how this is done, enter your word processor and call up the file ACAD.LIN. When it appears on the screen, you will see something similar to Figure 3.2.

Notice how the Boundary line type has been added to the list. AutoCAD has stored the information you supplied in response to the prompts as a two-line description. The first line is called the *header line*. The header line begins with an asterisk, followed immediately by the name of the line type (uppercase must be used), a comma, and the approximation of the line type using periods and underlines. This structure is required. Because you supplied the information in response to prompts, AutoCAD created the proper header-line structure for you. Now that you are working within the word processor, however, it is up to you to supply the correct structure for the header line. The next line consists of an uppercase A, a comma, and the numbers that represent the dashes, dots, and spaces. Notice that

```
*DASHED,__ __ __ __ __ __ __ __ __ __ __ __ __ __
A,.5,-.25
*HIDDEN,_ _ _ _ _ _ _ _ _ _ _ _ _ _ _ _ _ _ _ _ _ _
A,.25,-.125
*CENTER,____ _ ____ _ ____ - ____ - ____ - ____ - ____
A,1.25,-.25,.25,-.25
*PHANTOM,____ _ _ ____ _ _ ____ _ _ ____ _ _ ____
A,1.25,-.25,.25,-.25,.25,-.25
*DOT,.................................................
A,0,-.25
*DASHDOT,__ . __ . __ . __ . __ . __ . __ . __ . __
A,.5,-.25,0,-.25
*BORDER,__ __ . __ __ . __ __ . __ __ . __ __ . __ __
A,.5,-.25,.5,-.25,0,-.25
*DIVIDE,__ . . __ . . __ . . __ . . __ . . __
A,.5,-.25,0,-.25,0,-.25
*BOUNDARY,___ ... ___ ... ___ ... ___ ... ___ ...
A,.5,-.125,0,-.125,0,-.125,0,-.125




_
```

Figure 3.2   The Contents of the ACAD.LIN File

there is no comma at the end of the line of numbers, but there always is a carriage return.

Since we are here, why not try typing in another line type? Figure 3.3 illustrates another example, called Longdash. This line type consists of long dashes of one drawing unit each, separated by short spaces of 1/8 drawing unit. You can use the line-type description as given here or create variations on it. You can use it to emphasize other lines, or draw it as an extra-wide polyline, to make a fast *array* of solid rectangles.

CUSTOM HATCH PATTERNS

There are some similarities between the ASCII file descriptions that AutoCAD uses to construct its line types and those that AutoCAD uses to construct its hatch patterns.

When a hatch pattern is constructed, AutoCAD first draws a line type and then copies the line parallel to itself at a distance you specify. It continues to copy parallel lines until a specified area is filled. In addition, a single hatch pattern may be composed of more than one line-type

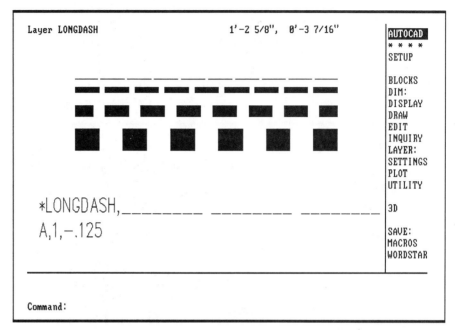

Figure 3.3 Longdash Line Type, Drawn as Various Polylines Along with Its Line-Type Description

description. Each line type in a hatch pattern is drawn and then copied parallel to itself, until all line types defined in the pattern are drawn.

As was the case with custom line types, you tell AutoCAD how to move its pen by means of a series of numbers that are separated by commas. However, with hatch patterns, you have to supply some extra information.

In hatch patterns that contain more than one line type, the various line types are usually drawn at different angles. It is the combination of the angles at which the line types are drawn; the starting position of the line types; their direction and distance from each other; and their pattern of dashes, dots, and spaces that combine to produce a virtually limitless number of patterns. Interestingly enough, a relatively simple set of descriptions can yield a surprisingly complex hatch pattern, as you will see.

This discussion begins with a look at AutoCAD's ASCII file of standard hatch patterns. We will examine the elements of a standard hatch pattern description and make changes to create a different pattern. We will present an example of how AutoCAD can be used as a tool for designing and developing custom hatch patterns from scratch.

The Structure of a Hatch-Pattern Description

AutoCAD's standard hatch patterns are contained in the file ACAD-.PAT. It can be found and should remain on the AutoCAD system-files subdirectory. It contains about 40 hatch-pattern descriptions.

To look at the file, enter your word processor and call up the file ACAD.PAT. The first few lines in the file should look something like this:

```
*ang1,Angle steel
0, 0,0, 0,.275, .2,-.075
90, 0,0, 0,.275, .2,-.075
*ansi31,ANSI Iron, Brick, Stone masonry
45, 0,0 0,.125
*ansi32,ANSI Steel
45, 0,0, 0,.375
45, .176776695,0, 0,.375
*ansi33,ANSI Bronze, Brass, Copper
45, 0,0, 0,.25
45, .176776695,0, 0,.25, .125,-.0625
```

Each hatch-pattern description begins with a header line. The header line has a structure that is reminiscent of the header line in line-type descriptions. That is, it begins with an asterisk (*), followed by the name of the pattern; unlike line-type names, hatch-pattern names in hatch-pattern descriptions are in lowercase only. The pattern name is followed by a comma, and the comma is followed by a short text description of the hatch pattern. This name and text description will appear in the listing of hatch patterns invoked by the user typing Auto-CAD's HATCH ? command. The description is optional, but I recommend that you supply one. If you choose not to supply a description, do not supply the comma after the pattern name either.

The line(s) following the header line contain the numbers that describe the various line types used to construct the hatch pattern. Each numerical line description occupies its own text line in the file. The numerical line descriptions adhere to a rigid structure. The first five numbers are required. As many as six additional numbers follow. The additional numbers describe noncontinuous line types and are optional. All numbers are separated by commas. Each numerical line description ends with a Return.

For example, this is the first hatch pattern in ACAD.PAT:

```
*ang1,Angle steel
0, 0,0, 0,.275, .2,-.075
90, 0,0, 0,.275, .2,-.075
```

The name of the hatch pattern is ang1 and the description is Angle steel. Because there are two numerical line descriptions below the hatch-pattern name, this hatch pattern is composed of two line types.

The first number in the numerical line description refers to the angle at which the line type is to be drawn. Subsequent parallel lines will be drawn at the same angle. In the Ang1 hatch pattern, the two lines are drawn at angles of zero and 90 degrees respectively.

The second number is the X-coordinate of the initial line's starting point. The third number is the Y-coordinate of the starting point. The starting point of the first line in a hatch pattern may be arbitrarily assigned and is frequently given coordinates of 0,0. The starting point is a reference point for determining the starting points of other lines in the pattern. In the Ang1 hatch pattern, both lines begin at point 0,0.

The fourth number, also a zero in this example, is the *offset number*. It will always be zero when the line type is continuous. It is given a nonzero value when the line type is composed of dashes and/or dots. Figures 3.4 through 3.6 illustrate the meaning of the offset number.

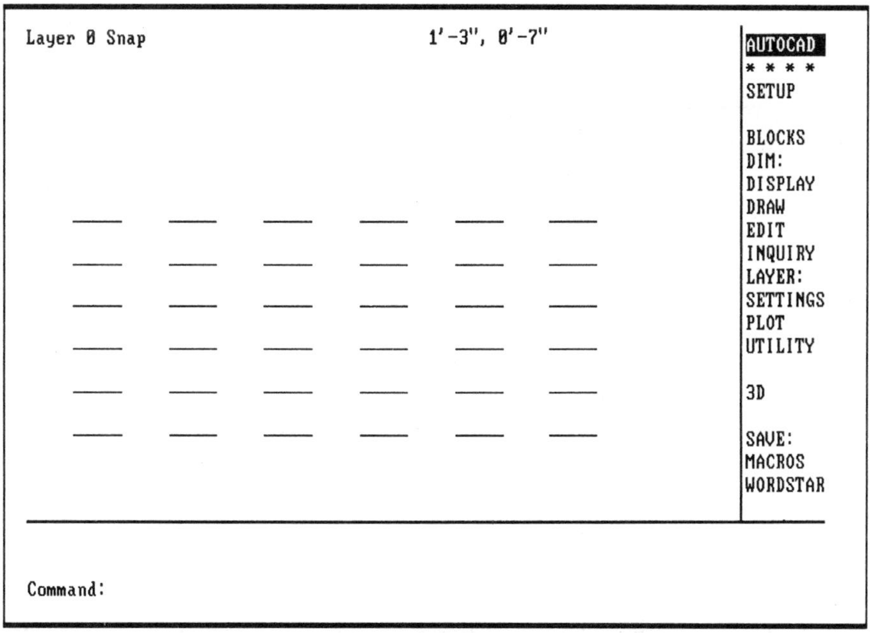

Figure 3.4   Dashed Lines at an Offset Value of Zero

ADVANCED TECHNIQUES IN AUTOCAD

```
Layer 0 Ortho Snap                    1'-3", 0'-4"              AUTOCAD
                                                               * * * *
                                                               SETUP

                                                               BLOCKS
                                                               DIM:
                                                               DISPLAY
                                                               DRAW
          ──   ──   ──   ──   ──                               EDIT
             ──   ──   ──   ──   ──                            INQUIRY
                                                               LAYER:
          ──   ──   ──   ──   ──   ──                          SETTINGS
             ──   ──   ──   ──   ──   ──                       PLOT
                                                               UTILITY
        ──   ──   ──   ──   ──   ──
                                                               3D
        ──   ──   ──   ──   ──   ──   ──
                                                               SAVE:
                                                               MACROS
                                                               WORDSTAR




Command:
```

Figure 3.5   Dashed Lines at an Offset Value of 1

```
Layer 0 Ortho Snap                    1'-3", 0'-3"              AUTOCAD
                                                               * * * *
                                                               SETUP

                                                               BLOCKS
                                                               DIM:
                                                               DISPLAY
          ──   ──   ──   ──   ──   ──                          DRAW
             ──   ──   ──   ──   ──   ──                        EDIT
                                                               INQUIRY
           ──   ──   ──   ──   ──   ──                         LAYER:
                                                               SETTINGS
             ──   ──   ──   ──   ──   ──                        PLOT
                                                               UTILITY
          ──   ──   ──   ──   ──   ──
                                                               3D
           ──   ──   ──   ──   ──
                                                               SAVE:
                                                               MACROS
                                                               WORDSTAR



Command:
```

Figure 3.6   Dashed Lines at an Offset Value of .5 Drawing Units

Figure 3.4 shows a set of parallel dashed lines. The length of each dash or space is one drawing unit. Because the offset value is zero, the dashes and spaces appear to stack on top of one another.

In Figure 3.5, the lines have been given an offset value of one drawing unit. This causes the dashes and spaces to line up differently.

In Figure 3.6, the lines have been given a fractional offset of .5 drawing units. This causes the dashes and spaces to overlap each other.

The fifth number in each numerical line description expresses the distance between the parallel lines. By definition, parallel lines must have some distance between them, so zero is not possible as a value for this line. In the case of the Ang1 hatch pattern, the distance is .275 drawing units.

The numbers that follow the fifth number move AutoCAD's pen up and down, exactly as was done in descriptions of custom line types. If there are no numbers after the fifth number, the line type is assumed to be continuous. In the Ang1 hatch pattern, the line type for both sets is composed of a dash .2 drawing units long and a space .075 drawing units long.

Hatch patterns allow a maximum of six pen motions per line type. The Ang1 hatch pattern uses two pen motions per line type. Here is the complete first numerical line description of the Ang1 hatch pattern:

0, 0,0, 0,.275, .2,-.075

We can read this pattern as follows: at an angle of zero degrees, starting at point 0,0, at an offset of zero, a dashed line type, pen down .2 units, pen up .075 units. The resultant pattern of parallel lines looks like that shown in Figure 3.7.

When you hatch using this pattern, AutoCAD will read this first line and fill the entities to be hatched with parallel lines according to this description. Then, it will move on to the next line in the hatch pattern and fill the entities again:

90, 0,0, 0,.275, .2,-.075

The parallel lines that result from this numerical line description look like those shown in Figure 3.8. When these two sets of lines are combined, they form the complete hatch pattern, as shown in Figure 3.9.

Creating New Hatch Patterns

We will now create a brand new hatch pattern. It is based on an existing standard hatch pattern, with a few alterations.

AutoCAD is delivered with a standard hatch pattern called Triang. It looks like a group of triangles pointed downward. We are going to create

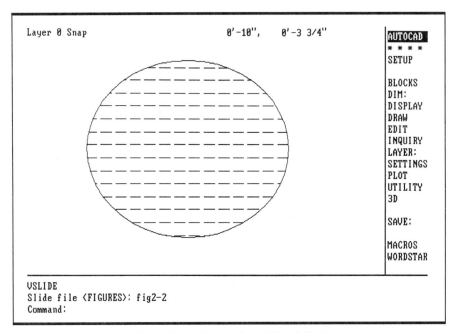

Figure 3.7 The First Set of Lines in the Ang1 Hatch Pattern

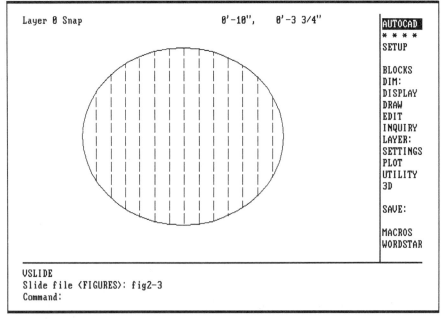

Figure 3.8 The Second Set of Lines in the Ang1 Hatch Pattern

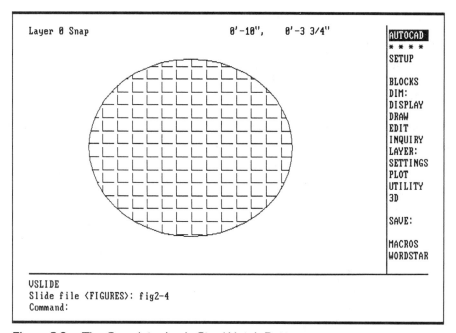

```
 Layer 0 Snap                    0'-10",    0'-3 3/4"    ┌─────────┐
                                                          │AUTOCAD  │
                                                          │* * * *  │
                                                          │SETUP    │
                                                          │         │
                                                          │BLOCKS   │
                                                          │DIM:     │
                                                          │DISPLAY  │
                                                          │DRAW     │
                                                          │EDIT     │
                                                          │INQUIRY  │
                                                          │LAYER:   │
                                                          │SETTINGS │
                                                          │PLOT     │
                                                          │UTILITY  │
                                                          │3D       │
                                                          │         │
                                                          │SAVE:    │
                                                          │         │
                                                          │MACROS   │
                                                          │WORDSTAR │

 VSLIDE
 Slide file <FIGURES>: fig2-4
 Command:
```

Figure 3.9   The Complete Angle Steel Hatch Pattern

the same pattern with the triangles pointed upward and place more space between them.

These are the elements of AutoCAD's Triang hatch pattern:

```
*triang,Equilateral triangles
60, 0,0, .1875,.324759526, .1875,-.1875
120, 0,0, .1875,.324759526, .1875,-.1875
0, -.09375,.162379763, .1875,.324759526, .1875,-.1875
```

The first numerical line description is saying, "At an angle of 60 degrees; starting at point 0,0; offset, .1875 drawing units; distance between the parallel lines, .324759526 drawing units; drawing a dashed line, pen down .1875 drawing units, pen up .1875 drawing units."

The author of this hatch pattern has done some math to arrive at the offset, the distance between the lines, and the up and down motion of the pen. In the case of the offset number and the motion of the pen, .1875 drawing units equal 3/16 inch. If the hatch pattern is used without scaling, it will produce triangles with sides measuring 3/16 inch, and the triangles will be spaced 3/16 inch apart.

In the case of the distance between the lines, 3/16 inch won't work. The distance between the lines, .324759526 drawing units, is twice the height of the triangles. Figure 3.10 shows how the first set of lines is drawn in AutoCAD.

The second set of lines is drawn in the same way, except that it is drawn at an angle of 120 degrees instead of 60. Figure 3.11 shows how the second set looks when it is added to the first.

The third line is drawn using the same elements, except that it is drawn at an angle of zero, and it does not start at the 0,0 point. The X-coordinate is equal to half of one side of the triangles, and the Y-coordinate is equal to the height of one of the triangles. This puts the line in the precise position needed to close up the triangles in the pattern. Figure 3.12 shows how the completed pattern looks.

If we wanted the triangles to point upward, we could simply rotate the hatch pattern 180 degrees. But for the sake of demonstration and practice, we will create another hatch pattern with triangles pointing upward. In addition, we will increase the space between the triangles.

First, on a new line in the file ACAD.PAT, type the required header line:

*triang2, Triangles pointing up

Press Return, and type the first numerical line description:

0, 0,0, 1, 1.732, .5,-1.5

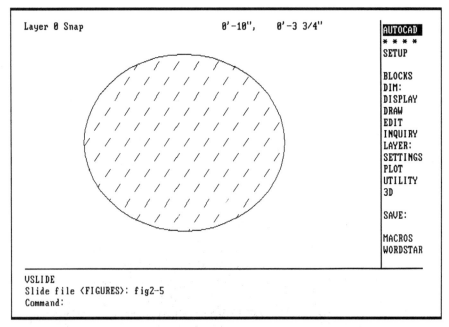

Figure 3.10   The First Set of Lines in AutoCAD's Triang Hatch Pattern

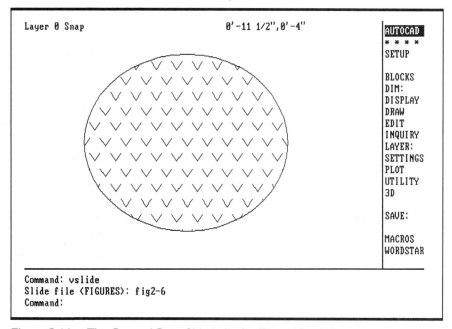

Figure 3.11   The Second Set of Lines in the Triang Hatch Pattern

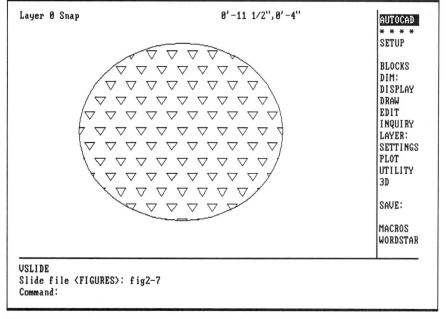

Figure 3.12   AutoCAD's Complete Triang Hatch Pattern

These elements will form the base of the triangles. The lines are drawn at an angle of zero, starting at point 0,0, and are offset by one drawing unit.

The distance between the lines is 1.732 drawing units. This value is double the sine of 60 degrees. Placing this distance between the lines causes the offset and distance values to work together to close the triangles. The line type is dashed, drawn pen down .5 drawing units and pen up 1.5 drawing units. Figure 3.13 shows how the first set of lines will appear on the screen.

The second set of lines is exactly the same, except that it is drawn at an angle of 60 degrees:

   60, 0,0, 1, 1.732, .5,-1.5

Figure 3.14 shows the second set of lines added to the first.

The third numerical line description is almost the same as the first two, except that the angle of the line is 120 degrees and the starting point has changed a bit. The third line must begin to the right of the other two, in order to close off the triangles. It will start at the X-

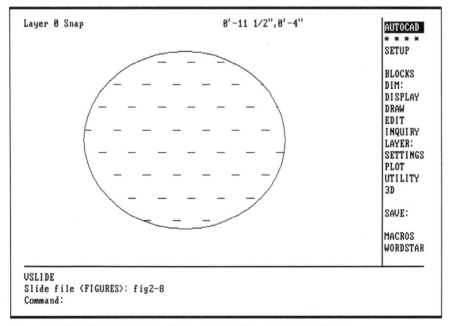

Figure 3.13   The First Set of Lines in the Triang2 Hatch Pattern

coordinate equal to the right side of the base of the triangles, and at the same Y-coordinate. That point is .5,0:

120, .5,0, 1, 1.732, .5,-1.5

Figure 3.15 shows the third set of lines added to the hatch pattern.

Now for something truly different. Use the same basic concept of dashed lines drawn at 0, 60, and 120 degrees. This time, however, alter the description in the following ways:

- Separate all the parallel lines by exactly the sine of 60 degrees.

- Set all the offsets to zero.

- Make all the dashes and spaces of equal length.

Here is this new hatch pattern description:

*trihex,Triangles plus hexagons
0, 0,0, 0, .866, .5,-.5
60, 0,0, 0, .866, .5,-.5
120, .5,0, 0, .866, .5,-.5

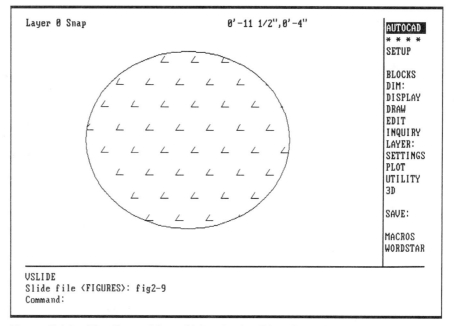

Figure 3.14   The Second Set of Lines in the Triang2 Hatch Pattern

Figure 3.16 shows the hatch pattern produced by this description. In this case, three simple line descriptions produce a rather complex pattern.

Using AutoCAD to Develop New Hatch Patterns

One of the most important things you can do when creating a new hatch pattern is to sketch the pattern before attempting to write the numerical line descriptions. You don't necessarily need to sketch the entire thing, just enough so that you can compute the necessary dashes, dots, angles, and offsets.

Because hatch patterns can require some complex geometrical math, it would be very useful if we had a special tool for developing the hatch pattern and making all the necessary calculations. Fortunately, we do have such a tool—AutoCAD.

In the next example we will use AutoCAD to sketch the hatch pattern and measure the distances and offsets necessary to create it. The hatch pattern we intend to create is a herringbone tweed; the finished

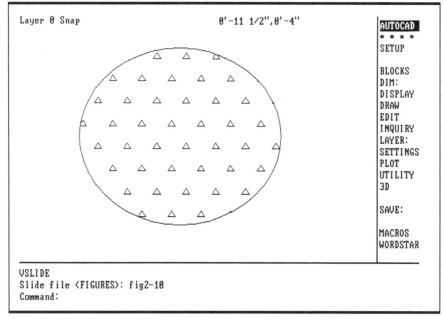

Figure 3.15   The Third, and Final, Set of Lines in the Triang2 Hatch Pattern

pattern is illustrated in Figure 3.17. Following is the complete tweed hatch pattern description:

    *tweed,Herringbone Tweed Pattern
    90, 0,0, 0, 1
    60, 0,0, .21650635, .125, 2, -2
    120, 0,0, -.21650635, .125, 2, -2

To prepare AutoCAD as a tool for helping create hatch patterns, begin a new AutoCAD drawing named Hatches. Because hatch patterns are defined using decimal drawing units, you may need to use the AutoCAD UNITS command to select default decimal drawing units. Also, because you will need as many decimal places of accuracy as possible, select the maximum number of decimal places, eight. For angle measures, select decimal degrees. Now, save the drawing, using AutoCAD's SAVE command.

A cursory analysis of the Tweed hatch pattern shows that at least one set of lines—vertical continuous line types—will be quite simple. The diagonal line types are a bit more complex.

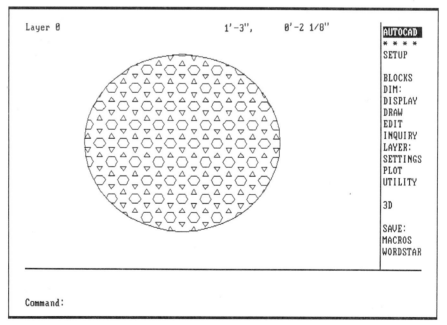

Figure 3.16   The Trihex Hatch Pattern

To begin, draw the vertical lines in the pattern. For simplicity's sake, space them exactly one drawing unit apart. Four vertical lines are enough to encompass the basic pattern. Figure 3.18 illustrates the four vertical lines.

The diagonal lines could be drawn at whatever angle you decide is visually appealing. For the sake of mathematical simplicity in this example, however, draw the diagonal lines at 60 degrees.

Because the diagonal lines will appear between every other set of vertical lines, they will be drawn as dashed line types. How long are the dashes and spaces? To find out, draw a line beginning at the low endpoint of the left vertical line. Use OSNAP to select the endpoint and enter the following at the keyboard:

@10<60

Then press Return twice. You have drawn a line that is ten drawing units long at an angle of 60 degrees. Ten drawing units is enough to be certain that the diagonal line will intersect all of the vertical line segments.

Zoom in and use AutoCAD's automatic dimensioning to measure the length of the line segment that falls between two vertical lines. Again, use OSNAP to select two intersections, as shown in Figure 3.19.

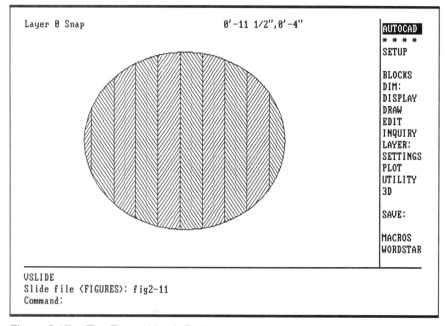

Figure 3.17 The Tweed Hatch Pattern

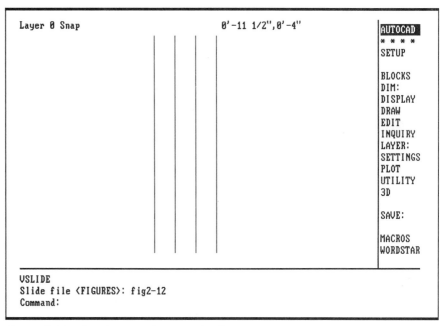

Figure 3.18   The Vertical Lines in the Tweed Hatch Pattern

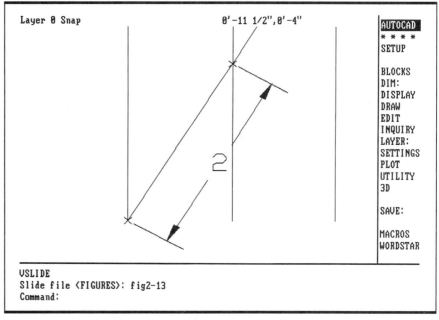

Figure 3.19   Measuring the Length of the Angled Line

When you measure the length of the angled line, you might be surprised to discover that the length of the diagonal line segment between two vertical lines is exactly two drawing units long. Since this is so, and the line continues at the same angle, the next space segment must also be two drawing units long.

The opposing diagonal line will be drawn at 120 degrees (the "mirror" of 60 degrees). It will also consist of alternating dashes and spaces, each two drawing units long.

How far apart should the parallel diagonal lines be? Again, you could choose any value you find visually appealing. For this example, however, select the value of 1/8 drawing unit or .125.

Next, use AutoCAD to copy the diagonal line segment. Issue the AutoCAD COPY command, select the line, and select any point as the base point of displacement. When AutoCAD prompts for the second point of displacement, enter

@0.125<150

and press Return.

The copy line is now located at a distance of 1/8 drawing unit from the original line. The angle of displacement is 150 degrees, that is, the original angle of the line plus 90 degrees. The two lines appear in the same relationship to each other as they would if they were part of a complete hatch pattern.

Notice that the copy line overlaps the first vertical line. In order to place the new line in the correct position, it must be offset. By how much?

Again, use AutoCAD's automatic dimensioning feature to measure the amount of overlap. Use OSNAP to select the endpoint, and then the intersection, as shown in Figure 3.20.

The amount of overlap is .21650635 drawing units. This value is the amount of offset needed for the dashed diagonal lines.

You are almost done. The final step is to determine the starting position and offset for the opposing diagonal lines, the ones at 120 degrees. This can be done logically.

The starting position is exactly the same: 0,0. The reason for this is that the dashed line leaves every other vertical column blank. Therefore, the 120-degree lines, drawn in the opposite direction and beginning at the same point as the 60-degree lines, will begin in a column left blank by the 60-degree lines.

Because the opposing diagonal line is the reverse of the first diagonal line, the offset for this line will also be reversed. In other words, the offset for the 120-degree lines will be negative, or -.21650635.

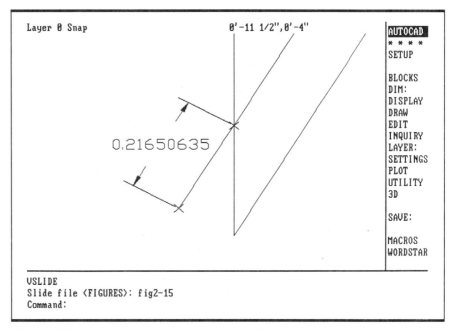

Figure 3.20 Measuring the Overlap of the Second Diagonal Line

The analysis is complete. AutoCAD has told you everything you need to know to create the Tweed hatch pattern. Enter your word processor and edit the file ACAD.PAT. Add the following lines to the bottom of the file. First, type the header line:

*tweed,Herringbone tweed pattern

Next, type the numerical description of the vertical lines, drawn at 90 degrees, starting at point 0,0, zero offset, one drawing unit apart, continuous line type:

90, 0,0, 0, 1

Next, describe the first set of diagonal lines, drawn at 60 degrees, starting at the same point, an offset of .21650635, .125 drawing units apart, pen down 2, pen up -2:

60, 0,0, .21650635, .125, 2, -2

Next, describe the last set of diagonal lines, drawn at 120 degrees, at the same starting position, distance, and line type (notice that the offset value is reversed):

120, 0,0, -.21650635, .125, 2, -2

This completes the Tweed hatch-pattern description. End the last line with a Return and save the file. Enter AutoCAD's Drawing Editor and hatch a circle using this pattern.

An Irregular Hatch Pattern—Concrete

Once I demonstrated AutoCAD to an architect, who was not at all impressed with AutoCAD's hatch pattern for concrete, which is a very regular pattern of alternating lines—one continuous, one dotted. I asked the architect what kind of a pattern would be preferable, and he answered, "Oh, you know, some dots, a few little lines, and a couple of rocks here and there."

So, here is a representation of that idea. I offer it to you as something you might want to try and improve upon, and as a demonstration that hatch patterns really can be just about anything, including random-looking mixtures of dots and lines and "rocks":

```
*concrete,Concrete material
35, 0,0, .3, .7, 0,-1
0, 0,0, 4, 6.928, .5,-7.5
60, 0,0, 4, 6.928, .5,-7.5
120, .5,0, 4, 6.928, .5,-7.5
70, 0,0, 0, 1.4, .125,-1.59
130, .125,0, 0, 1.7, .125,-1.48
```

The first numerical line description draws the dots:

```
35, 0,0, .3, .7, 0,-1
```

The rows are at an angle of 35 degrees, starting at 0,0, offset by .3 drawing units, .7 drawing units apart. Each line consists of dots separated by one drawing unit of space. Allocating nonroundable values for all spaces between the dots, including the offset, will help the final result appear to be random.

The next set of three lines is a variation on the earlier Triang2 hatch pattern:

```
0, 0,0, 4, 6.928, .5,-7.5
60, 0,0, 4, 6.928, .5,-7.5
120, .5,0, 4, 6.928, .5,-7.5
```

The value of the offset and the distance between the parallel lines have been increased by a factor of four in order to spread out the triangles that appear as part of the overall pattern. The lengths of the sides of the triangles are the same (nice and small), but the spaces between them have been increased. Before, the combined length of a line's dash and space totaled two drawing units. In these lines, the total must be four times that.

The next two lines bear little relationship to each other, except that the length of the dash in both cases is .125.

70, 0,0, 0, 1.4, .125,-1.59
130, .125,0, 0, 1.7, .125,-1.48

You can, if you wish, experiment with different angles, starting points, offset distances, and line types until they combine to form a pattern you prefer. Although the individual lines are always rendered in a repeating pattern, if the line elements are unrelated, they can appear random in the complete hatch pattern. Figure 3.21 illustrates this Concrete hatch pattern.

Studying the hatch patterns in ACAD.PAT is an excellent way to fine tune your skills at hatch-pattern definition. Here you will find a wide variety of relationships between lines, producing many interesting effects. Analyzing these existing patterns can help you develop ideas for patterns of your own. Creating your own hatch patterns gives you the ability to add your own unique touches to drawings (that is, apply textures to surfaces) without adding a lot of drawing time overhead.

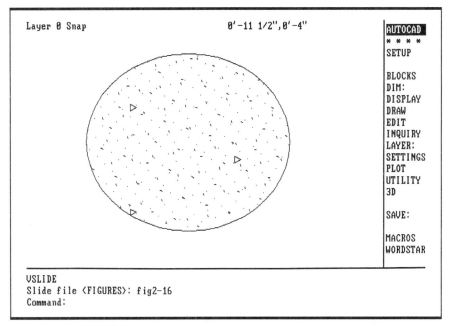

Figure 3.21   The Concrete Hatch Pattern

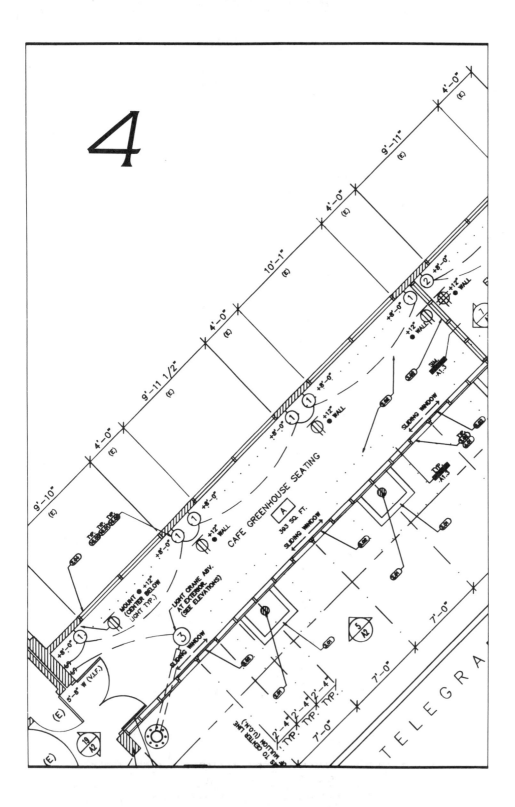

Chapter 4
Shape Files and
Text-Font Files

AUTOCAD SHAPE AND TEXT-FONT files are ASCII files with the extension SHP. You can name these files with any valid DOS file name. The files are edited using your word processor, and must be compiled before they can be used in a drawing. When a shape or text-font file is compiled, a new file is created. This new file is given the original file name plus the extension SHX. The SHX file is the file used by AutoCAD during a drawing session.

SHAPE FILES

Shape files contain basic drawing entities and symbols. By learning to create and compile these files, you can avoid having to create your shapes again and again. Instead, you can call up the appropriate file with a few simple steps.

Editing Shape Files

Since there is a possibility that your shape files may not work the very first time, it may be necessary to make a few trips back and forth between the word processor and AutoCAD's main menu to reedit and refine them. If you have the ability to access your word processor from inside AutoCAD's Drawing Editor, the following procedure is an efficient one:

1. Enter the Drawing Editor.

2. Call your word processor to create or edit the shape file.

3. Return to the Drawing Editor and issue an END command to return to AutoCAD's main menu.

4. At the main menu, select Task #7 (Compile a shape/text font description file).

5. AutoCAD prompts for the name of the shape file and proceeds with compilation.

6. After compiling, reenter the Drawing Editor.

7. Use the LOAD command to load the newly compiled shape file.

8. Use the SHAPE command to place shapes into the drawing.

9. If necessary, repeat steps 2 through 8.

By editing and compiling your shape files while inside AutoCAD, you save the time that it would take to reload AutoCAD from DOS. Also, if you have inserted a shape in a drawing, saved the drawing, changed the shape's description, and recompiled the shape file, the shape in the drawing is automatically updated to reflect those changes.

If you are unable to use your word processor while inside AutoCAD's Drawing Editor, you can at least save a few keystrokes using an endless-loop batch file (like the one described in Chapter 1) to move between AutoCAD and your word processor.

Shape-Description Elements

A single shape file can contain as many as 255 individual shape descriptions. Each shape description in a shape file contains at least two lines of ASCII text. The first line is a header line containing general information about the shape. The second line is a numerical description containing numbers that correspond to the movements of an imaginary pen. These pen movements create the final shape. The numbers describing the pen movements are called the *elements* of the numerical description. Each element in the shape description is separated from the others by a comma.

There is a limit of 2,000 elements in each numerical description in the shape file. Because so many elements are allowed per shape, it is possible for a shape's numerical description to occupy many lines of text in the shape file.

No line of text in a shape-description file can extend past column 80 (the rightmost column on most computer screens). If any line in your shape file is longer than this, the file will not compile.

It is easy to continue a long numerical description on multiple lines of text in the file. Simply end each line with the usual comma that follows an element and continue the description on the next line.

Hexadecimal Numbers In order for the shape file to function as fast as possible, it uses a special numerical counting system, called *hexadecimal,* in addition to the more common decimal counting system. While a decimal system is based on counting cycles of 10, a hexadecimal system is based on counting cycles of 16.

For example, in hexadecimal counting, the first ten integers are the same as decimal integers: 0, 1, 2, 3, 4, 5, 6, 7, 8, and 9. The hexadecimal system, however, substitutes the letter A for 10, B for 11, C for 12, D for 13, E for 14, and F for 15. After it reaches F, it continues with number 10. Number 10 in hexadecimal notation, therefore, has the same value as 16 in decimal notation.

Hexadecimal notation can become rather complex with such numbers as DD, 3F, and so on. Fortunately, the numbers 0 through F are all that are needed when writing shape descriptions.

Why bother using a hexadecimal number system? The reason has to do with the way in which MS-DOS computers handle bits of data, which is normally in groups of 16. A numbering system based on 16 rather than 10 is much more memory-efficient and increases computer speed, making the insertion of shapes as fast as possible and reducing the overall size of the AutoCAD drawing file.

Standard Line Lengths

Shape descriptions utilize other means to achieve speed and efficiency. AutoCAD shape descriptions can utilize 15 standard lengths for straight lines. These line lengths are expressed as whole numbers ranging from 1 drawing unit to 15 drawing units. Lines that have fractional lengths or lengths longer than 15 are considered nonstandard lines and are discussed separately in this chapter.

Standard Angles

AutoCAD shape files recognize 16 standard angles at which line segments may be drawn. These standard angles are represented in Figure 4.1. You will notice that angle zero in Figure 4.1 is AutoCAD's standard orientation for angle zero. The angle numbers increase in a counterclockwise direction, from zero through F. It is possible to produce nonstandard angles; they are discussed separately in this chapter.

Signal Elements

Certain elements in a shape description have special meanings and are reserved for that purpose. These numbers are called *signal elements*. They are as follows:

001 Brings the imaginary pen down. Pen movements that follow this element produce visible lines. This is the default at the start of each shape.

002 Brings the pen up. Pen movements that follow this element will not produce visible lines. This allows for the production of complex shapes with many line segments.

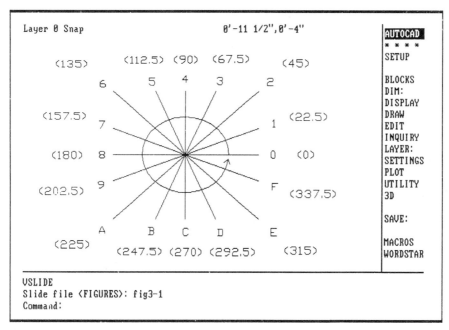

Figure 4.1   AutoCAD Shape File Standard Angles

003 Scales down (*shrinks*) the overall size of the shape. It must be
     followed by an additional element, a whole number by which
     all line lengths in the shape are divided. This allows for some
     additional flexibility while working with standard line lengths.

004 Scales up the overall size of the shape. It must be followed by
     a single element, a whole number by which all line lengths in
     the shape are multiplied.

005 Causes AutoCAD to store the current pen location in
     memory for quick recall later. Only one pen location at a time
     can be stored in this manner. If you wish that a second pen
     location be stored, you must first recall the previously stored
     location using signal element 006. Signal element 005 is often
     used for generating several line segments from a single
     reference point.

006 Causes AutoCAD to recall a previously noted pen location and
     position the pen there. Signal element 005 must have been
     previously issued.

007   Causes AutoCAD to include another shape in the current shape description. It is followed by the header line number of the additional shape to be drawn, starting at the current pen location. The referenced shape must be a member of the same shape file.

008   Causes AutoCAD to draw a single nonstandard line segment. It is followed by two elements indicating movement along an x-axis combined with movement along a y-axis.

009   Causes AutoCAD to draw a series of nonstandard line segments. It is followed by a series of pairs of elements, indicating pen movement along an x-axis combined with movement along a y-axis. The series is terminated with a special element pair, 0,0.

00A   Causes AutoCAD to produce a standard arc. It is followed by two elements. The elements following this element define the radius of the arc, whether the arc is clockwise or counterclockwise, the starting angle, and the arc length measured in octants (an arc spanning eight octants is a full circle).

00B   Causes AutoCAD to produce a nonarc. It is followed by elements that define the starting point, endpoint, starting angle, and length.

00C   Causes AutoCAD to draw a different type of nonstandard arc, called a *bulge arc*. It is followed by three elements that define x and y movement of the pen, which produces a straight line, and adds a *bulge factor*, which bends the line into an arc.

00D   Causes AutoCAD to draw a series of bulge arcs. The series is terminated by the special element pair 0,0.

0   This single zero signals the end of the numerical description. All shape descriptions end with a single zero.

Creating a Shape Description

To demonstrate how these various numbers work together in a shape description, here is an example of a simple shape description that might be included in an AutoCAD shape file. Figure 4.2 shows the kind of shape this shape description produces:

*1,6,EDGE
010,013,02D,013,010,0

The Header Line The first line in the example shape description

*1,6,EDGE

is the header line. This line employs a rigid and consistent structure. It contains four elements in the following order:

1. An asterisk. This symbol is used to identify the start of a new shape description in AutoCAD shape files.

2. A unique shape number. In our example, the shape number is the number 1, followed by a comma. No two shapes may have the same shape number. If they do, the file will not compile. Shape numbers, as long as they are unique to individual shapes, may be arbitrarily assigned. They need not be in sequence (although that is usually the most reasonable arrangement).

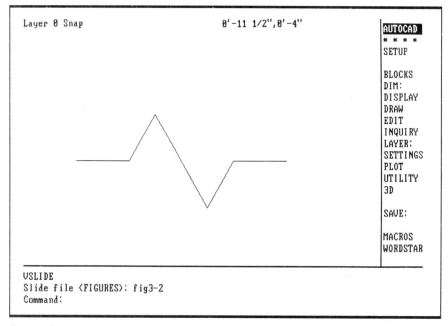

Figure 4.2 The Edge Shape

3. The number of numerical elements that define the shape. In this example, there are six numerical elements on the next line; hence, the number placed here is 6.

4. The shape's unique name. You will use this name to call the shape into your drawing. It must be in uppercase letters in the shape description, or the shape will not be usable. The example shape has been named EDGE.

The Numerical Description   The second line, the numerical description

010,013,02D,013,010,0

first describes a line segment one unit in length, drawn at AutoCAD's standard angle 0. Next, another one-unit line segment was drawn at AutoCAD's standard angle 3. A two-unit line segment was drawn at AutoCAD's standard angle D. Another one-unit line was drawn at angle 3. Finally, the last line segment was drawn, one unit long, at AutoCAD's standard angle 0, and a single zero signals the end of the shape description.

Notice that, with the exception of the zero at the end, the elements in this numerical description consist of groups of three numbers separated by commas.

Each element begins with a zero. This informs AutoCAD that we are dealing with hexadecimal numbers. If we were to skip the leading zero, AutoCAD would assume that we were using decimal numbers.

The second number in each element describes the length of a single line segment expressed in drawing units. The first line segment in this shape, for example, is one drawing unit long; the third line segment is two drawing units long.

The third number in each element describes the standard angle at which the line segment is drawn. The first line segment in this shape, for example, is drawn at the angle zero. The third segment is drawn at angle D. Figure 4.3 shows the example shape in AutoCAD, with each element code placed along the line it creates.

Creating and Compiling the Shape File   To place this example shape description into a shape file, do the following:

1. Enter your word processor.

2. Create a new file called EXAMPLE.SHP.

3. Enter the example shape description exactly as shown above. Enter a carriage return at the end of the second line of text.

4. Save the file to your AutoCAD system subdirectory.

5. At the AutoCAD main menu, select Task #7 (Compile shape/font description file).

6. Enter **EXAMPLE** as the name of the file to compile. The file extension is not necessary. Press Return. AutoCAD will respond

   Compiling shape/font description file

7. You will soon see the message

   Compilation successful. Output file EXAMPLE.shx contains 48 bytes

   If not, you will see an error message; check your original EXAMPLE .SHP file for errors and compile it again.

8. When the file is successfully compiled, enter AutoCAD's Drawing Editor and issue the AutoCAD LOAD command. At the prompt

   Name of shape file to load

   enter **EXAMPLE**.

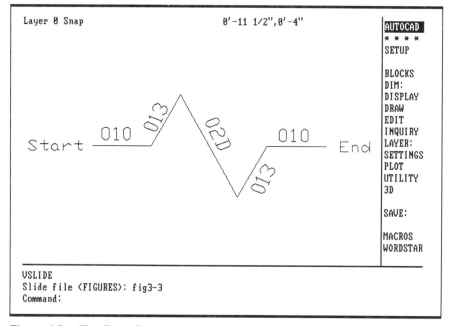

Figure 4.3   The Edge Shape with Description Elements Added

9. Next, issue the AutoCAD SHAPE command followed by the name of the shape, Edge. The shape can now be inserted anywhere in the drawing.

Complex Shape Descriptions

Some shape descriptions require more than movements of a pen. If the shape is composed of several line segments, it will be necessary to change the pen's location without producing a line. In addition, the relationships between the line segments of a more complex shape may require that the shape be drawn very large and then scaled down to fit within a drawing.

Pen Up, Pen Down, and Scaling Figure 4.4 illustrates a more complex shape that requires up and down movements of the pen as well as scaling. As mentioned earlier, we are required to express standard line segments in whole numbers. The Xbox shape description contains two short line segments surrounded by larger line segments. The smallest

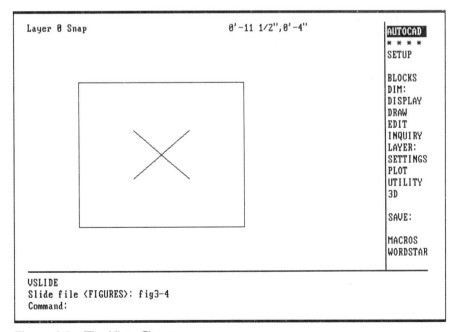

Figure 4.4 The Xbox Shape

standard line segment available to us is one drawing unit. Therefore, the sides of the box will have to be larger than one drawing unit—in fact, three drawing units. To simplify the process of scaling the shape at insertion time, this shape description will be scaled down by a factor of three, resulting in overall dimensions of one by one drawing unit.

Here is the shape description for the Xbox shape, shown in Figure 4.4:

*2,15,XBOX
003,3,030,034,038,03C,002,012,001,012,002,01C,001,016,0

The header line for Xbox follows the same structure as all header lines in shape descriptions: its shape number is 2, the number of elements in the numerical description is 15, and its name is spelled out in uppercase letters. The numerical description begins with these two elements:

003,3,

The first element in the numerical description is a signal element, 003, which means, "Divide all the lengths of the shape by the number that immediately follows." The element that follows, the number 3, reduces the overall size of the shape by a factor of 3. Because this factor of 3 in the second element is not describing any pen motion, it can be a simple decimal integer, and a leading zero is not necessary. This distinguishes it from the signal element 003.

The next four elements

030,034,038,03C,

describe a square, starting at the lower left and proceeding counter-clockwise along standard angles for zero, 90, 180, and 270 degrees. AutoCAD's pen finishes at its starting position.

To get the X in the center, the next element, signal element 002, lifts AutoCAD's pen. The element following 002 moves the pen without creating a visible line:

002,012,

The element 012 moves the pen one drawing unit at standard angle 2; that is, up and to the right at a 45-degree angle.

The next two elements lower the pen and draw one line:

001,012

The signal element 001 lowers AutoCAD's pen. The element 012 draws a line one drawing unit at 45 degrees.

The next two elements raise and move the pen again:

002,01C

This time the pen is moved one drawing unit straight down, at standard angle C.

The last three elements finish the numerical description:

001,016,0

The pen is lowered again and a line is drawn diagonally at standard angle 6, 135 degrees. Last, but certainly not least, the shape description finishes with a single zero.

At this point, you may rightly wonder how this shape description was able to move diagonally one drawing unit, and yet draw an X in the exact center of the square. After all, if the sides of the square are three drawing units each, the distance between opposite corners must be greater than three drawing units.

The answer lies in AutoCAD's special way of handling standard line lengths when drawn diagonally. AutoCAD automatically compensates by drawing these lines slightly longer than corresponding horizontal or vertical lines. In the case of shapes like Xbox, this can be very handy and can greatly simplify the shape description. However, as you might suspect, there are times when such automatic compensation can interfere with your intentions. Generating nonstandard lines is the way around such difficulties.

Octant Arcs Curved lines are added to shapes using standard arc segments, also known as *octant arcs*. An octant arc is a 45-degree arc. Larger arcs can be created by combining octant arcs. Eight octant arcs will form a full circle. You may combine octant arcs with line segments and scaling, as well as pen-up and pen-down motions, to produce a wide variety of useful shapes. The radius of an octant arc may be any whole number from 1 to 255, and octant arcs may be drawn either clockwise or counterclockwise. Figure 4.5 illustrates these arcs.

An octant arc begins at one of eight standard starting angles. These starting angles, called *octant angles*, are numbered 0 through 7, beginning with AutoCAD's standard angle 0, and moving in a counterclockwise direction. They are illustrated in Figure 4.6. Notice that the numbers for octant angles are different from those for the standard angles used to draw line segments.

Figure 4.7 illustrates an octant arc drawn at starting angle 1, with a radius of one drawing unit. Octant arcs may span any number of 45-degree octants. Figure 4.8 shows an octant arc starting at angle 1 and spanning four 45-degree octants. This yields an arc of 180 degrees.

A special signal element, 00A, is used in the shape description to indicate that an octant arc is to be drawn. The next two elements will

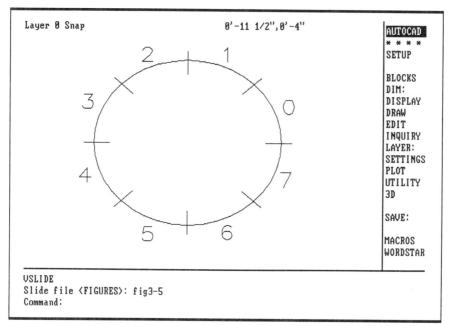

Figure 4.5   Standard Octant Arcs

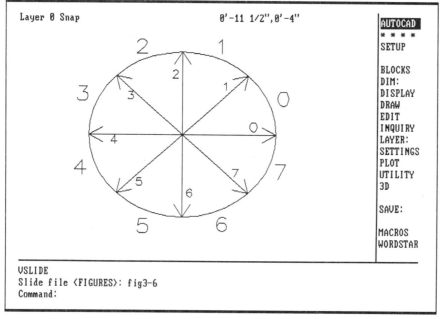

Figure 4.6   Octant-Arc Starting Angles

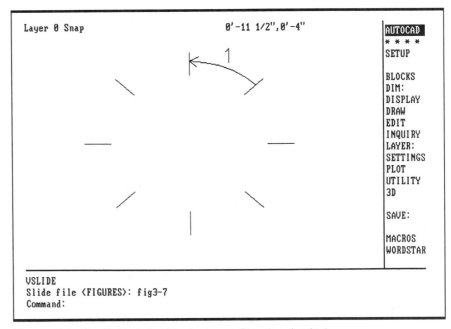

Figure 4.7 An Octant Arc Beginning at Starting Angle 1

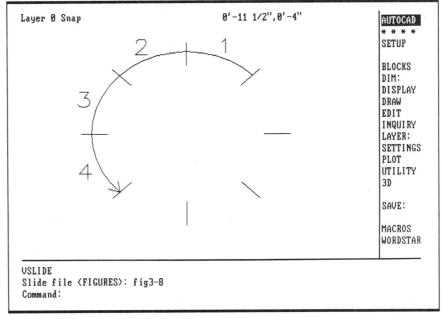

Figure 4.8 An Octant Arc Beginning at Starting Angle 1 and Spanning Four Octants

describe the arc. Use the first element as the radius of the arc. Use the second element to determine the direction of the arc (clockwise or counterclockwise), the starting angle of the octant arc (angle numbers 0 through 7), and the number of octants that the arc spans (1 through 8). For example, here is the syntax for drawing a 90-degree octant arc beginning at octant angle 1:

00A,1,-012

In this example, 00A signals the octant arc and 1 describes the radius.

The third element, – 012, begins with a negative-zero, indicating that the arc is to be drawn clockwise. (If this element were positive—zero without a minus sign—the arc would then be drawn counterclockwise.) The second number in this element, 1, indicates that the arc begins at octant angle 1. The third number, 2, indicates that the octant arc will span two octants.

Combining Elements of a Shape Description

You can use AutoCAD to design and draw the original sketch of a proposed shape, and also help determine whatever dimensions are required to translate line segments and arcs into elements of the shape description. The following example demonstrates this.

Figure 4.9 illustrates a shape called Insul, which combines octant arcs and line segments. This shape could be arrayed between parallel wall lines to add texture, indicating the presence of an insulated wall.

Begin the construction of this shape by sketching a rough version using AutoCAD elements. You will observe that the shape is a fairly simple one: two semicircles joined together with some straight lines.

For the sake of simplicity, draw the lines and semicircles using a length of one drawing unit as the radius of the arcs and the length of the line segments, and see how it works out. Figure 4.10 shows the preliminary drawing.

If you use AutoCAD's automatic dimensioning feature to discover the overall area of this basic design, you'll receive some good news: the design covers an area of four drawing units by four drawing units. If for any reason you don't like this overall size, you can adjust the lines and arcs until you have the exact shape you desire. Figure 4.11 shows the example sketch with AutoCAD's automatic dimensioning added.

It is fortunate that the basic overall dimension of this shape is four by four drawing units, because you can then scale down the overall shape description by a factor of four. By scaling the shape down in this fashion, you will create a shape with overall dimensions of one drawing unit by one drawing unit.

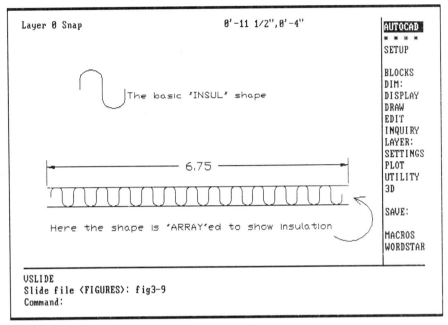

Figure 4.9   The Insul Shape

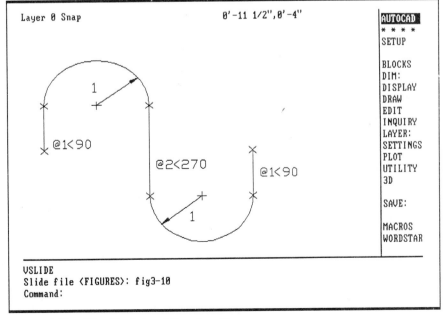

Figure 4.10   The Basic Insul Construction

ADVANCED TECHNIQUES IN AUTOCAD

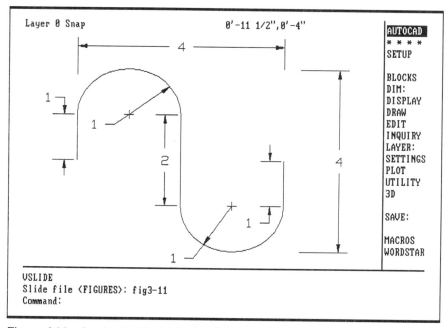

Figure 4.11   Insul with Dimensioning Added

One-by-one shapes are very flexible. For example, if you wish to insert the shape between wall lines that are 6½ inches apart, you could specify a shape height of 6.5 drawing units at insertion time. The one-by-one shape would then fit nicely between the wall lines. You can insert the same shape between thicker or thinner walls just by specifying a shape height equal to the thickness of the wall.

Here is the shape description for Insul:

*3,12,INSUL
003,4,014,00A,(001,-044),02C,00A,(001,044),014,0

The first two shape-description elements are scaling instructions:

003,4,

These two elements will reduce the final shape by a factor of four. The next element

014,

describes the first line segment, which is one drawing unit in length, and is drawn at AutoCAD's standard angle 4 (90 degrees).

The next element is the signal element 00A, followed by the elements that describe a single octant arc:

00A,1,-044,

The number 1 tells AutoCAD that the octant arc has a radius of one drawing unit. The next element describes the arc. It begins with – 0, which will produce a clockwise arc. The first 4 is the starting angle for the octant arc. The second 4 tells AutoCAD that this octant arc will span four octants, which makes it a 180-degree arc.

To make these octant-arc elements more readable at a later time, you can, if you choose, include them in parentheses:

00A,(1,-004),

The parentheses are optional, and they are ignored when the shape file is compiled.

The next element is another straight line segment:

02C,

Notice that it is two drawing units long, and drawn straight down (standard angle C). The next element describes another 180-degree arc:

00A,(001,044),

This arc is also drawn counterclockwise; therefore, the second element following 00A is positive. The last line segment is one drawing unit long at angle 4 (90 degrees):

014,

The shape description concludes with a single zero:

0

Try compiling the new EXAMPLE.SHP file with this description added. Then, insert it into a drawing. Notice that you can change the height of the shape.

Adjusting the Insertion Point   There is a drawback to this shape as it stands: if you want to insert it between two parallel wall lines, you must select an insertion point that is exactly midway between them, because the insertion point of the shape is the starting point of the shape description.

A better starting position for this shape would be its lower-leftmost point. By starting there, you could use AutoCAD's OSNAP to snap the shape to the endpoint of one of the wall lines, thus making it easier to insert.

You can change the insertion point of the shape easily by lifting AutoCAD's pen before actually creating visible lines. The extra elements to do this are added to the Insul shape description below (they are in italics here for emphasis only):

*3,15,INSUL
003,004,*002,024,001*,014,00A,(001,-044),02C,00A,(001,044),014,0

These extra elements lift the pen, move it two drawing units at angle 4, and lower the pen again to draw the shape. By lifting the pen and moving it two drawing units, you create an insertion point that is not the same as the start of the shape drawing itself.

Notice that you must change the total number of elements as shown in the header line. Three extra elements change the header from 12 to 15.

Add these extra elements to your description and notice how the shape drags across the screen at insertion time. Next, draw two parallel lines, each 20 drawing units long. Place them one drawing unit apart. Then try using OSNAP ENDP to snap the shape into position between the two horizontal lines. (Snap to the left endpoint of the lower line.) Accept the height of the shape as one drawing unit. The shape should settle neatly into position. Figure 4.12 illustrates this.

Next, use the AutoCAD ARRAY command to fill in the insulation pattern between the two lines. You will need to create an array with a single row and enough columns to extend the length of the lines. Here is where the overall shape dimensions of one-by-one again work to your advantage. To calculate the correct number of columns, follow these steps:

1. Divide the length of the wall lines in drawing units by the width of the shape. In this example, the result is 20 columns (20 divided by 1).

2. Determine the distance between the columns as equal to the width of the shape—in this case, one drawing unit. (The width of this shape is always equal to its height.)

This example works well because the lengths of the walls are divisible by even multiples of one drawing unit. But what happens when walls have fractional lengths? There are a couple of ways to handle this problem. One way is to move the final pattern slightly within the wall lines after the array is made. This may seem like cheating (and it is), but it often works very well, especially when two walls intersect and the patterns might otherwise overlap. Another solution to the problem is to

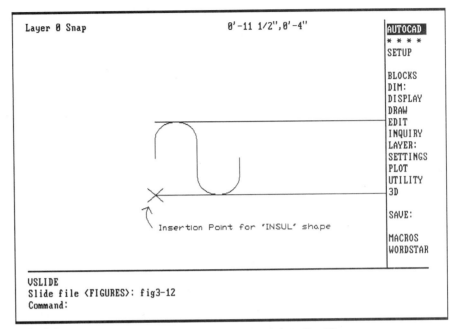

Figure 4.12   The Insul Shape After Snapping It into Position

create a couple of Insul shapes with different height-width ratios. For example, by using a smaller arc radius and compensating with longer line lengths, you can create a similar shape that is one drawing unit tall and only 1/2 drawing unit wide. This kind of shape will fit many fractional wall lengths. Here is the shape description of this narrow version of the shape, called Insul2:

*4,15,INSUL2
003,008,002,044,001,034,00A,(001,-044),06C,00A,(001,044),034,0

Figure 4.13 shows this shape with AutoCAD dimensioning added. Compare this with the shape description for the original Insul shape. Can you figure out why the numbers have changed as they have? Remember that the original size of the Insul2 shape (before it is scaled down) is eight units high and four units wide, in order to give us the proper one drawing unit to one-half drawing unit ratio after scaling.

If you were to compile this shape and insert it between the wall lines used in the previous example, your parameters for the array would be slightly different. With your inserted shape now one drawing unit tall, its width is only 1/2 drawing unit. Therefore, you would create a rectangular array with one row, 40 columns instead of 20, and the distance between columns of 1/2 drawing unit.

ADVANCED TECHNIQUES IN AUTOCAD

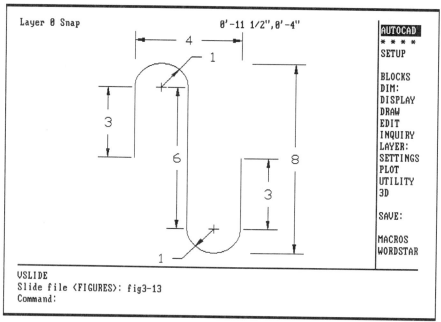

Figure 4.13   The Insul2 Shape

If you change your wall lengths to 21 drawing units, the parameters of your array would be the same, except that you would now need 42 columns in your array instead of 40.

This may seem complex when explained in printed words, but a little experimentation and practice with these shapes will make the concept clear. Try different wall lengths and widths in order to get the hang of creating these textured walls.

Shapes Using Nonstandard Lines and Arcs

It conserves memory space and drawing size to create shapes by means of standard line angles and lengths, octant arcs, and octant angles. This is all well and good, but at times it is very limiting. For cases where standard lines and arcs simply can't be used, there are ways to draw shape lines and move the pen in nonstandard ways. These nonstandard lines and arcs use up additional memory and slow down the process slightly.

Nonstandard Lines   AutoCAD shape files allow for nonstandard pen movement by means of a special signal element that instructs AutoCAD to move its pen to specific coordinate points. The coordinates are referenced by combining pen movements along the x-axis and y-axis. Lines of any length and any direction may be created by this means.

The signal element for this x-y pen movement is 008. This signal element is always followed by two additional elements. The first tells Auto-CAD how much movement takes place along the x-axis; the second element tells AutoCAD how much movement takes place along the y-axis. For example, the following sequence of elements tells AutoCAD to move the pen 16 drawing units to the right and 2 drawing units up:

008,16,2

Note that leading zeros were omitted here, so that AutoCAD will read the numbers as decimals, not hexadecimals. You can use hexadecimal numbers if you want; remember, however, that 16 units in hexadecimal is expressed as 010.

The range of pen movement for nonstandard lines is – 127 through + 127 drawing units. If the value of movement along the x-axis is negative, the pen moves to the left. If it is positive, the pen moves to the right. If the value of movement along the y-axis is negative, the pen moves down. If it is positive, the pen moves up.

Note that for positive numbers, the + symbol is optional, and is not included in the above example. Also, as in the case with octant arcs, you may include parentheses for readability. With parentheses added, the example elements are as follows:

008,(16,2)

Although two motion elements are used, only one line is generated using these elements. The line that results from this nonstandard motion will extend from the location of the pen when the 008 element is invoked to the point where the pen is located when the motion is complete. If the pen has been lifted by means of signal element 002, no line is drawn, and the pen is merely relocated.

Figure 4.14 shows a simple shape that includes two nonstandard diagonal lines. Here is the shape description that draws the Light shape shown in Figure 4.14:

*5,18,LIGHT
003,8,040,05C,008,(4,-14),08C,00A,(8,-4),084,008,(4,14),054,040,0

All of these elements have been demonstrated in earlier examples. After the header line, the numerical description begins with the element to scale down the shape by a factor of eight. Next, three straight line segments are drawn, beginning at the shape's insertion point. Then comes the 008 element, and within parentheses, the element to move

ADVANCED TECHNIQUES IN AUTOCAD

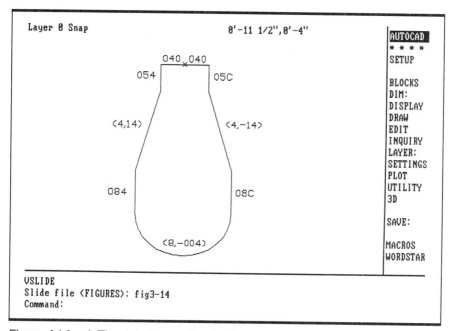

Figure 4.14   A Theatrical Lamp Symbol Drawn with Nonstandard Lines

the pen to the left 4 drawing units and down 14 drawing units. Again, notice that this movement simply locates the endpoint of the resulting line segment.

The shape continues: another standard line is drawn, followed by an octant arc and two more standard lines. Then, another nonstandard line is drawn. The syntax for this second nonstandard line is the same, although one of the values is different. Here the x-y movement is 4 drawing units to the right and 14 drawing units up. Two more standard lines finish off the shape and, as always, the shape description concludes with a single zero.

It is possible to draw a shape that consists entirely of nonstandard lines. Rather than reissue the 008 signal element over and over, you can use another signal element (009) to indicate a series of nonstandard x-y pen movements.

When this signal element is issued, a series of pairs of x-axis and y-axis movement elements follows. Any number of pairs of x-y movement elements can follow, but they must terminate with the special x-y movement elements, 0,0.

Here is an example shape description that contains a series of four nonstandard line movements, beginning with element number 4. This example shape is a simple narrow-diamond shape:

```
*6,21,DIAMD
003,12,020,009,(-1,-6),(-1,6),(1,6),(1,-6),(0,0),002,008,(-1,6),
001,0CC,0
```

This example includes a little bit of everything. It is scaled down by a factor of 12 to reduce its overall height from 12 drawing units to one drawing unit. First, a single standard line segment is drawn, two drawing units long at standard angle zero. A series of four nonstandard lines follows, using the appropriate x-y pen movement elements, which are terminated as required with the elements 0,0. Notice how each pair of x-y pen-movement elements is contained within a set of parentheses.

Following the nonstandard movement, the pen is lifted, and it backtracks by reversing its last movement. The 008 element works for this single nonstandard line movement. The element 001 lowers the pen again and a single standard vertical line is drawn, 12 drawing units in length.

The next-to-last element includes the hexadecimal number for 12 (C) to describe both the length of the line and its angle. (Notice that in this example, the numerical description extends to more than a single line of text.)

Nonstandard Arcs It is possible to create shape descriptions using arcs that do not begin on an octant angle, or whose total degrees are not a multiple of 45. There are two methods for doing this. One method creates an *offset arc;* the other method creates a *bulge arc.*

Offset Arcs An offset arc references the two nearest standard offset angles and draws the arc in relation to those angles. Offset arcs are signaled by element 00B. Element 00B is followed by five special elements that describe the offset arc.

The first three of these describe how the nonstandard arc is offset from the standard arc. The last two elements are the standard arc-description elements we have seen before.

For example, here are the numerical elements that describe a small, nonstandard arc that begins at 52 degrees and ends at 127 degrees, has a radius of 5 drawing units, and is drawn counterclockwise:

```
00B,(40,210,0,5,012)
```

The first element is 00B, signaling AutoCAD that an offset arc is to be described. The next two elements indicate the starting and ending offsets for this arc. These elements are calculated using the following formula:

1. Determine the starting angle of the offset arc. In our example, this is 52 degrees.

2. Determine the next lowest standard octant angle from the starting angle of the octant arc. In this example, this would be octant angle 1, 45 degrees.

3. Determine the difference in degrees between the starting angle of the offset arc and the octant angle. In this case, the difference between 52 degrees and 45 degrees is 7 degrees.

4. Having calculated this difference, multiply it by 256. In our example, this results in 1,792.

5. Divide the result by 45. In our example, this result is 40.82.

6. Drop the decimal portion of the number. In our example, this is 40.

Therefore, the starting offset for our example arc is 40. This is the numerical element that immediately follows element 00B.

The formula for calculating the offset for the endpoint of the arc is almost the same:

1. Determine the ending angle of the nonstandard arc. In our example, this is 127 degrees.

2. Determine the next lowest standard octant angle from the ending angle of the octant arc. In this example, this would be octant angle 2, 90 degrees.

3. Determine the difference in degrees between the ending angle of the offset arc and the octant angle. In this case, the difference between 127 degrees and 90 degrees is 37 degrees.

4. Having calculated this difference, multiply it by 256. In our example, this results in 9,472.

5. Divide the result by 45. In our example this results in 210.48.

6. Drop the decimal portion of the number. In our example, this is 210.

Therefore, the ending offset for the offset arc is 210. This is the second element in the offset-arc description.

The third element in the offset-arc description will always be zero. This zero simply indicates that the radius of the offset arc is less than the maximum allowable 255 drawing units.

The fourth and fifth elements in the offset-arc description are the same as if a standard arc were being drawn. In this case, the radius is five drawing units, so the fourth element is 5. The arc is drawn counter-clockwise, begins in octant 1, and spans a total of 2 octants, so the fifth element is 012.

Figure 4.15 illustrates a simple shape, called Cap, that includes this off-set arc. This is the complete shape description for Cap:

*7,24,CAP
003,10,002,008,(-1,5),001,0AC,002,020,001,0A4,002,008,(2,-1),001,
00B,(40,210,0,5,012),0

1. This shape is scaled by a factor of ten (**003,10,**).

2. The pen is lifted and moved one drawing unit to the left, five draw-ing units up (**002,008,(– 1,5),**).

3. The pen is lowered and a standard line segment is drawn ten drawing units at angle C (**001,0AC,**).

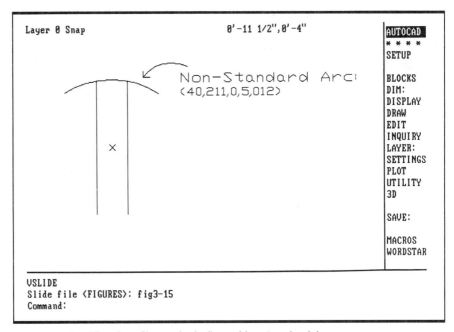

Figure 4.15 The Cap Shape, Including a Nonstandard Arc

4. The pen is again lifted, and moved two drawing units at angle 0 (002,020,).

5. The pen is lowered and a standard line segment is drawn ten drawing units at angle 4 (001,0A4,).

6. The pen is lifted and moved two drawing units to the right and one drawing unit down (002,008,(2, – 1),).

7. Finally, the pen is lowered and the offset arc is generated (001,00B,(40,210,0,5,012),0).

The secret to designing nonstandard shapes like this is to use Auto-CAD in the sketching and design process. In this example, the insertion point of the shape was used as the center point of the arc. The radius of the arc was determined by measuring from the insertion point to the endpoint of one of the vertical lines. After the arc was drawn, this center point was again referenced, using AutoCAD's angular dimensioning feature, to determine its starting and ending angles.

When AutoCAD first measured the radius, starting angle, and ending angle of the arc, these measurements were fractional. However, for purposes of calculating offsets, these fractional dimensions were rounded to the nearest whole number without problems.

Bulge Arcs   If all this calculating of offset arcs seems daunting, there is another method for producing a nonstandard arc if you have AutoCAD Version 2.5 or later, and your arc is 180 degrees or less. This second type of nonstandard arc is called a bulge arc. The following example uses this means to make a change in the theatrical lamp shape shown in Figure 4.14.

The process of creating a bulge arc involves drawing a nonstandard straight line segment using x-y movement as we have seen before, and then *bulging* it from its center point. The signal element for a single bulge arc is 00C.

The 00C element is followed by three elements:

1. The x-axis movement

2. The y-axis movement

3. The *bulge factor,* the amount of bulge to be applied to the line.

The following is an example of a bulge arc:

00C,(5,5,60)

In this example, first the line is drawn by moving the pen five drawing units to the right and five drawing units up. Then a bulge factor of 60 is applied to the line. Because the 60 is positive, the final arc will be drawn counterclockwise. If 60 had been negative, the final arc would have been drawn clockwise.

You can apply a bulge factor within a range from − 127 to + 127. Using the maximal or minimal value will result in a 180-degree arc. Arcs larger than 180 degrees will have to be drawn as standard arcs, as nonstandard arcs using offset calculations, or as a series of bulge arcs.

For a working example of a bulge arc, the following is the shape description of the Light shape again, drawn using a standard 180-degree octant arc (the elements for the octant arc are italicized for emphasis):

*5,18,LIGHT
003,8,040,05C,008,(4,-14),08C,*00A,(8,-004)*,084,008,(4,14),054,040,0

The next shape description substitutes a bulge arc, for a less rounded effect:

*5,19,LIGHT
003,8,040,05C,008,(4,-14),08C,*00C,(-16,0,-60)*,084,008,(4,14),054,040,0

Notice that because an extra element was used to generate the bulge arc, the number of elements in the header line is increased by one, from 18 to 19. Notice also that the bulge factor is negative, which results in the necessary clockwise arc. In Figure 4.16, the two shapes are compared.

As with nonstandard lines, there is a special signal element for defining a series of bulge arcs. This element is 00D. As with a series of nonstandard lines, any number of bulge-arc descriptions can follow this signal element, but the series must be terminated with the special elements 0,0. The following is an example of a shape description using a series of bulge arcs:

*8,18,CURLS
003,10,00D,(10,10,60),(10,10,-60),(3,14,120),(3,14,-120),(0,0),0

If you wish, you can apply a bulge factor of zero, which results in a straight line. This is very useful when connecting a continuous series of straight lines and bulge arcs into a continuous line. By using the zero bulge, you are spared the trouble of going back and forth between the various special elements to call nonstandard lines and bulge arcs. The following is an example of this:

*9,21,CURLS2
003,5,00D,(5,5,60),(5,5,-60),(5,0,0),(5,5,60),(5,5,-60),(0,0),0

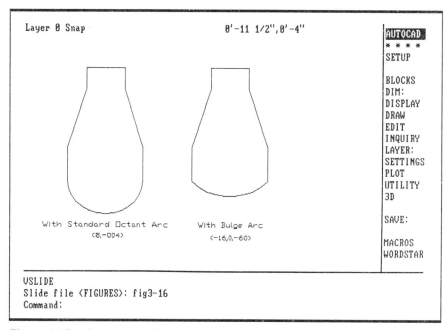

```
Layer 0 Snap                      0'-11 1/2",0'-4"            AUTOCAD
                                                             * * * *
                                                             SETUP

                                                             BLOCKS
                                                             DIM:
                                                             DISPLAY
                                                             DRAW
                                                             EDIT
                                                             INQUIRY
                                                             LAYER:
                                                             SETTINGS
                                                             PLOT
                                                             UTILITY
                                                             3D

       With Standard Octant Arc   With Bulge Arc             SAVE:
              (8,-004)                (-16,0,-60)
                                                             MACROS
                                                             WORDSTAR

VSLIDE
Slide file <FIGURES>: fig3-16
Command:
```

Figure 4.16   Octant-Arc Theatrical Lamp Compared to Bulge-Arc Theatrical
Lamp

Note how a straight line element is added within the series of bulge arcs
(5,0,0,) simply by supplying a bulge factor of zero.

How to Calculate the Correct Bulge Factor   Once you have designed
and dimensioned your shape using AutoCAD, you can continue to use
AutoCAD to determine the correct bulge factor. The following
describes this process:

1. Determine the angle of your arc. AutoCAD's autodimensioning feature is invaluable here. Draw scratch lines to connect the endpoints
   of the arc with the center of the arc, as shown in Figure 4.17.

2. After drawing your scratch lines, use AutoCAD's DIM ANG command to measure the angle formed by them. Figure 4.18 adds
   dimensions to the example drawing.

3. Divide the arc angle by 180, and multiply the result by 127. This
   yields the correct bulge factor.

If you choose to draw the arc clockwise, apply the bulge factor as a negative number; otherwise apply the bulge factor as a positive number.

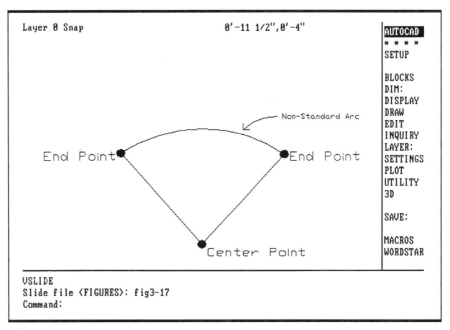

Figure 4.17   Connecting the Arc Center and Endpoints

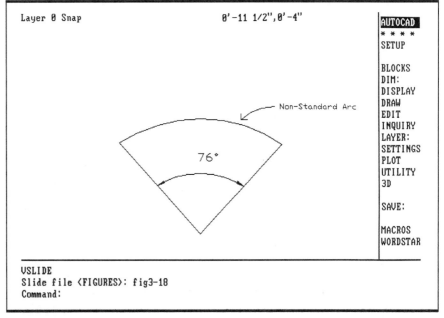

Figure 4.18   Arc Angle Determined by AutoCAD

This combination of autodimensioning and calculation can be made considerably easier and faster by using a short AutoLISP routine. For the sake of those who intend to design a lot of shapes using bulge arcs, such a routine is provided in Chapter 11, "Example AutoLISP Routines."

TEXT-FONT FILES

If you want to create text in AutoCAD using your own unique text font and you have perseverance, you can do so by means of a special type of shape file, called a *text-font file*. AutoCAD will read your custom text-font file and insert text with that font style into your drawings, using the same commands it uses to insert standard text.

Comparing Text-Font Files to Shape Files

Text-font files are similar to ordinary shape files. Like shape files, they have the file extension SHP. They are created and edited using your word processor. They can contain shape descriptions of each letter of the alphabet as well as numbers, punctuation marks, and any special characters that might be necessary to produce text in a drawing. For the most part, these shape descriptions use the same elements in the same way as those used in ordinary shape files.

Text-font files, however, contain certain special shape descriptions that distinguish them from ordinary shape files. For instance, a text-font file must begin with a special shape description that identifies the scaling, letter positioning, and orientation of the characters. A text-font file must contain a shape description for a line feed, which instructs Auto-CAD to move the pen a specific distance to a new line when entering repeated lines of text.

Unlike ordinary shape files, the shape numbers in the header line of a text-font file correspond to a set of standard number codes used to generate those text characters via the screen or printer. These codes are called ASCII codes. Table 4.1 contains the ASCII codes for text characters.

Because you use these standard ASCII codes, all text-font files are, in effect, prenumbered. For example, the shape number for an uppercase A is always 65.

The shape names in shape descriptions of text-font files are entered in lowercase, as opposed to the shape names in ordinary shape files, which are entered in uppercase. Also, because the standard numbering system in text-font files eliminates the need to name the shapes, when the text-font file is compiled, AutoCAD will ignore the lowercase shape

32 (space)	65 A	98 b
33 !	66 B	99 c
34 "	67 C	100 d
35 #	68 D	101 e
36 $	69 E	102 f
37 %	70 F	103 g
38 &	71 G	104 h
39 ' (apostrophe)	72 H	105 i
40 (	73 I	106 j
41)	74 J	107 k
42 *	75 K	108 l
43 +	76 L	109 m
44 , (comma)	77 M	110 n
45 - (hyphen)	78 N	111 o
46 . (period)	79 O	112 p
47 / (forward slash)	80 P	113 q
48 0	81 Q	114 r
49 1	82 R	115 s
50 2	83 S	116 t
51 3	84 T	117 u
52 4	85 U	118 v
53 5	86 V	119 w
54 6	87 W	120 x
55 7	88 X	121 y
56 8	89 Y	122 z
57 9	90 Z	123 [
58 : (colon)	91 [	124 | (vertical bar)
59 ; (semicolon)	92 \ (backslash)	125]
60 <	93]	126 ~ (tilde)
61 =	94 ^ (caret)	
62 >	95 (underscore)	
63 ?	96 ' (rev. apostrophe)	
64 @	97 a	

Table 4.1   The ASCII Codes for Text Characters

names, thus conserving space in the compiled file. The only reason to include shape names at all is to make individual text characters easier to locate for subsequent editing.

Scaling is handled differently in text-font files. In ordinary shape files, scaling is handled on a shape-by-shape basis. In text-font files, the entire file is scaled by means of a special shape description. Characters in a text-font file are often designed using a large scale, which allows complex characters to be rendered using whole numbers. Afterwards, the entire text-font file is scaled down to allow more flexibility in establishing text height at insertion time.

Like ordinary shape files, text-font files utilize source codes. It is useful to study the source code for the standard text-font files that come with AutoCAD. You can find these files on the AutoCAD Support Files disk in a separate subdirectory named SOURCE. Copy these files onto your hard disk before attempting to read them or make any changes. Do not work with the original files supplied by Autodesk.

Special Shape Descriptions in a Text-Font File

Two special shape descriptions signal AutoCAD that the file is a text-font file. The first identifies scaling, letter positioning, and orientation of the character, and the second is the line-feed description. Here is an example of the first special shape description in a text-font file:

```
*0,4,fontname
38,7,0,0
```

The header line contains the required shape number (zero), the number of numerical description elements (there are always four), and the name of the text font, always entered in lowercase. AutoCAD uses the numerical elements in this shape description to determine the scaling and orientation of the font:

1. The first element describes the maximum number of drawing units the uppercase letters extend above the baseline of the text. In this case the number is 38. This number may be different in your text-font file.

2. The second element describes the maximum number of drawing units that the lowercase letters may extend below the baseline of the text. In this case the number is 7. Again, this number may be different in your text-font file.

3. The third element is the orientation mode element. This number is zero if the text font is only horizontal. If the font contains optional pen motions for vertical orientation, the mode element is 2. No other numbers are used in this position.

4. The fourth element is the standard zero that finishes all shape descriptions.

Here is the second special shape description in a text-font file:

```
*10,5,lf
002,008,(0,-46),0
```

This is the line-feed shape description. It is always shape number 10. This shape description represents the downward motion of the pen when more than one line of text is entered. The motion is described by the signal element 002 and a nonstandard pen motion moving down the y-axis. It causes the pen to drop one line without drawing. In this example, the total pen motion required to drop one line is 46 drawing units. This motion includes 38 drawing units to account for the maximum height of the letters, plus 7 drawing units for the amount that lowercase letters may extend below the base line, plus an additional drawing unit.

Designing Text-Character Shapes

The process of creating a text-font file from scratch is time consuming. The first step is to create a shape description for each letter, number, punctuation mark, and symbol to be used in the font. All the shape-designing and describing techniques you have seen so far may be used to generate these text-character shape descriptions.

An effective way to test the accuracy of the shape descriptions in your text-font file is to create a special drawing that contains the characters you intend to include in your font file. Load your custom font file into this drawing via the AutoCAD STYLE command. As you edit characters or add them to your custom font file and recompile it, the characters in the drawing will be updated for you automatically. As you design your text characters and enter your shape-description elements, begin and end each shape description with the pen in the same position relative to the location of the text characters. In the example shape descriptions shown in this chapter, the pen drawing motions always begin in the lower-left corner and end in the lower right. There is some additional horizontal space added between the character and the ending position of the pen to allow space between the characters when they appear in text.

It is important that text characters be of consistent size. To help with this, create a template drawing of boxes into which you can draw your text characters. This template drawing should show you the maximum height and width of all the characters in the text-font file. Figure 4.19 shows an example of such a template.

Using the example template shown in Figure 4.19, uppercase characters would be drawn in the larger box and lowercase characters in the smaller box. Dimensioning lines were added in this example, so that you

ADVANCED TECHNIQUES IN AUTOCAD

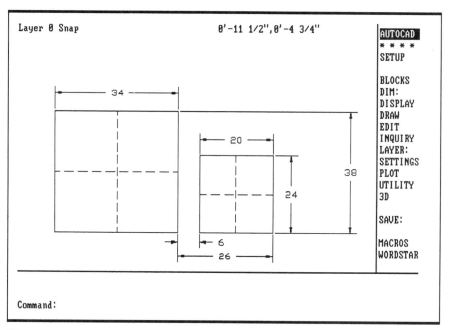

Figure 4.19   A Font Template

may see their relative sizes. A space of six drawing units is added in front of each box as a default spacing between the letters.

In this example, not all lowercase letters will remain within the boundaries of the small box. For instance, g and q will extend slightly below it.

The template drawing has a snap value of one drawing unit, which makes it easier to draw characters that can be dimensioned and translated into x-y pen movements accurately using whole numbers. The overall limits of this template are 136 units along the x-axis and 70 units along the y-axis. This allows extra room to insert text consisting of compiled character shapes and compare them with the original drawing. This example is not the only possibility for a template drawing. Feel free to experiment and develop the template that is just right for you.

Figure 4.20 shows a bold-outlined uppercase A, drawn in the example template. The following is the shape description that will produce the uppercase A shown in Figure 4.20:

```
*15,38,uca
009,(14,38),(6,0),(14,-38),(-7,0),(-4,11),(-12,0),(-4,-11),(-7,0),(0,0),
002,008,(13,17),001,009,(4,9),(4,-9),(-8,0),(0,0),002,008,(27,-17),0
```

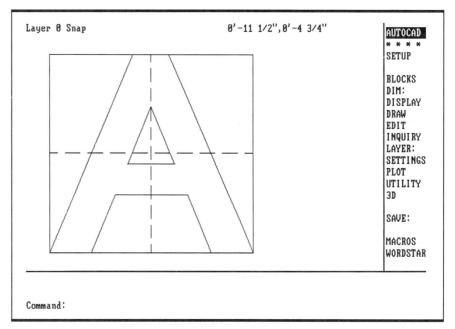

Figure 4.20 Designing an Uppercase A

Notice that this shape description is composed entirely of nonstandard line segments. The pen is lifted twice: the first time to draw the triangle in the center of the A and the second time to move the pen to its standard finishing position, which is six drawing units to the right of the lower-right corner of the letter. This allows space between the A and whatever letter may follow it.

Figure 4.21 shows this same letter A plus the x and y pen movements in the shape description that produce each line. Movement with the pen lifted is shown as dashed lines.

The lowercase letter a, which is more complex, is shown in Figure 4.22. The shape description for the lowercase a is as follows:

```
*16,64,lca
002,008,(15,0),001,034,00D,(-9,-3,-34),(-1,14,-110),(10,3,0),
(-1,2,37),(-8,-1,40),(-5,0,0),(4,5,-31),(11,0,-29),(4,-7,-42),
(0,-16,0),(-5,0,0),(0,0),002,008,(0,12),001,00D,(-9,-7,-71),
(0,4,-105),(9,3,0),(0,0),002,008,(9,-12),0
```

This shape description uses many bulge arcs to render the curves in the letter.

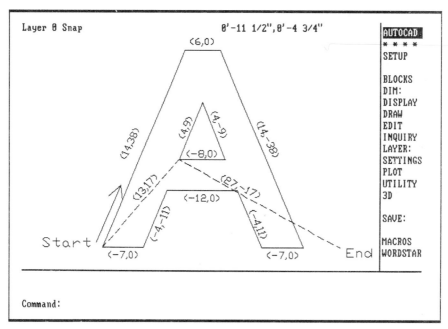

Figure 4.21 Uppercase A Showing AutoCAD Pen Movements

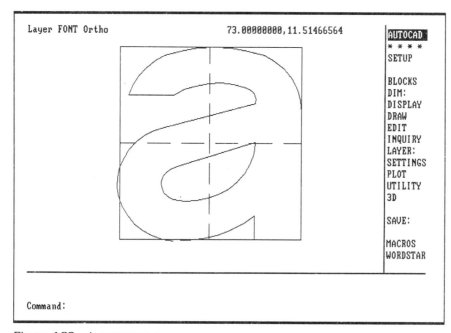

Figure 4.22 Lowercase a

A good procedure for creating letters with curves is as follows:

1. Draw the letter.

2. Once the letter looks just the way you want it, mark all endpoints of arcs for later reference. A small circle or x can be useful for doing this. Use AutoCAD's OSNAP command to make multiple copies of the mark at the endpoint of each arc.

3. Use AutoCAD to determine the bulge of each curved line in the character. Use the technique and formula that was given earlier in this chapter (or copy the AutoLISP routine for determining bulges, found in Chapter 13).

4. Make notes of the results and all the necessary shape-description elements.

5. Once the x-y pen movements and bulges have been determined, enter your word processor and type all the necessary elements for this character.

As was mentioned in the previous chapter, if your character is composed of both straight line segments and curves, it is easier to draw the straight line segments as bulge arcs with bulge factors of zero, rather than enter many signal elements for alternating arcs and straight lines. Figure 4.23 shows this lowercase character along with each set of pen-motion elements used to create its arcs and lines.

Dual-Orientation Text-Font Files

Once each character's shape description has been created and tested, special signal elements may be added to the description that will allow the font to be entered in either vertical or horizontal orientation. Text-font files that can be entered with either vertical or horizontal orientation are called *dual-orientation text-font files*.

In a dual-orientation text-font file, each shape description contains special optional pen-motion elements. AutoCAD ignores these optional elements unless the user specifies vertical text orientation when the font file is loaded into the drawing. These optional pen-motion elements are usually found at the beginning and end of each shape description. Their purpose is to lift and relocate the pen to the correct starting and finishing positions that orient the text vertically.

Figure 4.24 illustrates the extra pen motions necessary to adapt the uppercase A to vertical orientation. The optional pen-motion elements

ADVANCED TECHNIQUES IN AUTOCAD

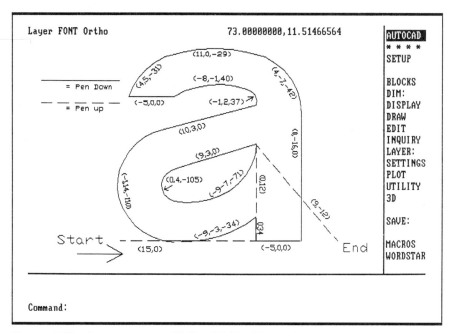

Figure 4.23   Lowercase a with Pen-Motion Elements

shown in Figure 4.24 are preceded by the special signal element 00E. The first element that follows this special signal element is ignored by Auto-CAD unless the user chooses vertical orientation when loading the text-font file. Subsequent elements are processed normally.

There is no special signal element for a series of optional pen motions. If you need to use such a series, each optional element must be preceded by the code 00E.

The following is the shape description for an uppercase A with optional vertical pen-motion elements added (italics are for emphasis only):

```
*65,49,uca
00E,002,00E,008,(-17,-38),001,009,(14,38),(6,0),(14,-38),(-7,0),
(-4,11),(-12,0),(-4,-11),(-7,0),(0,0),002,008,(13,17),001,009,
(4,9),(4,-9),(-8,0),(0,0),002,008,(27,-17),00E,008,(-13,-7),0
```

Notice that the total number of elements in the header line has been increased to account for these additional elements.

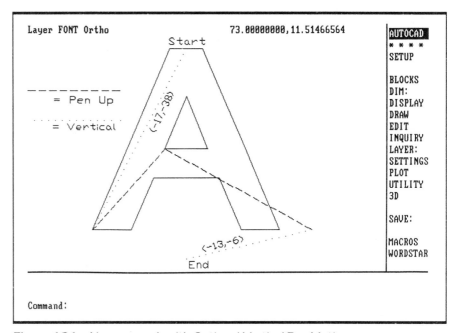

Figure 4.24   Uppercase A with Optional Vertical Pen Motion

At the end of this shape description, more optional pen motions relocate the pen to the lower-center position of the shape. Each shape description in the text-font file will begin, as this one does, with an optional pen motion straight down the height of the character. This causes the characters to line up vertically.

The optional pen motions required by your font file will depend on how you want your text characters to line up vertically: centered, left justified or right justified. In the above example, the pen motion is set to line up the characters along a vertical centerline.

Figure 4.25 shows a custom font for AutoCAD. Space does not permit a complete listing of source code in this book, but the code for this font is available on disk (see the coupon in the back of this book).

The keys to success in developing shape-description and text-font files are patience, persistence, and a willingness to experiment. There is some commercial software available that can be of some help with shape and font file development. See Appendix B of this book for details on third-party software.

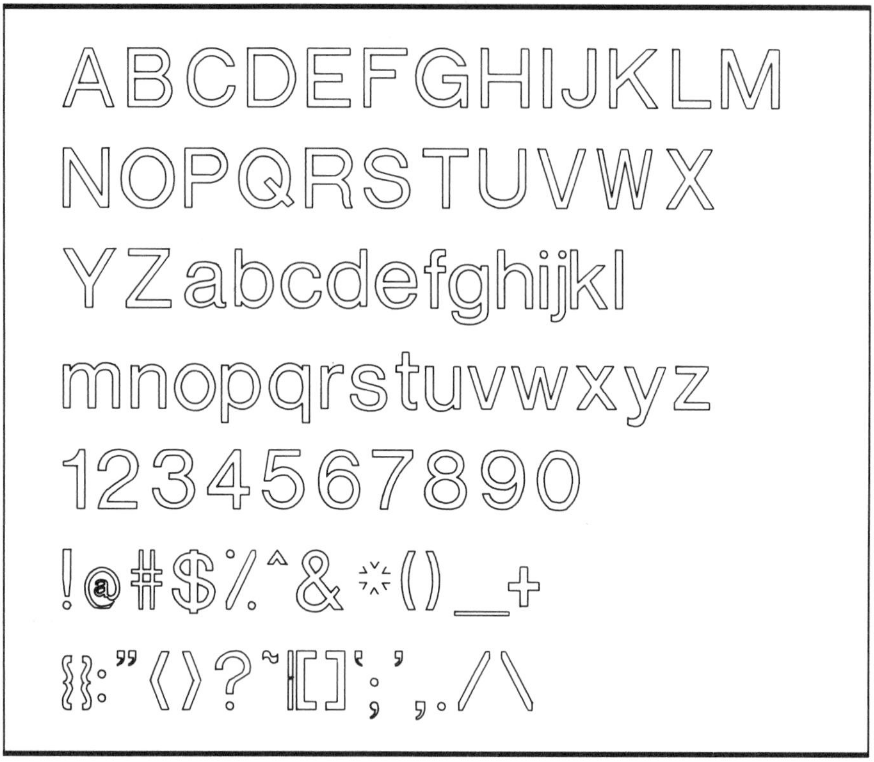

ABCDEFGHIJKLM
NOPQRSTUVWX
YZabcdefghijkl
mnopqrstuvwxyz
1234567890
!@#$%^&*()_+
{}:"<>?~[];',./\

Figure 4.25   A Sample Bold Outline Font

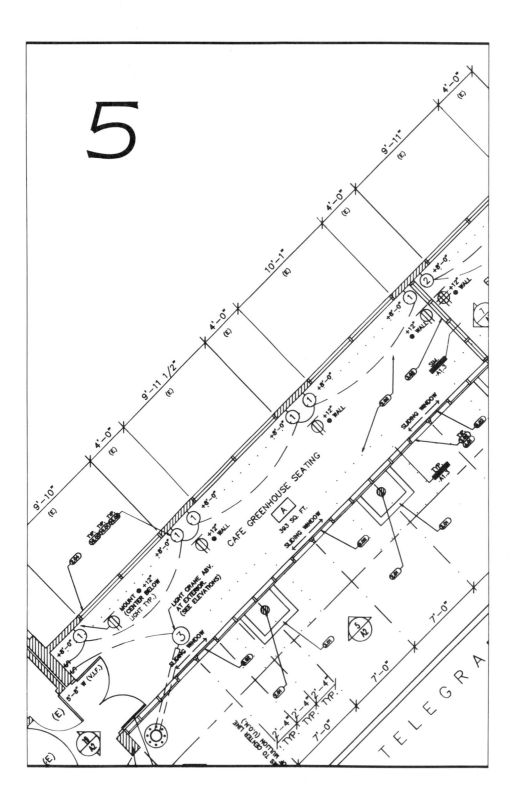

Chapter 5
Introduction to Custom Menus

THE CUSTOM MENU is one of the most powerful tools at your disposal for improving your AutoCAD drawing productivity. Custom menus enable you to eliminate unnecessary menu selections and repetitive keyboard entries. They are easily created and modified using your word processor.

Generally speaking, custom menus are used to handle the following types of procedures:

1. Grouping together frequently used AutoCAD commands, so that you no longer need to type them out at the keyboard or jump between screen menus to find them. For example, a custom menu might include LINE, ZOOM, and ERASE commands on the same screen. Another custom menu might combine the PLINE drawing command with certain specific PEDIT polyline-editing options.

2. Clarifying the on-screen command display by eliminating commands that are rarely (if ever) used. For example, if your editing consists almost entirely of using the ERASE, MOVE, COPY, BREAK, and CHANGE commands, you could create a special editing menu that displays only these commands, perhaps adding your most frequently used OSNAP overrides for extra convenience. Condensing the display in this fashion can save significant amounts of drawing time.

3. Combining specific commands and features, so that a single menu selection can execute a specific series of commands in sequence, including the typing of repeatedly invoked names (layers, blocks, shapes, and so on). A series of commands executed by means of a single menu selection is called a *macro*. For example, a custom menu might include a special series of layer-changing commands that sets any existing layer as current automatically, without going through the complete layer-changing routine at the keyboard.

This chapter will present techniques for accessing and changing the AutoCAD standard menu. Chapter 6 will examine the construction of custom menu macros in detail.

CREATING THE CUSTOM MENU

The purpose of a custom menu is to have a special version of Auto-CAD dedicated to your particular drawing needs, strengths, weaknesses, and area of specialization. There is no right or wrong way to organize a menu; there are only working principles that are useful, that actually work, and that produce beneficial results for you. The creation of a custom menu is by definition a subjective pursuit.

Knowing What You Want

Your most important asset when creating a custom menu is your knowledge of how you use AutoCAD. This may require some analysis, especially if you have been too busy creating drawings to spend much time watching and making notes on how you use the program. However, this knowledge is essential. A well-organized custom menu must be thoroughly thought out in advance. You could develop the custom menu by trial and error if you wish, but there are more efficient ways.

Get into the habit of making notes. For example, note which commands you use together frequently. You might be able to join these commands together in a macro and save a lot of time, especially if they are on different submenus. Do you use a lot of scratch lines? Do you usually select objects by windowing? Do you window zoom in one level and then zoom out again? These are examples of the kinds of AutoCAD techniques that can be made more efficient by means of custom menu macros. The more complete your notes and the more thorough your knowledge of how you use AutoCAD, the more powerful your custom menu will be.

When you are stringing a sequence of commands together for a custom menu macro, run through the command sequence step by step, preferably from the keyboard. Make a note of each step, the prompt, and the type of input required. Leave nothing out. Although this is tedious and slow, it will save you a great deal of time in the long run, because you will not have to make several journeys back and forth between AutoCAD and your word processor as you correct an improperly entered command sequence.

There is very little reason to attempt writing a custom menu until you have become familiar with the AutoCAD commands involved. When writing these menus, every letter, space, and punctuation mark becomes extremely important. There is simply no room for error. Without a working understanding of AutoCAD, you could write a custom menu that did not work and never figure out why.

You may eventually get to the point where you have many different menus to call upon, depending on the type of drawing you are doing. This is an acceptable and often useful practice. Several commercially available third-party software programs for AutoCAD make use of multiple menus. Once you have acquired some experience in this area, don't be afraid to experiment. A custom menu, even if it doesn't work, will not hurt AutoCAD.

Keep your notebook handy even after your custom menu has been created and seems to be working properly. Little surprises may still pop up from time to time. Note where they occur, under what circumstances, and what needs to be done.

Making a Copy of the AutoCAD Standard Menu

It is good practice to use a copy of AutoCAD's standard menu as a model that can be modified to create a custom menu of your own. Under no circumstances should you make any changes to the original menu that was supplied with AutoCAD. You will want to have an unchanged copy of the original menu available at all times, in case your editing goes awry and you need to return to a "tried-and-true" version of the screen menu.

Here is a DOS sequence that will create a copy of the AutoCAD standard menu for you to use:

1. Log onto the AutoCAD system subdirectory. For example, if your AutoCAD system files subdirectory is ACAD, you can enter the following command:

   CD ACAD

2. Place the AutoCAD Support Files disk in your computer's drive A.

3. If you are using AutoCAD Version 2.5 or later, enter the following command:

   COPY A:\SOURCE\ACAD.MNU CUSTOM.MNU

   If you are using an earlier version of AutoCAD, enter the following command:

   COPY A:ACAD.MNU CUSTOM.MNU

4. Watch for the message

1 file(s) copied

If you don't see this message, or an error message appears, check to be certain that the correct disk is in drive A and that you have typed the COPY command exactly as it appears above. Then try it again.

If you do see the "1 file(s) copied" message, it means that you now have a copy of the source code for the AutoCAD standard menu on your hard disk, in the same subdirectory as the AutoCAD system files. This file should remain there so that AutoCAD may find, compile, and load it easily. This new AutoCAD menu file has the name CUSTOM.MNU. You can safely make changes to CUSTOM.MNU using your word processor, confident that you will not affect your original ACAD menu.

Loading the Custom Menu

To load CUSTOM.MNU into the Drawing Editor, type the AutoCAD **MENU CUSTOM** command. The first time you do this, AutoCAD will compile the menu before it appears on the screen. This may take a minute or so. After compiling, a new file called CUSTOM.MNX is stored on the hard disk. This is the file that AutoCAD displays inside the Drawing Editor.

At this point, your custom menu looks exactly like the AutoCAD standard menu. AutoCAD will not recompile this menu unless you make a change to the original source-code file, CUSTOM.MNU. If you do edit the source code, AutoCAD will detect this and recompile it automatically the next time it loads the menu.

To return to the AutoCAD standard menu, simply type **MENU ACAD**. The standard menu will immediately return. Whatever menu was active at the time a drawing was last saved to disk is the menu that will be active when you reedit that drawing.

Eventually, you may wish to have your custom menu become the default menu for new drawings that you create. To do this, edit your prototype drawing, load the custom menu, and then save the drawing. If you are using multiple prototype drawings, you might consider creating a unique custom menu for each prototype drawing. Refer to Chapter 1 for information on prototype drawings.

There is no limit on the number of different custom menus you may have. However, be certain that each custom menu has its own unique name, to prevent one menu from overwriting another. Do not name any custom menu ACAD.MNU. To do so may well result in the loss of AutoCAD's standard menu.

THE SCREEN MENU STRUCTURE

The source-code files for AutoCAD menus are ASCII files, generally many lines long. When you first load the menu source code into your word processor, you will see a long list of AutoCAD commands and various symbols aligned on the leftmost column of the file.

Each line in a custom menu contains a specific command sequence, using one or more AutoCAD commands along with whatever options might be appropriate. Each sequence begins at the leftmost position and can continue to the right indefinitely. There is a special technique that will enable you to wrap long command sequences so that they are visible on the screen in their entirety. You will find that technique in the section entitled "The Plus Sign" later in this chapter.

Major Sections

AutoCAD menus are organized into seven *major sections*, which are identified by specific *section labels*. Each major section contains commands that relate to a particular hardware device. Here is a brief description of the seven major sections:

- **Screen** contains menu commands that appear on the monitor screen. This section is by far the largest major section in the Auto-CAD standard menu. Because it is very large and contains lots of AutoCAD commands, it is broken up into dozens of *menu subsections*.

- **Buttons** contains commands and functions that are executed by pressing buttons on the pointing device.

- **Tablet1**, **Tablet2**, **Tablet3**, and **Tablet4** each contain command sequences executed by touching areas on a digitizing tablet.

- **Aux1** contains commands that are executed by pressing the buttons of an auxiliary *function box* (an external hardware device displaying several buttons, which, when pressed, execute Auto-CAD commands).

These major sections of the menu are not commands. A custom menu is not required to have all these major sections.

Subsections

Major sections of the menu can contain many subsections. This is normally the case with the Screen major section, whose many subsections help control which part of the menu appears on the monitor at any given moment. Each menu subsection contains a list of the specific command sequences that will be executed when picked with the pointing device. These command sequences can include special syntax that controls the screen display of the various menu subsections.

Subsections of the Screen major section can contain as many text lines as there are lines available in your monitor's screen menu area. For example, many monitors display a maximum of 20 lines in the screen menu area. If your monitor is like this, each menu subsection in your Screen major section can be a maximum of 20 lines long. If any subsection is longer than the maximum displayed on your monitor, the extra lines are *wasted*—they will not appear.

Menu subsections are not required to contain the maximum number of lines. When a menu subsection has less than its maximum number of lines, the contents of the menu subsection are displayed, and any previous commands that are not overwritten by the new menu subsection will continue to appear on the screen. These previous commands will function normally if selected. Furthermore, you can cause the display of a menu subsection to begin on any line you choose. These display features can work to your advantage by causing frequently used command sequences to remain on the screen while different menu subsections are displayed.

Syntax

Your custom menus use special syntax to define how they will appear on the screen and how the command sequences will work. The elements of this syntax are summarized below.

Major Section Labels   Three asterisks identify the major sections of the menu. The three asterisks are followed by the major section *label* (in uppercase). Up to seven major section labels in an AutoCAD menu will appear in the leftmost margin of the menu file, heading their respective groups of commands, as shown below:

```
***BUTTONS
***SCREEN
***TABLET1
***TABLET2
***TABLET3
***TABLET4
***AUX1
```

Subsection Labels Two asterisks identify menu subsection labels, which contain related sets of command sequences. These labels, like the following, act as pointers for the AutoCAD menu processor:

**ERASE

In this example, a menu subsection called Erase is identified and given its label. You would expect that it contains commands, optional features, and/or probable prompt responses related to AutoCAD's ERASE command. The subsection label is not itself an ERASE command. It will not appear on the monitor screen. Every line that follows this subsection marker will appear on the screen until either another menu subsection label is encountered, a major section label is encountered, the maximum number of lines is used, or the menu file ends.

The subsection label can contain an optional number that will instruct the AutoCAD menu processor to begin the display of this subsection on a particular line. For example,

**ERASE 3

would indicate that this subsection begins on the third line of the screen menu area, leaving the first two lines intact. Any command sequences found on these two lines would remain active and accessible to the pointing device after the Erase subsection is displayed.

Subsection References The syntax that controls which menu subsection appears on the screen takes the following form:

$<key>=<subsection label>

When this special set of characters is encountered in the processing of any command sequence, it will cause the named menu subsection to appear on the screen. (Do not enter a space between the equal sign and its neighboring characters.)

As an example, if you wished for the Erase subsection to appear on the screen, at the appropriate point in the menu you would include the following characters:

$S=ERASE

You can see from this example that the command syntax for bringing up this menu subsection is $S = , followed by the name of the subsection. The letter S that appears after the dollar sign indicates that the subsection is part of the Screen major section. The character S is the Screen major section's *key character,* supplied between the dollar sign and the equal sign.

Other key characters are used for other major sections:

- **$B=** will access subsections of the Buttons major section.

- **$T1=**, **$T2=**, **$T3=**, and **$T4=** will access the subsections of the Tablet1, Tablet2, Tablet3, and Tablet4 major sections.

- **$A1=** will access the subsections of the Aux1 major section.

It is frequently useful to change the on-screen menu display while an AutoCAD command sequence is in progress. This syntax does not interrupt a command sequence in progress.

As menu subsections are displayed on the screen, AutoCAD keeps track of them, up to a maximum of eight. It is possible to backtrack through these menu-subsection references by means of the following syntax:

$S=

In this case, S is always used as the key character between the dollar sign and the equal sign. Each time these characters are issued without a subsection name, AutoCAD will recall the previous menu subsection and display it, until the maximum of eight has been recalled. Once it has backtracked through the previous eight subsections (or runs out of previous subsections, whichever comes first) this syntax has no effect.

As you debug your custom menu, you may discover that you have inadvertently created a menu subsection that offers no way to reference any other menu subsection, or perhaps does not allow you to return to the root menu. In this case, your only recourse is first to make a note of what happened (so you can later find the problem area and correct it using your word processor), and then type the AutoCAD MENU command, followed by either the name of the current menu or a new menu. When the menu is loaded, you will be at the start of the menu file again.

Brackets   Normally, you enclose the parts of the menu that appear on the screen in brackets. You may include up to eight characters, including spaces, within these brackets. The AutoCAD menu processor will display what it finds within brackets on the screen for you to pick. For example, when it finds

    [ERASE:]
    [FILLET:]
    [ZOOM ALL]

it will display

Erase:
Fillet:
Zoom all

The brackets are immediately followed by the sequence of commands and prompt responses to be executed when the characters within the brackets are selected with the pointing device.

Brackets are not absolutely required, although they usually make things easier to understand. If brackets are not used, the first eight characters on each command line will be displayed on the screen. When such nonbracketed characters are picked by the pointing device, it has the same effect as if the characters were typed at the keyboard. For example, suppose the following line appeared in a custom menu:

zoom w 0,0 12,12

This would have the same effect as typing out the same line at the keyboard, character for character, space for space. AutoCAD would respond by zooming in on a window with opposite corners at points 0,0 and 12,12. However, when the line is displayed on the screen, only the following characters (the first eight) would be visible:

zoom w 0

In this example, it is not clear what the command sequence does. The command might be easier to understand if it were preceded by a short tag enclosed in brackets, as in the following example:

[WZ 0/12]zoom w 0,0 12,12

In this example, WZ 0/12 would appear on the screen, and when picked with the pointing device, the command sequence following the brackets would be issued.

The Space and the Semicolon   As mentioned, every letter, punctuation mark, and space in a custom menu is read and interpreted by the Auto-CAD menu processor. A space character in the command sequence will nearly always function the same as if you pressed Return. This function of a space in the menu is just the same as the function of the Space bar in AutoCAD.

The semicolon can always be used to indicate the press of the Return key. In this book, all custom menu examples will use a semicolon rather than a space to indicate a Return, in order to eliminate ambiguity.

In some cases, it may be necessary to *force* AutoCAD to read a Return in a custom menu. For example, if you select an item from the menu in response to a prompt for a text entry (for example, the contents of a block attribute), AutoCAD will type the selected string, including any spaces it finds. In this case, a simple space will be read as part of the text string rather than as a Return. In cases like this, a Return must be forced with a semicolon.

AutoCAD's menu processor usually supplies an automatic Return at the end of each line in the menu file. Generally, this is what you want, but there are exceptions: if the line ends with a backslash, a control character, or a plus sign, AutoCAD does not supply an automatic Return. In cases where a line ends with one of these special characters and a Return is necessary as well, simply force the Return by adding a semicolon to the end of the line.

The Backslash   The backslash character is used whenever the command sequence must pause to accept input from the user. The backslash can accept input that is either digitized or typed from the keyboard. For example, the simple macro

> [ZOOM IN]ZOOM;W;\\

invokes the ZOOM command, issues a Return, invokes the Window option with the W, issues another Return (as you would if you were typing these commands at the keyboard), and finally pauses twice to get the coordinates of the corners of the zoom window from the user. No space follows the backslash, as no Return is necessary after the window corner selections.

The Caret   The caret identifies an AutoCAD control sequence within the menu. For example, ^C will be read by the AutoCAD menu processor as a CANCEL command. ^O will be read by the menu processor as the orthogonal mode toggle. (Do not enter a space between the caret and the letter, or AutoCAD will not read the control sequence correctly.) Any control sequence recognizable by AutoCAD can be used as part of a custom menu command sequence. Like menu subsection references, control sequences do not interrupt a command sequence in progress.

The Plus Sign   To extend a single menu command sequence over several lines in a custom menu, use the plus sign (+) at the end of each line that is to be continued. It can be inserted anywhere in the line, even in the middle of a word, if necessary. It is invisible to the AutoCAD menu interpreter, and can make the menu much easier to read and edit by allowing a long sequence of commands to appear on several lines in the menu file. There is no limit to the length of a command sequence.

When a long command sequence occupies many lines in this fashion, it is said to be *wrapped*. Command sequences that are wrapped do not reduce the maximum number of display lines available for use within that subsection. In other words, even though they occupy several text lines in the menu file, the AutoCAD menu processor sees wrapped command sequences as a single line. Thus, your maximum number of available display lines remains the same.

EXAMINING THE AUTOCAD STANDARD MENU

Now that you have made a copy (CUSTOM.MNU) of the AutoCAD standard menu, enter your word processor and take a look at it. At the moment, CUSTOM.MNU looks just like ACAD.MNU. You will find that it is a long ASCII file. The following example uses the menu for Version 2.5 of AutoCAD. If you are using a version of AutoCAD that is earlier than 2.5, your menu will not appear exactly as below, but the syntax elements will be the same.

Here are the opening lines of the menu source code for Version 2.5:

```
***BUTTONS
;
$S=OSNAPB
^C^C
^B
^O
^G
^D
^E
^T
***AUX1
;
$S=OSNAPB
^C^C
^B
^O
^G
^D
^E
```

```
^T
***SCREEN
**S
[AUTOCAD]$S=S
[* * * *]$S=OSNAPB
[SETUP] ^C ^C(load "setup") $S=UNITS

[BLOCKS]$S=X $S=BL
[DIM:]$S=X $S=DIM ^C ^CDIM
[DISPLAY]$S=X $S=DS
[DRAW]$S=X $S=DR
```

The first line signals the start of the Buttons section with three asterisks. The first button on the pointing device is always the Pick button; there is no way to change this. Therefore, the lines that follow the Buttons section label indicate the functions of the remaining buttons on the pointing device.

If you are using a three-button mouse, only the first two lines of this major section are operable; the remaining lines are ignored. If you are using a four-button digitizing puck, only the first three lines of this menu are operable.

In this menu, the second line (button 2) is a semicolon. Therefore, button number two on the pointing device issues a Return. The third line (button 3) invokes a menu subsection reference that will display another menu subsection. The characters $S=OSNAPB will cause the menu subsection labeled Osnapb to appear on the screen. Menu subsection Osnapb can be found beginning at line 217 of this menu. Here is how it looks:

```
**OSNAPB 3
[CENter]CENTER $S=
[ENDpoint]ENDPOINT $S=
[INSert]INSERT $S=
[INTersec]INTERSEC $S=
[MIDpoint]MIDPOINT $S=
[NEArest]NEAREST $S=
[NODe]NODE $S=
[PERpend]PERPEND $S=
[QUAdrant]QUADRANT $S=
[QUICK,]QUICK, ^Z
[TANgent]TANGENT $S=
[NONE]NONE $S=
[CANCEL:] ^C ^C$S=
```

```
[U:] ^C ^CU $S=
[REDO:] ^C ^CREDO $S=
[REDRAW:] ^C ^CREDRAW $S=
['SETVAR]'SETVAR $S=
[__LAST__]$S=
```

Note the number 3 that appears after the menu subsection label. This number indicates that the display of this menu subsection is to begin on the third display line of the Drawing Editor menu area. The first two lines of the previous menu subsection will remain on the screen when this menu subsection is displayed.

In the lines following the label, particular OSNAP features appear within brackets. Following each set of brackets, the referenced OSNAP feature is invoked, followed by a space (a semicolon could have been used instead), followed by the syntax to redisplay the previous menu.

Note the control sequence that comes after the brackets containing the word CANCEL (line 13 of the menu subsection). Here the symbol for Ctrl-C, ^C, appears twice. The repetition of the Cancel control sequence is a safety device. If this menu subsection were referenced from inside the AutoCAD dimensioning feature, for example, a single CANCEL command might not be enough to return us to the AutoCAD Command prompt. But two CANCELs will always work. In cases where a single CANCEL would be enough, repeating the Cancel control sequence has no effect.

Note that no space appears between these control characters and the menu subsection reference. This is because AutoCAD would read that space as a Return, and a Return at this point is not necessary.

When you write your own custom command sequences, begin each one with this double Ctrl-C. In this way you can always be sure that you are beginning each command sequence from the AutoCAD Command prompt, and not accidentally from within another AutoCAD command.

Returning to the beginning of CUSTOM.MNU, notice that another major section begins on line 11. This is the Aux1 section, for users with an auxiliary function box. Right now, the functions for the auxiliary function box are the same as for the pointing device buttons.

Line 21 contains the label of the major section that will be the immediate focus of the rest of this chapter, the Screen section. (Notice the three asterisks.) Immediately following the Screen section label is a menu subsection label called S. S is the menu subsection label for the AutoCAD root menu. Whenever you wish to jump immediately to the root menu, the following syntax, as shown on line 23 of the menu, will do the trick:

[AUTOCAD]$S=S

Line 24 displays four asterisks on the screen. The AutoCAD menu interpreter will not confuse them with a label, because they are within brackets. When these asterisks are selected, the command sequence will cause the display of the Osnapb menu subsection, just as button number 3 did in the Buttons major section.

Line 25, SETUP, contains a short AutoLISP command. The meaning of this command will be clear when you read about AutoLISP in Chapters 10 and 11.

Line 26 is empty and will display a blank line inside the Drawing Editor. If this blank space is selected, nothing will happen. Here, its purpose seems to be the improvement of the screen's appearance and to provide a neutral area on the screen display to help prevent SETUP from being picked accidentally.

Line 27, BLOCKS, is interesting because it references two menu subsections. The first menu subsection, X, can be found on line 43 of the file. Menu subsection X is 18 lines long, only the last three of which contain command sequences. The other lines are blank. Subsection X will begin its display on line 3 of the Drawing Editor menu area. When referenced, this menu subsection will clear any previously referenced menu subsections, except for the top two lines, and display its three command sequences on the lower part of the screen menu area.

The second menu subsection referenced by BLOCKS is subsection BL, which can be found on line 65. It looks like this:

```
**BL 3
[ATTDEF:]$S=X $S=ATTDEF ^C^CATTDEF
[BASE:]$S=X $S=BASE ^C^CBASE
[BLOCK:]$S=X $S=BLOCK ^C^CBLOCK
[INSERT:]$S=X $S=INSERT ^C^CINSERT
[MINSERT:]$S=X $S=MINSERT ^C^CMINSERT
[WBLOCK:]$S=X $S=WBLOCK ^C^CWBLOCK
```

This menu subsection also begins its display on the third line, again leaving the two top lines untouched. Because this menu subsection is only six lines long, the three lines at the bottom of menu subsection X will also remain on the screen.

Returning to menu subsection S, notice how menu subsection X combines with several different menu subsections. By using this technique, the command sequences that compose menu subsection X do not have to be copied onto many different menu subsections.

Moving through the menu, notice the following command sequence that appears on line 66:

```
[ATTDEF:]$S=X $S=ATTDEF ^C^CATTDEF
```

Notice how menu subsections in this example are referenced, the double cancel is issued (in case this item has been selected from inside another AutoCAD command), and the appropriate AutoCAD command is then invoked immediately. This command sequence causes the display of options for the ATTDEF command and invokes the command. The following lines follow the same procedure for other commands:

```
[BASE:]$S=X  $S=BASE ^C^CBASE
[BLOCK:]$S=X  $S=BLOCK ^C^CBLOCK
[INSERT:]$S=X  $S=INSERT ^C^CINSERT
[MINSERT:]$S=X  $S=MINSERT ^C^CMINSERT
[WBLOCK:]$S=X  $S=WBLOCK ^C^CWBLOCK
```

Sometimes there are too many options to fit in a single menu subsection. In such cases, AutoCAD uses a simple expedient, an example of which is found on line 95 of the menu:

```
[next]$S=DR2
```

It occurs within a menu subsection labeled DR. Although the brackets say [next], all that occurs is a simple menu subsection reference to a menu subsection that contains related commands. As you might expect, the menu subsection DR2 contains the following line:

```
[previous]$S=DR
```

Compare this command sequence to another command sequence on the DR2 menu subsection:

```
[__LAST__]$S=DR
```

Here, the command sequence is exactly the same as the one after [previous] and it has exactly the same result. This may appear redundant, but different users respond to different kinds of displays. Sometimes it's a good idea to offer a choice of on-screen prompts; if you don't need two displays for the same submenu reference or command sequence, you can delete the unnecessary one and replace it with another, more useful command sequence.

Skipping to line 237 of CUSTOM.MNU, you will find the following:

```
**BLOCK 3
[BLOCK:] ^C ^CBLOCK
?


Window
Last
Previous
```

Crossing
Remove
Add

Here the Block menu subsection contains the AutoCAD BLOCK command. On the following lines, the ? option (for obtaining a list of referenced block names) along with all the optional responses to object selection options are listed. They are not contained in brackets. Brackets are not necessary here, becuase the selection of one of these options has the same effect as typing it at the keyboard. No semicolon is necessary; AutoCAD's menu processor automatically supplies a Return at the end of each line in the menu file.

An alternative method for displaying these object selection options would be

[Window]W;
[Last]L;
[Previous]P;
[Crossing]C;
[Remove]R;
[Add]A;

This method would yield exactly the same result, with AutoCAD typing only the first key letter of the selection option, followed by a Return. In this example, semicolons force the Return. Because a semicolon was included at the end of each line, AutoCAD's menu processor does not supply an automatic Return.

Neither of these two display methods has a significant advantage over the other. When creating a custom menu, use whichever method you prefer.

FIRST CHANGES TO THE CUSTOM MENU

In this section, you will practice making changes to CUSTOM.MNU in order to clarify frequently used on-screen display and group commands. The following example demonstrates this technique by making some changes to the menu subsections that contain AutoCAD's entity drawing commands. These subsections are labeled **DR and **DR2. In AutoCAD Version 2.6, these subsections can be found on CUSTOM.MNU lines 81 through 113. In their original form, they look like this:

```
**DR 3
[ARC]$S=X $S=ARC
[ATTDEF:]$S=X $S=ATTDEF ^C^CATTDEF
```

[CIRCLE]$S=X $S=CIRCLE
[DONUT:]$S=X $S=DONUT ^C^CDONUT
[DTEXT:]$S=X $S=DTEXT ^C^CDTEXT
[ELLIPSE:]$S=X $S=ELLIPSE ^C^CELLIPSE
[HATCH:]$S=X $S=HATCH ^C^CHATCH
[INSERT:]$S=X $S=INSERT ^C^CINSERT
[LINE:]$S=X $S=LINE ^C^CLINE
[MINSERT:]$S=X $S=MINSERT ^C^CMINSERT
[OFFSET:]$S=X $S=OFFSET ^C^COFFSET
[PLINE:]$S=X $S=PLINE ^C^CPLINE

[next]$S=DR2
**DR2 3
[POINT:]$S=X $S=POINT ^C^CPOINT
[POLYGON:]$S=X $S=POLYGON ^C^CPOLYGON
[SHAPE:]$S=X $S=SHAPE ^C^CSHAPE
[SKETCH:]$S=X $S=SKETCH ^C^CSKETCH
[SOLID:]$S=X $S=SOLID ^C^CSOLID
[TEXT:]$S=X $S=TEXT ^C^CTEXT
[TRACE:]$S=X $S=TRACE ^C^CTRACE
[3DLINE:]$S=X $S=3DLINE ^C^C3DLINE
[3DFACE:]$S=X $S=3DFACE ^C^C3DFACE

[previous]$S=DR

[__LAST__]$S=DR

The menu in the following example will change the order in which drawing commands are displayed on these two subsections, placing more frequently used commands on the first subsection (DR), less frequently used commands on the second subsection (DR2), and eliminating commands that are either never used or more easily found elsewhere on the menu.

Begin by making a list of the drawing commands, grouping them under four headings: Never Selected, Found Elsewhere, Seldom Selected, and Often Selected. A list of this type might look like the following:

Never Selected:
  MINSERT
  SKETCH
  TRACE

Found Elsewhere:
   INSERT (found on Blocks subsection)
   OFFSET (found on Edit subsection #2)
   3DLINE (found on 3D subsection)
   3DFACE (found on 3D subsection)
Seldom Selected:
   ATTDEF
   DONUT
   DTEXT
   ELLIPSE
   SHAPE
Often Selected:
   ARC
   CIRCLE
   LINE
   HATCH
   PLINE
   POINT
   POLYGON
   SOLID
   TEXT

Having thus determined priorities for selecting entity drawing commands, your next step is to note the original locations of all references to other menu subsections. In general, you will want to keep these menu-subsection references on their original lines as you delete some commands and move others around. However, you can move them if there is a good reason, and you don't disturb the operation of the menu file.

In the original version of CUSTOM.MNU, the menu-subsection reference [next] occurs on line 14 of subsection DR. Likewise, the menu-subsection reference [previous] occurs on line 15 of subsection DR2. The menu-subsection reference [__LAST__] occurs on line 17 of DR2. In this example, you will keep the reference [next] where it is, but you will move [previous] and [__LAST__] up one line, to lines 14 and 16 of DR2, respectively. This change will make the operation of the drawing command menus much smoother.

In addition, you will add two lines to DR, making it a total of 16 lines long. On line 16 of DR, you will add the following new reference:

   [__LAST__]$S=S

This additional reference is based on the notion that when you are on the first screen of the entity drawing menu, you got there from the main menu, and that is where you intend to go when you pick this reference. If you did not add these additional lines, the reference [__LAST__] from DR2 would remain on the screen. DR2's version of this reference will have no effect when on DR (this occurs in the standard AutoCAD menu).

Commands from other subsections can be added here to good advantage. For example, it may be useful to place the ERASE command on line 13 of both the DR and DR2 subsections, just before the menu subsection references. (Placing the command on the same line in both of these subsections will allow you to find it in a consistent place in the display.) This will allow you to erase entities a little more quickly, rather than first accessing the editing commands subsection and returning to the entity drawing commands subsection. The ERASE command can be found on the menu subsection labeled ED. Copy it (don't move it) to line 13 of DR and DR2.

After you have completed the processes of deleting the Never Selected and Found Elsewhere commands, and have moved the Often Selected commands to DR and the Seldom Selected commands to DR2, the menu subsections will look like this:

```
**DR 3
[ARC]$S=X  $S=ARC
[CIRCLE]$S=X  $S=CIRCLE

[LINE:]$S=X  $S=LINE ^C^CLINE
[PLINE:]$S=X  $S=PLINE ^C^CPLINE

[POINT:]$S=X  $S=POINT ^C^CPOINT
[POLYGON:]$S=X  $S=POLYGON ^C^CPOLYGON

[TEXT:]$S=X  $S=TEXT ^C^CTEXT
[HATCH:]$S=X  $S=HATCH ^C^CHATCH

[ERASE:]$S=X  $S=ERASE ^C^CERASE
[next]$S=DR2

[__LAST__]$S=S
**DR2 3
[ATTDEF:]$S=X  $S=ATTDEF ^C^CATTDEF

[DONUT:]$S=X  $S=DONUT ^C^CDONUT

[DTEXT:]$S=X  $S=DTEXT ^C^CDTEXT

[ELLIPSE:]$S=X  $S=ELLIPSE ^C^CELLIPSE
```

[SHAPE:]$S=X $S=SHAPE ^C^CSHAPE

[SOLID:]$S=X $S=SOLID ^C^CSOLID

[ERASE:]$S=X $S=ERASE ^C^CERASE
[previous]$S=DR

[__LAST__]$S=DR

   In this example arrangement, there isn't enough room to put space between all the commands on DR, so commands like ARC and CIRCLE, LINE and PLINE, POINT and POLYGON, and HATCH and TEXT have been arranged in pairs.
   In addition to placing the more frequently used commands "up front" in the menu structure, you have created some space between them, making inadvertent command selection more difficult. You have saved a little drawing time by putting an extra ERASE command in a more convenient location. Figures 5.1 and 5.2 show how these new entity drawing menus will appear on the screen.

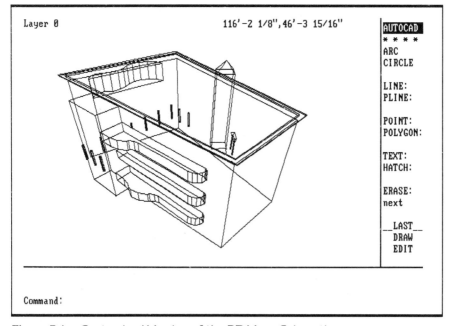

Figure 5.1   Customized Version of the DR Menu Subsection

This technique can be applied to any menu subsection; editing commands, display commands, utility commands are all candidates for this kind of treatment. As you consolidate your custom menu, seconds of time saved will begin to add up significantly. There are ways to save even more time by means of custom menu macros, discussed in the next chapter.

CUSTOMIZATION USING THE DIGITIZER

If you use a digitizing tablet as your input device, you can make the process of drawing much more efficient by means of custom tablet menus. AutoCAD allows you to specify up to four separate areas of your tablet as menu areas as well as a remaining area to be used as the screen pointing area. These menu areas are rectangular in shape, but they may be arranged on the tablet in any way you choose. With a well-organized set of tablet menus, you can bypass the hierarchical screen menu altogether.

Once each tablet menu area is defined, it may be partitioned to contain as many smaller rectangular boxes as you choose. The boxes within

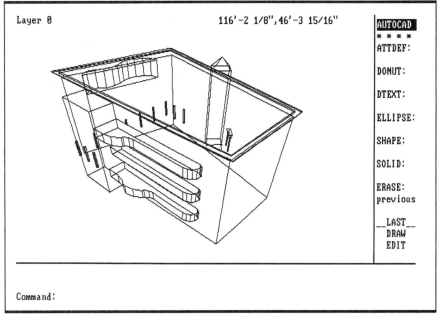

Figure 5.2   Customized Version of the DR2 Menu Subsection

ADVANCED TECHNIQUES IN AUTOCAD

a tablet menu area are numbered by AutoCAD automatically, beginning with number one in the upper left, continuing horizontally, row by row, and ending with the box in the lower right. Each one of the boxes can be designated as a particular AutoCAD command, setting, or macro.

Figure 5.3 shows a typical arrangement of a digitizer tablet divided into four tablet menus and a screen pointing area. Figure 5.4 shows a tablet menu area partitioned into 30 boxes (five columns by six rows).

Designing the Template

The first step in creating a custom digitizing tablet is to design a model of your tablet menu areas, their location on the digitizing tablet, the number of boxes in each, and the location on the tablet of the screen pointing area.

Once you have settled on an arrangement of tablet menu areas and commands, you can create a *template*, a drawing of your arrangement. Label each box in the menu area with its intended AutoCAD command or command sequence. You can, if you wish, make some boxes larger than others by having the same command apply to adjacent boxes.

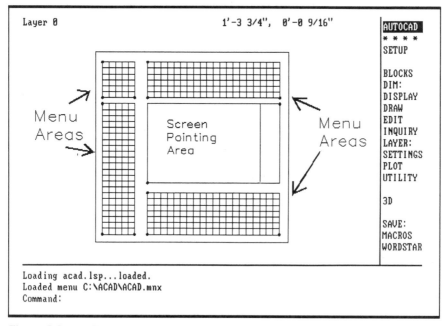

Figure 5.3   A Typical Tablet Menu Configuration

The arrangement of commands on your template drawing should be made so that a minimum of pen motion is required to move from command to command. Related commands should be grouped together. Commands frequently used in sequence should be located near each other, if not actually strung together in macros.

Of course, you use AutoCAD to draw the template. When your template design is satisfactory, plot it out at the correct scale. Fasten the template onto the surface of your digitizing tablet.

To prevent your template from wearing out too quickly, you may consider laminating it. If you don't want to laminate it, another trick is to use AutoCAD's MIRROR command to *flip* the finished template, plotting it in reverse on sturdy clear vellum. Then simply reverse the vellum when fastening the template to your digitizing tablet.

Configuring the Tablet

When your template is in place, you are ready to configure AutoCAD to respond to your custom tablet menus. You tell AutoCAD about your

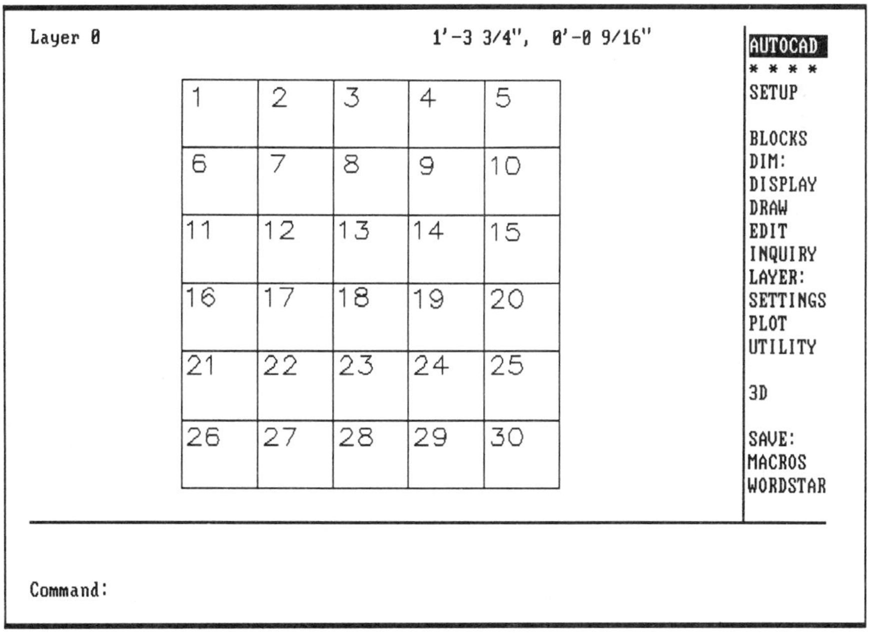

Figure 5.4   Tablet Menu Area with Numbered Boxes

arrangement of tablet menu areas by means of the TABLET CFG command. When you issue this command, AutoCAD will prompt

Enter number of tablet menus desired (0-4):

After you enter the appropriate number of tablet menus, AutoCAD prompts you to enter the upper-left corner, lower-left corner, and lower-right corner of each tablet menu area. Respond by digitizing the requested points on your template drawing. The set of three points must form a 90-degree angle, or AutoCAD will request a new set of points. The tablet menu areas must not overlap each other.

After you enter the location of each tablet menu area, AutoCAD prompts

Enter the number of columns for menu area *n*:

Respond with the number of vertical columns in the menu area. AutoCAD next prompts

Enter the number of rows for menu area *n*:

Respond with the number of horizontal rows in the menu area. Continue this process until all your tablet menu areas are defined. AutoCAD then prompts

Digitize lower left corner of screen pointing area:

Respond by digitizing the appropriate point. AutoCAD prompts

Digitize upper right corner of screen pointing area:

Respond by digitizing the appropriate point. Do not overlap the screen pointing and tablet menu areas.

Placing Commands on the Digitizing Tablet

Once your digitizing tablet has been configured, you may assign Auto-CAD commands, settings, macros, and so on to the labeled menu area boxes. This is done by editing the Tablet1 through Tablet4 major sections of CUSTOM.MNU.

CUSTOM.MNU, because it is a copy of AutoCAD's standard menu, has already assigned Tablet sections 2, 3, and 4 to various AutoCAD commands and settings. These assignments correspond to a standard template that is sent to users who return their software registration card to Autodesk. It is a very nice premium and a powerful incentive for registration. If you are using AutoCAD's standard template, only Tablet section 1 should be edited. Leave the others alone. If you are using your own template, these sections can be overwritten.

In AutoCAD's standard menu, Tablet section 1 has room for 200 user-definable commands. Figure 5.4 illustrates a considerably smaller tablet menu area with five columns and six rows. Boxes in this tablet menu are numbered from 1 to 30. Using this example, menu section Tablet1 will contain 30 text lines. The first text line corresponds to box number 1, the second line to box number 2, and so on through all the boxes.

Figure 5.5 illustrates a possible arrangement of AutoCAD LAYER commands and options in the example tablet menu area. In order to correspond to the illustrated menu area, the Tablet1 section of the menu file should be as follows:

```
***TABLET1
^C^CLAYER;
^C^CLAYER;
;
;
[ ]
^C^CLAYER;
^C^CLAYER;
;
;
[ ]
S;
COLOR;
CEILING;
FOUNDATION;
[ ]*;
N;
LTYPE;
DOORS;
FURNITURE;
?;
OFF;
FREEZE;
ELEC;
PLUMB;
Y;
ON;
THAW;
FLOOR;
WINDOW;
N;
```

In this example, notice how some command boxes in the tablet menu were enlarged simply by repeating the same command in adjacent boxes.

The fifth and tenth lines of this section contain empty brackets. This is a convenient way of indicating an empty box, although a blank line will do just as well. On a tablet menu, if a pair of brackets is found at the beginning of a line, the brackets along with anything contained within them are ignored.

Line 15 contains a pair of brackets followed by an asterisk. These brackets are necessary in order to move the asterisk off the leftmost column of the file. The asterisk is an appropriate response to some prompts within the LAYER command, but if the asterisk appears on the menu file's leftmost column, the menu processor will misinterpret it as the beginning of a new subsection. In this case, the potential problem is solved by the empty brackets.

Boxes in a tablet menu area can contain macros, such as those described in the next chapter. Long command sequences may be wrapped around several text lines for easy editing, and all custom menu syntax (that is, screen menu changes) can be used where desired in the tablet sections of the custom menu file.

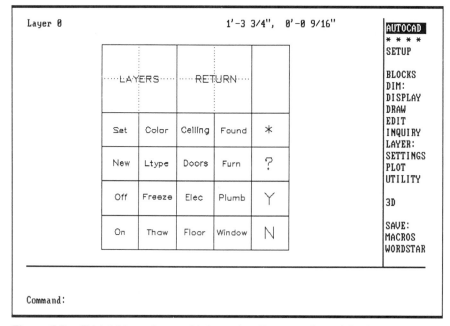

Figure 5.5   Tablet Menu Area with Layering Commands and Options

Multiple template designs are possible as well. The configuration of the digitizing tablet is stored as part of the drawing; so if you wish to use more than one template design, you will need a prototype drawing for each. If you use a consistent template design, you can change commands assigned to the boxes by loading different custom menus.

CREATING A NEW MENU SUBSECTION

To assist you in the process of creating macros, this section will demonstrate the technique for creating a new menu subsection in the Screen major section of CUSTOM.MNU. The subsection created here will be called Macros. You can use it to store the custom menu macros discussed in the next chapter.

Using your word processor, return to the beginning of the Screen major section of CUSTOM.MNU. The first menu subsection in this section is subsection S.

Once you have found this menu subsection, locate the cursor on any convenient blank line. (Line 19 in the S menu subsection is usually blank. If it is, place the cursor there.) Once you are on a blank line in the S menu subsection, beginning at the leftmost column, type in the following:

[MACROS] ^C ^C$S=X $S=MACROS

This now-familiar syntax will first cause the word MACROS to appear on the screen. Next, a double cancel is invoked to cancel any command that might be active when the Macros subsection is picked. Next, the menu subsection references for the X menu subsection, followed by the Macros menu subsection, are invoked.

The next step is to create the Macros menu subsection. Go to the end of the Screen major section. In the Version 2.5 menu, the major section after Screen is Tablet1. Therefore, you can find the Tablet1 major section label using your word processor and skip to the end of the line just preceding this label. Once you've located the end of Screen, press Return. This should open up a new line just above Tablet1, with the cursor positioned in the leftmost column. If this is so, type the following:

**MACROS 3

Now, press Return two or three times, save the new menu file, and you are finished.

As you gain experience and your macros become more numerous, you may wish to move or copy them to other, already existing menu subsections in the custom menu file. This is fine, but remember not to exceed the maximum number of lines your screen allows, and remember that menu subsections can be combined. When adding lines to a menu subsection, be careful that you don't overwrite any necessary command sequence displayed from a previous menu subsection accidentally.

To test the command sequences you just entered, enter AutoCAD's Drawing Editor and type the MENU CUSTOM command. AutoCAD will recompile your custom menu. In a moment or so, your custom menu will appear. Try selecting your new commands and see what happens. If things don't work out, enter your word processor and check to see that your command sequences were entered correctly. Then return to the Drawing Editor, type MENU CUSTOM once again, and select your menu subsection once more.

Remember, you can never hurt AutoCAD with a custom menu. Sometimes you can get into trouble with command sequences that don't operate as you anticipate, but you are never far from help. In case of absolute disaster, you can always get back to AutoCAD's standard menu by typing the MENU ACAD command at the keyboard, so, don't be afraid to experiment. Experimentation is your best learning device.

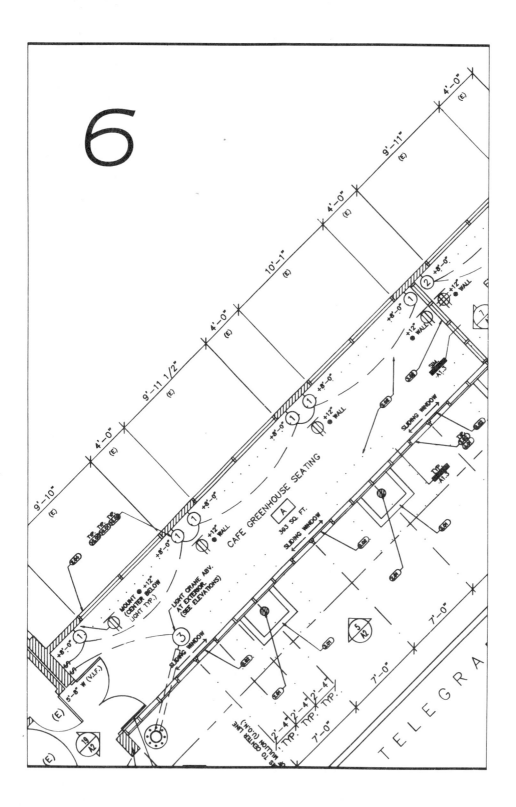

Chapter 6
Custom Menu Macros

A *MACRO* IS A SERIES OF commands and options that will execute in sequence from a single menu or tablet selection. The purpose of the macro is to save time and promote drawing efficiency. For example, a macro based on AutoCAD's layer commands might set any existing layer as current without going through all the keystrokes required to change a layer at the keyboard.

When do you need a macro? Whenever you find yourself jumping around between menus on the same screen or typing the same things over and over at the keyboard, you are looking at an opportunity to create a powerful, time-saving macro.

This chapter presents some examples of general-purpose macros that can be added to the screen menu or included in a command box on a tablet menu. Use them as the basis for constructing more specific macros geared to your own individual needs.

UTILITY MACROS

It is quite possible that some of your more useful macros will be related to the process of managing your drawing file rather than creating and editing drawing entities. Layers, blocks, named entities, and the like often require a series of commands and laborious keyboard input to process. Placing these "management" command sequences and named entities within a macro can save considerable time and improve overall drawing efficiency.

Layer Macros

Layer changing is one of those things that can seem to take forever. Here are some macros that speed up the movement between layers. These examples use layers named Red, Yellow, Blue, and Green.

To begin, place the following subsection reference on your drawing or editing menu:

    [LayerSet] ^ C ^ C$S=LSET

This macro cancels any current operation and references a menu sub-section named Lset, which contains macros that set any one of the example layers current:

```
**LSET 3

[red]LAYER;S;RED;;$S=
[yellow]LAYER;S;YELLOW;;$S=
[blue]LAYER;S;BLUE;;$S=
[green]LAYER;S;GREEN;;$S=
[0]LAYER;S;0;;$S=


[LASTMENU]$S=
[ROOTMENU]$S=S
```

Using this menu subsection, you can pick the layer of your choice from the screen menu; the layer is immediately set current, and you are returned to the menu subsection you came from. This is a lot faster than using off-the-shelf AutoCAD. When you use this technique, the drawing must already contain the referenced layers. This technique will work best for layers found in a prototype drawing.

Notice the need for the double semicolon in these macros. This is because AutoCAD requires an extra Return at the conclusion of the LAYER command to restore the AutoCAD prompt.

You can easily compose variations on this theme, such as

```
[LayerOn]^C^C$S=LSON

[LayerOff]^C^C$S=LSOFF
```

which will transfer you to menu subsections for turning layers on and off, respectively.

The following is the menu subsection for turning layers off (compare it to the LSET subsection):

```
**LSOFF 3

[red]LAYER;OFF;RED;;$S=
[yellow]LAYER;OFF;YELLOW;;$S=
[blue]LAYER;OFF;BLUE;;$S=
[green]LAYER;OFF;GREEN;;$S=

[0]LAYER;OFF;0;;$S=

[ALL]LAYER;OFF;*;;;;$S=
```

[LayerOn]^C$S=LSON

[LASTMENU]$S=
[ROOTMENU]$S=S

In addition to turning off individual layers, the ALL command on the ninth line of this menu subsection will turn off all the layers except the one that is current. The macro labeled ALL can tell which layer is current because AutoCAD's default answer to the prompt

Really want to turn the current layer off?

is no. An extra Return is added in the macro as the response to this prompt. The result is that the current layer is left on while all the others go off. The reference to the Lson subsection is repeated on this display for convenience.

The following is the Lson subsection, which utilizes the same general technique:

**LSON 3

[red]^CLAYER;ON;RED;;$S=
[yellow]^CLAYER;ON;YELLOW;;$S=
[blue]^CLAYER;ON;BLUE;;$S=
[green]^CLAYER;ON;GREEN;;$S=

[0]^CLAYER;ON;0;;$S=

[ALL]^CLAYER;ON;*;;$S=

[LayerOff]^C$S=LSOFF

On each of these layer menu subsections, the names of the layers appear in the same position. This provides consistency when the menu is displayed and reduces the chance of selection error.

If you have more layers in your drawing than you have room for on a single menu subsection, the technique of using additional subsection references labeled *next* and *previous* will work just fine here. Examples of these references can be found in Chapter 5. In such a case, you may wish to alphabetize the layer names or display the names with the most-often selected first and the least-often selected last. Choose an arrangement that helps you locate the layer names as quickly as possible.

When using multiple displays of layer names, remove the $S= syntax from the command sequence on succeeding lists of layer names.

Instead, show a direct reference to appropriate originating menu subsections on each menu subsection, such as

[DRAW]^C^C$S=DRAW

[EDIT]^C^C$S=EDIT

[ROOTMENU]^C^C$S=S

Using the $S= syntax on succeeding lists of layer names will only return you to the previous list of layer names, something that could prove inconvenient.

Menu Subsections to Save Keystrokes

Listing names on menu subsections is a technique that can be applied to several commands that require typing names. For example, the following is a command sequence for the HATCH command. It invokes the command and immediately references the Hatch menu subsection:

[HATCH:]^CHATCH $S=HATCH

In the following example, the subsection reference is changed to a custom subsection label:

[HATCH:]^C^CHATCH $S=HP

When the HATCH command is invoked, the first prompt displayed is

Pattern (? or name/U,style):

At the same time the user is presented with this prompt, the new menu subsection, HP, lists favorite hatch-pattern names:

```
**HP 3
[angle ]angle;$S=HATCH
[brick ]brick;$S=HATCH
[concrete]concrete;$S=HATCH
[cork ]cork;$S=HATCH
[cross ]cross;$S=HATCH
[dots ]dots;$S=HATCH
[escher ]escher;$S=HATCH
[grate ]grate;$S=HATCH
[honeycmb]honey;$S=HATCH
[houndsth]hound;$S=HATCH
[net3 ]net3;$S=HATCH
[stars ]stars;$S=HATCH
```

```
[triang ]triang;$S=HATCH
[trihex]trihex;$S=HATCH
[tweed ]tweed;$S=HATCH

[continue]$S=HATCH
[ROOTMENU]^C^C$S=S
```

This subsection makes it easy to select from a group of frequently used hatch-pattern names and eliminates the need to type them out. Each pattern name on the list includes a reference to the standard Hatch menu subsection; thus, once the name is selected, you can continue through the remaining prompts as usual. Also included on this subsection is a special reference, [continue], which takes you to the Hatch menu subsection without making a selection from the list. This is needed for those times when the desired pattern does not appear on the list. An additional reference cancels everything and returns you to the root menu, in case the HATCH command was selected by accident.

This technique can be used to replace any sequence of commands that requires repeated typing of standard data. For instance, this technique can be applied to shape names, saved views, and block names.

Quick Undo

If you are using AutoCAD Version 2.5 or later, you are at an advantage in case a command accidentally goes awry. You can place the following simple UNDO macro, which will cause an immediate undo of the last command sequence, all over your menu landscape. This macro will even undo complex macro sequences.

```
[UNDO]^C^CUNDO;;
```

Quick Zoom In and Out

Here are two simple but extremely useful "quickies" that can be used with a wide variety of drawing and editing commands:

```
[ZOOMIN]^C^CZOOM;W;\\
```

```
[ZOOMOUT]^C^CZOOM;P;
```

They first cancel any current command that might be in place, and then invoke the ZOOM command. ZOOMIN goes on to select the Window option with a W, and then pauses twice for the user to mark the window. ZOOMOUT takes the user to the previous view. You can add these to your drawing and editing menu subsections, as appropriate. They can save you time if you zoom in and out a lot.

As your experience with custom menus grows, you may try placing these macros on their own menu subsection, similar to the X menu subsection, as well as combining this one menu subsection with various short drawing and editing menus.

ZOOMIN and ZOOMOUT are examples of the best kinds of macros. They are quick, easy to implement, and they do an effective and time-saving job. You will find that in many ways simple macros like these, rather than long complex macros that are specialized, are your most valuable ones.

Quickly Clear the Screen

The following macro erases all the visible entities in a drawing that measures 1,020 drawing units horizontally and 780 drawing units vertically:

    [ZAP]^C^CERASE;W;0,0;1020,780;REDRAW;

    [OOPS!!!]^C^COOPS;

This macro first invokes a window erase, and then references the exact coordinates of the limits of the prototype drawing area automatically. It then issues a redraw. The AutoCAD OOPS command can recover the screen, so it is a worthwhile companion macro.

The next example is a safer variation of ZAP:

    [SAVE-ZAP]^C^CSAVE;;ERASE;W;0,0;1020,780;REDRAW;

This macro takes a little longer, but the SAVE command before the screen erase, followed by two Returns, first saves the drawing to disk under the current name, then clears the screen.

The following macro will pause to accept a name for the file to be saved before the screen clears:

    [SAVE-ZAP]^C^CSAVE;\ERASE;W;30,30;1020,780;REDRAW;

On occasion this macro can be quite handy; for instance, by saving a series of simple drawings under different file names and clearing the screen automatically, you can quickly create a series of several blocks written to outside drawing files. This is much faster than using the BLOCK and WBLOCK commands.

Rotating the Crosshairs

The following macro will rotate the crosshairs to any user-specified angle, using the point 0,0 as the base point of rotation:

[+ ANGLE]^C^CSNAP;R;0,0;\

If you rotate the crosshairs to standard reference angles, you can do it quickly by placing macros like the following in their own menu subsection:

*CHRSHRS 3

[ROTATE]
[CROSS]
[HAIRS]

[ANG-10]^C^CSNAP;R;0,0;10;
[ANG-25]^C^CSNAP;R;0,0;25;
[ANG-30]^C^CSNAP;R;0,0;30;
[ANG-45]^C^CSNAP;R;0,0;45;
[ANG-60]^C^CSNAP;R;0,0;60;
[ANG-80]^C^CSNAP;R;0,0;80;

The following macro quickly resets the crosshairs to normal position:

[+ RESET]^C^CSNAP;R;0,0;0;

Word Processor Macros

If you have already modified ACAD.PGP to include a command to call your word processor, the following macros will make using this command easier:

[WORDPROC]^C^CWP;

The word WORDPROC will appear in the screen menu area. The command sequence cancels any current command and issues the command for accessing the word processor (WP, in this case).

If your word processor allows document names at the command line, the following variation on this macro helps edit CUSTOM.MNU:

[EDITMENU]^C^CWP;CUSTOM.MNU;MENU;CUSTOM;

This macro invokes the WP command and follows it immediately with the answer to the "File to Edit?" prompt. Then, upon your return to the

Drawing Editor, the macro picks up where it left off, invoking the MENU command followed by the menu name. Using this macro, you can complete the entire editing cycle with a single menu selection.

If your word processor command does allow file names at the command line, the following macro will help when editing CUSTOM.MNU:

[EDITMENU]^C^CWP;MENU;CUSTOM;

MACROS THAT AID THE EDITING PROCESS

The editing process in AutoCAD frequently involves several commands in sequence—selecting the editing command, selecting the object (sometimes selecting the means by which objects can be selected for edits), plus various editing parameters that must be specified after an object or objects are selected. As you gain experience and develop your own style for using AutoCAD, you will notice that certain sequences of commands repeat themselves. These repeating sequences can and should be combined into macros.

Quick Selection

The following macro from AutoCAD's standard menu invokes the ERASE command and references the Erase subsection:

[ERASE:]^C^CERASE;$S=ERASE

If you often select objects to erase by means of a window, or if you often wish to erase the last object drawn, these macros will save you considerable time. They can be added underneath the standard ERASE command on your custom menu:

[window]^C^CERASE;W;\\;
[last]^C^CERASE;L;;

These macros do not reference the Erase subsection because it is not necessary. Instead, they invoke the desired selection mechanism along with the command. If you select

window

you return to the screen and can window the objects you wish to erase, which will then immediately vanish. If you select

last

the last entity drawn will disappear from the screen immediately.

Since both macros cause selected objects to disappear from the screen immediately, they require a bit of caution. If you ever do erase more than you intended, the OOPS or UNDO command will reverse the effect of these macros.

Notice that two semicolons are needed after the L (for last); they indicate the extra Returns needed to end the object selection process. It is easy to forget these extra Returns.

The following macros apply the same principle to the MOVE and COPY commands:

```
[COPY:]^C^CCOPY;$S=COPY
[ window]^C^CCOPY;W;\\;\\
[ last]^C^CCOPY;L;;\\

[MOVE:]^C^CMOVE;$S=MOVE
[ window]^C^CMOVE;W;\\;\\
[ last]^C^CMOVE;L;;\\
```

Extra backslashes in these macros pause and accept user input for the points of displacement. The display words

window

and

last

are indented within their brackets when they are added underneath the standard versions of these commands to improve the screen appearance. Figure 6.1 shows how these additions might look on a custom menu.

If you are using AutoCAD 2.18 or earlier, you can add syntax to these macros that will invoke the dynamic dragging feature automatically, as shown in the following lines:

```
[ window]^C^CCOPY;W;\\;\DRAG;\
[ last]^C^CCOPY;L;;\DRAG;\

[ window]^C^CMOVE;W;\\;\DRAG;\
[ last]^C^CMOVE;L;;\DRAG;\
```

Notice that the DRAG; syntax appears immediately after the backslash for user selection of the base point of displacement. A Return, in the form of a semicolon, is required after the word DRAG in order to switch on AutoCAD's dragging mode.

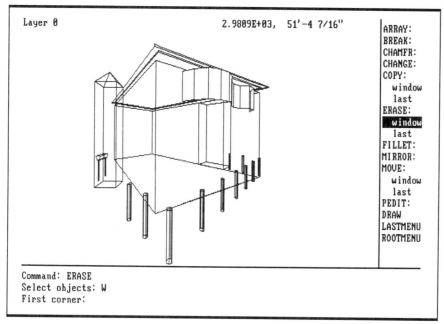

Figure 6.1   A Custom Menu Including Editing Macros

If you are using AutoCAD Version 2.5 or later, dragging in commands such as COPY or MOVE is the standard default state. If you like, you can still include the DRAG; syntax in the macro, but it will have no visible effect.

Combining Drawing and Editing Commands

The following macro draws a line segment and then makes a copy of it immediately (it helps draw parallel lines):

[PARALINE]^C^CLINE;\\;COPY;L;;\\

It combines some unrelated commands. After the standard cancel, the LINE command is invoked and two backslashes are inserted for user input of the endpoints of the line. The COPY command is then invoked, and the L option (for last) is selected automatically. Next, an extra Return tells AutoCAD that no more selection is necessary. Finally, the macro pauses to get the points of displacement from the user. This macro can seem remarkably fast if you're used to performing this process with off-the-shelf AutoCAD.

If you are using AutoCAD Version 2.18 or earlier, you may wish to invoke the dynamic dragging feature, as in the following macro:

[PARALINE]^C^CLINE;\\;COPY;L;;\DRAG;\

If you are using AutoCAD Version 2.5 or later, the following macro can be reworked using AutoCAD's OFFSET command:

[WALL]^C^CLINE;\\;$S=OFFSET;OFFSET;

This macro will draw a single line segment and immediately invoke the OFFSET command. When the macro ends following the invocation of the OFFSET command, all normal command options will be prompted as usual, so a menu subsection reference to the Offset menu subsection is included within the macro.

The next macro takes takes advantage of the multiple-copy option of the COPY command in AutoCAD Version 2.5:

[MANYLINE]^C^CLINE;\\;COPY;L;;M;\

Notice here that the macro ends with the selection of the base point of displacement. This allows the user to make any number of copies immediately after drawing the line.

The following variation on the theme uses block insertion with multiple copies:

[MANYBLKS]^C^CINSERT;\\\\\COPY;L;;M;

Notice the series of five backslashes after the INSERT command. These backslashes allow for user input to select

1. The block name

2. The insertion point

3. The x-scale factor

4. The y-scale factor

5. The rotation angle

All five of these backslashes are required. No Return is necessary to end the INSERT command, so the COPY command is issued immediately after the fifth backslash, followed by the L option (for last), the extra finishing Return, and the M option (for multiple). The macro ends after the selection of the M option, so that the user is free to select as many copies of the inserted block as needed.

Combining Editing and Display Commands

Any series of AutoCAD commands and references can be combined into macros, not just those that are intuitively related. In the examples that follow, editing and display commands are combined, eliminating the need to move between screen menus.

Cleaning Corners   After drawing some intersecting sets of parallel lines, you can use macros to help clean up the corners. The following macro uses the FILLET command to clean a simple corner formed by intersecting sets of parallel lines. It works with AutoCAD versions that have OSNAP capability:

[CORNER1]^C^CFILLET;R;0;;INT;\@;;INT;\@;

Figures 6.2 and 6.3 illustrate how this command might work. This macro sets the fillet radius to zero automatically, just in case it is not already zero. The macro then repeats the FILLET command by means of an extra Return. Next, OSNAP INTER is invoked, and a backslash pauses the macro for the user to select an intersection. Once the intersection is selected, AutoCAD automatically reselects the same point to complete the fillet, using the @ symbol, which references the last selected point. The FILLET command is again invoked by means of an extra Return, and the process repeats, filleting the second intersection.

If you need to fillet lines that are not intersecting, you can, using a slightly different macro. The following macro will work for both inter-

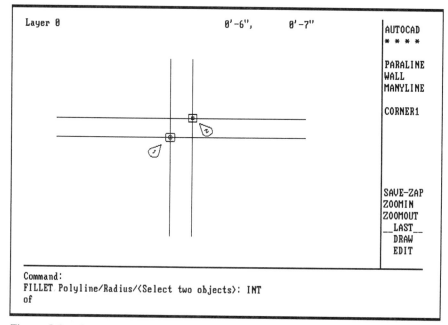

Figure 6.2   Selecting Points for Macro Corner Clean-Up

secting and nonintersecting wall lines, but it requires two line picks per fillet, four picks altogether.

[CORNER2]^C^CFILLET;R;0;;NEAR;\NEAR;\;NEAR;\NEAR;\

This macro sets the fillet radius to 0 and uses the OSNAP NEAR to help pick the lines to be filleted. Four lines need to be selected, but the OSNAP NEAR makes the selection easier by not requiring quite so much exactitude. Notice how the semicolon is used to repeat the FILLET command after the second backslash in this macro. Figures 6.4 and 6.5 show how intersecting and nonintersecting lines can be picked using this alternate corner clean-up macro.

For those cases where the lines and corners are close together and the intersections are difficult to pick, the following macros begin with an automatic window zoom, which enables you to get close to the corner you wish to clean up. For example:

[CORNER1]^C^CZOOM;W;\\FILLET;R;0;;INT;\@;;INT;\@;ZOOM;P;

[CORNER2]^C^CZOOM;W;\\FILLET;R;0;;NEAR;\NEAR;\+
;NEAR;\NEAR;\ZOOM;P;

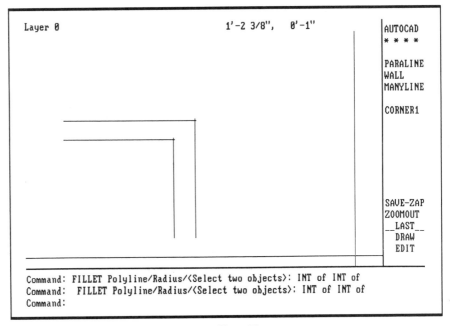

Figure 6.3   After the Macro Corner Clean-Up

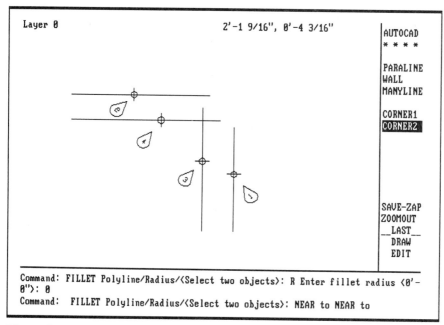

Figure 6.4 Cleaning Up Both Intersecting and Nonintersecting Wall Lines with a Macro

When finished, these macros automatically zoom back out to the previous view.

When editing a large, complex drawing, you may wish to use the zoom feature of these macros only occasionally. If such is the case, instead of placing the zooms within the macro, place the ZOOMIN and ZOOMOUT macros on the same menu subsection as your corner clean-up macros. With this configuration, you may use zoom as you wish or not use it at all.

An alternative approach for selection of objects in a complex drawing is to reduce the size of the Osnap aperture box temporarily. Use Auto-CAD's APERTURE command within the macro to shrink the aperture temporarily and then restore it to normal again.

The following macros demonstrate this principle. They assume that the current Osnap aperture size is ten pixels; they reduce the aperture size to five pixels temporarily, execute the macro normally, and then reinstate the previous ten-pixel aperture size:

```
[CORNER1]^C^CAPERTURE;5;FILLET;R;0;;INT;\@;+
;INT;\@;APERTURE;10;
```

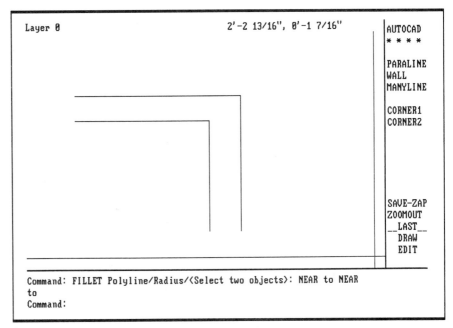

Figure 6.5 The Results of the Clean-Up Using CORNER2

[CORNER2]^C^CAPERTURE;5;FILLET;R;0;;NEAR;\NEAR;\+
;NEAR;\NEAR;\APERTURE;10;

You may wish to experiment with different size values.

Cleaning an Open-T Macros that clean up open-T intersections use the same fundamental techniques as described in the previous section.

[OPEN-T]^C^CBREAK;NEAR;\@;\FILLET;R;0;;INT;\@;;INT;\@;

This macro invokes the BREAK command so that you can break the line segment that must disappear for the open-T. OSNAP NEAR again helps out by requiring less exactitude. Two points on this line are needed, but notice that the second break point is automatically invoked using the @ symbol, followed by a Return. (This technique can be used to split any breakable entity into two or more segments.) After making the line break, the fillet radius is set to 0. The filleting process used is the same as the filleting process described in the previous section. Figures 6.6 and 6.7 show the point selections that will clean up an open-T intersection.

If your lines are close together and you find the segments are hard to select, even using OSNAP, you could easily add zooms or change the

ADVANCED TECHNIQUES IN AUTOCAD

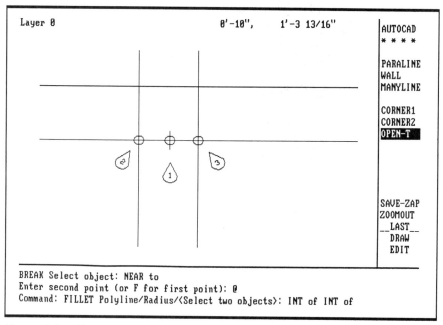

Figure 6.6   Cleaning Up an Open-T with a Macro

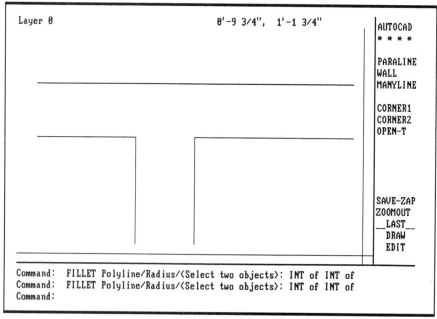

Figure 6.7   The Result of Clean-Up Using OPEN-T

aperture size as described in the previous section. In the following examples, the open-T macro is repeated, once using added zooms and a second time with added aperture changes:

[OPEN-T]^C^CZOOM;W;\\BREAK;NEAR;\@;+
FILLET;R;0;;INT;\@;;INT;\@;ZOOM;P;

[OPEN-T]^C^CAPERTURE;5;BREAK;NEAR;\@;+
FILLET;R;0;;INT;\@;;INT;\@;APERTURE;10;

Notice that the second macro uses the plus sign to wrap the command sequence to the text line underneath.

Cleaning a Cross Intersection
The next two macros clean up an open-cross intersection. The first example will work in AutoCAD Version 2.5 and later.

[CROSS2.5]^C^CTRIM;C;\\;NEAR;\NEAR;\NEAR;\NEAR;\;

This macro combines the TRIM command with the crossing window option to select four wall lines. Following that, a touch of each inner line segment causes it to disappear. Figures 6.8, 6.9, and 6.10 show the point picks the macro requires.

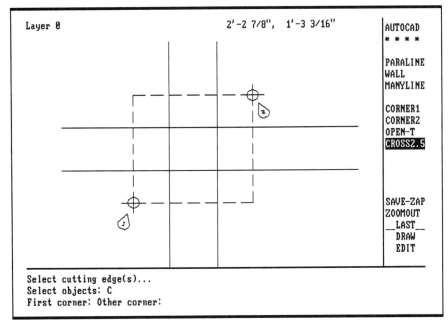

Figure 6.8   Cleaning Up an Open-Cross Intersection (Version 2.5), Step One

ADVANCED TECHNIQUES IN AUTOCAD

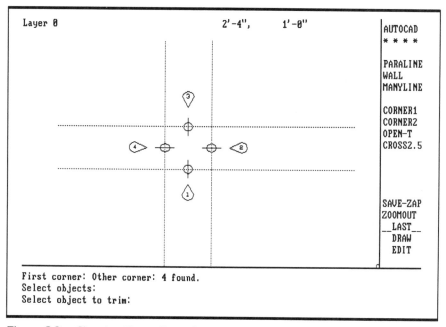

Figure 6.9   Cleaning Up an Open-Cross Intersection (Version 2.5), Step Two

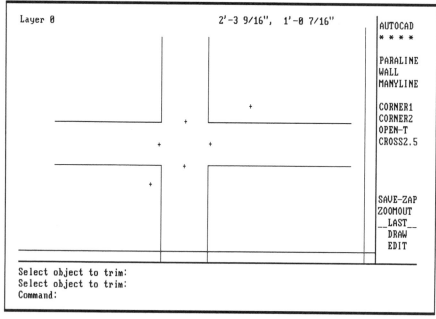

Figure 6.10   The Result of Cleaning Up an Open-Cross Intersection (Version 2.5)

In the following examples, the same macro is repeated, once using added zooms and a second time using added aperture changes:

[CROSS2.5]^C^CZOOM;W;\\TRIM;C;\\;NEAR;\NEAR;+
\NEAR;\NEAR;\;ZOOM;P;

[CROSS2.5]^C^CAPERTURE;5;TRIM;C;\\;NEAR;\NEAR;+
\NEAR;\NEAR;\;APERTURE;10;

The following is an example of a macro that will clean up an open-cross intersection in AutoCAD Version 2.18 and earlier. This macro uses the BREAK command to clear out the cross.

[CROS2.18]^C^CBREAK;NEAR;\@;;NEAR;\@;;NEAR;\@;+
;NEAR;\@;FILLET;R;0;;INT;\@;;INT;\@;;INT;\@;;INT;\@;

This macro begins with the BREAK command, and the OSNAP NEAR helps the user select one of the inner line segments to be broken. The @ symbol selects the same point again, breaking the line. This sequence is repeated three times, breaking the other inner line segments. Next, the FILLET command is invoked and the user selects the four intersections, with the aid of the OSNAP INTERSECT command. This process is repeated for the other three line segments to be cleaned up, thus trimming out the cross. While this macro is a little less efficient than the Version 2.5 command macro, it is still much easier than manual AutoCAD. This macro will also work in AutoCAD Version 2.5 and later. Figures 6.11, 6.12, and 6.13 show the point picks that the macro requires.

The following examples show this macro repeated with optional zooming and a change of the aperture size:

[CROS2.18]^C^CZOOM;W;\\BREAK;NEAR;\@;+
;NEAR;\@;;NEAR;\@;;NEAR;\@;+
FILLET;R;0;;INT;\@;;INT;\@;;INT;\@;;INT;\@;ZOOM;P;

[CROS2.18]^C^CAPERTURE;5;BREAK;NEAR;\@;+
;NEAR;\@;;NEAR;\@;;NEAR;\@;+
FILLET;R;0;;INT;\@;;INT;\@;;INT;\@;;INT;\@;APERTURE;10;

MACROS FOR BLOCK OPERATIONS

Block insertion is always command intensive, requiring a block name as well as insertion parameters. Macros can be very helpful in this regard, as the examples in this section demonstrate.

ADVANCED TECHNIQUES IN AUTOCAD

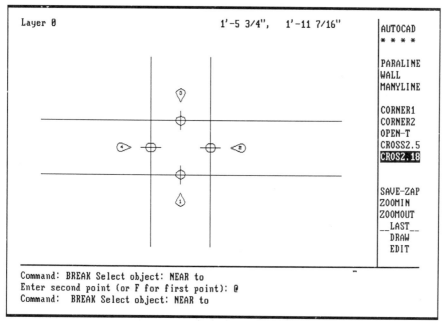

Figure 6.11   Cleaning Up an Open-Cross Intersection (Version 2.18 and Earlier), Step One

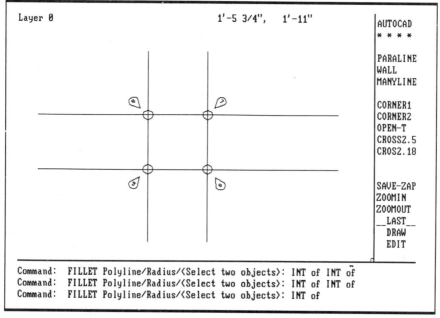

Figure 6.12   Cleaning Up an Open-Cross Intersection (Version 2.18 and Earlier), Step Two

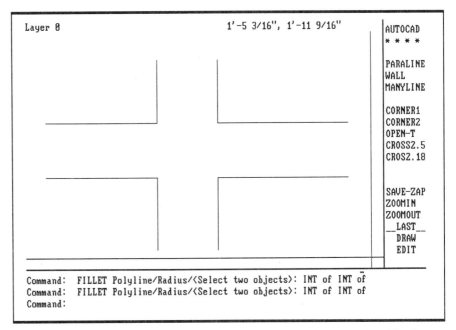

Figure 6.13 The Result of Cleaning Up an Open-Cross Intersection (Version 2.18 and Earlier)

Inserting Blocks

Macros are helpful when inserting standard blocks or shapes. The following example shows a subsection labeled Furn, which contains a few macros that insert blocks. This example assumes that the drawing file contains some blocks named for a few standard pieces of furniture (door1, window, sofa, table, and chair). You should substitute your own block names to use these macros:

```
**FURN 3

[door1]^C^CINSERT;door1;NEAR;\DRAG;\\DRAG;\
[window]^C^CINSERT;window;DRAG;\DRAG;\DRAG;\
[sofa]^C^CINSERT;sofa;DRAG;\DRAG;\DRAG;\
[table]^C^CINSERT;table;DRAG;\DRAG;\DRAG;\
[chair]^C^CINSERT;chair;DRAG;\DRAG;\DRAG;\
```

The first macro displays the name of the block, door1, on the screen. The INSERT command is invoked and the door1 block is spelled out within the command sequence, as if typed at the keyboard. OSNAP NEAR ensures that the door is seated on a point on the wall line. The x- and y-scale factors

ADVANCED TECHNIQUES IN AUTOCAD

are automatically dragged, but if you wish, you can enter exact values for the door dimensions.

The door1 block was designed with some very special features. When the block was originally created, it was drawn to measure one drawing unit by one drawing unit. The block is illustrated in Figure 6.14.

That's a very small door, but it's also very easy to scale to a variety of door widths. For example, using this one-unit door, if you enter x- and y-scales of 30, you will insert a 30-inch door. Later, if you use x- and y-scales of 28, you will insert a 28-inch door. Different scale factors will always result in an equal number of door-inches when the block is inserted. This process is illustrated in Figure 6.15.

After the door is inserted, it may be rotated to any angle. Whenever you insert door1 using this macro, you have the choice of either dragging the rotation of the block or entering the exact angle of the wall at the keyboard.

This same technique can be used to insert any frequentlycalled block, as in the following examples from the Furn menu subsection:

```
[window]^CINSERT;window;DRAG;\DRAG;\DRAG;\
[sofa]^CINSERT;sofa;DRAG;\DRAG;\DRAG;\
```

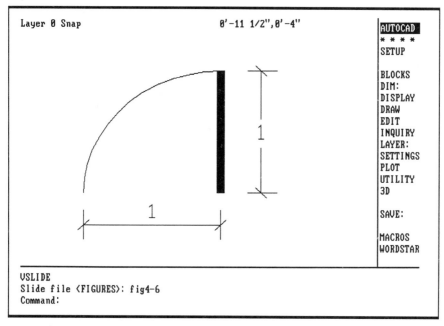

Figure 6.14   The Door1 Block, with Dimensioning Added

```
[table]^CINSERT;table;DRAG;\DRAG;\DRAG;\
[chair]^CINSERT;chair;DRAG;\DRAG;\DRAG;\
```

All these blocks are originally one drawing unit by one drawing unit; you can therefore enter whatever specific lengths and widths you wish. The chair and table blocks are illustrated in Figure 6.16.

Inserting Blocks with Attributes

You can take this block insertion routine a step further. What if the door1 block included attributes? Suppose you find that you enter the same kinds of attribute data frequently? Why not use a menu subsection to select attribute data instead of typing it out?

In the following example, assume that the door1 block has three attributes: 1) door frame specifications, 2) materials specifications, and 3) hardware specifications. Further assume that you have standard codes for this data that you enter each time you insert a door block.

The first step is to add an additional menu subsection reference to the DOOR insertion macro:

```
[DOOR]^C^CINSERT;door1;NEAR;\DRAG;\\DRAG;\$S=DSPECS
```

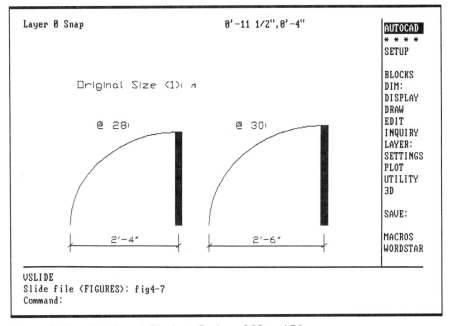

Figure 6.15   The Door1 Block at Scales of 28 and 30

Now the macro inserts the door and immediately references a new menu subsection named Dspecs. This new menu subsection might look something like the following:

**DSPECS 3

[Hardw:]
[BRASS]brass;
[ALUMINUM]aluminum;
[STAINLSS]stainless steel;

[Specs:]
[ALUMINUM]Aluminum;
[OAK]Oak;
[MAPLE]Maple;
[PLYWOOD]Plywood;

[Frame:]
[ALUMINUM]Aluminum;
[OAK]Oak;

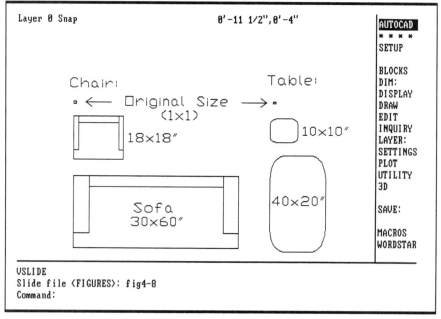

Figure 6.16   Furniture Blocks, Original Size and Scaled

[MAPLE]Maple;
[PINE]Pine;

[FURNMENU]^C^C$S=FURN

This menu allows you to pick standard specifications regarding the door's hardware, material specifications, and frame specifications. You simply use your pointing device to highlight the specific attribute you wish to apply to any particular door and pick it. The standard data is entered into each attribute without typing. Figure 6.17 illustrates this process.

The technique illustrated here will work for any set of standard attribute data attached to any block. If any block contains nonstandard attribute data, you are not forced to pick something from the menu; you can still enter exceptional data using the keyboard and move on to the next attribute.

In this example, when you have picked the last attribute (frame specifications), a menu subsection reference returns you automatically to the original Furn menu subsection that contains your original insertion macro, setting you up to insert more if you wish.

When different block attributes are listed on the same menu subsection, they should be listed in the *reverse order of their original setup*,

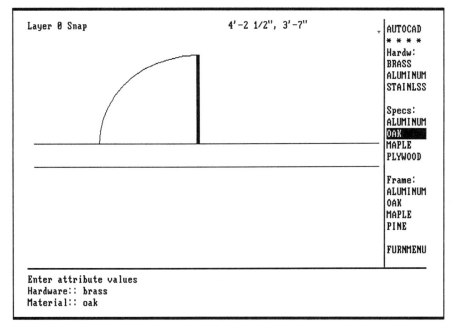

Figure 6.17 Picking Attributes from a Screen Menu

because AutoCAD will prompt for attribute data beginning with the last attribute and ending with the first. You will want to include the menu subsection reference that returns you to your original subsection only after your response to the last prompt. In this example, the frame specifications attribute was the first attribute created for the door1 block. Therefore, on the attribute data menu, it is the last set of attribute data. The menu subsection reference to return to the Furn subsection comes immediately after the response to this last entry.

Certainly, you will have many possibilities for different standard attribute data, and it may be necessary to place a series of attribute data on more than one menu subsection. This is fine; simply include the appropriate menu subsection reference on any attribute data line that requires it.

At the bottom of each attribute data menu subsection, be sure to include an independent menu subsection reference that does not insert attribute data, but simply references the next menu subsection. This technique is like the next and previous references you saw earlier. In this way, the user will be able to move through the menu structure even when typing nonstandard data from the keyboard. It is also worthwhile to include an independent reference to the original block-inserting menu on each attribute data menu subsection, in case you decide to cancel the process altogether.

Finally, notice that the semicolons following the attribute data are not optional; they are required. Because AutoCAD allows spaces to be considered as part of the attribute data, spaces will not be read by the menu processor as Returns. The semicolon is always considered a Return when it appears in any menu command sequence. This also means that you cannot include a semicolon as part of your standard attribute data unless you skip the menu and type it at the keyboard.

Editing around the Inserted Block

Once the door has been placed on the wall line, you can use another macro to help trim the wall around the door:

```
[TRIMDOOR]^C^CLINE;NEAR;\PERP;\;+
;NEAR;\PERP;\;TRIM;\\;\\;
```

This macro may look long and complex, but it only combines techniques you have seen before. First, it invokes the LINE command to draw two short line segments perpendicular to the original wall lines. OSNAP

NEAR helps find a point on one wall line, and PERP helps locate the perpendicular point on the opposite wall line. This process is repeated; hence the two semicolons before the second NEAR: the first finishes the LINE command, and the second repeats it. Figures 6.18, 6.19, and 6.20 illustrate the process.

After the lines are drawn, the macro employs the TRIM command. First the two small line segments just drawn are selected by the user as the cutting edges. Then the wall line segments are selected and trimmed out.

As with the previous macros, you can add zooms or aperture size changes to make the selection process easier if you like:

[TRIMDOOR]^C^CZOOM;W;\\LINE;NEAR;\PERP;\;+
;NEAR;\PERP;\;TRIM;\\;\\;ZOOM;P;

[TRIMDOOR]^C^CAPERTURE;5;LINE;NEAR;\PERP;\;+
;NEAR;\PERP;\;TRIM;\\;\\;APERTURE;10;

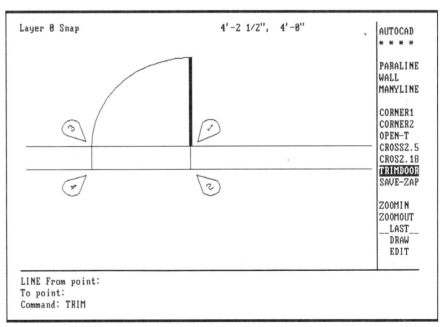

Figure 6.18   Trimming the Wall Around the Door—Drawing the Perpendicular Lines

ADVANCED TECHNIQUES IN AUTOCAD

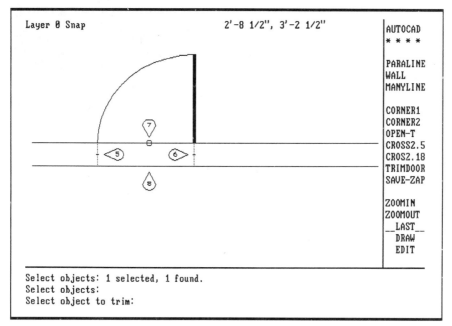

Figure 6.19   Breaking Out the Wall Sections

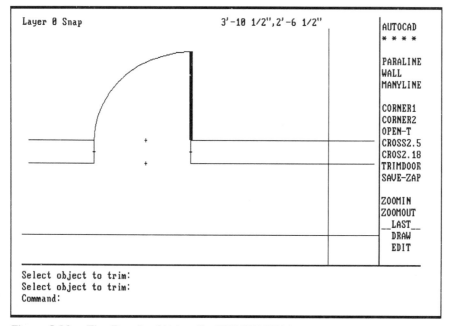

Figure 6.20   The Result of Using the TRIMDOOR Macro

ENHANCED MACROS

The macros demonstrated in this chapter can be greatly enhanced by combining them with AutoLISP functions. The next two chapters introduce the fundamentals of AutoLISP; Chapter 9 will demonstrate how AutoLISP functions can be used to create more powerful macros.

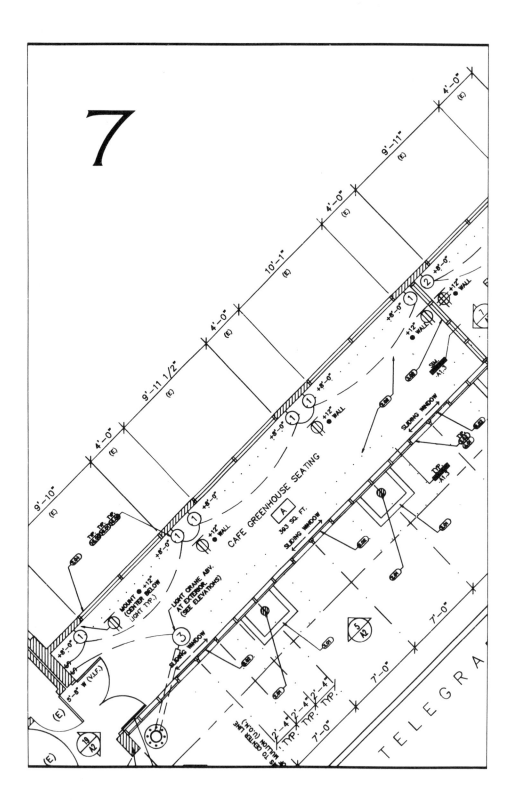

Chapter 7
Introduction to AutoLISP

AUTOLISP IS A SPECIAL LANGUAGE used to write instructions carried out by AutoCAD. AutoCAD instructions that have been written in Auto-LISP are called *LISP routines*. LISP routines are contained in ASCII files that are called *LISP files*. LISP files can have any name that is a valid DOS file name, and they always have the file extension LSP.

LISP routines are your single most powerful tool for optimizing Auto-CAD performance. LISP routines enable the AutoCAD user to "auto-mate" AutoCAD. They have many possible applications, including the creation of new and unique AutoCAD commands (Chapter 8), the inser-tion of special drawing and calculating functions in custom menu macros (Chapter 9), and the development of applications that automatically carry out detailed graphics analysis and drawing inside AutoCAD's Drawing Editor (Chapters 10 through 12).

LISP routines quickly perform calculations and analysis of data used to generate drawing entities on the monitor screen. They analyze existing drawing entities or create new entities by invoking AutoCAD com-mands directly. The entities created by LISP routines are the same as any created by the user, except that with AutoLISP, the process is faster and easier. LISP routines greatly enhance the production of com-plex drawings, as well as eliminating unnecessary menu selections and repetitive keyboard entries.

AutoLISP is not a true programming language, such as PASCAL, FORTRAN, COBOL, or C, because many of the functions in the AutoLISP language can be used only to create instructions that are carried out by AutoCAD. However, AutoLISP does share many of its functions and its overall syntax structure with its parent programming language, Com-mon LISP. Common LISP is itself just one dialect of a programming lan-guage that has many different dialects—MacLISP, UCI LISP, InterLISP, and Franz LISP are just a few.

Although AutoLISP is a limited programming language, it uses many con-ventional control structures that are common to all programming lan-guages. Readers with some experience in programming will recognize such control structures as "if-then-else" statements and controlled loops.

Since AutoLISP is a small language, limited in scope, it is easy for non-programmers to learn. In fact, if you have never written a computer program before, AutoLISP is an excellent, nonthreatening way to get a taste of programming's rewards and frustrations. A unique and deep satisfaction comes from creating a computer program that accomplishes a time-consuming, tedious, or complex task quickly and easily. With this satisfaction comes the potential for increased productivity and business profits.

Is it profitable to use AutoLISP? It certainly can be. A small LISP routine may take a beginner 10 hours to develop. If that LISP routine saves only 30 minutes of drawing time per day, it will pay for itself in a month, and you will profit long afterward.

It's true that programming can occasionally be frustrating. Often the development of an AutoLISP routine is marked by a grinding process of *debugging*—getting rid of problems that interfere with the routine's ability to achieve its intended results. The solution to one problem can reveal another problem waiting underneath. A program may have to be tested several times before it runs correctly. This process notwithstanding, it is still overwhelmingly advantageous to make use of the power of AutoLISP.

Once you have learned the *syntax*, or language rules, of AutoLISP, LISP routines are fairly easy to create and modify with your word processor. However, a useful LISP routine must be thought out in advance. You could, if you wish, develop a LISP routine by trial and error, but there are more efficient ways.

The process of developing a LISP routine is similar to that of developing a custom menu macro. In one sense, a LISP routine is really a complex macro. The instructions contained in a LISP routine are executed in sequence; they build on each other, the results of previous instructions being used to carry out subsequent instructions. A LISP routine, however, can handle more sophisticated instruction sets than a simple macro.

As in the development of macros, the first step in writing any LISP routine is to sit down with a pencil and paper and describe in plain English exactly what it is that you would like the LISP routine to do. This exercise is extremely important as a time-saving and error-preventing device. It will help you organize your thoughts and wishes, and by referring to it later, you can keep yourself on track regarding what it is you are attempting to create. Programmers refer to this plain-English version of a routine as *pseudocode*. It's simply good organization; no other single step will save you more time or prevent more errors.

When developing the pseudocode for your LISP routine, you should manually go over the process from the keyboard, as much as possible.

You can enter most AutoLISP instructions from the AutoCAD command prompt. This pretesting procedure will help you spot problems early in the developmental process and save you lots of time in debugging. Make notes of every step you take and how it was accomplished. Note what calculations were involved and on what the figures were based; in short, note everything that relates to the drawing you wish to produce or the process you wish the LISP routine to accomplish.

You can collect ideas for useful LISP routines by keeping a notepad handy during your drawing sessions. Keep a record of how you use AutoCAD. Note where you are slowing down to make mathematical calculations, for instance. Note if you find yourself drawing certain types of objects repeatedly. Can this drawing process be automated, at least in part? These notes will be the seedbed for your LISP routines. They will tell you exactly how you can benefit from AutoLISP.

Even after your LISP routines seem to be working perfectly, keep the notepad handy to jot down any little surprises that might pop up days or even weeks later, perhaps when a new user tries out the same routines. Note where they occurred, under what circumstances, and what needs to be done to correct the problem. Don't rely on memory alone to guide you as you move between AutoCAD and your word processor.

As you learn and acquire more experience, the number of bugs in your LISP routines will certainly diminish. But all experienced programmers learn to be patient with both the machine and, more importantly, themselves.

SYNTAX CONVENTIONS

The syntax of AutoLISP is built on certain conventional ways of organizing computer instructions in ASCII files. These structures make it possible for AutoCAD, by way of the AutoLISP interpreter, to read the ASCII files and execute the instructions contained in them. These syntax structures are relatively few in number, especially when compared to ordinary spoken languages. They also tend to be more rigid, with fewer exceptions and little tolerance for slight variances. Syntax structures are summarized in this section.

Functions

Some AutoCAD users are surprised to discover that AutoCAD has a built-in math calculator. This internal calculator is accessible from the command prompt and illustrates the fundamental instruction format in AutoLISP, the *function*.

For example, imagine that you are drawing a complex mechanical part; to draw the next curve, you need to know the quotient of 84.037 divided by 2.56. You have several options. You could do it in your head if you're mathematically inclined, you could stop what you're doing and work it out on paper, or you could turn to that trusty little calculator you keep next to the computer keyboard. Perhaps you could call up some memory-resident computer utility, if you have one that works with AutoCAD. Another option is to use AutoCAD itself, by typing the following at the AutoCAD command prompt:

(/ 84.037 2.56)

After you press Return, AutoCAD will instantly provide the answer: 32.826950.

When you use AutoCAD to perform math like this, you are accessing AutoCAD's *AutoLISP interpreter* and offering it a *function*, which it then *evaluates*. After the AutoLISP interpreter evaluates the function, it returns a *result*—in this example, the number 32.826950.

The structure of this simple math function follows certain general rules that apply to all AutoLISP functions. These general rules are as follows:

- The AutoLISP function is contained within parentheses. All parentheses in LISP routines are matched, or *balanced;* that is, a pair of parentheses surrounds the individual function.

- The function reads from left to right.

- The first thing inside the parentheses is the *function operator,* which is a command to the AutoLISP interpreter to do something. In the example, the command was to perform a division. The function operator for this command is the forward slash symbol (/).

- The function operator is followed by any necessary function *arguments*. Arguments are individual items of information that are required by the AutoLISP interpreter to accomplish the purpose of the function. In the example, the AutoLISP interpreter needs two numbers in order to perform a division, so the forward slash is followed by these two arguments.

- The function operator and its arguments are separated by at least one space, so the AutoLISP interpreter can tell where one ends and the next one begins.

- Extra spaces and carriage returns within and between functions are not required and are therefore ignored by the AutoLISP interpreter. This means that a function can occupy many lines in an ASCII file.

- Functions use standard ASCII characters. They are not case sensitive; when typing out AutoLISP functions you can use either upper- or lowercase characters, or mix upper- and lowercase together. This book usually uses uppercase for function names in regular text; as you will see, the names are usually *entered* in lowercase, with uppercase reserved for purposes of emphasis in the LISP file.

The above example of an AutoLISP function, translated into English, says, "Perform a division. Take 84.037 and divide it by 2.56." In all division functions, the first number is divided by the second; in mathematical terms, the first number following the operator is the dividend, and the second number is the divisor.

The following is the function for addition, using the same numbers for its arguments:

(+ 84.037 2.56)

In English this means, "Perform an addition. Take 84.037 and add 2.56 to it." If you type this out at the AutoCAD command prompt, AutoCAD will return the result, 86.597.

The following function performs subtraction. Notice how the subtraction is carried out:

(– 84.037 2.56)

In English this means, "Perform a subtraction. Take 84.037 and subtract 2.56 from it." In all subtraction functions, the second number is subtracted from the first. In this case, the result returned by AutoCAD is 81.477.

The following function performs multiplication:

(* 84.037 2.56)

AutoLISP contains dozens of useful predefined functions. Different functions require different types and quantities of arguments; many functions have arguments that are optional. The next chapter examines several of these functions.

Memory Variables

Memory variables are the basic means by which a computer can organize, remember, and later recall information. All programming languages depend on the manipulation of memory variables.

AutoLISP memory variables work in the following way:

1. A portion of the computer's random-access memory is set aside as a place to hold AutoLISP's memory variables.

2. When a memory variable is created, it is given a *variable name*.

3. When the memory variable has been created and named, it can then receive a *value*, the specific piece of information that is associated with its name. When the name of a memory variable has a value, the variable is said to be *bound* to that value.

4. While a memory variable is bound to a value, subsequent functions can make use of the memory variable by using the memory-variable name. As these functions are evaluated, whenever the memory variable's name is encountered, the AutoLISP interpreter substitutes the value of the memory variable for the name.

Because of memory variables, one set of general instructions can be used on many different sets of data. Without memory variables, LISP routines would have to be reedited each time the data changed.

AutoLISP uses a special function to create memory variables and bind them to values. This function is the SETQ function, which requires a minimum of two arguments. The first argument is the name of the memory variable. The second is the value to which the memory variable is bound. Here is an example of this function:

```
(setq x 2)
```

Translated into English, this function means, "Create a memory variable. Give it the name x. It contains the integer 2."

Once AutoLISP has evaluated this function, the following function becomes valid:

```
(* 2.36 x)
```

AutoLISP will substitute 2 for x in this function, and will multiply 2.36 by 2, returning the result, 4.72.

If you wish, you can use the SETQ function to assign a new value to x:

```
(setq x 3)
```

The memory variable x has already been created. Repeating the function with the same name and a new value does not create a second memory variable with the same name, but merely binds x to a new value, 3. Now the multiplication function will return a new result:

```
(* 2.36 x)
```

AutoLISP will substitute 3 for x in this function and then return the result, 7.08.

You can find out the value of a memory variable quickly if you type an exclamation point followed by the memory-variable name at the AutoCAD command prompt. For example, if you have assigned a value to the memory variable x, type the following at the AutoCAD command prompt:

!x

AutoCAD will respond with the current value of the memory variable x.

Memory-variable names contain no spaces or punctuation marks, always begin with a letter (not a number), and can have as many characters as you like, up to the limit of available memory. However, your LISP routines will be processed more quickly and you will conserve computer memory space if you keep them short, preferably six characters or fewer.

type of value they contain. For example, you might choose to store angle information in memory variables with names like ang (such as xang, yang, ang1, or ang2). Likewise, you may choose to store coordinate-point information using memory variables with names like pt (such as xpt, ypt, pt1, or pt2).

A memory variable whose value never changes is called a *constant*. AutoLISP makes use of only one constant, *pi*. The value of pi is always approximately 3.1415926. The advantage of this constant is that pi is easier to type than 3.1415926. Also, because the actual value of the constant pi computes to an infinite number of decimal places, using the constant is more accurate than using the decimal value.

LISP routines often perform a calculation and store the result in a memory variable. For example, consider the following AutoLISP function:

(setq m (/ 4 2))

This function divides four by two and assigns the result of this computation to the new memory variable m. This example demonstrates a fairly common structure for basic AutoLISP functions.

Nesting

The results returned by functions can be used as the arguments of other functions in a process called *nesting*. For example, here is a valid AutoLISP function:

(+ 1 1)

As you have seen, the plus sign is the function operator for addition, and the arguments are 1 and 1. The function will return a value of 2. Now observe the following nested function:

$$(* 2.36 (+ 1 1))$$

Note how the addition function is nested within a multiplication function. These combined functions return a result of 4.72. The function that adds 1 and 1 exists on what is called the *second level* of nesting, because it is nested within only one other function. Notice how the parentheses that surround the multiplication function also surround the entire addition function, including its set of parentheses.

You can build deep levels of functions within functions. The AutoLISP command interpreter can trace nested functions up to 100 levels deep. The AutoLISP interpreter will evaluate nested functions beginning with the deepest level. Here is an example of the addition function nested three levels deep:

$$(- (* 2.36 (+ 1 1)) 2)$$

This function returns the result 2.72 after a three-level computation. First, the integer 1 is added to 1, returning the result 2. Next, 2 is multiplied by 2.36, which returns the result 4.72. Finally, 2 is subtracted from 4.72, which returns the final result, 2.72.

The parentheses are arranged in matched pairs surrounding each function. Careful arrangement of these parentheses requires a little practice and alertness, but it will be worth it—nesting is a powerful AutoLISP technique.

System Variables

AutoLISP makes use of certain special memory variables called *system variables*. A system variable contains values related to the AutoCAD drawing environment and the state of the current drawing. AutoLISP comes supplied with dozens of these predefined system variables.

For example, the system variable ORTHOMODE contains a value of either 0 or 1. When the value of ORTHOMODE is 0, AutoCAD's orthogonal mode is off. When the value of ORTHOMODE is 1, AutoCAD's orthogonal mode is on.

System variables can be changed by means of a special AutoLISP function, SETVAR. For example,

```
(setvar "ORTHOMODE" 1)
```

sets the value of ORTHOMODE to 1. When ORTHOMODE has a value of 1, AutoCAD's orthogonal mode is toggled on. This is the same as if you toggled on Ortho mode with a keyboard function key (F8 on most systems). The AutoLISP function GETVAR is related to SETVAR. For example,

(getvar "ORTHOMODE")

will return the current value of AutoCAD's ORTHOMODE system variable but will not change it. This is handy when a LISP routine needs to find out the value of a system variable.

System variables are extremely valuable when you are creating LISP routines that change AutoCAD drawing parameters. A list of all the current AutoCAD system variables can be found in Appendix A of the *AutoCAD Reference Manual* (Version 2.5).

Radians

AutoLISP does not use degrees for measuring angles; instead, it uses a system of *radians*. Fortunately, angle degrees can be converted to radians using a simple formula: divide the angle degrees by 180 and multiply the result by pi. In AutoLISP, the mathematics is as follows:

(* pi (/ angle 180))

Converting a large set of angle degrees to radians is not as cumbersome as it first seems, because you can define a special AutoLISP function that will do it for you automatically. Chapter 8 (as well as the *AutoLISP Programmer's Reference*) presents a function, DTR, that converts angle degrees to radians and radians to angle degrees.

FUNDAMENTAL AUTOLISP DATA TYPES

The data used by AutoLISP can be grouped into *data types*. These are categories of data that are distinguished by what they can and cannot do when referenced and used within LISP routines. The following are brief descriptions of AutoLISP data types and their functions.

Entity Names

Each drawing entity created in AutoCAD is listed in a special database along with all information required to reproduce that entity. A straight line, for example, is stored as a *line entity* along with information that describes its starting point, ending point, and drawing-layer location. More complex entities have longer lists of information associated with them.

Using AutoLISP, it is possible to select an entity from the drawing database. Special functions return the selected entity and the defining data as a list. (See the definition of a list later in this section.) The first item on a list of this type is the *entity name*, a special data type reserved for handling the list of definition data and distinguishing it from other selected entities. Once selected and assigned an entity name, an item on the definition list can be extracted and manipulated by AutoLISP. This technique is demonstrated in Chapter 12.

File Descriptors

Special functions in AutoLISP can open a file on disk for information storage or read the information contained in disk files. When a file is opened under AutoLISP, it is assigned a special data type, called a *file descriptor*, which acts as a pointer to that file, keeping track of its physical location on the disk for storage and access, and distinguishing it from any other selected files. This technique is demonstrated in Chapter 11.

Integers and Reals

AutoLISP recognizes two forms of numerical data: *integers* and *reals*. Integers are whole numbers only. They can be processed quickly but are limited in range. Any whole number from -32768 to $+32767$ is a valid integer. Using an integer outside that range produces an error message.

The result of using integers is also an integer. For example, the following function uses integers:

(/ 35 2)

The result returned by this function is 17, not 17.5. This is because both 35 and 2 are expressed as integers, and therefore the result can only be another integer.

Reals are more flexible, although they process a bit more slowly. Here, the same function uses two reals instead of two integers:

(/ 35.0 2.0)

The result returned by this function is mathematically correct: 17.5, another real.

Reals are easily identified because they always include a decimal point; integers never do. If a real has a value of less than 1, its decimal point is preceded by a leading zero. For example, 0.5 is a valid real, and .5 is not.

You can combine integers and reals in the same function:

(/ 35.0 2)

The result returned by this function is also 17.5. When integers and reals are combined in the same function, the result is always a real.

A good rule of thumb regarding integers and reals is this: Use integers when you are sure that you need only whole numbers in your processing, and that these numbers (as well as the results of calculations using these numbers) will stay within the allowed range for integers. Do this for speed and memory efficiency. In all other cases, or when in doubt, use reals.

Lists

In AutoLISP, a *list* is any group of individual items of information enclosed by a matched set of parentheses. The items are separated from each other by at least one space. Items on a list can be numbers, characters, function operators, arguments, or even other lists. They derive their meaning from the nature of their contents and the context in which they appear. Thus, a function is a list composed of a function operator and its arguments. The length of a list is the number of individual items it contains. Lists can be any length.

AutoLISP treats x-y coordinate information as a list of two numbers that indicates a coordinate point. For example, given the list

(1.25 2.75)

AutoLISP assumes that the first number is the x-coordinate and the second number is the y-coordinate. In AutoCAD Version 2.6, a third number on the list would be recognized as the z-coordinate of a 3-D point.

Strings

Strings are sequences of one or more characters (letters, numbers, and punctuation marks) that do not require mathematical processing. A string is always surrounded by quotation marks. For instance, consider the following AutoLISP SETQ function:

(setq x "This is a string")

This function takes the sequence of characters "This is a string" and stores it in memory variable x.

Strings can be any length; the computer allocates memory for them as needed. However, because they can use up a lot of computer memory quickly, long strings can really slow down processing. Keep your strings as short as possible.

Strings are often used as computer prompts for the user, which is why they can be so cryptic at times. Computer programs attempt to strike a balance between processing speed and prompt clarity, often with mixed results.

Try typing the above example function at the AutoCAD command prompt. Then type !x and press Return. Try using various strings. Remember to include the quotation marks.

Symbols

The term *symbol* is a general term used to describe ASCII characters that stand for something else. Memory-variable names are symbols; so are function operators. A string is different from a symbol because it is literal, representing only itself. Likewise, a number is different from a symbol because it can only represent its own value.

The characters that make up a symbol can include any combination of ASCII letters, numbers, and punctuation marks except the following:

().'";

These punctuation marks have special meaning in AutoLISP.

Selection Sets

AutoLISP allows you to select groups of entities. A group of entities can be given a name, called a *selection set*, and can then be acted upon as a group. The manipulation of selection sets is demonstrated in Chapter 12.

MANAGING AUTOLISP ROUTINES IN AUTOCAD

AutoLISP routines are contained in separate files on disk; thus, they require some simple management before they can be used within Auto-CAD. The file contents must be loaded before they can be executed, and sufficient memory must be allocated for their use.

Loading AutoLISP Routines

LISP routines are executed when LISP files are loaded into an area of memory reserved for that purpose by AutoCAD. This loading process is accomplished by using the special AutoLISP function called LOAD, as in the following example:

```
(load "filename")
```

This function would cause AutoCAD to look for the file FILENAME.LSP on the default subdirectory. If found, the entire contents of FILENAME- .LSP would be loaded into memory and the expressions it contains would be evaluated. It is possible to load LISP routines from different subdirectories using the full path name of the file. For example, the file FILENAME.LSP, if located on foreign subdirectory \ACAD\LISPFILE, could be loaded as follows:

(load "c:/acad/lispfile/filename")

Notice that in the above syntax, the forward slash (/) is used to separate subdirectory names in the full path name of the LISP file. This is because the backslash (\) has a special meaning in AutoLISP; it is reserved for designating special control characters in strings.

Stack and Heap Areas

AutoLISP files are loaded entirely into memory before they can be executed. Because of this, it is necessary to allow sufficient room in memory to hold all their variable names, functions, prompt strings, and so on. If you load several LISP files in succession (or even one really big one), you may get this error message from the AutoLISP interpreter:

insufficient node space

You can make more room for your LISP routines by including the following two DOS commands in your AUTOEXEC.BAT file (or by typing them at the DOS prompt) before you run AutoCAD:

SET LISPHEAP = 35000
SET LISPSTACK = 10000

The total of these two numbers cannot exceed 45,000. You may not have to use numbers this big, or you may eventually find that you have to juggle these values around. The value of LISPHEAP is usually set as the larger of the two, especially if you define many functions and memory variables. If you nest your functions deeply, or if your LISP routine repeats the same calculation many times before returning a final result, you may have to increase the LISPSTACK number. Setting up these values in DOS has no effect on programs other than AutoCAD.

MAKING A LISP FILE MORE READABLE

The AutoLISP interpreter will read and execute any LISP routine as long as the function syntax is correct. However, the human reader must also be able to understand what the LISP routine intends to accomplish; it is not always easy to decipher what is going on among the various AutoLISP functions, arguments, symbols, and parentheses. Fortunately, there are two ways to make a LISP routine more easily understandable to the human reader, as well as to the AutoLISP interpreter: comments and indentation.

Comments

You can place plain-English explanations and comments within your LISP routines that will be ignored by the AutoLISP interpreter. To do this, simply precede each line of comment with a semicolon. Descriptive text lines preceded by a semicolon are called *comments*. Here is an example:

```
; This function assigns a value of 2 to the memory variable x:
(setq x 2)
```

AutoLISP will read the function, but ignore the comment above it because a semicolon precedes the comment. Comments may begin anywhere on a line; everything following a semicolon on any one line is ignored.

As a general rule, place comments in the LISP file to explain the meanings and operations of functions that are not readily apparent, and as an aid to yourself for editing or debugging the LISP file at a later date. There is no limit on the number of comments in a LISP file, but they do enlarge the file and slow the process of loading it into the computer's memory. You may wish to work with two copies of your LISP file, one with extensive comments for editing and one without comments for loading and executing.

Indentation

When several nested functions are strung together in a LISP file, it can become difficult to read, especially if there are many. One way to help sort things out is to arrange parentheses within the LISP file in such a way as to isolate specific functions, as in the following valid AutoLISP function:

```
(setq m
    (/ (+ x y) 2
    )
)
```

When arranged in this fashion, the right parenthesis of the shallowest function has been placed on a new line, directly underneath its corresponding left mate. The deeper function has been indented on the page, and its corresponding right parenthesis has also been indented below its left mate. The deepest function has been left alone. By having mates share the same degree of indentation, this layout helps the eye to isolate specific functions and their arguments and to see which sets of parentheses belong together. If a parenthesis had been accidentally left out, it would be fairly easy to spot.

The AutoLISP interpreter has no trouble with this arrangement as long as at least one space separates data items on any given text line. The following example repeats the previous example, showing required spaces as underlines:

```
(setq_m
    (/_( + _x_y)_2
    )
)
```

This kind of arrangement of functions is optional and somewhat subjective. For example, you may not wish to indent your LISP files unless the function is more than two or three levels deep or involves some special, complex analysis. The key issue here is to make the files as easy to read and analyze as possible. As you acquire more experience, you will undoubtedly settle on a layout method that works best for you. However, if your LISP files are going to be read by someone else, you should make every possible effort to keep them clear.

GETTING OUT OF TROUBLE

Not every LISP routine works the first time. Some LISP routines will function but achieve unintended results. Others may simply fail to function. The AutoLISP documentation provides a complete list of error messages and their meanings. The following two techniques, the console break and the unbalanced function prompt, help you handle a LISP routine that performs in an unexpected way.

Console Break with Ctrl-C

In the midst of executing a lengthy LISP routine, you may wish to abort the process if, for instance, the routine is offering incorrect or unintelligible results, or if it appears to stop processing altogether. You can abort a LISP routine by pressing Ctrl-C or Ctrl-Break. This will cause the LISP routine to cease execution after it has evaluated the current function. AutoCAD will also display the message

Error: Console Break

Once you have aborted a LISP routine, you are returned to the AutoCAD command prompt, where you may take any corrective action required.

The Unbalanced Function Prompt

There is a likelihood that, as you build more and more complex functions with deeper and deeper levels of nesting, you may accidentally leave out a parenthesis or two. This will cause your AutoLISP routine to produce strange results. In such an event, the following prompt may replace the familiar AutoCAD command prompt:

n>

The n will be the number of right parentheses that are still needed in order to have an equal number of left and right parentheses in the LISP routine.

If you ever encounter this strange and persistent little prompt, there is only one way to get rid of it and return to the AutoCAD command prompt: type that same number of right parentheses at the keyboard, and press Return. Although this will return you to the normal AutoCAD command prompt, you should not attempt to run the LISP routine that caused the trouble. First return to your word processor, locate the places where the missing right parentheses belong, and add them. Then return to AutoCAD and reload the LISP file. This will ensure that your LISP routine runs properly.

If you find that this prompt persists even after you have typed the correct number of right parentheses, the cause is probably a missing quotation mark. Once the AutoLISP interpreter encounters a quotation mark, everything that follows, including right parentheses, is treated as part of a string. This includes the parentheses that you type at the keyboard. The solution is to type a set of quotation marks followed by the correct number of right parentheses.

It will help if you use nesting levels sparingly at first until you have the AutoLISP routine working. Once the file is working, you can go back and nest functions to reduce the number of needed memory variables and use your LISPHEAP space more efficiently.

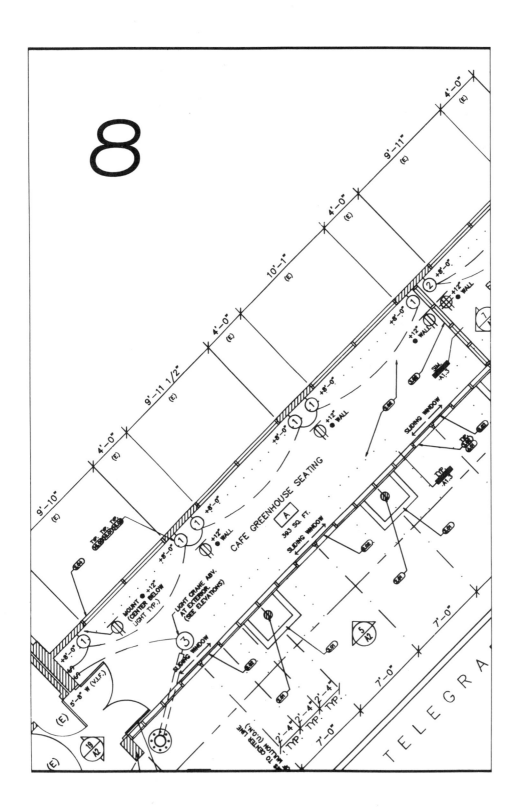

Chapter 8
Fundamental AutoLISP
Functions

THIS CHAPTER EXPLAINS some of the predefined AutoLISP functions. Although the functions presented here are certainly not all the available predefined functions, they are the most commonly used, and with them, it is possible for a beginner to construct a wide variety of Auto-LISP routines. In addition, once you have had a chance to understand these functions and to practice using them, other functions presented in the *AutoLISP Programmer's Reference* will be easier to understand and use.

The functions presented here are arranged according to broad categories of purpose. Some functions can be used for more than one purpose. In such cases, this is noted and the function is then listed according to how it is used in this book's example routines.

As you read through this chapter, you may find it helpful to type out the example functions at the AutoCAD command prompt. This will allow you to see the data that these functions return. Note that the brackets shown in the syntax sections for these functions are only used to make compound terms more readable; you do not enter them.

MATH FUNCTIONS

In addition to the four-function math we have already seen, Auto-LISP contains other math functions that expand the power of its built-in calculator.

The 1+ Function

Syntax: (1 + *number*)

This math function requires a single argument, a number. It returns the argument incremented by 1. It is the equivalent of the function (+ *number* 1).

If the argument of this function is an integer, the function will return an integer result. If the argument is a real, the result will also be a real. For example,

(1+ 5)

returns 6, and

(1+ 5.0)

returns 6.000000.

This function is useful in situations where a single memory variable is incremented by 1 repeatedly throughout the processing of a LISP routine. You will see examples of this in later sections.

The 1– Function

Syntax: (1– *number*)

This function returns its argument decreased by 1. It is the opposite of the 1+ function. Its arguments and results follow the rules explained in the 1+ function description. This function is useful in situations where a single memory variable is decreased by 1 repeatedly throughout the processing of a LISP routine.

ABS

Syntax: (abs *number*)

The ABS function returns the absolute value of its argument as a single number, integer or real. If the argument is an integer, the function returns an integer; if the argument is a real, it returns a real. For example,

(abs –1)

returns 1. This function is useful for quickly converting negative values to their positive equivalents.

COS

Syntax: (cos *angle*)

The COS function returns the cosine of its argument, which is assumed to be an angle expressed in radians. The function returns a real number. For example,

(cos 1.57076)

returns the cosine of 90 degrees.

EXPT

Syntax: (expt [*base number*] [*power*])

The EXPT function returns the number supplied as its first argument raised to the power given in the second argument. Both arguments are required. If both arguments are integers, the result is also an integer. If one or both arguments are reals, the result is a real. For example,

(expt 3 3)

returns 27, and

(expt 3.0 3)

returns 27.000000. The power of 2 squares the number. For example,

(expt 5 2)

returns 25.

GCD

Syntax: (gcd *number number*)

The GCD function returns the greatest common denominator of the two numbers used as its arguments; for example,

(gcd 54 81)

returns 27. If both arguments are integers, the function returns an integer. If one or both are reals, the function returns a real. Both arguments are required.

SIN

Syntax: (sin *angle*)

The SIN function returns the sine of its argument, which is assumed to be an angle expressed in radians. This argument is required. The function returns a real number. For example,

(sin 1.57076)

returns a sine of 90 degrees.

SQRT

Syntax: (sqrt *number*)

The SQRT function returns the square root of its single argument. The argument can be any real number or integer. The square root returned is always a real; for example,

(sqrt 25)

returns 5.000000.

FUNCTIONS THAT PROMPT
THE USER FOR INFORMATION

The following functions pause execution of a LISP routine and wait for the user to supply the needed information before execution continues.

GETANGLE

Syntax: (getangle [*ref point*] [*prompt*])

The GETANGLE function pauses and waits for the user to supply angle information. GETANGLE requires no arguments, but two optional arguments may be supplied. The more important of these arguments is a prompt that can be displayed for the user. With or without the optional arguments, the GETANGLE function allows the user either to select two points on the screen as input for the angle information or to enter the angle directly from the keyboard.

Keyboard-supplied angle information is entered using whatever angle-unit format has been currently set by the AutoCAD UNITS command. However, once the angle measurement has been entered, GETANGLE always returns that angle measurement converted to radians.

If the user elects to enter the angle by means of two digitized points, after the first point is selected, a "rubber-band" line will appear between that point and the current location of the crosshairs. When the second point is selected, AutoCAD will automatically measure the absolute angle formed by the two points and return that angle measurement expressed in radians. The following are two examples of this function:

(getangle)
(getangle "Enter two points to show the desired angle: ")

Both of these functions will accept two points from the user. The second function, because it includes a prompt specifically asking for angle information, is likely to be more useful than the first, which offers no help to the user.

When used within a LISP file, the screen display of the prompt may be enhanced by the use of a special control character at the beginning of the prompt, as in the following example:

(getangle "\nEnter two points to show the desired angle: ")

Note that \n has been entered as the first character in the prompt. This special character inserts a carriage return just before the display of the prompt, causing the prompt to appear on its own line. This greatly improves readability.

Functions such as GETANGLE frequently take user-supplied information and store it in a memory variable, as in the following example:

(setq ang1 (getangle "\nEnter two points to show the desired angle: "))

Here, the GETANGLE function is nested within a SETQ function. This nested function causes the LISP routine to pause, receive the user-supplied starting-point information, and then store the coordinate information in a memory variable named ang1.

You can demonstrate this function for yourself. At the AutoCAD command prompt, enter the example function carefully. Notice how AutoCAD displays the prompt and pauses to accept your angle information. Pick two points, and then enter

!ang1

AutoCAD will respond with the angle of the points you selected, expressed in radians.

If the optional reference-point argument is included, GETANGLE assumes that this is the first selected reference point. For example, consider the following AutoLISP function:

(getangle '(0 0) "\nEnter an angle: ")

The point 0,0 is referenced as an argument for GETANGLE. When the user supplies angle information for the memory variable ang1, the correct angle information can be supplied with a single selection. Notice that in all cases where information is supplied by means of picking reference points, these points are not stored by the system automatically.

In the above example, the absolute coordinate points 0,0 have been supplied as the first reference point. When absolute coordinate points are supplied in this fashion, they are presented as a list of two integers or reals. This list must be preceded by the single quote character; it cannot be presented simply as a list of two integers or reals.

The single quote character is shorthand for another special AutoLISP function, QUOTE. The QUOTE function is handy when you are supplying literal information to AutoCAD, and could have been used for the example presented here. It is explained more fully in the "Special Functions" section later in this chapter.

You can also use a memory variable containing point information as the optional reference-point argument, as in this example:

```
(setq x '(0 0))
(getangle x "\nEnter an angle: ")
```

Because the GETANGLE function returns the angle information expressed as radians, you may think that it can be used to convert angle information from the current unit format to radians. It can, but it will work only for angle information entered by the user. Because this function pauses the execution of the LISP routine, you cannot supply another LISP function as a response to GETANGLE (or to any other GET-type function, for that matter). This severely limits GETANGLE as a conversion device.

If later in the routine, you wish to use the angle information obtained by GETANGLE in the current AutoCAD angle-unit format—that is, in response to an AutoCAD command prompt—you must reconvert the stored radians to the current format.

GETDIST

Syntax: (getdist [*ref point*] [*prompt*])

All the syntax rules we have seen with the GETANGLE function apply as well to the GETDIST function. The GETDIST function returns the distance between the two points instead of the angle. This information is always returned as a real number.

Keyboard entry of a real number is also accepted as a response to this function:

```
(setq x (getdist "\nEnter the distance: "))
```

In response to the prompt in this example, the user may supply either two points or a real number. Notice that in the following example, the optional reference-point argument is used to create a rubber-band screen display:

```
(setq dist (getdist '(0 0) "\nEnter distance from base point: "))
```

The GETDIST function is similar to the GETANGLE function examined previously. In the above example, the memory variable dist contains the distance between the base point 0,0 and the selected point. As before, the selected point is not stored automatically in memory.

GETINT

Syntax: (getint *prompt*)

GETINT pauses for input and displays a prompt if you wish, but it will only accept integers (whole numbers in a range from – 32768 to 32767) from the user. It will ignore all noninteger input. Its syntax is similar to GETPOINT. Consider the following example:

(setq x (getint "\nEnter a WHOLE NUMBER (-32768 to 32767): "))

Notice that a pair of parentheses appears within the prompt's set of quotation marks. This is valid. AutoLISP will not attempt to process these parentheses as a function because they appear inside the quotation marks and therefore are understood to be part of the prompt.

GETPOINT

Syntax: (getpoint [*ref point*] [*prompt*])

The GETPOINT function pauses the execution of the LISP routine and waits to receive x-y coordinate information from the user. This information can be entered from the keyboard using any valid coordinate-entry method, or the information may be entered by picking a point with a digitizing device.

Here is an example of typical AutoLISP function syntax using GET-POINT with the prompt argument:

(getpoint "\nEnter the starting point: ")

When this function occurs within a LISP routine, execution pauses, the prompt is displayed, and AutoCAD pauses until the user supplies some valid coordinate-point information.

As with GETANGLE and GETDIST, a reference-point argument may be added to GETPOINT. This argument is used in cases where the user is likely to supply the coordinate information by picking the point with the digitizing device.

For example, let's assume that the user has already responded to the previous example function, and that coordinate information for a starting point has been stored in the memory variable x. The following example function would then become valid:

(setq y (getpoint x "\nEnter the next point: "))

This nested function displays the prompt and pauses to get coordinate information to be stored in memory variable y. The GETPOINT function contains an additional argument following the operator—in this case, the memory variable x. AutoCAD substitutes the coordinate information stored in memory variable x in place of x itself.

When coordinate information is supplied as the first argument of the GETPOINT function, AutoCAD will draw a rubber-band line from the referenced coordinate points to the current location of the crosshairs. You can demonstrate this rubber-band line technique by typing the above example at the AutoCAD command prompt. AutoCAD will pause and wait for you to enter a point.

GETREAL

Syntax: (getreal *prompt*)

GETREAL accepts any numerical input of up to 16 significant digits. Here is an example of its use:

(setq x (getreal "\nEnter any number: "))

GETREAL will not accept a number that is less than one unless it is preceded by a leading zero. For example, this is a valid response to GETREAL:

0.25

This is not:

.25

If the user enters an integer in response to the GETREAL function, the integer is converted to a real.

GETSTRING

Syntax: (getstring *value prompt*)

The GETSTRING function works like all the other GET-type functions, pausing to accept any sequence of keyboard characters and then returning them as a literal string. In the example

(setq x (getstring "\nWhat is your first name? "))

the sequence of characters supplied by the user will be terminated by pressing the Space bar or Return, as is normal in AutoCAD. However, there may often be cases where a space must be included as part of the character string. In such a case, a special optional argument is used, as in the following example:

(setq x (getstring 1 "\nWhat is your full name? "))

Here, the integer 1 was supplied immediately following the function operator. If any valid argument is supplied here (such as an integer or a memory variable that actually contains some value), the user's response can be terminated only by pressing Return. This allows spaces to be used as part of the user's response.

PROMPT

Syntax: (prompt *"message"*)

The PROMPT function simply displays a prompt in the AutoCAD command prompt area. It does not pause the execution of the LISP routine or wait for any user-supplied information. It is useful when a particular confirming message needs to be sent to the user. It requires a single argument, and this argument must be contained within quotation marks. Here is an example:

(prompt "This function was typed in correctly.")

If this function were typed at the AutoCAD command prompt, Auto-CAD would display the message contained in the quotation marks.

FUNCTIONS THAT USE COORDINATE INFORMATION

Once the user has supplied coordinate-point information, AutoLISP can use several functions to perform calculations based on it. This section presents these functions.

ANGLE

Syntax: (angle [*first point*] [*second point*])

The ANGLE function requires two arguments. It will accept two x-y coordinate information sets and return the absolute angle formed by the points. The angle will always be measured from the first point following the function operator, and the angle information is always expressed in radians.

The ANGLE function, because it requires no user input, does not pause execution of an AutoLISP routine. It will accept the result of other AutoLISP functions as its arguments.

For most purposes, the x-y coordinate information used as the arguments for this function will be supplied by memory variables. For example, consider the following little LISP routine:

```
(setq x (getpoint "\nEnter first point: "))
(setq y (getpoint "\nEnter second point: "))
(setq ang (angle x y))
```

The result of this routine is the creation of three memory variables: x, which contains the coordinates of the first selected point; y, which contains the coordinates of the second selected point; and ang, which contains the absolute angle formed by these points, expressed as radians.

Arguments for the ANGLE function could also be quoted literally, as in the following example:

```
(setq ang (angle '(0 0) '(4.657 7.893)))
```

Literal quotes and memory variables can be combined as arguments of this function. The following example computes an angle in this fashion:

```
(setq x (getpoint "\nEnter reference point from 0,0: "))
(setq ang (angle '(0,0) x))
```

CAR

The CAR function returns the first item found on any data list. In AutoLISP, it is often used to extract x-coordinate information from point variables. For example, consider the following two functions:

```
(setq x '(6.25 12.5))
(car x)
```

Here, the memory variable x is being used to store the coordinate points 6.25 and 12.5. The second function, (car x), returns 6.25.

CADR

The CADR function extracts the second item found on any data list. In AutoLISP it comes in handy when you are extracting the y-coordinate from a point variable. Using the above example, the function

(cadr x)

would return y-coordinate 12.5.

CADDR

AutoCAD Version 2.6 introduced 3-D points with z-coordinates. In AutoLISP, each of these points is represented as a list of three real numbers. The CADDR function will extract the third item on any data list. For instance, in this example (caddr x) returns z-coordinate 7.9:

(setq x (6.25 12.5 7.9))
(caddr x)

DISTANCE

Syntax: (distance [*first point*] [*second point*])

The DISTANCE function requires two arguments: it will accept two sets of valid x-y coordinate information and return the distance between the two points. This distance is expressed as a real number, regardless of current drawing units set by AutoCAD's UNITS command. The DISTANCE function does not pause execution of an AutoLISP routine, and it will accept the result of other AutoLISP functions as its arguments.

In many cases, the x- and y-coordinate information used as the arguments for this function will be supplied by memory variables. Consider the following LISP routine:

(setq x (getpoint "\nEnter first point: "))
(setq y (getpoint "\nEnter second point: "))
(setq dist (distance x y))

The result of this routine is the creation of three memory variables: x, which contains the coordinates of the first selected point; y, which contains the coordinates of the second selected point; and dist, which contains the exact distance between the two points, expressed as a real number.

Arguments for the DISTANCE function can be quoted lists of two or three real numbers, as in the following example:

(setq dist (distance '(0 0) '(4.657 7.893)))

A literal quote can be combined with a memory variable, as in the following example:

```
(setq x (getpoint "\nEnter reference point from 0,0: "))
(setq dist (distance '(0,0) x))
```

INTERS

Syntax: (inters *point point point point nil*)

The INTERS function requires four arguments and may also have an optional fifth argument. The first and second arguments are coordinate points that describe the endpoints of a straight line. The third and fourth arguments are coordinate points that describe the endpoints of a second line. The function returns a list of two reals, the x-y coordinates of the point at which the two lines intersect. If the two lines do not intersect, this function returns nil. For example, the function

```
(inters '(0 0) '(2 2) '(2 0) '(0 2))
```

returns the intersection point

```
(1.000000 1.000000)
```

The fifth optional argument is a nil value. If this nil value is present, the lines are considered infinite in length and the intersection point will be returned, even if that point does not exist on the lines. For example, because the extra nil value is present in the following function:

```
(inters '(0 0) '(1 2) '(3 0) '(2 2) nil)
```

it returns this intersection point:

```
(1.500000 3.000000)
```

However, in the function

```
(inters '(0 0) '(1 2) '(3 0) '(2 2))
```

the same coordinates return nil, because the optional nil value is not present and the intersection point does not exist on the lines.

LIST

The LIST function is used to create data lists of any length. In Auto-LISP, it is frequently used to create point variables containing lists of x-y or x-y-z coordinate information. Consider the following functions:

```
(setq x 6.25)
(setq y 12.5)
```

(setq z 7.9)
(setq pt1 (list x y))
(setq pt2 (list x y z))

In this example, a list of x-y coordinate information is created by means of the LIST function and stored to memory variable pt1. The second LIST function is used to create memory variable pt2, containing x-y-z coordinate information.

MAPCAR

Syntax: (mapcar 'function list list...)

The MAPCAR function quotes another AutoLISP function as its first argument and applies that function to the data lists that follow as additional arguments. For instance, the function

(mapcar '+'(2 3)'(5 6))

returns

(7 9)

In this example, MAPCAR applied the + function to the lists that followed. Thus, it took the integer 2 from the first list and added it to the integer 5 from the second list; then it took the integer 3 from the first list and added it to the integer 6 from the second list.

MAPCAR always returns a list of its results. Although MAPCAR may be used to apply functions to lists of any data, it is especially useful when you wish to change a known set of coordinate points by a known amount. For example, imagine that point 5.75,6.75 is stored in memory variable x, and you wish to add two drawing units to both coordinates. You would use the following MAPCAR function:

(setq y (mapcar '+'(2 2)'(5.75 6.75)))

This would return the point 7.75,8.75 as a list of two reals, stored in memory variable y. The new memory variable could then be used where point information was required.

Whenever you use MAPCAR, you must supply at least as many list arguments as the number of arguments required by the quoted function. In cases where a quoted function will cause data lists to act upon each other, take care that the data lists contain an equal number of individual items of information. Otherwise, erroneous information may result. For instance, in

(mapcar '+ '(1 2) '(3 3 6))

MAPCAR will add the first two items in each quoted list together, but will disregard the third item in the second list. Thus, the function will return

(4 5)

If your intended result was a list of three items including the integer 6, the following function would work:

(mapcar ′+ ′(1 2 0) ′(3 4 5))

It would return

(4 5 6)

OSNAP

Syntax: (osnap [*point*] [*snap mode*])

The OSNAP function applies AutoCAD snap values to a drawing entity found at a particular point. If the referenced point is a 2-D point (a list of two reals), a 2-D point is returned. If the referenced point is a 3-D point, a 3-D point is returned. The following example assumes that a line has been drawn from point 0,0 to point 12,12. The function shown here returns the midpoint of that line:

(osnap ′(0 0) ″midp″)

If a 3-D line were drawn from point 0,0,0 to point 12,12,12, the following function would return the midpoint of that line:

(osnap ′(0 0 0) ″midp″)

If no object snap point is found using the specified snap mode, the function returns nil.

You may combine several object snap modes if you wish. For example, the following function is valid:

(snap ′(0 0 0) ″midp,cent,perp″)

In this case, the AutoLISP interpreter would test each snap mode in sequence until an object snap point was found. Otherwise, nil would be returned.

POLAR

Syntax: (polar [*ref point*] [*angle*] [*distance*])

The POLAR function returns x-y coordinate information. It is extremely powerful because it allows AutoCAD to pick points automatically. This function requires three arguments in the following order:

1. A starting reference point

2. A reference angle, expressed in radians

3. A reference distance from the starting reference point

In plain English, this function says, "Find a point. The point will be located relative to a given reference point, at a given angle, and at a given distance." For example, the following two functions create two variables:

```
(setq pt1 (getpoint "\nEnter the reference point: "))
(setq pt2 (polar pt1 1.57076 12))
```

The first function uses SETQ and GETPOINT to store the user-supplied reference point in the memory variable pt1. The second uses SETQ and POLAR to store additional point information in memory variable pt2. Pt2 contains the x-y coordinates of a point that is 12 units from pt1 at an angle of 90 degrees (1.57076 is 90 degrees expressed in radians).

Other functions and memory variables can be used as any or all of the arguments of this function.

LOGICAL FUNCTIONS

AutoLISP logical functions compare two or more sets of information to determine whether a given relationship between them is true or false. The following examples demonstrate how this works.

The = Function

Syntax: (= *data data*)

The = function determines whether its arguments are equal. If the arguments are equal, the function returns T for true. If the arguments are not equal, the function returns nil. For example,

(= 1 1.0)

compares the integer 1 with the real number 1.0. Because they are equal, the function returns T. The following function returns nil because the numbers are not equal:

(= 2 2.1)

The = function will compare strings as well as numbers, as in these examples:

(= "dog" "dog")
(= "dog" "cat")
(= "dog" "DOG")

The first function returns T, and the other two return nil.

At least two arguments must be supplied with this function. It is permissible to compare more than two arguments, but they must all be equal for the function to return T. Otherwise, it will return nil.

The / = Function

Syntax: (/ = *data data*)

The / = function determines whether its arguments are *not* equal. If the arguments are not equal, the function returns T for true. If the arguments *are* equal, the function returns nil. For example,

(/ = 1 2)

compares the integer 1 with the integer 2. Because they are not equal, the function returns T. The function

(/ = 2 2.0)

returns nil because the numbers are equal.

The / = function will compare strings as well as numbers, as in the following example:

(/ = "dog" "dog")
(/ = "dog" "cat")
(/ = "dog" "DOG")

The first function returns nil, and the other two return T.

The / = function requires two arguments and does not permit more than two arguments. It cannot be used to compare lists.

The > Function

Syntax: (> *number number*)

The > function compares two numbers to determine if the first number is greater than the second. If the first number is indeed greater, the function returns T. Otherwise, it returns nil.

At least two arguments must be supplied with this function. It is permissible to compare more than two arguments, but each argument must be greater than the argument to its right for the function to return T. Only numerical values may be used as arguments.

The < Function

Syntax: (< *number number*)

The < function compares two numbers to determine if the first number is less than the second. If the first number is indeed less, the function returns T. Otherwise, it returns nil.

At least two arguments must be supplied with this function. It is permissible to compare more than two arguments, but each argument must be less than the argument to its right for the function to return T. Only numerical values may be used as arguments.

The > = Function

Syntax: (> = *number number*)

The > = function compares two numbers to determine if the first number is greater than or equal to the second. If the first number is indeed greater than or equal to the second, the function returns T. Otherwise, it returns nil.

At least two arguments must be supplied with this function. It is permissible to compare more than two arguments, but each argument must be greater than or equal to the argument to its right for the function to return T. Only numerical values may be used as arguments.

The < = Function

Syntax: (< = *number number*)

The < function compares two numbers to determine if the first number is less than or equal to the second. If the first number is indeed less than or equal to the second, the function returns T. Otherwise, it returns nil.

At least two arguments must be supplied with this function. It is permissible to compare more than two arguments, but each argument must be less than or equal to the argument to its right for the function to return T. Only numerical values may be used as arguments.

AND

Syntax: (and [*logical function*] [*logical function*]...)

The AND function evaluates two or more logical functions. If all the logical functions return T, the AND function returns T; if one or more functions return nil, AND returns nil. Logical functions that operate on strings can be evaluated along with logical functions that operate on numbers. For example, the function

(and (= "dog" "dog") (/ = 1 3))

returns T because both of its nested logical functions return T. The function

(and (= "dog" "dog") (> 3 2.9) (> = 2.1 1 0.5 1.0) (/ = "cat" "DOG"))

returns nil because the third logical function nested inside returns nil, while the other three return T.

EQUAL

The EQUAL function is similar to the = function, but it is used to compare more complex data, such as lists, that must be evaluated by the LISP interpreter before they can be compared. For example, given these memory-variable bindings:

(setq pt1 '(0 0))
(setq pt2 '(1 1))
(setq pt3 '(0 0))

only the following functions will return T:

(equal pt1 pt3)
(equal pt3 pt1)

All other comparisons will return nil. The function

(= pt1 pt3)

will also return nil, because the = function can only compare numbers and strings, not lists.

NOT

Syntax: (not [*logical function*])

The NOT function will return T if the nested logical function returns nil. It reverses the effect of the inner function. For example, the function

(not (= "cat" "dog"))

returns T because "cat" is not equal to "dog".

This function is especially useful as the "not equal to" function for complex data. For example, given these memory-variable bindings:

(setq pt1 '(0 0))
(setq pt2 '(1 1))
(setq pt3 '(0 0))

the following function returns T:

(not (equal pt1 pt2))

The following function returns nil:

(not (equal pt1 pt3))

OR

Syntax: (or [*logical function*] [*logical function*])

The OR function evaluates two or more logical functions. If at least one returns T, the OR function returns T. If all the functions return nil, OR returns nil as well.

Logical functions that operate on strings can be evaluated along with logical functions that operate on numbers. For example, the function

(or (= "dog" "swordfish") (/ = 1 3))

will return T because one of its nested logical functions returns T. The function

(or (/ = "dog" "dog") (< 3 2.9) (> = 2.1 1 1.0 3) (= "cat" "DOG"))

returns nil because all of the functions nested inside return nil.

FUNCTIONS USED IN CONTROL STRUCTURES

Computers excel at two basic processes: They can make either/or-type decisions, and they can do the same thing over and over again. A *control structure* is the means by which AutoLISP routines accomplish these kinds of tasks. AutoLISP can be instructed to perform either one specified set of functions or an alternative set, or it can perform the same set of functions over and over until it is specifically told to stop.

The two functions used to accomplish this are IF and WHILE. They can be nested within each other or within themselves, and they can be used with logical conditions that are joined by means of the AND or OR function. Using them in this manner, you can produce some very sophisticated "thinking."

IF

Syntax: (if [*logical expression*] [*function if true*] [*function if false*])

The IF function requires two arguments and may also use a third one. The first argument is always a logical function. The second is a function that is evaluated if the logical function returns T. If the logical function evaluates to nil, this second function will not be evaluated.

In the following example, the IF function evaluates the logical function (= 1 1):

(if (= 1 1) (prompt "One equals one"))

It returns T. Because the logical function returns T, the following PROMPT function is evaluated. AutoCAD displays the message "One equals one" in the command prompt area.

If there is no third argument and the logical expression evaluates to nil, the IF function will also evaluate to nil. In other words, nothing will happen. However, if there is a third argument (which must be another function) and the logical expression evaluates to nil, the third argument will be evaluated instead of the second argument. In the example

(if (= 1 2) (prompt "1 equals 2") (prompt "1 does not equal 2"))

the logical function returns nil. The first PROMPT function is ignored, and the second PROMPT function is evaluated instead. AutoCAD will display this message:

One does not equal two.

WHILE

Syntax: (while [*logical expression*] [*function while true*])

The AutoLISP WHILE function requires two arguments. These arguments are also AutoLISP functions. The first argument is always a logical function of some sort. The second argument is a function that is evaluated repeatedly as long as the first logical function returns T. As soon as the logical function returns nil, the second argument is no longer evaluated. For instance, in

(setq x 1)
(while (< x 10) (setq x (1 + x)))

the first function binds the memory variable x to the value of 1. The second function, WHILE, evaluates x to determine if it is less than 10. Because it is, the function (1 + x) is evaluated, and the new value, 2, is stored to x. Now the WHILE function reevaluates x, and because x is still less than 10, the function to increment x repeats. This continues until x equals 10 and the WHILE function ceases. If you would like to demonstrate the WHILE function, type the above two functions at the Auto-CAD command prompt and observe the results.

Note that during the repeated execution of tasks inside a WHILE function, something must eventually take place that will cause the logical condition to evaluate to nil. If the logical condition never evaluates to nil, the repeated tasks will continue indefinitely in an endless loop. (When caught in an endless loop, your only recourse is to end it all with a console break.)

FUNCTIONS THAT USE STRINGS

Literal strings, such as prompts to the user or text information, can be acted upon in specific ways. For instance, you may wish to combine a message to the user with the result of a function, or you may wish to use only part of a longer string stored in memory. The following functions offer "cut and paste" operations on strings:

STRCASE

Syntax: (strcase *string upper/lower*)

The STRCASE function will convert all the characters in a string to either upper- or lowercase. It accepts two arguments. The first argument is the string to be converted. If the second argument is present and not nil, all characters will be converted to lowercase. If the second argument is omitted or nil, the characters in the string will be converted to uppercase. For example,

(strcase "Convert This")

returns

CONVERT THIS

The function

(strcase "Convert This" 1)

returns

convert this

This function is useful for comparing strings in which case is unimportant as a factor in the comparison, as in

(setq yn (getstring "\nPress Y for yes: "))
(if (= (strcase yn) "Y") (prompt "YES"))

Although the prompt in the GETSTRING function asks for an uppercase Y, the IF function will work whether an upper- or lowercase y is pressed. Without the nested STRCASE function, only an uppercase Y would work.

STRCAT

Syntax: (strcat *string1 string2*...)

The STRCAT function will connect, or *concatenate*, two or more strings. For example, given the following memory-variable bindings

(setq x "These two strings form")
(setq y " a complete sentence.")

the function

(strcat x y)

returns this:

These two strings form a complete sentence.

The STRCAT function is useful when you wish to display messages for the user based on data that was entered earlier or resulted from internal calculation.

This function will concatenate strings only. It cannot be used to concatenate numbers or to connect strings with numbers. If you wish to concatenate strings with numbers, you can use other functions to convert numerical data to string data. These functions are explained in the next section of this chapter.

SUBST

Syntax: (subst *'new 'old list*)

The SUBST function searches the list supplied as its third argument. It will replace every occurrence of the item supplied as its second argument (the old item) with the item supplied as its first argument (the new item). For example, in this sequence of functions:

(setq a '(This list is unchanged))
(setq b 'changed)
(setq a (subst b 'unchanged a))

the SUBST function will return this:

(THIS LIST IS CHANGED)

SUBSTR

Syntax: (substr *string start length*)

The SUBSTR function will return a *substring*, a portion of the string supplied as its first argument, starting with the character position indicated in the second argument and continuing for the length of characters indicated in the third argument. For example, with the functions

(setq x "This will be a substring soon.")
(substr x 14 11)

the SUBSTR function will return

"a substring"

Both the starting-position and the length arguments must be positive integers. The starting-position argument is required. If the length argument is omitted, the substring will continue to the end of the specified string.

FUNCTIONS THAT CHANGE DATA TYPES

String data and numerical data are handled in different ways. Numerical data cannot be concatenated with string data. String data cannot be used as arguments for mathematical functions. Sometimes, in the course of a LISP routine, it may be necessary to convert string data to numerical data (and vice versa) in order for the AutoLISP interpreter to handle the data appropriately. The following functions allow you to change the data types.

ATOF

Syntax: (atof *string*)

The ATOF function converts string data to real numbers. The string data presented as the argument of this function must be a numeral of some sort. For instance, in the example

```
(setq x "7.75")
(1 + (atof x))
```

the second function returns 8.750000. AutoLISP is able to perform a mathematical function on the string data after it has been converted by the nested ATOF function.

ATOI

Syntax: (atoi *number*)

The ATOI function converts string data to an integer. The string data presented as the argument of this function must be a numeral of some sort. In the example

```
(setq x "7")
(1 + (atoi x))
```

the second function returns 8.

If the argument of ATOI contains a decimal point, the decimal portion of the argument is ignored. The number is not rounded. Thus, if the value of x were the string "7.75", the second function would still return 8.

FIX

The FIX function will convert a real to an integer. In converting, the decimal portion of the real is ignored. The number is not rounded. For example,

```
(fix 6.75)
```

returns 6.

FLOAT

The FLOAT function converts an integer to a real. For example,

(float 6)

returns 6.000000.

ITOA

Syntax: (itoa *integer*)

The ITOA function returns an integer converted to a string. For example,

(itoa 1)

returns 1. This function is helpful when you are concatenating strings with numbers, as in the following example:

(setq x (getint "\nEnter an integer: "))
(prompt (strcat "The value of x is " (itoa x)))

RTOS

Syntax: (rtos *string*)

The RTOS function converts reals to strings. For example

(rtos 7.0)

returns "7.000000".

SPECIAL FUNCTIONS

Three AutoLISP functions have special purposes that do not fall into any category. They are the functions DEFUN, COMMAND, and QUOTE.

DEFUN

Syntax: (defun [*name(arguments)*] [*other functions*])

Just in case you can't do what you would like with one of AutoLISP's predefined functions, AutoLISP provides you with the means to create additional functions of your own.

DEFUN is the AutoLISP function that does this. It is one of AutoLISP's most powerful functions. It will create brand-new functions. DEFUN requires two arguments: the name of the new function operator being created (including any arguments the function requires) and a description, using one or more AutoLISP functions, of what the new function does.

Using DEFUN   To demonstrate how the DEFUN function works, this section will guide you though the creation of a useful new AutoLISP function. Consider the following scenario: You are producing a drawing, and you wish to begin a line at a point that is midway between two existing objects. You don't know exactly how far apart the objects are, and no current entity occupies that point, so OSNAP won't help.

One way to solve the problem might be to draw a scratch line between the two objects, use OSNAP to find the midpoint of the scratch line, draw the new line, and finally erase the scratch line. But there is a faster and easier way, if you first define a simple AutoLISP function that will work like a fancy OSNAP override. The function you are about to define locates the midpoint between any two points without bothering to create and erase the scratch line.

Here is how you create the function:

1. Show AutoCAD which two points to use. Two SETQ functions with nested GETPOINT functions will do that:

   ```
   (setq pt1 (getpoint "\nEnter first point: "))
   (setq pt2 (getpoint "\nEnter second point: "))
   ```

   Any valid point-entry mechanism, including OSNAP overrides, will be accepted as a valid response to these functions.

2. Compute the distance between the two points. The DISTANCE function does the trick:

   ```
   (distance pt1 pt2)
   ```

3. You will also need to know what half that distance is, so divide the distance in two by nesting the DISTANCE function inside a simple division function:

   ```
   (/ (distance pt1 pt2) 2)
   ```

4. Compute the angle between the two points. The ANGLE function works nicely here:

   ```
   (angle pt1 pt2)
   ```

5. Establish a point that is half the distance between the two points, at the angle formed by the two points, starting from the first point. The new point will be handled nicely by the POLAR function, with the previous calculating functions nested inside:

```
(polar pt1
        (angle pt1 pt2)
        (/ (distance pt1 pt2) 2)
)
```

6. Use AutoLISP's DEFUN function to apply a function name to all of this. Here is the complete function, named MID:

```
(defun mid ( )
            (setq pt1
                    (getpoint "\nEnter first point: ")
            )
            (setq pt2
                    (getpoint "\nEnter second point: ")
            )
            (polar pt1
                    (angle pt1 pt2)
                    (/ (distance pt1 pt2) 2)
            )
)
```

7. Enter your word processor and open a new ASCII file called MID.LSP. Type the MID function into this file.

8. Save the file to the AutoCAD system subdirectory.

9. Enter AutoCAD's Drawing Editor. At the command prompt, type

(load "mid")

10. AutoCAD responds with

MID

Once the function is defined and loaded, it can be used to draw any entity starting midway between two existing entities. The following sequence demonstrates how to use it:

1. Enter the LINE command.

2. In response to AutoCAD's "From point:" prompt, enter

(mid)

3. A new prompt appears:

Enter first point:

4. Select the first reference point. Use OSNAP if you wish.

5. A new prompt appears:

Enter second point:

6. Select the second reference point. Again, use OSNAP if you wish.

The new midpoint appears where it should, and the LINE command continues normally, rubber-banding from the new referenced point.

This function can be called at the start of any AutoCAD command that expects a point. It is an example of AutoLISP at its best, creating a simple, fast routine that saves drawing time and simplifies the drawing process.

Saving New Functions   It would be inconvenient to reload new AutoLISP function definitions each time you entered the Drawing Editor. Auto-CAD uses a special LISP file to remember frequently used new AutoCAD commands and AutoLISP functions. This special LISP file is named ACAD.LSP. Every time the user enters the AutoCAD Drawing Editor, AutoCAD searches the system subdirectory for this file and, if it finds it, loads it into memory and evaluates the functions it contains.

If ACAD.LSP is already on your AutoCAD system subdirectory, copy MID.LSP into it. Otherwise, you can simply rename MID.LSP as ACAD.LSP. Once this is done, the MID function will be available to you at the start of each drawing session.

For a crowning touch, place a reference to the MID function on the Osnap menu subsection, so that your new function can be referenced like any other OSNAP override:

[MIDspace](mid);$S =

Creating New AutoCAD Commands   The ability to define new functions is an extremely powerful feature of AutoLISP, especially when you are developing groups of AutoLISP instructions that are to be included in AutoLISP routines. However, a more powerful application of the DEFUN function can be used to create brand-new AutoCAD commands.

Creating new AutoCAD commands requires almost the same syntax as creating AutoLISP functions: you begin by using AutoLISP's DEFUN function, but substitute a special syntax for the name of the function operator. This special syntax requires that you precede the name of the command with C:, which informs the AutoLISP interpreter that an AutoCAD command, not an AutoLISP function, is being created. In the following example, you will create an AutoCAD command that divides a number by the value of pi automatically. This command will be named DPI:

```
(defun C:DPI( )
        (setq q
                (/ (getreal "\nEnter number to be divided by PI: ") pi)
        )
)
```

To test the new AutoCAD command, create a new ASCII file called DPI.LSP and enter the AutoCAD command definition as it appears above. Save the file to the AutoCAD system subdirectory and enter the Drawing Editor. Load the file, using the following command:

(load "dpi")

AutoCAD responds with

C:DPI

This response tells you that the new command has been defined. Next, enter the new command:

DPI

Notice that parentheses are not required. AutoCAD responds with

Enter number to be divided by pi:

Enter this number:

3.141593

AutoCAD responds with

1.000000

In addition to calculating the correct quotient of pi, AutoCAD stores the result in memory variable q. If you later wish to use this number in response to an AutoCAD prompt, simply enter

!q

and the current value of q will be entered by AutoCAD in response to the prompt.

COMMAND

Syntax: (command ["*AutoCAD command*"]
           [*command options and prompt responses*])

Any AutoCAD command can be called from within a LISP routine. AutoLISP can use the results of its automatic processing as responses to the normal prompts that occur as part of the command sequence. The name of the AutoCAD command, as well as any necessary responses, are the arguments of the COMMAND function. For instance, in the following example

```
(command "LINE" "0,0" "5,5" "")
```

the LINE command and the coordinate information are contained in quotation marks and are thus treated as literal strings by the AutoLISP interpreter. This example function will cause a line to be drawn from coordinate point 0,0 to coordinate point 5,5. The third set of quotation marks, which contains nothing, is the equivalent of pressing Return (necessary, in this case, to end the LINE command).

You can demonstrate this to yourself by typing the above function at the AutoCAD command prompt. The line will be drawn between the points specified.

Using this function can be tricky, because it requires that all the necessary command responses be known and presented in sequence. AutoLISP functions and memory variables can be used as responses to commands called by this function. For instance, this series of functions will cause a line to be drawn from point 0,0 to point 5,5:

```
(setq x "0,0")
(setq y "5,5")
(command "LINE" x y "")
```

Handling Angle Information in the COMMAND Function   The following syntax will also cause a line to be drawn from point 0,0 to point 5,5. It is more complex, and demonstrates how the POLAR function, combined with math functions, can calculate line distance and orientation:

```
(command "LINE
         (setq x (0 0))
         (polar x
                (dtr 45)
                (sqrt (* (expt 5.0 2) 2))
         )
         ""

)
```

In this COMMAND function, the line begins at point 0,0. At the same time, the starting point is stored to the memory variable x. The endpoint is found using the POLAR function, which references point x at an angle of 45 degrees and a distance equal to the square root of 5 squared times 2.

Notice how the 45-degree angle is handled in this example. The POLAR function expects its angle argument to be expressed in radians. The DTR function is applied to the integer 45 in order to convert 45 degrees to the equivalent number in radians. This function is *not* a predefined AutoLISP function; you must define it before it can be used in AutoLISP. It can be found in the *AutoCAD Programmer's Reference*, and is repeated here for convenience:

(defun dtr(a) (* pi (/ a 180.0)))

Note that the DTR function is defined with the letter a inside the parentheses following the operator name. This informs the AutoLISP interpreter that DTR requires a single argument, symbolized by a. Next comes the math for the conversion, using a. Notice how the letter a works here. Once you have defined a function that uses arguments, you must be consistent and inform AutoLISP of exactly what to do with the arguments.

Once DTR is defined, it can be used whenever AutoLISP functions expect angle information; in this case, the POLAR function requires the radian angle. However, although AutoLISP functions require angle information expressed in radians, AutoCAD *commands* that prompt for angle information, even when called from inside AutoLISP, expect angle information expressed in the current angle-unit format.

This can require some additional converting. For example, consider a situation in which you have prompted the user for an angle using GETANGLE and stored that information to a memory variable:

(setq x (getangle "\nEnter the desired angle: "))

No matter how the user enters the angle information in response to this prompt, the memory variable x contains the information in radians. Later, if you wish to use this information as part of an AutoCAD command (for example, ROTATE), the syntax

(command "ROTATE" "L" "" "0,0" x)

would *not work*, because the memory variable x is not supplying information to an AutoLISP function; rather, it is a response to an AutoCAD command prompt (for the angle of rotation). In order to use the value of x in this case, it must be converted back to degrees. The following function will do the job:

(defun rtd(a) (* (/ a pi) 180))

ADVANCED TECHNIQUES IN AUTOCAD

The math in the RTD function is the reverse of the math in the DTR function. Once this function is loaded, the following syntax would work with the memory variable x:

(command "ROTATE" "L" "" "0,0" (rtd x))

Most of the example LISP routines used in this book make use of these two functions. Therefore, add them to ACAD.LSP so that they will be available in all your drawing sessions.

QUOTE

Syntax: (quote *data*)

The QUOTE function requires a single argument, and it returns that argument without any evaluation. For example

(quote swordfish)

returns SWORDFISH, and

(quote 1+1)

returns 1+1.

(quote 0,0)

returns 0,0.

There is an alternative syntax for this function that can be used only within a LISP file or nested within another function. Instead of the function operator within parentheses, you can type a single apostrophe, as in the following examples:

'swordfish
'1+1
'0,0

This will be understood by the AutoLISP interpreter as the QUOTE function. This is the only case of a function that doesn't require parentheses. Its purpose is to save keystrokes when you are typing. You cannot, however, use this alternative syntax at the AutoCAD command prompt; you must use the QUOTE function operator within parentheses.

Be careful with the QUOTE function. The argument to this function cannot use spaces unless the entire argument is contained within parentheses of its own. Do not attempt either of the following:

'Here are four words
(quote Here are four words)

AutoLISP will see only

(quote Here)

The rest will cause an error message. You can, however, enter this:

'(Here are four words)
(quote (Here are four words))

The function will return

(HERE ARE FOUR WORDS)

This function is useful when literal information needs to be supplied and there is a possibility that it might be misinterpreted by the AutoLISP interpreter as a function or an error, or might otherwise be subject to an attempt at evaluation. You have seen this function earlier when a list of coordinate-point information was quoted as a reference-point argument within the GETANGLE function. It was also used to provide lists of data as arguments to the MAPCAR function.

AutoLISP functions can produce some remarkably sophisticated results by working together in sequence and by means of nesting. They can use information supplied by the user or calculate information and pass it on to other functions. Your ability to use AutoLISP effectively is based on how you combine these predefined functions and create new functions using them. The following chapters present many examples of how these functions work together, beginning in Chapter 9 with their use within custom menu macros, followed by the development of complex AutoLISP routines in Chapters 10 through 12 and Appendix A.

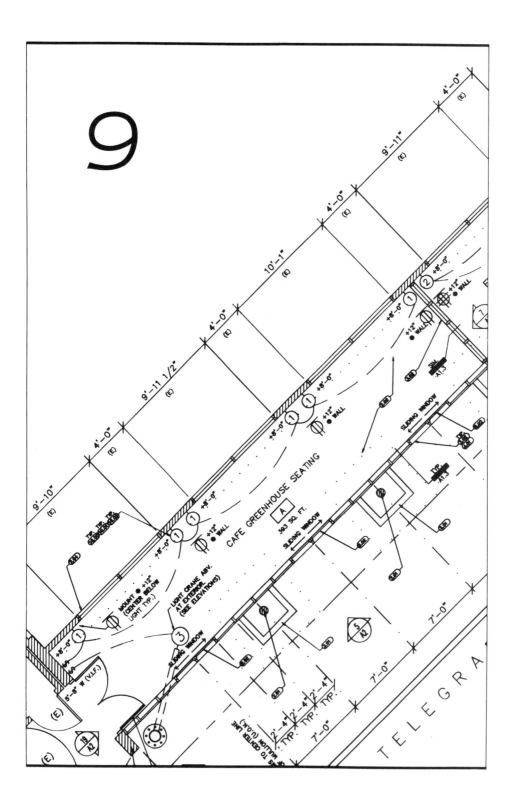

Chapter 9
Enhanced Macros with AutoLISP

AUTOLISP FUNCTIONS can be entered from the keyboard in response to AutoCAD command prompts. The result returned by the function will be seen by AutoCAD as the response to the prompt. Because of this feature, AutoLISP functions can also be included in custom menu macros in order to enhance their power. This chapter presents some examples of how AutoLISP functions can be included in macros.

UTILITY MACROS

It is possible that some of your most useful macros will be related not to creating entities, but rather to managing the drawing environment. AutoCAD's system variables provide a convenient means of doing this within menu macros, as the following examples demonstrate.

Incremental Snap

The following macros can cause the snap value to increase or decrease according to a set amount. If the grid is visible and set to zero, these macros will reset the snap value without a redraw, thus saving time. (Issuing a REDRAW command will change the appearance of the grid.) These macros allow you to snap up or snap down in a stepwise fashion:

```
[SnapUp] ^ C ^ C(setvar "SNAPUNIT" +
(mapcar '+ (getvar "SNAPUNIT") '(1 1)));
[SnapDn] ^ C ^ C(setvar "SNAPUNIT" +
(mapcar '- (getvar "SNAPUNIT") '(1 1)));
```

The deepest function, (getvar "SNAPUNIT"), is evaluated first, returning the current snap value in the form of a list that contains the x and y snap values as real numbers. For example, if the current snap value is set to 3 drawing units, the list returned by this function is

(3.000000 3.000000)

The MAPCAR function also returns a list of two real numbers, which are calculated by taking the numbers in the list returned by GETVAR and adding the corresponding numbers found in MAPCAR's quoted list to each of them:

(mapcar ' + (getvar "SNAPUNIT") '(1 1))

Using this example, if the current snap value is 3, MAPCAR would add the list (1 1) to the list (3.000000 3.000000) and return the list (4.000000 4.000000). The outermost function, SETVAR, takes this new list and assigns it to the system variable SNAPUNIT.

You can set the amount of increment or decrement to any value you wish by changing the value of the quoted list in the MAPCAR function. Or, if you prefer, you can vary the incremental/decremental value by means of the GETREAL function, as in the following examples:

[SnapUp] ^ C ^ C(setq x (getreal "Increment Snap by: "));\ +
(setvar "SNAPUNIT" (mapcar ' + (getvar "SNAPUNIT") (list x x)));
[SnapDn] ^ C ^ C(setq x (getreal "Decrement Snap by: "));\ +
(setvar "SNAPUNIT" (mapcar '- (getvar "SNAPUNIT") (list x x)));

In these examples, the GETREAL function obtains a real number from the user and stores it to memory variable x. Instead of using a quoted list, the MAPCAR function uses a list made from this variable by means of the nested LIST function. The result is a quick change of the snap value.

Simple Toggle Macros

You can create a simple menu macro that will toggle the display of the screen blips, as in the following example, which uses the IF function combined with GETVAR and SETVAR:

[BLIPS] ^ C ^ C(if (= (getvar "BLIPMODE") 0) +
(setvar "BLIPMODE" 1) (setvar "BLIPMODE" 0))

Here, the IF function first evaluates whether the current value of the system variable BLIPMODE is zero (meaning that blips are not displayed on the screen):

(= (getvar "BLIPMODE") 0)

The inner GETVAR function obtains the value of the system variable BLIPMODE. The outer = function returns T if the value of BLIPMODE is currently zero.

If BLIPMODE equals zero, the next function sets its value to 1 (meaning that blips will now be displayed):

(setvar "BLIPMODE" 1)

If BLIPMODE does not equal zero, then it must already equal 1. In this case, the third function, the "else" function, is evaluated, setting the value of BLIPMODE to zero:

(setvar "BLIPMODE" 0))

The extra right parenthesis seen after this function is the closing parenthesis of the original IF function.

This principle can be applied to any system variable that has on/off properties, as in the following:

[ANGLEDIR] ^ C ^ C(if (= (getvar "ANGDIR") 0) +
(setvar "ANGDIR" 1) (setvar "ANGDIR" 0))
[AXIS] ^ C ^ C(if (= (getvar "AXISMODE") 0) +
(setvar "AXISMODE" 1) (setvar "AXISMODE" 0))
[FILLS] ^ C ^ C(if (= (getvar "FILLMODE") 0) +
(setvar "FILLMODE" 1) (setvar "FILLMODE" 0))
[HIGHLITE] ^ C ^ C(if (= (getvar "HIGHLIGHT") 0) +
(setvar "HIGHLIGHT" 1) (setvar "HIGHLIGHT" 0))
[LIMITS] ^ C ^ C(if (= (getvar "LIMCHECK") 0) +
(setvar "LIMCHECK" 1) (setvar "LIMCHECK" 0))
[QTEXT] ^ C ^ C(if (= (getvar "QTEXTMODE") 0) +
(setvar "QTEXTMODE" 1) (setvar "QTEXTMODE" 0))

Toggle Between Two Chosen Values

If a system variable has more than two possible variables associated with it, it is still possible to toggle between any two chosen values for that system variable. The following example toggles a nonzero fillet radius to zero, and then toggles it back to its original value:

[FRAD = 0/X] ^ C ^ C(if (/ = (getvar "FILLETRAD") 0) +
(setq fr1 (getvar "FILLETRAD")) (setq fr1 0)) +
(if (/ = (getvar "FILLETRAD") 0) (setq fr2 (getvar "FILLETRAD"))) +
(if (/ = fr1 0) (setvar "FILLETRAD" 0) (setvar "FILLETRAD" fr2))

To use this toggle, first set a nonzero fillet radius of your choice using the FILLET R command. Then, when you wish to toggle the radius to zero, select FRAD = 0/X from the screen menu. Each time you reselect this macro, it will switch the fillet radius value. You can change the value of the nonzero radius at any time using the FILLET R command. This macro will work only if you have first set a nonzero fillet radius. Otherwise, you might wind up toggling between zero and zero.

The FRAD = 0/X macro works by first checking to see if the fillet radius is not zero. If it isn't, it stores the value of the fillet radius to memory variable fr1. However, if the value of the fillet radius is zero, the macro stores the value of zero to fr1.

Next, another IF function checks the unchanged fillet radius again. If the value is not zero, its stores the value of the fillet radius to the memory variable fr2. If the fillet radius is zero, however, this second IF function does nothing.

Finally, a third IF function checks the value of fr1. If fr1 is not zero, it sets the value of FILLETRAD to zero. If the value of fr1 is zero, however, it sets the value of FILLETRAD to the value of fr2.

This technique will work for any active memory variable, not just system variables, in case you wish to toggle a memory variable between two values.

EDITING MACROS

The process of editing is often cumbersome because of the large number of editing possibilities within each command. AutoLISP functions can be used to reset the drawing environment within an editing function, or to make a single point do the work of two or more, as in the following examples.

Array at an Angle

AutoCAD's rectangular array normally copies objects at angles of zero and 90 degrees. However, it is possible to produce a rectangular array at any angle you choose, using the following two macros. These macros work because the rectangular array actually orients itself according to the current snap orientation, whether or not the snap is actually on. By resetting this orientation, you can array at any chosen angle.

Figures 9.1 through 9.3 demonstrate the process of creating a rectangular array, five rows by five columns, at an angle of 45 degrees. The following macro does the job:

```
[A-ARRAY] ^ C ^ C(setq oldang (getvar "SNAPANG")); +
(setvar "SNAPANG" (dtr (getreal "Angle of Array: ")));\ARRAY;
```

The macro A-ARRAY begins by storing the current snap orientation to the memory variable oldang. This step will allow you to reset the

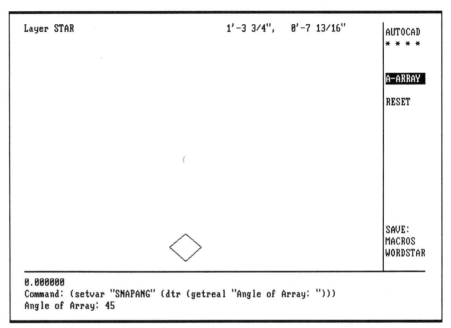

Figure 9.1 Selecting the Angle of Array

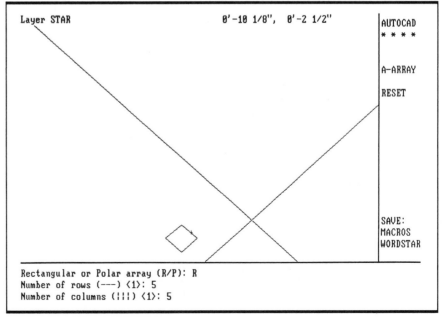

Figure 9.2 Selecting Parameters of the Array (Crosshairs Have Now Rotated)

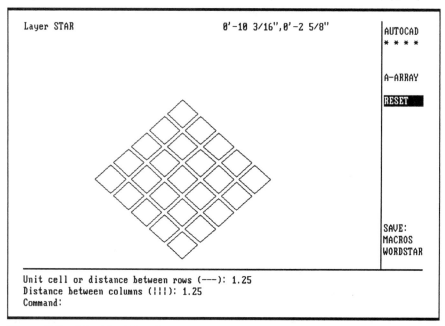

```
Layer STAR                          0'-10 3/16",0'-2 5/8"     AUTOCAD
                                                              * * * *

                                                              A-ARRAY

                                                              RESET







                                                              SAVE:
                                                              MACROS
                                                              WORDSTAR

Unit cell or distance between rows (---): 1.25
Distance between columns (|||): 1.25
Command:
```

Figure 9.3   The Final Result

original snap orientation later. Next, the function GETREAL prompts for the new angle. The angle, entered as a real number, is converted to radians using the DTR function described in Chapter 7. Then the SETVAR function stores the converted value to the system variable SNAPANG. After that, the ARRAY command is issued. Enter responses for a rectangular array with parameters of your choosing, and the array is made at the requested angle.

In this macro, the GETREAL function is used with an optional prompt to remind the user that an angle value must be entered. However, you are not allowed to begin this or any prompt with the special character \n. This is because the backslash character is always seen by the menu processor as a pause for user input; thus, if it is used in the prompt, the GETREAL function would not continue.

It would be convenient if this macro were to continue with an automatic reset of SNAPANG. The value was stored in the memory variable oldang for this purpose. However, the prompt sequence of the ARRAY command varies, depending on whether a value of 1 is entered for either rows or columns. In addition, the process of selecting objects to array can be complex at times. Therefore, in order to allow for variations in the prompt sequence of the ARRAY command, a separate macro is employed to reset the orientation of the crosshairs:

[RESET] ^ C ^ C(if (/ = oldang nil) (setvar "SNAPANG" (dtr organg))); +
(setq oldang nil);

This macro checks to see if the value of oldang is nil. If so, oldang was never initialized. In such a case, the SETVAR function need not be evaluated. This prevents problems if the RESET macro were selected by accident. If oldang has a value, the SETVAR function converts the value to radians and stores it to the system variable SNAPANG. Once SNAPANG is reset, oldang is reset to nil.

Door Insert and Auto-Trim

The following example uses AutoLISP functions to combine two macros presented in Chapter 5, DOOR and TRIMDOOR. Since the insertion of a door into a wall almost always requires wall breaks, combining these macros and making them more automatic can be a real time saver. This technique can be used anytime an INSERT command must be followed by a clean-up routine.

For convenience, here are the two original macros seen in Chapter 5:

[DOOR] ^ C ^ CINSERT;door1;NEAR;\DRAG;\\DRAG;\
[TRIMDOOR] ^ CLINE;NEAR;\PERP;\;;NEAR;\PERP;\;TRIM;\\;\\;

Figures 9.4 through 9.7 illustrate the process of inserting a door with automatic clean-up. The following macro accomplishes this task:

[DOOR] ^ C ^ C(setvar "BLIPMODE" 0);INSERT;door1;NEAR;\ +
(setq x (getreal "Enter door width: "));\(abs x);NEAR;\ +
$S = DSPECS \\\$S = FURN (setq y +
(getvar "LASTPOINT"));LINE;!y; +
(setq z (getpoint y "Enter opposite wall line: "));PERP;\;; +
(polar y (- (angle y z) (dtr 90)) x); +
(polar z (- (angle y z) (dtr 90)) x);; +
BREAK;(polar y (- (angle y z) (dtr 90)) (/ x 2));F;!z; +
(polar y (- (angle y z) (dtr 90)) x);; +
(polar z (- (angle y z) (dtr 90)) (/ x 2));F;!z; +
(polar z (- (angle y z) (dtr 90)) x);(setvar "BLIPMODE" 1);

At first glance, this macro may appear quite complex, but when broken down into its separate parts it becomes easier to understand.

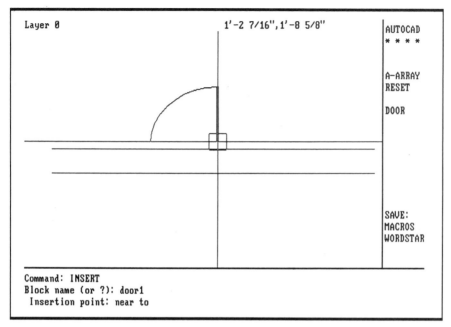

Figure 9.4   The Enhanced DOOR Macro—Placing the Block on the Wall Line

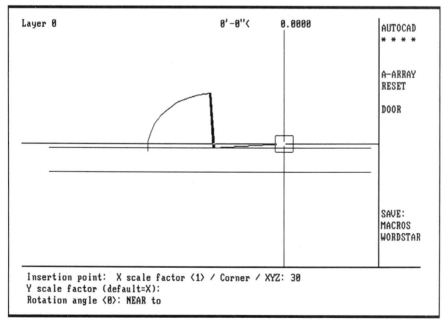

Figure 9.5   The Enhanced DOOR Macro—Selecting the Rotation Angle

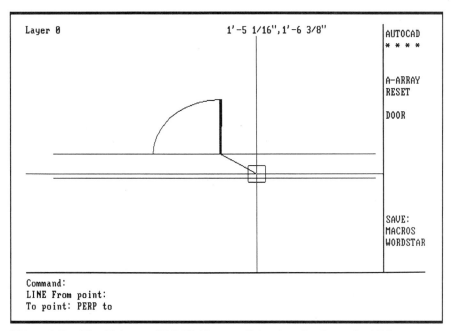

Figure 9.6 The Enhanced DOOR Macro—Selecting the Opposite Wall

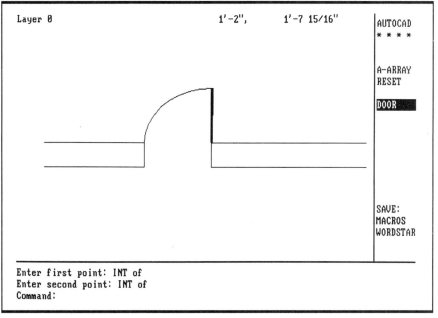

Figure 9.7 The Enhanced DOOR Macro—The Wall Is Trimmed Automatically

First, in order to improve the screen display, the macro turns the screen blips off temporarily. The following is the AutoLISP function that accomplishes this:

```
(setvar "BLIPMODE" 0);
```

In your own application, you may choose to keep the blips on, or they might already be off; in either case, omit this function.

Next, the INSERT command is invoked, followed by the name of the block, door1. The block is inserted using the OSNAP override NEAR to ensure that the block sits squarely on the wall line:

```
INSERT;door1;NEAR;\
```

Next, the GETREAL function prompts the user to enter the width of the door from the keyboard. The number entered by the user becomes the x-scale factor of the door. This number is stored in memory variable x:

```
(setq x (getreal "Enter door width: "));\
```

The original door1 block was drawn upright, with the door opening on the left. The user may reverse this orientation and show a door opening on the right by simply entering the width of the door as a negative number. This *flips* the door block, so that it opens on the right.

In order to allow for the possibility that the user may enter the door as a negative number, some extra analysis must be performed within this macro. Regardless of the value of the x-scale factor, the y-scale factor must remain a positive number with the same absolute value as x. If the y-scale factor were permitted to remain a negative value along with the x-scale factor, the door1 block would *flip* over along the opposing axis, and the result would be an upside-down block, not a reversed one. If this principle is not clear to you, you can demonstrate it by entering the block from the keyboard and observing the results for various positive and negative x- and y-scale factors.

To keep the value of the y-scale factor positive, this macro invokes the following function, which returns the absolute value of x in response to AutoCAD's prompt for the y-scale factor of the block:

```
(abs x);
```

The INSERT command continues normally, not at all interrupted by these AutoLISP functions. The rotation angle of the door must be selected next. The block rotates on the screen to aid the user in selecting the correct angle. The OSNAP override NEAR assures that the exact angle is found by snapping to a point on the original wall line.

Because door1 has three attributes, and those attributes can be selected off the screen, a new menu subsection reference is included at this point, as was seen in the original version of this macro:

$S = DSPECS \\\$S = FURN

The original door1 block had three attributes, so three additional back-slashes are included here. Include as many backslashes as you have attributes. The block attributes may be selected from the screen menu or entered at the keyboard.

After the attributes have been selected, another menu reference returns the original menu subsection to the screen. In this example, the original macro was on the Furn menu subsection. Be certain that you include one space after the menu reference. Of course, if your block has no attributes, these menu references and extra backslashes are not used.

The block is now completely inserted. AutoCAD remembers the origi-nal block insertion point by means of the following function:

(setq y (getvar "LASTPOINT"));

Technically, the last point picked was the reference point that deter-mined the rotation angle of the block. However, that point was used only as a reference point to calculate an angle and is not considered part of the actual drawing. The point contained in the system variable LAST-POINT is the last drawing point selected, the insertion point of the block.

Finally, the user selects the opposite wall line by touching it anywhere. The OSNAP override PERP will cause a line to be drawn from the door insertion point (point y) perpendicular to the opposite wall line. The end-point of this short line segment is stored in memory variable z. The fol-lowing function accomplishes this:

(setq z (getpoint y "Enter opposite wall line: "));PERP;\;;

Figure 9.8 shows the location of points that have been stored in mem-ory variables.

From this point on, the process continues without further intervention from the user. The second perpendicular line segment is drawn, and the LINE command is repeated by means of an extra semicolon. The starting point of the second line is found by the following POLAR function:

(polar y (- (angle y z) (dtr 90)) x);

In this example, the first function evaluated is the ANGLE function, which returns the angle formed by points y and z. This angle is 90 degrees greater than the true angle needed, so AutoLISP subtracts

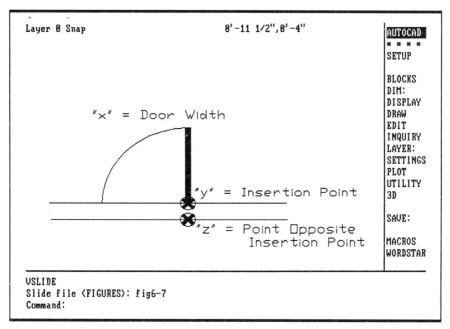

Figure 9.8 Stored Points When Inserting the Automatic-Trim Door

90 degrees from the angle automatically. Since the ANGLE function returns its result in radians, the DTR function, which also returns radians, is applied to 90. The subtraction takes place, and the result is the correct reference angle from point y, expressed in radians.

The distance is the width of the door, stored in memory variable x. If x happens to be negative, that is fine; the reference distance will reverse itself, yielding the same orientation as the door.

The LINE command continues, expecting another point. The next point is found using almost the same POLAR function, except that this time, the base reference point is z, not y:

```
(polar z (- (angle y z) (dtr 90)) x);;
```

After this function, an extra semicolon finishes the LINE command. The BREAK command follows, using the same POLAR function again, this time beginning with point y, and specifying half of the distance x:

```
BREAK;(polar y (- (angle y z) (dtr 90)) (/ x 2));
```

The F option is invoked automatically, and point y is again selected as the first break point:

```
F;!y;
```

The second break point is the starting point of the second perpendicular line segment. The function that found that point before finds it again:

(polar y (- (angle y z) (dtr 90)) x);;

An extra semicolon repeats the BREAK command, and the entire BREAK command sequence is repeated, this time starting with point z:

(polar z (- (angle y z) (dtr 90)) (/ x 2));F;!z; +
(polar z (- (angle y z) (dtr 90)) x);

Finally, if the screen blips were turned off, it's time to turn them back on:

(setvar "BLIPMODE" 1);

This completes the enhanced DOOR macro. As you have seen, many AutoLISP functions are used in its creation. It must be constructed carefully. However, it presents considerable rewards, in that it allows a door block of any size and orientation to be inserted on any set of parallel wall lines, and trims the lines automatically, based on the information provided during the INSERT command. It does this using a single generic door block. If you insert blocks and trim, you can construct your own variation on this macro to make the process more automatic.

Enhanced Open-T Trim

The following example demonstrates a simple AutoLISP enhancement to the OPEN-T macro seen earlier. That macro cleaned up the intersecting wall lines in an open-T intersection:

[OPEN-T] ^ C ^ CBREAK;NEAR;\@;FILLET;R;0;;INT;\@;;INT;\@;

The macro requires that the user pick three points to clean up the open-T figure: the line to break and the two intersections to fillet the open-T. You can eliminate the first point pick by using AutoLISP functions. When AutoLISP functions are inserted in the macro, the two point picks shown in Figure 9.9 are all that need be selected. The enhanced OPEN-T macro is shown here:

[OPEN-T] ^ C ^ C(setq x (getpoint "Enter first intersection: "));INT;\ +
(setq y (getpoint "Enter second intersection: "));INT;\BREAK; +
(polar x (angle x y) (/ (distance x y) 2));@;FILLET;R;0;;!x;!x;;!y;!y;

This macro invokes AutoLISP's SETQ and GETPOINT functions to aid the user in selecting the two intersections of the open-T. Notice how the OSNAP override INT is also invoked between the AutoLISP SETQ function and the backslash for user input. Both intersections are obtained

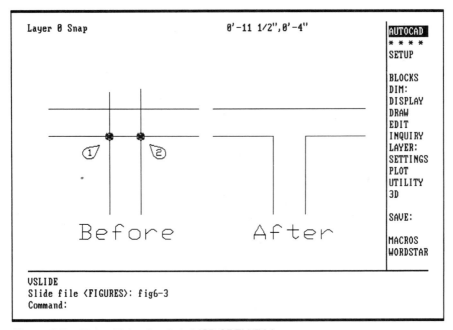

Figure 9.9　Point Picks for AutoLISP OPEN-T Macro

using this technique, and the point information is stored in memory variables x and y.

Once the points have been selected, this macro becomes fully automatic. The line to break is selected automatically by AutoLISP's POLAR function. The correct line is found, using point x as a polar reference point, at the angle formed by points x and y, and at half the distance between points x and y. The following AutoLISP function accomplishes this:

(polar x (angle x y) (/ (distance x y) 2))

The angle argument of the POLAR function is provided by the nested ANGLE function:

(angle x y)

The distance argument of the POLAR function is provided by two nested functions. The DISTANCE function

(distance x y)

is nested within a math function that divides it in half:

(/ (distance x y) 2)

After this complete POLAR function is invoked, the point is selected again (using AutoCAD's @ syntax) and the break is made.

Next, AutoCAD's FILLET command is invoked, and the points x and y are again selected (twice each), using the the exclamation-point syntax followed by the variable name. The fillets are then made, completing the open-T.

Take special notice of all the semicolons used in this macro. Some of them represent returns after AutoLISP functions, some represent returns after OSNAP overrides, and one repeats a previously invoked FILLET command.

You can test this macro by typing it "as is" on your custom menu Macros subsection. Then draw some walls and try cleaning them up. Reducing point selection from three points to two can make a noticeable difference in the macro's ease of use.

Enhanced Cross Trim

The following example applies the same basic technique to the CROSS macro, reducing its original six picks to four. The following is the original version of this macro:

[CROSS] ^ C ^ CTRIM;C;\\;NEAR;\NEAR;\NEAR;\NEAR;\;

Figure 9.10 illustrates the point picks required for the enhanced version of the CROSS macro. Although the enhanced CROSS macro is much longer than the OPEN-T macro, the basic technique is the same. Note the prompts, which remind the user to pick the points in a clockwise circular fashion. This must be done in order for the macro to work. Here is the enhanced CROSS macro:

```
[CROSS] ^ C ^ C(setq w (getpoint "Enter first intersection: "));INT;\ +
(setq x (getpoint "2nd intersection (move clockwise): "));INT;\ +
(setq y (getpoint "3rd intersection (move clockwise): "));INT;\ +
(setq z (getpoint "4th intersection (move clockwise): "));INT;\ +
BREAK;(polar w (angle w x) (/ (distance w x) 2));F;!w;!x; +
;(polar x (angle x y) (/ (distance x y) 2));F;!x;!y; +
;(polar y (angle y z) (/ (distance y z) 2));F;!y;!z; +
;(polar z (angle z w) (/ (distance z w) 2));F;!z;!w;
```

The plus signs in this macro are used not only to wrap the macro line, but also to group related commands together on the same text line. This procedure improves the macro's readability.

Once the four intersection points have been selected, the POLAR function can be used to locate the points midway between them. Using this point, the line is selected for the BREAK command, the F option is invoked, and the two intersection points become the break points. This process is repeated for the remaining lines. Picking the points in a circular fashion ensures that the memory variables are bound to the correct points.

DRAWING MACROS

Macros can simplify the drawing process when certain drawing entities are constructed around mathematical relationships between points, or in cases where a drawing command is followed by an editing command to create a complex shape. The following examples demonstrate these techniques.

Drawing a Complex Shape

AutoLISP-enhanced macros can be used to construct complex entities based on minimal user input. For example, the following macro draws a

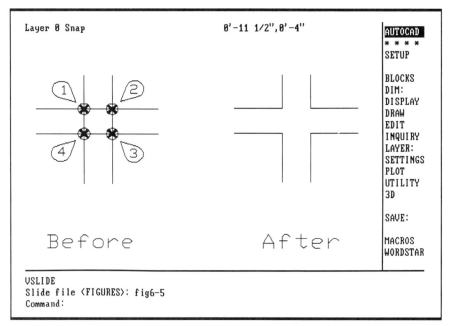

Figure 9.10   Point Picks for the Enhanced CROSS Macro

five-pointed star, once the user has supplied the starting point and the length of one side:

```
[5PSTAR] ^ C ^ C(SETQ X (getpoint "Top of star: "));\ +
(setq y (getdist x "Length of one side: "));\ +
PLINE;!x;(polar x (dtr 288) (* y 0.381967)); +
(polar (getvar "LASTPOINT") (dtr 0) (* y 0.381967)); +
(polar (getvar "LASTPOINT") (dtr 216) (* y 0.381967)); +
(polar (getvar "LASTPOINT") (dtr 288) (* y 0.381967)); +
(polar (getvar "LASTPOINT") (dtr 144) (* y 0.381967)); +
(polar (getvar "LASTPOINT") (dtr 216) (* y 0.381967)); +
(polar (getvar "LASTPOINT") (dtr 72) (* y 0.381967)); +
(polar (getvar "LASTPOINT") (dtr 144) (* y 0.381967)); +
(polar (getvar "LASTPOINT") (dtr 0) (* y 0.381967));c;
```

This macro is illustrated in Figures 9.11 and 9.12.

In this macro, the GETPOINT function binds the memory variable x to the user-selected starting point. The GETDIST function binds the memory variable y to the length of one side of the star. Notice that the GETDIST function, by referencing x, can accept either keyboard input or

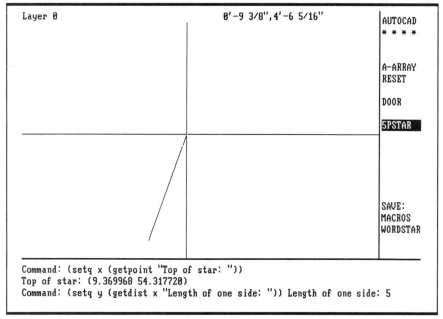

Figure 9.11 Drawing with the 5PSTAR Macro, Showing a Side Length of Five Drawing Units

ADVANCED TECHNIQUES IN AUTOCAD

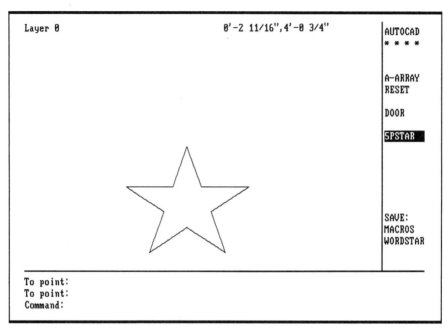

Figure 9.12 The Result of the 5PSTAR Macro

digitized input. Once these variables have values, the PLINE command is invoked and the ten line segments forming the star are drawn using the POLAR function, which continually references the LASTPOINT system variable and the length supplied by the user, multiplied by a factor of 0.381967.

This macro makes use of the DTR function to convert angles expressed in degrees to radians automatically. This makes reading and editing this macro easier for those not used to radians. Likewise, shapes can be drawn with pen-up and pen-down motions, simply by ending the LINE command and beginning the next LINE command with an additional POLAR function. The following example draws a common drafting symbol, illustrated in Figures 9.13 and 9.14.

```
[DBOX] ^ C ^ C(setq x (getpoint "Enter first corner: "));\ +
(setq y (getdist x "Enter length of one side: "));\ +
(setq z (/ (sqrt (* (expt y 2) 2)) 2)); +
PLINE;!x;(polar x (r 45) y);; +
PLINE;(polar (getvar "LASTPOINT") (r 225) (/ y 2.0)); +
(polar (getvar "LASTPOINT") (r 135) (/ (- y z) 2)); +
(polar (getvar "LASTPOINT") (r 180) (/ y 2.0));; +
ARRAY;@;!x;;P;(polar x (r 90) z);4;360;Y;
```

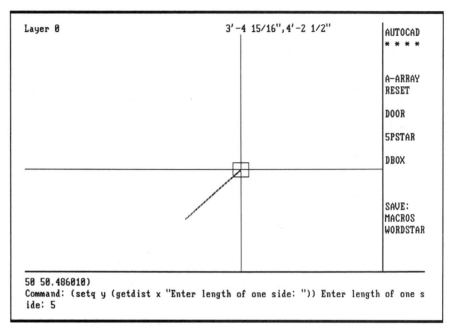

Figure 9.13 Drawing with the DBOX Macro, Showing a Side Length of Five Drawing Units

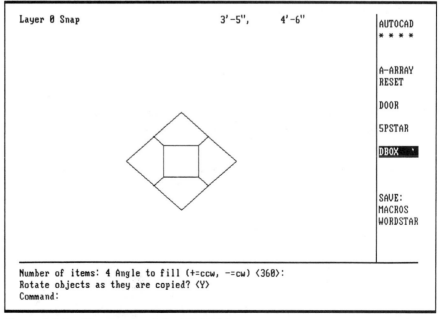

Figure 9.14 The Result of the DBOX Macro

In this macro, the user is prompted for a lower corner of the shape and the length of one side. The next function computes one half of the diagonal measurement of the outer square and stores the amount to memory variable z. Next, the PLINE command draws one side of the box. A second PLINE command is issued and one small diagonal line, as well as one side of the inner box, are drawn. The ARRAY command selects the objects just drawn, using the @ symbol to reference the last polyline drawn and the memory variable x to find the first line drawn. The centerpoint of the array is found by using the POLAR function to reference point x at an angle of 90 degrees and at a distance of z. The array completes the shape.

As this example shows, AutoLISP functions combined with AutoCAD drawing commands can be used to construct virtually any shape.

Multiple Lines from a Single Point

The following example uses the ARRAY command to create a specified number of lines joined at a specified point:

[M-LINE] ^ C ^ CLINE;(setq x (getpoint));\\; +
(setq y (getint "Number of Lines? "));\ARRAY;L;;P;!x;!y;360;Y;

Figures 9.15 and 9.16 illustrate this process. The GETPOINT function is used to select the starting point of the line, and at the same time, store that point information to memory variable x. At the completion of the LINE command, the user is prompted for the number of lines desired. This information is stored in memory variable y, and the array is quickly made.

More complex arrays can be created using the following variation on the M-LINE macro:

[MPLINE1] ^ C ^ C(setq x (getpoint "Enter Center Point: "));\PLINE;
[MPLINE2] ^ C ^ C(if (/ = x nil) (setq y (getint "Number of Copies? ")) +
(command));\ARRAY;L;;P;!x;!y;360;Y;(setq x nil);

In this case, two macros are used in sequence. The first prompts for the array center point and then invokes the PLINE command. This sequence allows the center point to be either on the polyline or offset from it. The macro ends with the PLINE command to allow maximum flexibility in creating a polyline figure. When the user has finished drawing the polyline figure, the selection of the second macro prompts for the number of copies desired. After the user has entered the number of copies, the array is made.

Notice in the second macro that an IF function is used to determine if the value of x is nil. If it is, the MPLINE1 macro has not yet been executed;

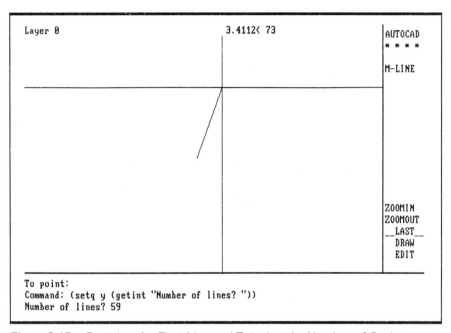

Figure 9.15   Drawing the First Line and Entering the Number of Copies

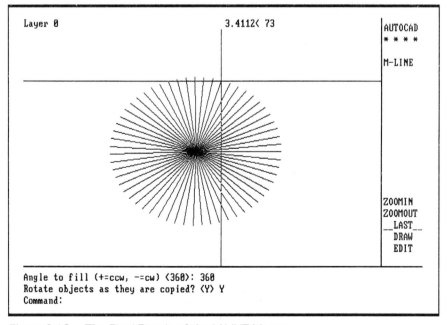

Figure 9.16   The Final Result of the M-LINE Macro

in such a case, the "else" function (in this example, the COMMAND function) is executed instead of the GETINT function. The COMMAND function
called without arguments has the effect of pressing Ctrl-C at the keyboard, thus canceling the command. This is a safeguard in case the
MPLINE2 macro is ever selected by accident. Once the array has been
made, the last AutoLISP function in MPLINE2 resets the value of x to nil.

Quick Elevation Change for 3-D

The following macro allows you to change the elevation setting while
drawing 3-D lines:

[CNGELEV]'SETVAR;ELEVATION;

This macro simply pauses execution of the 3DLINE command long
enough for you to enter a new elevation at the keyboard. CNGELEV
does not begin with the normal double cancel, because you do not intend
to cancel the command in progress. The SETVAR command must be
preceded by the apostrophe to make it transparent to the 3DLINE command in progress.

The following macro does the same thing, but it also allows you to set
the new elevation by pointing to the endpoint of an existing line:

[NEWELEV]'SETVAR;ELEVATION;(initget 16); +
(caddr (getpoint "Elevation of? (select endpoint): "));END;

This macro uses three AutoLISP functions. The first function, (initget
16), allows the following GETPOINT function to return 3-D coordinate
information, rather than its standard 2-D coordinate information. Notice
how the INITGET function does not interrupt the flow of the command
sequence, because it always returns nil.

The GETPOINT function is nested within the CADDR function, which
returns only the z-coordinate of the selected endpoint. This z-coordinate
is used as the response to the command 'SETVAR ELEVATION. OSNAP
END is used to ensure a clean pick on an existing endpoint. Once the line's
endpoint is selected, the new value for ELEVATION is immediately set,
and the current 3DLINE or 3DFACE command picks up where it left off.

10

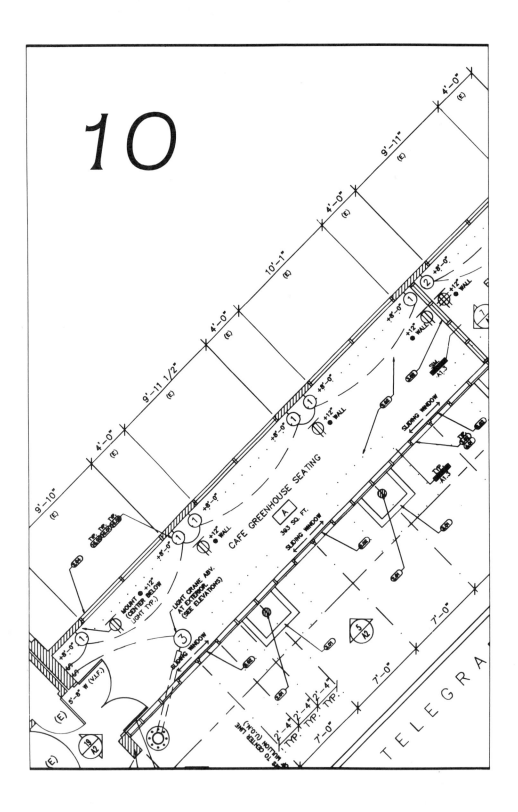

Chapter 10
Writing LISP Files

AS YOU LEARNED IN CHAPTER 7, a LISP routine is a set of related Auto-LISP functions that, when evaluated in sequence, perform a given task. This set of AutoLISP functions is contained in an ASCII file called a *LISP file*. LISP files can be named with any valid DOS file name. They always have the extension LSP. Using your word processor, you can create LISP files as you would any other ASCII files. The ACAD.LSP file is a LISP file; its contents are an example of a LISP routine, albeit a short one.

LISP files are loaded into a part of memory reserved by AutoCAD for that purpose. Once loaded, AutoCAD's AutoLISP interpreter evaluates all the functions in the LISP file. The functions are evaluated one after another, from top to bottom within the file. As each function is evaluated, its deepest level of nesting is evaluated first, the next-deepest level next, and so on to the shallowest level.

A good LISP routine should accomplish its tasks as quickly and efficiently as possible. It should also be well organized and structured, so that any subsequent process of making changes or correcting problems is as easy as possible. A good way to structure a LISP routine is to use the DEFUN function to define new AutoLISP functions and Auto-CAD commands, and then use these new functions and commands to execute its processes. The new functions and commands will come into existence when the LISP file is loaded. There are several good reasons to write LISP routines that are based on defining new functions:

- Defining functions results in better program organization, with a complex process broken down into simple steps, each step handled by a defined function.

- Defined properly, a function is *portable*—functions defined in one LISP routine can be used in other LISP routines that are loaded later.

- When a LISP routine is based on defined functions, its problems are easier to locate, making the process of debugging faster.

When a LISP routine requires the user to supply information, at least one of its functions should offer clear and concise prompts. A good LISP routine will ask the user for the absolute minimum amount of information necessary. Since the point of a LISP routine is to save time and simplify AutoCAD, the less information the user is required to supply, the better. AutoLISP's predefined functions for inputting points, distances, angles, and so on make the process of writing this part of a LISP routine fairly simple. A good LISP routine will also define other functions that perform calculations and analysis based on the user-supplied information. This calculation and analysis can be made invisible to the user, so that the LISP routine works as quickly as possible.

Finally, a good LISP routine defines at least one function that displays the results of its processing in a form that the user can quickly understand. This often takes the form of new entities drawn automatically by AutoCAD, or it can simply be the displaying of computation results in the command prompt area.

A BASIC LISP ROUTINE

The following example demonstrates how a LISP routine is put together. This fundamental routine creates a new AutoCAD command that produces two lines, which are offset from a user-supplied centerline. Once you have created this routine, you will add enhancements that will allow it to draw a series of such offset lines, trimming the intersections as it goes. Combining a routine like this with AutoCAD's snap setting will make subsequent centerline dimensioning much easier.

Writing the Pseudocode

The first step of development is to specify, in plain English, exactly what the routine does. In doing so, look for ways to break down the overall task of the LISP routine into a series of small, simple tasks that lead to the desired result.

This LISP routine will define two new AutoLISP functions: a function that prompts the user for the distance between the lines and the endpoints of the centerline, and a function that draws parallel lines that are offset from the user-supplied centerline.

In this example, the new AutoLISP functions are arbitrarily named PRLINF (short for parallel line information) and PRLDRW (for parallel line drawing). Here is a more detailed English description of the PRLINF function, breaking it down into a series of smaller steps:

1. If the user has not previously defined the distance between the lines, prompt the user to enter the distance.

2. If the distance was entered before, offer it as a current default and allow it to be changed.

3. Store the value entered by the user in a memory variable named dist.

This establishes the mechanism of the prompting function. The next task is to establish the mechanism for the drawing function:

4. Prompt the user for two points, which will form the endpoints of the centerline. Store this point information in memory variables named sp and ep.

5. To determine the correct amount of offset, calculate the angle formed by the endpoints of the centerline.

6. Add 90 degrees to this angle.

7. Offset a new line starting point from the centerline starting point, at this new angle, at half the user-specified distance.

8. Offset a new endpoint from the endpoint of the centerline, using the same calculated angle and half of the user-specified distance.

9. Draw a line between the two new points.

10. Subtract 90 degrees from the angle formed by the endpoints of the centerline.

11. Offset a second starting point and endpoint using the new angle, again at half the value of the user-defined distance.

12. Draw the second line between the second set of points.

Figure 10.1 illustrates the process of calculating the offset lines.

The PRLINF Function

Having defined the LISP routine in plain English, you are now ready to translate it into AutoLISP. The complete PRLINF function is shown in Figure 10.2. This function prompts the user for the distance between the lines and the endpoints of the centerline. You begin by defining the function operator name, PRLINF, and indicating that it does not require any arguments in order to execute:

```
(defun prlinf( )
```

ADVANCED TECHNIQUES IN AUTOCAD

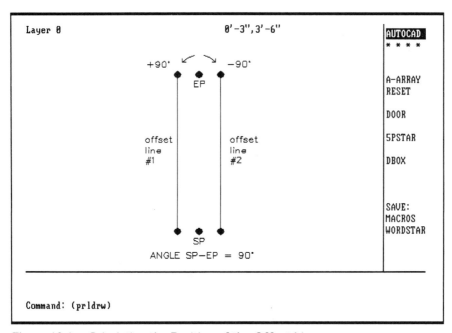

Figure 10.1   Calculating the Position of the Offset Lines

```
; * -- Define the PRLINF function:
    (defun prlinf()
; * -- Test for the value of init:
    (if
        (<= init 0)
; * -- Prompt if init is zero:
        (while
            (<= init 0)
            (setq init
                (getreal "\nPlease enter distance between lines: ")
            )
        ) ; End WHILE
; * -- Prompt if init is not zero:
        (setq init
            (getreal
                (strcat "\nPlease enter distance between lines <"
                    (rtos dist)
                    ">: "
                )
            )
        ) ; End SETQ
    ) ; End of IF function
; * -- Set values of init or dist based on the value of init:
    (if
        (<= init 0)
        (setq init dist)
        (setq dist init)
    )
) ; End of PRLINF function
```

Figure 10.2   The PRLINF Function

PRLINF first tests the value of a memory variable named init to determine if it is equal to or less than zero:

```
(if
  (< = init 0)
```

If init has yet to be bound to a value, the logical "less than or equal to" function will evaluate to nil. Nil is considered to be less than zero by the AutoLISP interpreter. This function will return T (for true) if init has yet to be bound to a value; values of zero or less will also cause it to return T.

Two different prompt functions may be presented to the user, depending on whether or not init is less than zero or equal to nil. If init is zero or less, or nil, the first prompt function is offered:

```
(while
  (< = init 0)
  (setq init
    (getreal "\nPlease enter distance between lines: ")
  )
)
```

This prompts the user to enter a new value for init. At first, another IF function may seem to be the function to use, but the WHILE function makes more sense. WHILE ensures that the user cannot accidentally skip past this function while leaving init with a value of nil or zero; the prompt will repeat over and over until some value greater than zero has been assigned. It is a good idea to write LISP routines in a way that prevents possible input errors. This process is called *error trapping*, and it helps ensure that a LISP routine will not return bad data in the event of an unforeseen user response.

In this example, the WHILE function first tests the value of init with the same logical function that is used by the shallower IF function:

```
(< = init 0)
```

This function continues to return T if the current value of init is nil, or zero, or less than zero. When init is finally given a value greater than zero, the logical function will return nil. As long as the function returns T, the prompting function GETREAL continues to execute.

The GETREAL function prompts the user to enter a real number and then stores that number in the memory variable init. Notice how the nesting of functions works here. The GETREAL function is nested inside the SETQ function, which is nested inside the WHILE function; this efficiently combines the prompting, obtaining, storing, and error-trapping mechanisms.

The GETREAL function cannot be used to change the value of init, because once init has a nonzero value, the WHILE function will no longer execute. Thus, it is necessary to have another function change the value of init whenever the user desires a new value for the distance between the lines. The original IF function allows for an alternative func-tion to execute if its original test function did not return T (that is, if init was bound to a value greater than zero). In this example, the alternative prompt function is as follows:

```
(setq init
  (getreal
    (strcat "\nPlease enter distance between lines <"
      (rtos dist)
      ">: "
    )
  )
)
```

This alternate GETREAL function uses several nested functions to display to the user the currently stored value of init as a default, and at the same time prompt the user for a new value. The two deepest func-tions, RTOS nested inside STRCAT, create the prompt:

```
(strcat "\nPlease enter distance between lines <"
  (rtos dist)
  ">: "
```

The prompt is assembled from three character strings concatenated by means of the STRCAT function. The three character strings are as follows:

- "\nPlease enter distance between lines <" is a literal character string that is contained within quotation marks. It will be displayed, as is, following a carriage return.

- (rtos dist) takes the previously entered value of dist, a real number, and converts the value to string-type information. Numbers must be converted to non-number strings if they are to be linked together with other strings.

- ">: " is another set of literal characters contained within quotes. It closes off the entire string sequence and aids in its appearance.

To illustrate how these strings link together, imagine that the user had previously used this function and entered a value of six drawing units as the distance between the lines. The next time the prompt appeared, it would look like this:

Please enter distance between lines <6>:

The figure enclosed in the angled brackets would inform the user that six drawing units is the current default. The user may accept the default response with a Return, or enter a new value.

The next function reacts to the user's response:

```
(if
    (< = init 0)
    (setq init dist)
    (setq dist init)
)
```

Here, another IF function tests the value of init for the last time. How this function works may not be immediately clear when you are reading it on paper. Here is what it does: if init had been zero or less to begin with, the routine would never have reached this point—it would still be executing the WHILE function. Once init had a value, however, the LISP routine would arrive at this IF function.

If init has become nil once again, the user has entered a Return in response to the prompt that showed the default. Therefore, the LISP routine will do one of two things:

- If init has become nil, LISP will give it the value of dist, which must exist and must contain some real number.

- If init has a value, it will bind dist to that value for use in the remainder of the routine. It will also make the value of dist the current default.

This completes the PRLINF function. Remember that a final right parenthesis must be added at the end to close off the initial DEFUN function, which contains all these prompting and analysis functions.

The PRLDRW Function

The PRLDRW function will draw the parallel lines and offset them correctly for the centerline, based on the information the user has supplied in the PRLDRW function. The entire PRLINF function is shown in Figure 10.3. You begin by giving this function the operator name PRLDRW and indicating that it requires no arguments in order to execute:

```
(defun prldrw( )
```

```
; * -- Define the function:
  (defun prldrw()
; * -- Get start and endpoints of centerline:
      (setq sp
        (getpoint "\nEnter starting point: ")
      )
      (setq ep
        (getpoint sp "\nEnter endpoint: ")
      )
; * -- Calculate and draw the first line:
      (command "LINE"
                (polar sp
                        (+ (angle sp ep) (dtr 90))
                        (/ dist 2)
                )
                (polar ep
                        (+ (angle sp ep) (dtr 90))
                        (/ dist 2)
                )
                ""
      ) ; End of Line command
; * -- Calculate and draw the second line:
      (command "LINE"
                (polar sp
                        (- (angle sp ep) (dtr 90))
                        (/ dist 2)
                )
                (polar ep
                        (- (angle sp ep) (dtr 90))
                        (/ dist 2)
                )
                ""
      )
  ) ; End of PRLDRW function
```

Figure 10.3   The PRLDRW Function

The following two functions pick up a starting point and an endpoint, storing the coordinate information in memory variables named sp and ep:

```
(setq sp
  (getpoint "\nEnter starting point: ")
)
(setq ep
  (getpoint sp "\nEnter endpoint: ")
)
```

Again, the prompting GETPOINT functions are nested within SETQ functions, which allows the computer to "remember" the information being obtained. The second function, which prompts for the endpoint ep, uses the point information just obtained in the memory variable sp to create a rubber-band line. This is done as a convenience for the user.

Next, additional points are found, and a line is drawn between them:

```
(command "LINE"
  (polar sp
```

```
          ( + (angle sp ep) (dtr 90))
          (/ dist 2)
      )
      (polar ep
          ( + (angle sp ep) (dtr 90))
          (/ dist 2)
      )
      ""
  ) ; End of Line command
```

To draw the lines, the routine must first compute the angle formed by the user-specified points. This function does the job:

(angle sp ep)

The angle will be expressed in radians. You can determine the two off-set angles for the parallel lines by adding 90 degrees to this angle and then subtracting 90 degrees from it as well. When doing this math, you must also use radians to express angles.

The DTR function, defined in the previous chapter, helps here. To express 90 degrees as radians, you can use the following function:

(dtr 90)

If you attempt to run this routine without previously defining the DTR function, you will receive the error message, "Error: null function." If the DTR function has been placed in ACAD.LSP, it will have been loaded automatically and will be available for your use.

The angle functions are nested inside the functions that compute the offset angles:

(+ (angle sp ep) (dtr 90))
(- (angle sp ep) (dtr 90))

Since the drawn lines are offset from a centerline, the distance between the centerline and each of these lines will be half of the total distance selected by the user. This is computed easily:

(/ dist 2)

You can determine the starting point of the first drawn line by using these computed angle and distance functions inside the AutoLISP POLAR function. It locates a new point relative to the user-supplied starting point, at the first computed offset angle, and at a distance of one-half of the user-supplied distance:

(polar sp   **; the initial reference point**

```
    ( + (angle sp ep) (dtr 90))          ; the angle to offset
    (/ dist 2)                           ; the distance to offset
)
```

The next POLAR function does the same thing, starting with the user-supplied endpoint:

```
(polar ep                               ; the initial reference point
    ( + (angle sp ep) (dtr 90))          ; the angle to offset
    (/ dist 2)                           ; the distance to offset
)
```

The starting and ending points for the other drawn line are identified in the same way, this time using subtraction to calculate the offset angle:

```
(polar sp                               ; the initial reference point
    (- (angle sp ep) (dtr 90))           ; the angle to offset
    (/ dist 2)                           ; the distance to offset
)
(polar ep                               ; the initial reference point
    (- (angle sp ep) (dtr 90))           ; the angle to offset
    (/ dist 2)                           ; the distance to offset
)
```

These functions return point information, so you can easily nest them inside two LINE commands. AutoCAD will draw the lines between the calculated points.

Notice that two sets of quotation marks end each of the LINE commands. This symbol, two double quotes with nothing between them, is the AutoLISP equivalent of a Return. It is necessary here as a response to the final "To point:" prompt in AutoCAD's LINE command. As always, a final right parenthesis is also necessary to close off the original DEFUN function, which created the PRLDRW function.

The next step is to create, load, and execute the LISP file that contains these functions:

1. Create an ASCII file called PARALINE.LSP to contain the PRLINF and PRLDRW functions. This file should be located on the AutoCAD system subdirectory.

2. If necessary, add the DTR function to ACAD.LSP.

3. Enter AutoCAD's Drawing Editor by typing

   (LOAD "PARALINE")

   AutoCAD responds with "(prldrw)".

4. Enter

(prlinf)

You will then be prompted for the distance between the lines and the endpoints of the centerline.

5. Enter

(prldrw)

AutoCAD will draw two lines at the specified distance and offset from the centerline.

ENHANCEMENTS TO PARALINE.LSP

The next version of the PARALINE.LSP file builds new functions using the functions you have defined previously. It will create a continuous series of parallel lines along a centerline and trim the corners as it goes. Using this routine, if you wish to close the figure, you can pick the original starting point (using a snap value or an Osnap override) and AutoCAD will trim the final corners automatically. After you have defined the new functions, you will create an AutoCAD command, PARALINE, to execute these functions.

If you are using AutoCAD Version 2.6 or later, you can add a further enhancement that will cause this routine to mimic the LINE command: you can add extra functions that will close and trim the figure if the user enters c or C in response to the "To point:" prompt.

When this LISP routine has finished processing, you will have generated several sets of parallel line segments from a single AutoCAD command. Each individual line segment can be independently moved, copied, erased, and so on. This is great for moving walls, in cases where AutoCAD's STRETCH command might throw off the parallel orientation or the width. The key to this LISP routine is AutoLISP's ability to reassign the same memory variables to different data as the lines are being created.

Pseudocode for Enhanced PARALINE.LSP

Begin developing this new LISP routine with more pseudocode:

1. Use the functions PRLINF and PRLDRW to create the first set of parallel lines.

2. Store the starting point in an additional memory variable named spx, in case the lines are closed at the conclusion of the routine.

3. Store the starting points of the offset lines to memory variables named osp1 and osp2.

4. Store the endpoints of the offset lines to memory variables named oep1 and oep2.

5. Save the starting and ending points of the first set of offset lines to extra memory variables, in case the lines are to be closed later.

6. Prompt the user for another endpoint.

7. As long as the user does not enter a Return or the original centerline's starting point in response to the prompt for an additional endpoint, continue to repeat the next nine steps (steps 8 through 16).

8. Store the point to a memory variable named ep2.

9. Repeat all offset drawing calculations based on points ep and ep2.

10. Store the new offset starting points to memory variables named osp3 and osp4.

11. Store the new offset endpoints to memory variables named oep3 and oep4.

12. Determine the point at which the current lines intersect with the previous lines, and store these lines to memory variables named int1-3 and int2-4.

13. Erase the previous lines. Draw them again from their starting points to the intersection points.

14. Erase the current lines. Draw them again from the intersection points to the current endpoints.

15. Redefine osp3 as osp1, osp4 as osp2, oep3 as oep1, and oep4 as oep2. (By redefining these points, the same command can repeat and the correct intersection point can be recalculated.)

16. Prompt again for an additional endpoint.

17. If the user enters a Return in response to the prompt for new coordinate points, end the command.

18. If the user enters the original starting point (still stored in memory variable spx), erase and trim the lines as before, drawing a new set of lines between the intersection points of the last set of lines with the original set of lines.

This process may seem complex when described in words, but it is actually quite simple. Figures 10.4 through 10.11 illustrate what is happening.

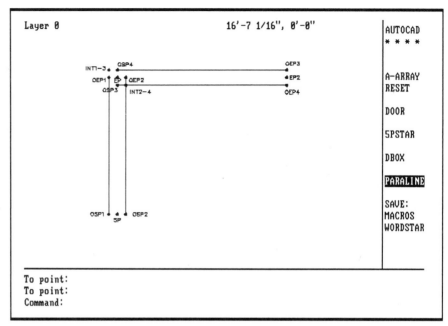

Figure 10.4 The First Two Sets of Parallel Lines, with Points and Memory Variables Noted

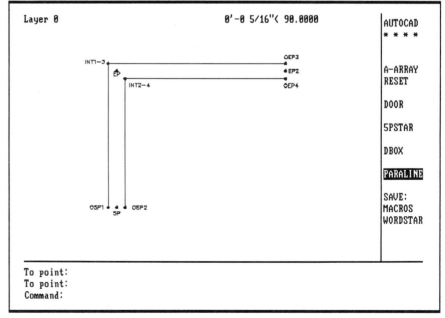

Figure 10.5 The Lines are Erased and Redrawn

ADVANCED TECHNIQUES IN AUTOCAD

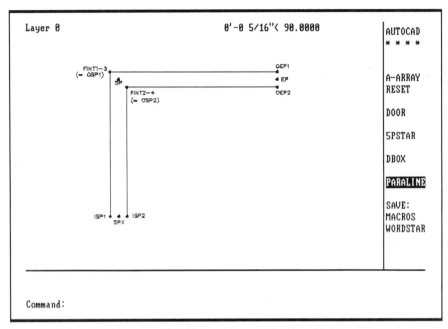

Figure 10.6   The Memory Variables are Bound to New Points

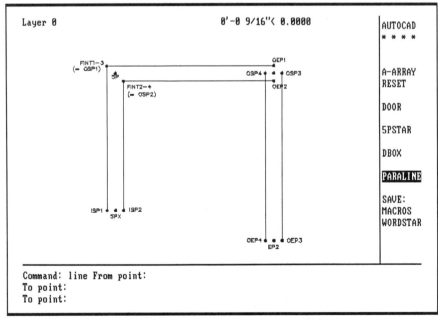

Figure 10.7   A New Endpoint Is Selected; the Remaining Memory Variables
                 Are Rebound

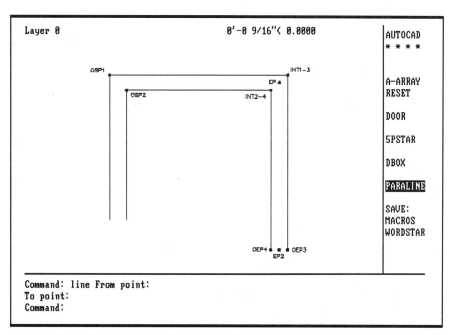

Figure 10.8   The Lines Are Erased and Redrawn

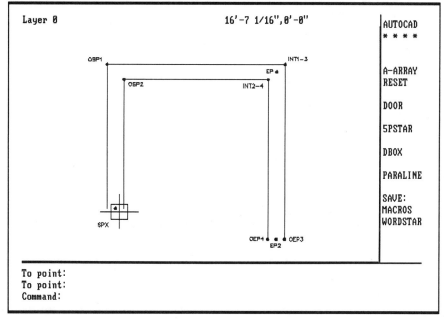

Figure 10.9   The User Selects the Original Starting Point

ADVANCED TECHNIQUES IN AUTOCAD

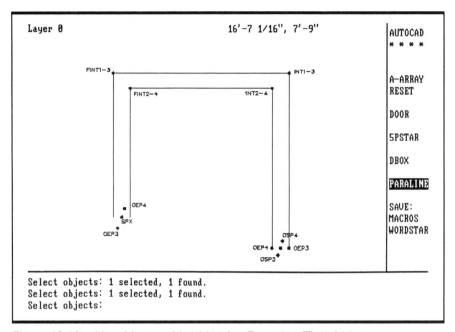

Figure 10.10   New Memory Variables Are Bound to Their Values

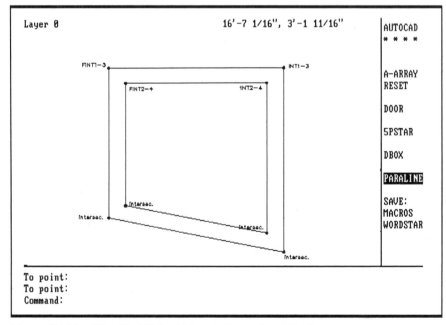

Figure 10.11   The Final Set of Lines Is Erased and Redrawn

Functions in Enhanced PARALINE.LSP

The enhanced PARALINE.LSP routine shown in Figure 10.12 contains all the routines you need to perform the actions you have just described in pseudocode. PRLINF and PRLDRW are familiar to you, although some additional memory variables have been added to PRLDRW. This LISP routine will work in AutoCAD Version 2.18 and later. As mentioned earlier, additional enhancements can be added if you are using AutoCAD Version 2.6 or later; they are explained in the next section. For now, let's work through this LISP routine step by step.

As you know, PRLINF obtains a value to be used for the distance between the parallel lines, and the PRLDRW function draws the first set of parallel lines. Because you may need the initial centerline starting point later (in order to close the figure), store it in a special memory variable named spx by adding the following function to PRLDRW:

```
(setq spx sp)
```

PRLDRW continues by drawing the offset lines and storing their starting and ending points to memory variables. It will use these to determine where the lines will intersect with the next set of parallel lines:

```
(command "LINE"
  (setq osp1
    (polar sp
      (+ (angle sp ep) (dtr 90))
      (/ dist 2)
    )
  )
  (setq oep1
    (polar ep
      (+ (angle sp ep) (dtr 90))
      (/ dist 2)
    )
  )
  ""
)
(command "LINE"
  (setq osp2
    (polar sp
      (- (angle sp ep) (dtr 90))
      (/ dist 2)
    )
  )
  (setq oep2
```

```
(defun prlinf()
; * -- Test for the value of init:
    (if
          (<= init 0)
; * -- Prompt if init is zero:
          (while
              (<= init 0)
              (setq init
                   (getreal "\nPlease enter distance between lines: ")
              )
          )
; * -- Prompt if init is not zero:
          (setq init
              (getreal
                   (strcat "\nPlease enter distance between lines <"
                           (rtos dist)
                           ">: "
                   )
              )
          )
    ) ; End of IF function
; * -- Set values of init or dist based on the current value of init:
    (if
          (<= init 0)
          (setq init dist)
          (setq dist init)
    )
  ) ; End of PRLINF function
(defun prldrw()
; * -- Save the starting point and endpoint for additional trimming
; * -- later:
    (setq spx sp)
; * -- Draw the lines, save information to variables
    (command "LINE"
          (setq osp1
              (polar sp
                      (+ (angle sp ep) (dtr 90))
                      (/ dist 2)
              )
          )
          (setq oep1
              (polar ep
                      (+ (angle sp ep) (dtr 90))
                      (/ dist 2)
              )
          )
          ""
    )
    (command "LINE"
          (setq osp2
              (polar sp
                      (- (angle sp ep) (dtr 90))
                      (/ dist 2)
              )
          )
          (setq oep2
              (polar ep
                      (- (angle sp ep) (dtr 90))
                      (/ dist 2)
              )
          )
          ""
```

Figure 10.12   The Enhanced PARALINE.LSP Routine

```
        )
    (setq isp1 osp1
          iep1 oep1
          isp2 osp2
          iep2 oep2
    )
)
; * -- End of PRLDRW function
(defun getmor()
; * -- Temporarily set the blips to their original value:
    (setvar "BLIPMODE" oldblp)
; * -- Prompt the user for the next endpoint and store it to ep2:
    (setq ep2
      (getpoint ep "\nTo Point: ")
    )
; * -- Turn the blips back off:
    (setvar "BLIPMODE" 0)
; * -- Check the value of ep2.  If ep2 is not nil or
; * -- the original starting point, spx, draw and trim the lines.
; * -- If it is spx, close the polygon.  If ep2 is nil, do nothing:
    (if
      (and
        (not (equal ep2 nil))
        (not (equal ep2 spx))
      )
      (drw1)
      (if
        (or
          (equal ep2 spx)
        )
        (closer)
      )
    )
)

; * -- End of GETMOR function
(defun drw1()
; * -- Define the new memory variable osp3 as the offset starting point
; * -- of one of the parallel lines:
    (setq osp3
      (polar ep
             (+ (angle ep ep2) (dtr 90))
             (/ dist 2)
      )
    )
; * -- Define memory variable osp4 as its counterpart:
    (setq osp4
      (polar ep
             (- (angle ep ep2) (dtr 90))
             (/ dist 2)
      )
    )
; * -- Define the new memory variable oep1 as the offset endpoint of
; * -- the first parallel line:
    (setq oep3
      (polar ep2
             (+ (angle ep ep2) (dtr 90))
             (/ dist 2)
      )
    )
; * -- Define memory variable oep2 as its counterpart:
    (setq oep4
      (polar ep2
```

Figure 10.12   The Enhanced PARALINE.LSP Routine (continued)

```
                        (- (angle ep ep2) (dtr 90))
                        (/ dist 2)
                      )
                    )
; * -- Define memory variable int1-3 as the point of intersection between
; * -- lines 1 and 3:
       (setq int1-3 (inters osp1 oep1 osp3 oep3 nil))
; * -- Define memory variable int2-4 as the point of intersection between
; * -- lines 2 and 4:
       (setq int2-4 (inters osp2 oep2 osp4 oep4 nil))
; * -- If the memory variables fint1-3 and fint2-4 are nil,
; * -- Initialize them with the current values of int1-3 and int2-4:
       (if (= fint1-3 nil)
        (setq fint1-3 int1-3
              fint2-4 int2-4
        )
       )
; * -- Erase the original lines:
       (command "ERASE"
         "L"
         " "
       )
       (command "ERASE"
         "L"
         " "
       )
; * -- Draw new lines using the new intersection points:
       (command "LINE"
         osp1
         int1-3
         " "
       )
       (command "LINE"
         osp2
         int2-4
         " "
       )
       (command "LINE"
         int1-3
         oep3
         " "
       )
       (command "LINE"
         int2-4
         oep4
         " "
       )
; * -- Reinitialize new memory variables, updating the starting and
; * -- endpoints of the centerline; the starting points of the
; * -- offset lines (as the intersection points) and the endpoints
; * -- of the offset lines:
       (setq sp ep
             ep ep2
             osp1 int1-3
             osp2 int2-4
             oep1 oep3
             oep2 oep4
       )
)
; * -- End of DRW1 function
(defun closer()
; * -- Define the new osp3 as the offset starting point of the first
; * -- parallel line, using the unchanged ep as the reference point
; * -- this time, and also referencing the original starting point,
```

Figure 10.12   The Enhanced PARALINE.LSP Routine (continued)

```
; * -- spx, in order to determine the angle of the final centerline:
    (setq osp3
      (polar ep
             (+ (angle ep spx) (dtr 90))
             (/ dist 2)
      )
    )
; * -- Define memory variable osp4 as its counterpart:
    (setq osp4
      (polar ep
             (- (angle ep spx) (dtr 90))
             (/ dist 2)
      )
    )
; * -- Define the new memory variable oep3 as the offset endpoint of
; * -- one of the final parallel lines. Use the original starting point:
    (setq oep3
      (polar spx
             (+ (angle ep spx) (dtr 90))
             (/ dist 2)
      )
    )
; * -- Define memory variable oep2 as its counterpart:
    (setq oep4
      (polar spx
             (- (angle ep spx) (dtr 90))
             (/ dist 2)
      )
    )
; * -- Erase the lines on either end of the final lines:
    (command "ERASE"
      oep1
      ""
    )
    (command "ERASE"
      oep2
      ""
    )
    (command "ERASE"
      isp1
      ""
    )
    (command "ERASE"
      isp2
      ""
    )
; * -- Draw new lines from the most recent intersection,
; * -- to the starting point of the final lines (an intersection point),
; * -- to the endpoint of the final lines (also an intersection point),
; * -- to the initial intersection point, int1-3:
    (command "LINE"
      int1-3
      (inters osp1 oep1 osp3 oep3 nil)
      (inters osp3 oep3 isp1 iep1 nil)
      fint1-3
      ""
    )
; * -- Do the same for the parallel mate:
    (command "LINE"
      int2-4
      (inters osp2 oep2 osp4 oep4 nil)
      (inters osp4 oep4 isp2 iep2 nil)
      fint2-4
      ""
```

Figure 10.12 The Enhanced PARALINE.LSP Routine (continued)

ADVANCED TECHNIQUES IN AUTOCAD

```
      )
  ) ; end of CLOSER function
  (defun C:PARALINE()
    (setq oldblp
      (getvar "BLIPMODE")
    )
    (setq oldech
      (getvar "CMDECHO")
    )
    (setvar "CMDECHO" 0)
  ; * -- Reset the values of ep2, int1-3, and int2-4
  ; * -- to their starting values:
    (setq ep2 '0,0
          fint1-3 nil
          fint2-4 nil
    )
    (prlinf)
    (setvar "BLIPMODE" 0)
    (prldrw)
  ; * -- Check the value of ep2.  If ep2 is not nil or spx,
  ; * -- prompt for the next endpoint.  If ep2 is nil or spx,
  ; * -- end the function:
    (while
      (and
        (not (equal ep2 nil))
        (not (equal ep2 spx))
      )
      (getmor)
    )
    (setvar "BLIPMODE" oldblp)
    (setvar "CMDECHO" oldech)
  ); End of C:PARALINE function
```

Figure 10.12   The Enhanced PARALINE.LSP Routine (continued)

```
        (polar ep
          (- (angle sp ep) (dtr 90))
          (/ dist 2)
        )
      )
      ""
    )
```

When this process is complete, save these starting and ending points to additional memory variables:

```
    (setq isp1 osp1
      iep1 oep1
      isp2 osp2
      iep2 oep2
    )
```

These extra variables will be employed if the user elects to close off the figure. The first set of variables defining these points cannot be used, because they will become bound to different values as the routine progresses.

With PRLINF and PRLDRW defined to handle the first set of parallel lines, the next step is to define the function that will prompt for the second set (and subsequent sets) of parallel lines. This function is arbitrarily named GETMOR.

This LISP routine does most of its processing with the blips turned off. However, if the blips were on before PARALINE was invoked, and you would like to have them turned on again after PARALINE, place this small function here:

(setvar "BLIPMODE" oldblp)

The oldblp memory variable contains the original value of the BLIPMODE system variable. The oldblp memory variable is initialized early in the execution of this routine, even though it has not yet appeared in the text of this LISP file. It is initialized in the C:PARALINE function, which is defined later in this LISP routine. We can use a memory variable that is yet to be initialized because the SETVAR function is nested inside a DEFUN function. AutoLISP "takes it on faith" that memory variables and other expressions used in the DEFUN function will evaluate correctly when the defined function is actually executed. In this case, the GETMOR function will be evaluated from within the C:PARALINE function.

It would be a mistake to attempt to initialize oldblp here. If you do so, the memory variable will be reinitialized each time GETMOR is executed. This could easily cause incorrect information to be stored in the memory variable, not to mention slowing down the program.

After the user selects the point ep2, the blips are turned back off:

(setvar "BLIPMODE" 0)

Next, the LISP routine must check the response the user gave to the prompt for point ep2. If the user pressed Return instead of supplying coordinate-point information, ep2 will have a value of nil; therefore, nothing need be done. You must structure the function in a way that causes nothing to happen if a Return was entered by the user.

On the other hand, if coordinate-point information was supplied by the user, you must first find out if the supplied coordinate points were the same as the original starting point stored in memory variable spx. If the coordinate points are the same, the LISP routine must close the polygon and trim the lines at all the intersection points. If the coordinate points are not the same, the LISP routine must draw an additional set of parallel lines and trim them at their points of intersection.

Although this may seem complex when written out this way, Auto-LISP can perform this analysis quite efficiently. First, the routine checks the value of ep2 to determine that it is not nil or spx:

```
(if
  (and
    (not (equal ep2 nil))
    (not (equal ep2 spx))
  )
(drw1)
```

This IF function tests two logical functions at the same time, because the two functions are nested within an AND function, which is what IF actually tests. The AND function will return T only if both of the logical functions nested inside it return T. If either logical function returns nil, the AND function will return nil as well.

These kinds of logical evaluations often require a bit of figuring out— you must determine whether using the AND function or the OR function is best. If the OR function had been used here instead of AND, it would have returned T if either one of the inner logical functions had returned T. This is not at all what you want, because the next function draws additional lines using ep2, and it trims a pair of intersections based on the assumption that a new endpoint has been entered. Using AND ensures that the next function will execute only if non-nil and non-spx coordinate information has been entered.

The drawing function that follows AND, DRW1, is defined next in this LISP file. AutoLISP accepts it as a valid function for now, because you are currently defining the GETMOR function. As before, you must define this function before it is executed.

If ep2 is nil or equal to spx, the second function nested in this IF function will execute. It will first determine to which value ep2 is bound. If ep2 is equal to spx, then it is time to close the figure. If it is not equal to spx, it must be nil, because that is the only other possibility at this point. If ep2 is nil, nothing need happen.

Here you can make use of another IF function, which will cause the LISP routine to close the figure if ep2 is equal to spx. There is no second function within this second IF function, because you don't want anything to happen if ep2 is nil:

```
(if
  (equal ep2 spx)
  (closer)
)     ; End of inner IF function
)     ; End of outer IF function
```

```
)          ; End of GETMOR function
```

This is the end of the GETMOR function, so three parentheses close off all the open functions, as the comments indicate.

The next step is to define the DRW1 and CLOSER functions. DRW1 takes the memory-variable information, draws the correct parallel lines, and trims them to their intersections. To do this, it first obtains the off-set starting and ending points of the new parallel lines. It stores them in memory variables named osp3, osp4, oep3, and oep4:

```
(defun drw1( )
  (setq osp3
    (polar ep
      ( + (angle ep ep2) (dtr 90))
      (/ dist 2)
    )
  )
  (setq osp4
    (polar ep
      (- (angle ep ep2) (dtr 90))
      (/ dist 2)
    )
  )
  (setq oep3
    (polar ep2
      ( + (angle ep ep2) (dtr 90))
      (/ dist 2)
    )
  )
  (setq oep4
    (polar ep2
      (- (angle ep ep2) (dtr 90))
      (/ dist 2)
    )
  )
```

The next step is to use this new information to correctly trim the resulting lines. To do this, the routine must determine the intersection points of the offset lines:

```
(setq int1-3 (inters osp1 oep1 osp3 oep3 nil))
(setq int2-4 (inters osp2 oep2 osp4 oep4 nil))
```

The INTERS function finds the intersection of lines 1 and 3 and stores that point to memory variable int1-3. The intersection point of lines 2 and 4 is found with the same mechanism, and the point is stored to memory variable int2-4.

Later, these memory variables may be bound to new values. However, if the figure is closed, you will need to access these points to trim the final set of lines properly. Therefore, store these points again to the special memory variables fint1-3 and fint2-4:

```
(if ( = fint1-3 nil)
  (setq fint1-3 int1-3
     fint2-4 int2-4
  )
)
```

The first set of intersection points that is found must be stored to fint1-3 and fint2-4. These will be used to close off the polygon should the user supply the original starting point. To prevent fint1-3 and fint2-4 from being updated each time the user supplies a new endpoint, an IF function tests to see if the current value of fint1-3 happens to be nil. If it is, fint1-3 and fint2-4 have not yet been initialized, and the memory variables int1-3 and int2-4 must contain the first set of intersection points. The SETQ function therefore initializes fint1-3 and fint2-4, binding them to the coordinate points contained in int1-3 and int2-4.

However, if fint1-3 is not nil, then fint1-3 and fint2-4 must already contain values, and these values must be the first set of intersection points. In this case, the function does nothing.

The previous set of lines can now be erased and redrawn from their starting points to the new intersection points:

```
(command "ERASE"
   "L"
   ""
)
(command "ERASE"
   "L"
   ""
)
(command "LINE"
   osp1
   int1-3
   ""
)
(command "LINE"
   osp2
   int2-4
```

```
    ""
)
```

The current set of lines can be drawn next, from the intersection points to the current endpoints:

```
(command "LINE"
  int1-3
  oep3
  ""
)
(command "LINE"
  int2-4
  oep4
  ""
)
```

Having trimmed the lines, this function's final step will bind the memory variables to new values, so that the same set of commands can be repeated using new line segments:

```
(setq sp ep
      ep ep2
      osp1 int1-3
      osp2 int2-4
      oep1 oep3
      oep2 oep4
  )
) ; End of DRW1 function
```

First, the value in ep is copied to sp, making it the new starting point of the centerline. Then ep2 is renamed ep, making it the new endpoint of the centerline. Memory variable ep2 is thus free to be redefined when the user enters new coordinate information or makes ep2 nil by entering a Return.

Just as the centerline points have been renamed, so must the offset points be renamed. Line 3 will become the new line 1; its offset starting point becomes the point value of int1-3. Line 4 become the new line 2; its offset starting point becomes the point value of int2-4. The offset endpoint of the new line 1 is the offset endpoint of the old line 3. The offset endpoint of the new line 2 is the offset endpoint of the old line 4.

This ends the DRW1 function. Next, you must define the CLOSER function, which will close off the figure if the user enters the original starting point in response to the prompt for ep2. In this function, the centerline starting and ending points of the final lines are already defined. They are ep (the last endpoint) and spx (the original starting point). Offset points for lines 1 and 2 have been defined by the renaming functions just seen, so you begin by using ep and spx to create the final offset points for lines 3 and 4:

```
(defun closer( )
  (setq osp3
    (polar ep
      ( + (angle ep spx) (dtr 90))
      (/ dist 2)
    )
  )
  (setq osp4
    (polar ep
      (- (angle ep spx) (dtr 90))
      (/ dist 2)
    )
  )
  (setq oep3
    (polar spx
      ( + (angle ep spx) (dtr 90))
      (/ dist 2)
    )
  )
  (setq oep4
    (polar spx
      (- (angle ep spx) (dtr 90))
      (/ dist 2)
    )
  )
```

Once these points are established, the intersection points can be determined. Since these final lines are drawn to close up the figure, both the previous set of lines and the original set of lines must be updated to reflect the intersections involved. Both sets of lines are therefore erased:

```
(command "ERASE"
  oep1
  ""
)
(command "ERASE"
  oep2
```

```
    ""
)
(command "ERASE"
  isp1
    ""
)
(command "ERASE"
  isp2
    ""
)
```

Four separate ERASE commands are used to find these lines; the lines are selected and erased individually. This avoids problems that can occur with different display devices when AutoLISP attempts to select entities that are close together. Even though exact points are specified by means of memory variables, if the objects are very close on the display screen, the wrong line may sometimes be found. Using four separate ERASE commands prevents this. Fortunately, because this is AutoLISP, the commands are invoked quite rapidly.

With these lines erased, two sets of lines can now be drawn. Drawing begins at the starting point of the previous set of lines and proceeds to the intersection of the previous and final lines, then to the intersection of the final and the original set of lines, and finally, to the endpoints of the original set of lines. These lines are quickly drawn with the following functions:

```
(command "LINE"
  int1-3
  (inters osp1 oep1 osp3 oep3 nil)
  (inters osp3 oep3 isp1 iep1 nil)
  fint1-3
    ""
)
(command "LINE"
  int2-4
  (inters osp2 oep2 osp4 oep4 nil)
  (inters osp4 oep4 isp2 iep2 nil)
  fint2-4
    ""
)
) ; End of CLOSER function
```

Notice how the INTERS function can be used as an argument for the LINE command. This is possible because the command is now complete, and these points need not be stored to memory variables.

All of the functions used in the enhanced PARALINE.LSP routine are now defined. Now you must define the AutoCAD command that uses these functions:

(defun C:PARALINE( )

To improve the appearance of the screen while the PARALINE command executes, store the current value of the BLIPMODE and CMDECHO system variables to the memory variables oldblp and oldech, respectively. This will enable you to turn them off and restore them to their original state at will:

```
(setq oldblp
   (getvar "BLIPMODE")
)
(setq oldech
   (getvar "CMDECHO")
)
(setvar "CMDECHO" 0)
```

Each time you reinvoke this command, you must be certain that the memory variables used in its control structures are set to values that allow for the proper execution of all its functions. Therefore, the value of ep2 must be set to a value other than nil, in case the user previously ended the command with a Return (which has the effect of binding ep2 to a nil value). If this variable is allowed to remain nil, the looping functions will not work. Binding ep2 to point 0,0 will ensure that there is no problem. Similarly, the values of fint1-3 and fint2-4 must be set to nil so that they will receive the value of the first set of intersections:

```
(setq ep2 '0,0
   fint1-3 nil
   fint2-4 nil
)
```

Once everything is set up, you can execute your first defined function:

(prlinf)

Next, turn the blips off:

(setvar "BLIPMODE" 0)

Draw the first set of lines:

(prldrw)

As long as the user does not enter a Return or the original starting point, execute the GETMOR function:

```
(while
  (and
    (not (equal ep2 nil))
    (not (equal ep2 spx))
  )
  (getmor)
)
```

GETMOR handles the execution of the DRW1 and CLOSER functions, so the only thing left at this point is to reset the values of BLIPMODE and CMDECHO at the conclusion of PARALINE:

```
(setvar "BLIPMODE" oldblp)
(setvar "CMDECHO" oldech)
); End of C:PARALINE function
```

PARALINE will not replace OFFSET, but it does have its advantages. It's more intuitive, allows for the easy movement of its line segments, draws its lines from a single command, and aids in centerline dimensioning. It also demonstrates the principles of good LISP-routine design.

For Users of Version 2.6 +

If you are using AutoCAD Version 2.6 or later, a new AutoLISP function, INITGET, will allow you to close the figure generated by this LISP routine by typing the letter c or C in response to the "To point:" prompt. The INITGET function's syntax is

```
(initget "C")
```

This function should be placed within the GETMOR function as follows:

```
(defun getmor( )
  (setvar "BLIPMODE" oldblp)
  (initget "C")                    ; Add INITGET here and
                                   ; continue the function with
                                   ; the following additional lines:

  (setq ep2
    (getpoint ep "\nTo Point: ")
  )
  (setvar "BLIPMODE" 0)
```

ADVANCED TECHNIQUES IN AUTOCAD

```
; * - If ep2 is not nil, "c", "C", or the original starting
; point spx, draw and fillet the lines. If ep2 is
; spx, "c", or "C", close the polygon.
; If ep2 is nil, do nothing:

    (if
      (and
        (not (equal ep2 nil))
        (not (equal ep2 spx))
        (not (equal ep2 "c"))          ; Add this new line
        (not (equal ep2 "C"))          ; Add this new line
      )
      (drw1)
      (if
        (or                            ; Add this new OR function -
                                       ;  any one of the following
                                       ;  functions, if true, must
                                       ; cause the figure to close:

          (equal ep2 spx)
          (equal ep2 "c")              ; Add this new line
          (equal ep2 "C")              ; Add this new line
        )
        (closer)
      )
    )
  )
) ; End of GETMOR function
```

When used in this fashion, the INITGET function allows the user to respond to the GETPOINT function with the letter c or C. Other non-point responses will not be allowed.

INITGET works only for the first GET-type function encountered after it has been evaluated. Therefore, it must be reinvoked before each GET function that needs it. In the LISP routine PARALINE.LSP, the GET-MOR function is contained in a loop; thus, INITGET is reevaluated each time the loop evaluates GETMOR.

If you use the INITGET function to close the figure, all of the logical functions in the LISP routine must account for the possibility of ep2 having a value of either C or c. Therefore, the looping WHILE function in C:PARALINE must be changed:

```
(while
  (and
    (not (equal ep2 nil))
```

```
        (not (equal ep2 spx))
        (not (equal ep2 "c"))          ; Add this
        (not (equal ep2 "C"))          ; Add this
      )
    (getmor)
  )
```

USING PARALINE.LSP
TO CREATE SLOTS.LSP

Other figures that require parallel lines are candidates for additional LISP routines that can share some of the functions presented so far. The following LISP routine is an example—it draws slots. Since this LISP routine will use functions that were defined in PARALINE.LSP, it could be attached to the end of PARALINE.LSP, and both routines could be loaded at once. Or, if you prefer, these extra functions could be stored in a separate LISP file. If you choose to store them separately, remember that PARALINE.LSP will have to be loaded before these LISP routines will work. Another alternative, somewhat less efficient, is to repeat the PRLINF and PRLDRW functions in both LISP files. However, this will greatly increase the time required to load both of them.

Pseudocode for SLOTS.LSP

Here is the plain-English version of what these new functions do:

1. Prompt for and draw parallel lines as before.

2. Using the memory variables created in the previous functions, add two 180-degree arcs on either end of the parallel lines.

This process is illustrated in Figure 10.13.

To do this, two additional functions can be added to PARALINE.LSP. These functions are SLTDRW and C:SLOT, shown in Figure 10.14. Note that the SLTDRW function uses the functions defined in PARALINE.LSP.

Functions in SLOTS.LSP

The SLTDRW function uses the previous PRLINF and PRLDRW functions to draw parallel lines. When they are drawn, the ARC command uses the memory variables that were set in the preceding functions to connect the starting and ending points with arcs.

ADVANCED TECHNIQUES IN AUTOCAD

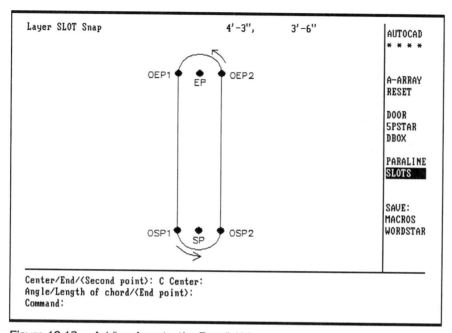

Layer SLOT Snap   4'-3",   3'-6"

Center/End/<Second point>: C Center:
Angle/Length of chord/<End point>:
Command:

Figure 10.13   Adding Arcs to the Parallel Lines

Notice the order in which the starting and ending points of the arcs are selected. This example assumes the AutoCAD default; the arcs are drawn counterclockwise. If you have changed your AutoCAD configuration to clockwise arcs, you will need to reverse these points. Also notice that the second argument of the ARC command is the letter c contained in quotes. This is just the same as if the letter c had been entered at the keyboard in response to the AutoCAD prompt "Center/End/ <second point>:." In this case, the c informs AutoCAD that the next point is the center of the arc.

The C:SLOT function loads the new SLOT command. It follows the same structure as the C:PARALINE function, which loads the PARALINE command.

PLACING LISP ROUTINES
ON A CUSTOM MENU

You can simplify the process of loading LISP routines if you include the LOAD function as part of a custom menu macro:

[PARALINE] ^ C ^ C(load "PARALINE");PARALINE;

```
; * -- Define function SLTDRW:
(defun sltdrw()
; * -- Collect distance information
    (prlinf)
; * -- Draw the lines
    (prldrw)
; * -- Draw arcs on either end:
    (command "ARC"
                ospl
                "C"
                spx
                osp2
    )
    (command "ARC"
                oep2
                "C"
                ep
                oepl
    )
) ; End of SLTDRW function
; * -- Define SLOT command
(defun C:SLOT()
; * -- Store blips and echo:
    (setq oldblp
            (getvar "BLIPMODE")
    )
    (setq oldech
            (getvar "CMDECHO")
    )
; * -- Turn them off:
    (setvar "CMDECHO" 0)
    (setvar "BLIPMODE" 0)
; * -- Draw the slots:
    (sltdrw)
; * -- Reset blips and echo:
    (setvar "BLIPMODE" oldblp)
    (setvar "CMDECHO" oldech)
) ; End of function C:SLOT
```

Figure 10.14   The SLTDRW and C:SLOT Functions

This macro will load the LISP routine and execute the command automatically. Unfortunately, there is a problem with this—since you only need to load the LISP routine once, it will waste time and accomplish nothing if you reload it every time you pick this menu command.

Solving this problem is a matter of adding an IF function and a SETQ function to the macro:

**[PARALINE] ^ C ^ C(if (= prl nil) (load "PARALINE")); +
(setq prl 1);PARALINE;**

The IF function will check to see if the memory variable prl is bound to nil. If it is, PARALINE.LSP has not been loaded, and the LOAD function is evaluated. Immediately after PARALINE.LSP is loaded, prl is bound to a value of 1, and the command is executed. The next time this macro is selected, the loading function will not be evaluated, because prl is no longer nil. When variables such as prl are used in this manner, they are referred to as *flag variables*.

If you create several LISP routines and wish to load them by using custom menu macros, note that there are a few different ways to handle flag variables and the loading of LISP files:

- A separate flag variable may be used for each LISP routine. If you wind up with dozens of LISP routines, this would mean that an equal number of flag variables take up space in the heap area. If you have room in memory and you need to load several different LISP routines in any given drawing session, this is acceptable. However, it is not particularly efficient—it does consume some extra memory space.

- To reduce the number of flag variables, combine several related LISP routines into a larger LISP file. Then the LISP routines can be loaded all at once, and several macros can share a single flag variable. Although this will undoubtedly increase the initial loading time, once the big file is loaded, you need not worry about it again. This is a good technique if you use several related commands regularly, if memory space is at a premium and you can't afford extra flag variables, or if many of your LISP routines share the same functions.

- You can eliminate the need for flag variables by placing *all* of your LISP routines within the ACAD.LSP file and having them all load automatically at the beginning of every drawing session. This dramatically increases the time you must spend at the beginning of each drawing session, while the message "loading acad.lsp..." appears in the command prompt area. However, once the big ACAD.LSP file is finally loaded, it's loaded, and you needn't wait for any further loading throughout the drawing session. This technique is recommended if you use the same LISP routines during every drawing session; you might as well get the loading process over with right away.

If you develop several LISP files that share the same set of basic LISP functions, you can speed up the process of loading them, and save some memory space, by placing the shared LISP functions in ACAD.LSP and loading the supplementary functions as needed.

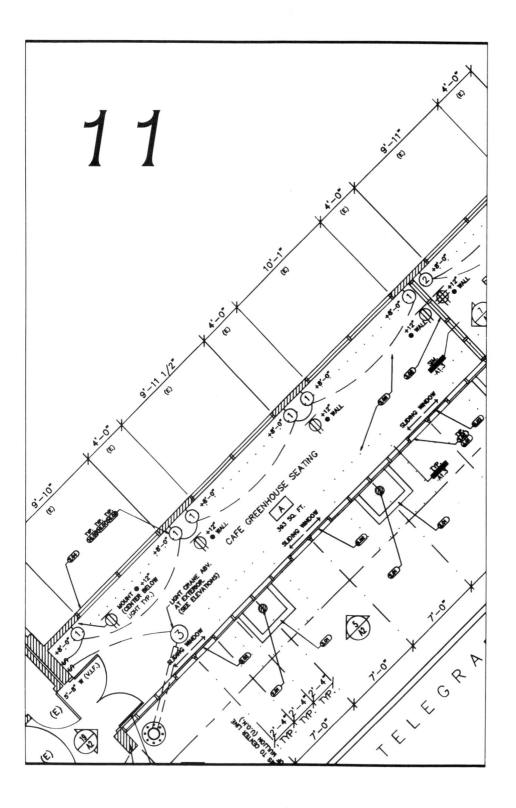

Chapter 11
Example LISP Routines

BLOCKS AND SHAPES WORK WELL when you insert repeatedly drawn objects into a drawing. However, some of these objects require slightly different drawing parameters each time. In such a situation, you can draw from scratch each time or maintain what might become an uncomfortably large block library. A third option is to write an AutoLISP routine that will incorporate common drawing elements with a new set of drawing parameters each time it is invoked. The following examples demonstrate techniques for creating such LISP routines.

PARALLEL ARCS AND CURVED SLOTS

The parallel line techniques presented in the previous chapter can be used to generate figures that use curved parallel lines. The LISP routine presented here, CSLOT.LSP, uses a three-point arc to generate a curved slot shape. This technique need not be limited to three-point arcs—it can be modified to include other means of drawing arcs in AutoCAD as well. To demonstrate this kind of modification, a variation on this routine, using a start-center-endpoint arc, follows the discussion of CSLOT.LSP.

CSLOT.LSP defines three new functions: ARCDRW, to draw the arcs; ENDSLT, to close the ends with line segments; and C:CSLOT, to create the AutoCAD command that executes the functions. It also uses the PRLINF function from C:PARALINE, which establishes the distance between parallel straight lines.

Pseudocode for CSLOT.LSP

Here is the complete LISP routine in English:

1. Prompt the user for the distance between the arcs, and offer a default if a value has been previously set. (This is PRLINF.)

2. Temporarily turn the blips on.

3. Prompt the user for three points to determine an arc. Draw the arc between these points.

4. Using the arc, reference the center point of its radius.

5. Store the coordinates of the center point to memory variable cp.

6. If the radius of the arc is less than the distance between the arcs, warn the user.

7. Erase the centerline arc. (Note: As an option, you can change the arc's layer, line type, or whatever properties you wish. Simply supply the appropriate AutoCAD command in the LISP routine.)

8. Draw two concentric arcs, referencing the original points and the center point, at half the user-specified distance.

9. Connect the endpoints of the arcs with line segments.

The CSLOT.LSP Routine

Figure 11.1 shows the entire CSLOT.LSP routine, which performs all of the steps just described in pseudocode. The first seven lines of this function are standard AutoLISP functions you have seen before. The PRLINF function (which must be previously loaded) gets the distance between the arc lines, and the GETPOINT functions in ARCINF get the three arc points. Then the ARC command draws the reference arc.

Next, a memory variable is initialized, containing half of the user-specified distance between the arcs:

```
(setq dist2 (/ dist 2))
```

If memory-variable space is at a premium, this math could be nested inside subsequent functions instead of being assigned to the memory variable dist2.

Next, another memory variable is initialized, which contains the x-y coordinates of the center point of the radius. To find the center point, we use the OSNAP function. This function applies the Osnap override CENTER to the arc just drawn. By nesting it with the SETQ function, it will be saved to the memory variable cp:

```
(setq cp
  (osnap ep "center")
)
```

Now a decision must be made. In some cases, the radius of the centerline arc might be less than the distance between the two final arcs. In such a case, a warning can be displayed, using the PROMPT function:

```
(if
  (< (distance cp sp) dist)
```

```
; * -- Define ARCDRW function
(defun arcdrw ()
; * -- Collect distance between arcs. (Note: PRLINF function
;       must be already loaded.):
  (prlinf)
; * -- Turn on blips:
  (setvar "BLIPMODE" oldblp)
; * -- Get three points for centerline arc:
  (setq sp (getpoint "\nCenterline Arc Start Point: "))
  (setq mp (getpoint "\nCenterline Arc Second Point: "))
  (setq ep (getpoint "\nCenterline Arc End Point: "))
; * -- Turn blips off
  (setvar "BLIPMODE" 0)
; * -- Draw the centerline arc:
  (command "ARC" sp mp ep)
; * -- Set a memory variable for half the user-specified distance:
  (setq dist2 (/ dist 2))
; * -- Reference the arc center point using Osnap:
  (setq cp
        (osnap ep "center")
  )
; * -- If the arc radius is less that the distance, warn the user, but
;       continue with the command:
  (if
     (< (distance cp sp) dist)
     (prompt
       "\nArcs too wide -- Inner arc may be reversed.
     )
  )
; * -- Erase the centerline arc. (Or, substitute another command if
;       you wish to keep it and just change it. Omit the command if
;       you wish to keep it):
  (command "ERASE" "l" "")
; * -- Draw the offset arcs:
  (command "ARC"
     (polar sp (angle sp cp) dist2)
     (polar mp (angle mp cp) dist2)
     (polar ep (angle ep cp) dist2)
  )
  (command "ARC"
     (polar sp (angle cp sp) dist2)
     (polar mp (angle cp mp) dist2)
     (polar ep (angle cp ep) dist2)
  )
) ; End of ARCDRW function
; * -- Define ENDSLT function
(defun endslt()
; * -- Connect the ends of the arcs with line segments:
  (command "LINE"
     osp
     isp
     ""
  (command "LINE"
     iep
     oep
     ""
  )

) ; End of ENDSLT function
; * -- Define C:CSLOT function (AutoCAD command)
(defun C:CSLOT ()
; * -- Save screen values:
  (setq oldblp
```

Figure 11.1   The CSLOT.LSP Routine

ADVANCED TECHNIQUES IN AUTOCAD

```
    (getvar "BLIPMODE")
  )
  (setq oldech
    (getvar "CMDECHO")
  )
;  * -- Turn off command echo:
  (setvar "CMDECHO" 0)
;  * -- Draw curved slots:
  (arcdrw)
  (endslt)
;  * -- Restore screen values:
  (setvar "BLIPMODE" oldblp)
  (setvar "CMDECHO" oldech)
) ; End of C:CSLOT function
```

Figure 11.1   The CSLOT.LSP Routine (continued)

```
(prompt
   "\nArcs too wide — Inner arc may be reversed."
)
)
```

The command is allowed to continue, however, since the inner arc may not be reversed in all cases. Next, the centerline arc is erased:

```
(command "ERASE" "L" "")
```

Two new arcs are drawn. The POLAR function references all the correct points. Notice how the memory variable cp is used to determine the correct reference angle on all six points:

```
(command "ARC"
   (polar sp (angle sp cp) dist2)
   (polar mp (angle mp cp) dist2)
   (polar ep (angle ep cp) dist2)
)
(command "ARC"
   (polar sp (angle cp sp) dist2)
   (polar mp (angle cp mp) dist2)
   (polar ep (angle cp ep) dist2)
)
) ; End of ARCDRW function
```

The ARCDRW function can be used in a variety of LISP routines in which parallel arcs are required. In this example, the figure is finished off with a simple function that connects the starting and ending points of the arcs, ENDSLT:

```
(defun endslt( )
   (command "LINE"
```

```
      osp
      isp
      ""
  )
  (command "LINE"
      iep
      oep
      ""

  )
) ; End of ENDSLT function
```

It is a simple task to define the new CSLOT AutoCAD command to execute these functions. (The C:CSLOT function contains functions you have seen before in Chapter 10.)

The AutoCAD ARCDRW Function (S-C-A Variation)

The following variation on the ARCDRW function employs a start-center-angle arc instead of a three-point arc. In this case, because the center point is entered directly by the user, the initial centerline arc need not be drawn, and the two offset arcs can be drawn immediately:

```
; * — Define ARCDRW function (S-C-A version)
(defun arcdrw ( )
; * — Get starting point, center point, included angle:
    (setq sp (getpoint "\nCenterline Arc Start Point: "))
    (setq cp (getpoint "\nArc Center Point: "))
    (setq iang (getreal "\nArc Included Angle: "))
; * – Turn blips off:
    (setvar "BLIPMODE" 0)
; * – Warn user if radius is less than distance between arcs:
    (if
      (< (distance cp sp) dist)
      (prompt
        "\nArcs too wide – Inner arc may be reversed."
      )
    )
; * — Divide distance in half and save to dist2:
    (setq dist2 (/ dist 2))
; * — Draw the arcs
    (command "ARC"
        (polar sp (angle sp cp) dist2)
```

```
      "C"
      cp
      "A"
       iang
    )
    (command "ARC"
      (polar sp (angle cp sp) dist2)
      "C"
      cp
      "A"
      iang
    )
  ) ; End of ARCDRW function
```

In this variation, GETREAL is used to get the included angle from the user. The user enters this number in whatever current angle format was selected with the UNITS command.

Note that when this memory variable is referenced as an argument to the ARC command, it is not converted to radians. Inside a LISP routine, when an angle measurement is given as a literal argument to an AutoCAD command, conversion to radians is not required. The argument should be supplied in the current format that was selected with the UNITS command. This is because arguments to an AutoCAD command, including the values of memory variables, are understood by AutoCAD as typed keyboard responses to prompts.

This situation is an exception to the general rule about requiring radians inside LISP routines. It applies only to literal arguments for AutoCAD commands. Notice how the POLAR function is used to get the arc's starting point:

```
   (polar sp (angle cp sp) dist2)
```

Here, the nested ANGLE function, which returns radians, is *not* an argument to the ARC command, but rather an argument to the POLAR function. The POLAR function returns coordinate information that is accepted as the argument to the ARC command.

ANALYSIS AND DECISION MAKING: ZIGZAG.LSP

The next LISP routine demonstrates AutoLISP's ability to analyze user information and make decisions based on that information. ZIGZAG.LSP creates an AutoCAD command called ZIGZAG, which prompts the user for two endpoints and the number of corners to be used. It then analyzes this information and draws a staircase-like line between the endpoints.

ZIGZAG.LSP defines four functions: ZZINF, which prompts the user for the required information; ZZCALC, which does the analysis; ZZDRW, which draws the staircase; and C:ZIGZAG, which creates the AutoCAD command that executes these functions.

Pseudocode for ZIGZAG.LSP

The pseudocode for this routine contains the following steps:

1. Prompt the user for a starting point and endpoint.

2. Store the coordinate information in memory variables sp and ep.

3. Prompt the user for the number of corners in the final figure.

4. Store the corner information in memory variable nc.

5. If the x-coordinate of sp is less than the x-coordinate of ep, then the horizontal lines in the figure will be drawn from left to right, or at angle 0. If the opposite is true, the horizontal lines in the figure will be drawn from right to left, or at angle 180.

6. In a similar manner, if the y-coordinate of sp is less than the y-coordinate of ep, the vertical lines in the figure will be drawn from top to bottom, or at angle 270. If the opposite is true, the vertical lines in the figure will be drawn from bottom to top, or at angle 90. Figure 11.2 illustrates this process.

7. To determine the length of the horizontal and vertical lines, first reference a new point. The x-coordinate of this point will be the same as the x-coordinate of sp. The y-coordinate of this point will be the the same as the y-coordinate of ep. Store these coordinates to the memory variable np. Figure 11.3 illustrates this process.

8. Measure the distance between sp and np. Divide the distance by the number of corners. This yields the length of the horizontal lines. Store this value to a memory variable called step.

9. Measure the distance between ep and np. Divide the distance by the number of corners. This yields the length of the vertical lines. Store this value to a memory variable called riser. Figure 11.4 illustrates this process.

10. Reference a new point for drawing the lines relative to sp, at the angle defined by yang, and at the distance defined by riser.

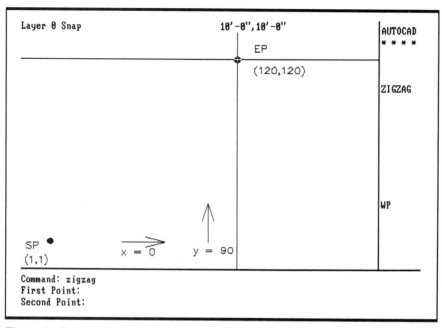

Figure 11.2 Determining the Correct Angle of the Line Segments

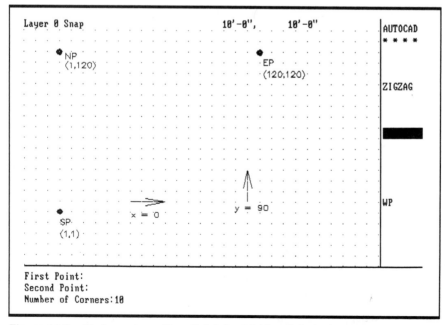

Figure 11.3 Referencing a New Point for Making Calculations

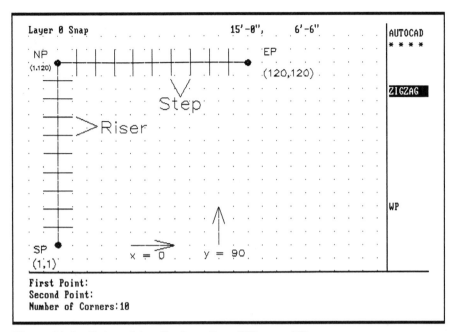

Figure 11.4　Determining the Lengths of Step and Riser

11. Store the coordinate information in the memory variable pt1.

12. Reference a second point for drawing the lines relative to pt1, at the angle defined by xang, and at the distance defined by step.

13. Store the coordinate information in the memory variable pt2. Figure 11.5 shows this process.

14. Initialize a special memory variable that will be updated each time a step-riser combination is drawn. This will control the loop that draws the figure. Call this memory variable case, and give it an initial value of zero.

15. When the value of case is less than the value of nc, continue to repeat the following steps (steps 16 through 20).

16. Draw a line from sp, to pt1, to pt2.

17. Store the new coordinate information to sp; the new sp will contain the value of pt2.

18. Store the new coordinate information to pt1; the new pt1 will be relative to the new sp, at the angle yang, and at the distance defined by riser.

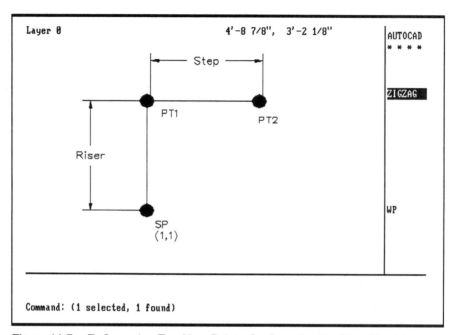

Figure 11.5 Referencing Two New Points for Drawing the First Two Lines

19. Store new coordinate information to pt2; the new pt2 will be relative to the new pt1, at the angle xang, and at the distance defined by step. Figure 11.6 illustrates this process.

20. Increment the value of the memory variable named case by 1.

The ZIGZAG.LSP Routine

The AutoLISP functions that perform these steps are contained in the ZIGZAG.LSP routine, shown in Figure 11.7. Figure 11.8 shows four lines drawn with this routine.

The first function in this routine, ZZINFO, is straightforward; it includes functions that you have seen and analyzed before. The next function, ZZCALC, will perform all the calculations necessary for a computer to draw a simple zigzag line. It is an excellent example of the analytical power of AutoLISP.

The IF functions make a decision regarding the angles at which the zigzag line is drawn. The first IF function evaluates the following condition:

(< (car sp) (car ep))

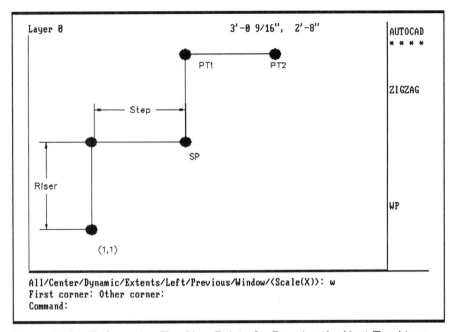

Figure 11.6   Referencing Two New Points for Drawing the Next Two Lines

The ZZINFO function has set up the variables sp and ep; now the CAR function will isolate the x-coordinates of these points. The two CAR functions are nested inside a "less-than" function to determine if the x-coordinate of the starting point is less than the x-coordinate of the endpoint. If this function returns true, AutoLISP will execute the next function, which sets the angle for drawing the horizontal lines to zero:

(setq xang 0)

If the "less-than" function returns false, AutoLISP will instead execute the second function, which sets the angle for drawing the horizontal lines to 180 degrees:

(setq xang (dtr 180))

Notice that 180 degrees is changed to radians inside this second function.

The second IF function does the same thing, but it operates on the y-coordinates of the starting point and the endpoint using the CADR function. It determines if the y-coordinate of the starting point is less than the y-coordinate of the endpoint. If the result is true, AutoLISP creates a memory variable called yang and gives it a value of 90 degrees

ADVANCED TECHNIQUES IN AUTOCAD

```
; * -- Define ZZINF function
(defun zzinf ()
; * -- Get starting point, ending point, number of corners:
  (setq sp
       (getpoint "\nFirst Point:")
  )
  (setq ep
       (getpoint "\nSecond Point:")
  )
  (setq nc
       (getint "\nNumber of Corners:")
  )
) ; End of ZZINF function
; * -- Define ZZCALC function
(defun zzcalc ()
; * -- Calculate angles for line segments:
  (if
     (< (car sp) (car ep))
     (setq xang 0)
     (setq xang (dtr 180))
  )
  (if
     (< (cadr sp) (cadr ep))
     (setq yang (dtr 90))
     (setq yang (dtr 270))
  )
; * -- Find reference point and calculate length of line segments:
  (setq cp
       (list
          (car sp)
          (cadr ep)
       )
  )
  (setq riser
       (/ (distance sp cp) nc)
  )
  (setq step
       (/ (distance cp ep) nc)
  )
; * -- Find drawing points
  (setq pt1
       (polar sp yang riser)
  )
  (setq pt2
       (polar pt1 xang step)
  )
; * -- Initialize loop counter
  (setq case 0)
) ; End of ZZCALC function
; * -- Define ZZDRW function
(defun zzdrw ()
; * -- Loop to draw corners and update variables
  (while
     (< case nc)
; * -- Draw a corner
     (command "LINE"
          sp
          pt1
          pt2
          ""
     )
; * -- Update memory variables
     (setq case
```

Figure 11.7   The ZIGZAG.LSP Routine

```
            (1+ case)
        )
    (setq sp pt2)
    (setq pt1
            (polar sp yang riser)
    )
    (setq pt2
            (polar pt1 xang step)
    )
    ) ; End of WHILE function
) ; End of ZZDRW function
; Define C:ZIGZAG function
(defun C:ZIGZAG ()
; * -- Save screen values:
    (setq oldblp
        (getvar "BLIPMODE")
    )
    (setq oldech
        (getvar "CMDECHO")
    )
; * -- Turn off command echo:
    (setvar "CMDECHO" 0)
; * -- Get information:
(zzinf)
; * -- Turn off blips:
    (setvar "BLIPMODE" 0)
; * -- Calculate and draw staircase:
(zzcalc)
(zzdrw)
; * -- Restore screen values:
    (setvar "BLIPMODE" oldblp)
    (setvar "CMDECHO" oldech)
) ; End of C:ZIGZAG function
```

Figure 11.7   The ZIGZAG.LSP Routine (continued)

(expressed in radians). If the result is false, however, AutoLISP gives yang a value of 270 degrees, also expressed in radians:

```
(if
    (< (cadr sp) (cadr ep))
    (setq yang (dtr 90))
    (setq yang (dtr 270))
)
```

Now that AutoLISP knows the directions in which to draw its line segments, it needs to know how long those segments will be. To calculate this, AutoLISP must first identify another point. It creates a memory variable called cp and places within it the values of the x-coordinate of the starting point and the y-coordinate of the endpoint. This results in three points that form a right angle, with point cp marking the location of that angle.

A nested LIST function inside a SETQ function performs this process. The LIST function contains a CAR and a CADR function as its arguments.

ADVANCED TECHNIQUES IN AUTOCAD

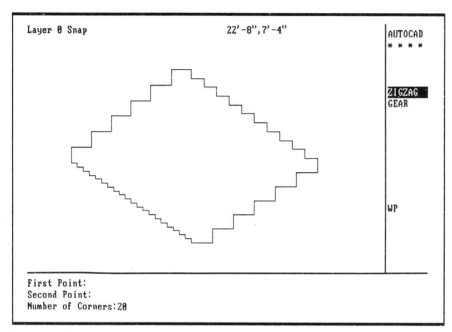

Figure 11.8   Four Zigzag Lines Drawn with ZIGZAG.LSP

The result is new coordinate information:

```
(setq cp
  (list
    (car sp)
    (cadr ep)
  )
)
```

AutoLISP then calculates the distance between the starting point and cp automatically. It also calculates the distance between the endpoint and cp. The functions that do this are nested within a math function that divides each total distance by the number of corners supplied by the user. The result of the math is stored in memory variables riser and step:

```
(setq riser
  (/ (distance sp cp) nc)
)
(setq step
  (/ (distance cp ep) nc)
)
```

The next step creates two intermediate points. They are calculated using the POLAR function and draw on previously calculated variables. The first point, pt1, is determined to be relative to the starting point, at an angle equal to the value of yang, and at a distance equal to the value of riser. Then another intermediate point is calculated in relation to the just-created pt1, at an angle equal to the value of xang, and at a distance equal to the value of step. This point is saved to memory variable pt2:

```
(setq pt1
   (polar sp yang riser)
)
(setq pt2
   (polar pt1 xang step)
)
```

Finally, this function is going to loop several times. AutoLISP needs to know when to end the looping process, so you must set up a special variable that will be incremented by 1 each time AutoLISP executes the loop functions. When this variable equals the number of corners, the loop will end:

```
(setq case 0)
```

The next function, ZZDRW, draws the lines and updates the variables as necessary. As long as the value of case is less than the value of nc, the loop will continue:

```
(while
   (< case nc)
```

The following lines call the AutoCAD LINE command and then draw the line using the calculated memory variables:

```
(command "LINE"
   sp
   pt1
   pt2
   ""
)
```

This function takes the previously defined variable, case, and increments it by 1 for each time through the loop:

```
(setq case
   (1 + case)
)
```

Next, AutoLISP changes the values of some of its variables so that it can draw the next corner. It redefines the starting point sp, giving it the values contained in the variable pt2, and then it redefines the variable pt1 using the POLAR function. The new pt1 is relative to the new sp at the angle of yang and the distance of riser. The function then redefines pt2 using the POLAR function, setting the new pt2 relative to the new pt1, at the angle of xang and at the distance of step:

```
(setq sp pt2)
(setq pt1
   (polar sp yang riser)
)
(setq pt2
   (polar pt1 xang step)
)
) ; End of WHILE function
) ; End of ZZDRW function
```

The final function in this routine, C:ZIGZAG, creates the new Auto-CAD command ZIGZAG by using familiar AutoLISP functions. You have seen this done before in Chapter 10.

USING FIXED FORMULAS: GEAR.LSP

This LISP routine draws a typical machinery gear. It uses formulas taken from a machinist's handbook and is an example of how standard math calculations can be built into new AutoCAD commands. The LISP routine GEAR.LSP contains four functions: GRINF, which gets the required information from the user; GRCALC, which performs the standard calculations; GRDRW, which draws the resulting gear; and C:GEAR, which creates a new AutoCAD command, GEAR, to execute the functions. GEAR.LSP will work on AutoCAD Version 2.5 and later. A variation for Version 2.18 and an enhancement for Version 2.6 follow the presentation of this routine.

Pseudocode for GEAR.LSP

The GEAR.LSP routine is defined in English by these steps:

1. Prompt the user for the center point of the gear.

2. Save the center-point coordinates to the memory variable cp.

3. Prompt the user for the pitch circle of the gear by means of a point pick.

4. Save the coordinate information to the memory variable pc.

5. Prompt the user for the number of gear teeth.

6. Save the number of teeth to the memory variable teeth.

7. If the number of teeth is less than 14, display an error message and again prompt the user for the number of teeth.

8. Regardless of where the user has set the pitch circle, correct its coordinates so that the center point and the pitch-circle coordinates have the same y-coordinate. (This will simplify angle calculations.)

9. Calculate the diametral pitch of the gear.

10. Calculate the length of half the end of a tooth.

11. Calculate the distance between the pitch circle and the end of a tooth.

12. Calculate the length of the side of a tooth.

13. Draw half of a tooth using the results of these calculations.

14. Mirror what was drawn to create a whole tooth.

15. Perform a circular array based on the user-specified number of teeth.

Figures 11.9 and 11.10 illustrate the process of drawing a 6-inch gear with 36 teeth.

The GEAR.LSP Routine

The entire GEAR.LSP routine is shown in Figure 11.11. The routine begins with the GRINF function, which asks for three items of information: the center point of the gear, a point defining its pitch circle, and the number of teeth. This function is straightforward and uses familiar prompting syntax. A small error trap prevents the user from inadvertently entering less than 14 for the number of teeth, which would be too few teeth for this type of gear.

```
(while
  (< teeth 14)
  (setq teeth
    (getint "\nMust be at least 14 teeth: ")
  )
)
```

ADVANCED TECHNIQUES IN AUTOCAD

```
Layer 0 Snap                        14'-4",      1'-8"        AUTOCAD
 .    .    .    .    .    .    .    .    .    .    .    .      * * * *

 .    .    .    .    .    .    .    .    .    .    .    .
                                                             ZIGZAG
 .    .    .    .    .    .    .    .    .    .    .    .      GEAR

 .    .    .    .    .    .    .    .    .    .    .    .

 .    .    .    .    CP•■—— 6" ——■• PC   .    .    .    .

 .    .    .    .    .    .    .    .    .    .    .    .

 .    .    .    .    .    .    .    .    .    .    .    .      WP

 .    .    .    .    .    .    .    .    .    .    .    .

 .    .    .    .    .    .    .    .    .    .    .    .


Center of Gear:
Pitch Circle:
Number of teeth: 36
```

Figure 11.9   The Beginning of GEAR.LSP

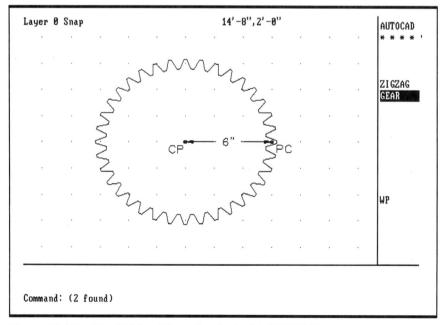

```
Layer 0 Snap                     14'-8",2'-0"                 AUTOCAD
 .    .    .    .    .    .    .    .    .    .    .           * * * * '

                                                             ZIGZAG
                                                             GEAR


                CP•■—— 6" ——■• PC


                                                             WP


Command: (2 found)
```

Figure 11.10   The Finished Gear Created with GEAR.LSP

```
(defun grinf()
; * -- Get center, pitch circle, and number of teeth
    (setq cp
        (getpoint "\nCenter of Gear: ")
    )
    (setq pc
        (getpoint cp "\nPitch Circle: ")
    )
    (setq teeth
        (getint "\nNumber of teeth: ")
    )
; * -- Error trap for incorrect number of teeth
    (while
        (< teeth 14)
        (setq teeth
            (getint "\nMust be at least 14 teeth: ")
        )
    )
) ; End of GRINF function
; * -- Define GRCALC function
(defun grcalc()
; * -- Correct pitch circle coordinates to common y-coordinate
    (setq pc
        (polar cp
            0
            (distance cp pc)
        )
    )
; * -- Formula to calculate diametral pitch
    (setq dptch
        (/ teeth (* 2.0 (distance cp pc))
        )
    )
; * -- Formula to calculate the height of a tooth

    (setq htooth
        (/ 0.32 dptch)
    )
; * -- Formula to calculate tooth extension beyond pitch circle
    (setq xtooth
        (/ 1.0 dptch)
    )
; * -- Formula to calculate the length of a tooth side.
    (setq side
        (* (/ 2.257 dptch) 1.0642)
    )
) ; End of GRCALC function
; Define GRDRW function
(defun grdrw()
; * -- Draw one half of the tooth
    (command "PLINE"
        (polar pc
            0

            xtooth
    )
    "A"
    "CE"
    cp
    "L"
    htooth
    "L"
    (polar (getvar "lastpoint")
        (dtr 160)
        side
```

Figure 11.11   The GEAR.LSP Routine

ADVANCED TECHNIQUES IN AUTOCAD

```
            )
            "A"
            "CE"
            cp
            "L"
            htooth
            ""
        )
    ; * -- Mirror the half-tooth
      (command "MIRROR"
         "L"
         ""
         pc
         cp
         "n"
      )
    ; * -- Array the tooth
      (command "ARRAY"
            "c"
            (polar pc
                   (dtr 135)
                   side
            )
            (polar pc
                   (dtr 315)
                   side
            )
            ""
            "P"
            cp
            teeth
            ""
            ""
         )
) ; End of GRDRW function
; Define C:GEAR function
(defun C:GEAR ()
; * -- Get gear information
      (grinf)
; * -- Set screen values
      (setq oldblp
            (getvar "BLIPMODE")
      )
      (setq oldech
            (getvar "CMDECHO")
      )
      (setvar "BLIPMODE" 0)
      (setvar "CMDECHO" 0)
; * -- Calculate & draw gear
      (grcalc)
      (grdrw)
; * -- Restore screen
      (setvar "BLIPMODE" oldblp)
      (setvar "CMDECHO" oldech)
) ; End of C:GEAR function
```

Figure 11.11   The GEAR.LSP Routine (continued)

The GRCALC function follows GRINF. It first corrects the location of the pitch-circle point, placing it on the same y-axis as the center point. This is done simply by referencing a new point at angle zero, with the same distance as that between the center point cp and the point pc supplied by the user. Relocating point pc at angle zero from point cp will greatly simplify the subsequent calculations, making the rest of the routine easier to write and increasing its overall speed. Notice how the POLAR function, nested inside a SETQ function, reinitializes point pc:

```
(setq pc
  (polar cp
    0
    (distance cp pc)
  )
)
```

The formulas that follow are all standard. First, the diametral pitch of the gear is calculated by dividing the diameter of the pitch circle by the number of teeth:

```
(setq dptch
  (/ teeth (* 2.0 (distance cp pc))
  )
)
```

The height of a tooth is calculated by dividing 0.32 by the diametral pitch:

```
(setq htooth
  (/ 0.32 dptch)
)
```

The amount of tooth that extends beyond the pitch circle is calculated by dividing 1 by the diametral pitch:

```
(setq xtooth
  (/ 1.0 dptch)
)
```

The length of the tooth's side is calculated by dividing 2.257 by the diametral pitch, and multiplying the result by 1.0642:

```
(setq side
  (* (/ 2.257 dptch) 1.0642)
)
```

Now that the gear elements are calculated and stored to memory variables, AutoLISP can automatically draw the gear. The GRDRW function will do this. It begins by drawing a "half-tooth." The starting point is referenced from point pc, at the angle zero, and at the distance xtooth. Literal characters, contained in quotes, are passed to AutoCAD's PLINE command: "A" to draw an arc, "CE" to reference the arc's center point as the memory variable cp, and "L" to indicate the chord length of the arc as the distance htooth.

The PLINE command continues with another "L" to indicate that a line is now drawn, and a POLAR function to reference the endpoint of the line, starting from the end of the arc at an angle of 160 degrees, with the distance defined as the length of a tooth side. Where did the 160-degree angle come from? Remember, the tooth is "lying on its side" at angle zero. To draw the correct 20-degree angle at the correct orientation, you need to draw a line from right to left (an angle of 180 degrees) minus 20 degrees, which would be 160 degrees.

To complete the half-tooth, a final arc is drawn using the command sequence used for the previous arc:

```
(command "PLINE"
  (polar pc
    0
    xtooth
  )
  "A"
  "CE"
  cp
  "L"
  htooth
  "L"
  (polar (getvar "lastpoint")
    (dtr 160)
    side
  )
  "A"
  "CE"
  cp
  "L"
  htooth
  ""
)
```

Once the half-tooth is complete, the MIRROR command makes it a whole tooth easily:

```
(command "MIRROR"
  "L"
  ""
  pc
  cp
  "n"
)
```

Once the whole tooth is drawn, the ARRAY command turns one tooth into a whole gear:

```
(command "ARRAY"
  "c"
  (polar pc
    (dtr 135)
    side
  )
  (polar pc
    (dtr 315)
    side
  )
  ""
  "P"
  cp
  teeth
  ""
  ""

)
```

The C:GEAR function uses familiar functions to change the CMDECHO and BLIPMODE values, draw the gear, and reset them. This completes the LISP routine.

You may or may not need to draw gears, but if you construct certain basic drawings that require variable parameters, or if your drawings are based on mathematical calculations, building them into a LISP routine will make your job a much simpler one. Generally speaking, if you are using a calculator to help create AutoCAD drawings, consider placing those calculations in a LISP routine instead.

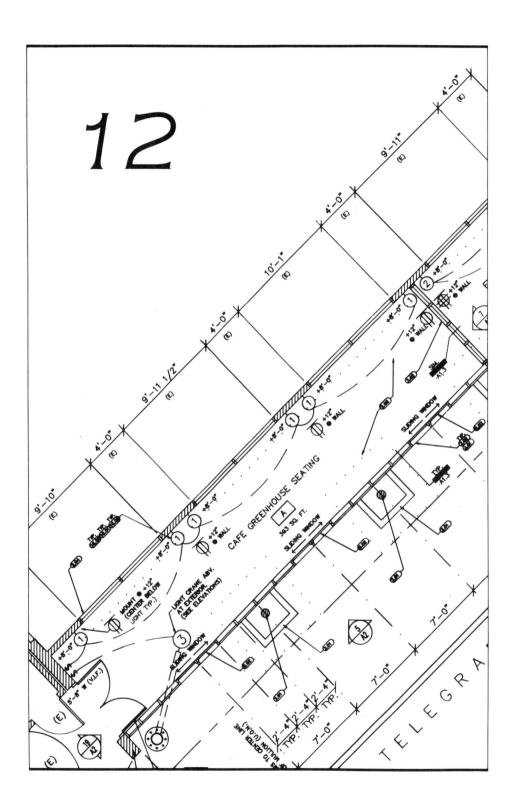

Chapter 12
Advanced AutoLISP Usage

THIS CHAPTER EXAMINES ADVANCED USES of AutoLISP: writing to and reading from files on disk, and direct access to the AutoCAD drawing database. These functions require AutoCAD Version 2.5 or later. They offer you powerful new ways to make the drawing process easier and more efficient.

WRITING INFORMATION TO DISK

The following LISP routine, STAIRS.LSP, draws a simple, straight staircase that looks realistic in 3-D. From the parameters supplied by the user, the routine draws a single step. The stair step is then defined as a block, and the block is copied at increasing elevations. This method works because AutoLISP can define unique block names automatically.

STAIRS.LSP opens and reads a file that contains the name of a block. The block name ends in a number, and it is changed simply by incrementing that number. The LISP routine then saves the block name to the file for later use. This procedure ensures that the LISP routine will always create a unique block name.

To work with the block-name file, AutoLISP must first make the file's contents available for reading or writing by *opening* the file. The Auto-LISP OPEN function is used to do this. OPEN returns a *file descriptor* if it successfully opens the file, or nil if it is not successful. DOS uses the file descriptor to locate the file once it has been opened. The file descriptor must be saved to a memory variable in order to be used inside a LISP routine.

A file may be opened in one of three *modes*, which govern how the file's data is handled:

- *Read-only* mode allows AutoCAD to read the contents of the file, but the file cannot be modified. The file must already exist on disk to be opened in this mode. For example, to open the BLOCKS.MEM file for reading, this syntax is required:

(setq x (open "BLOCKS.MEM" "r"))

As you can see, the OPEN function is followed first by the name of the file and then by a lowercase r within quotes. This second argument is the mode argument for a read-only file; it must be in lowercase.

- *Write-only* mode allows AutoCAD to open a new file and write information to it if a file with the specified name does not already exist on disk. If a file with the specified name *does* already exist, AutoCAD opens a file that overwrites the contents of the existing file. To open BLOCKS.MEM for writing, the syntax is as follows:

(setq x (open "BLOCKS.MEM" "w"))

In this example, the mode argument "r" has changed to "w," making the file a write-only file.

- *Appendable* mode allows AutoCAD to create a new file and add information to it if no file with the specified name exists on disk. If a file with the specified name does exist, AutoCAD opens the file and adds new data at the end of the file, after any data that is already there. To open BLOCKS.MEM for appending, the syntax is as follows:

(setq x (open "BLOCKS.MEM" "a"))

The mode argument "a" makes BLOCKS.MEM an appendable file.

Pseudocode for STAIRS.LSP

The pseudocode for STAIRS.LSP contains the following steps:

1. Prompt the user for the following information: the lower-left point of the staircase, the height of the riser, the depth of the step, the width of the staircase, and the total number of steps. Figure 12.1 illustrates this sequence.

2. Look on the disk for a file named BLOCKS.MEM, containing a generic block name ("$$" plus a number). If it is found, open the file as a read-only file, read the name, and increase the number by one. If it is not found, initialize a new generic block name, "$$1."

3. Initialize memory variables for all the points needed to draw the first step of the staircase.

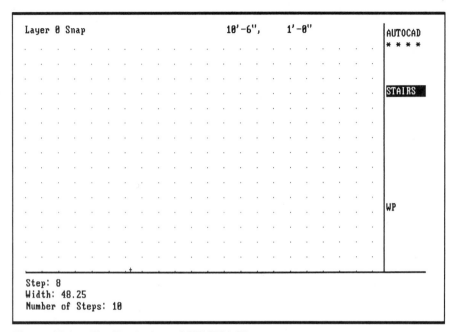

Figure 12.1 The Beginning of STAIRS.LSP

4. Initialize a counter memory variable to keep track of the number of steps drawn.

5. Initialize an elevation memory variable to keep track of the total height of the staircase.

6. Draw the first step and save it as a block with the new block name.

7. While the number of steps is less than the number requested by the user, repeat the next two steps (steps 8 and 9).

8. Update the current elevation, insertion point, and step count.

9. Insert the step block at the new insertion point.

10. When the staircase is finished, close BLOCKS.MEM if it is open.

11. Reopen BLOCKS.MEM as a write-only file, write the current generic block name to it, and close it again.

Figure 12.2 illustrates the result of this LISP routine in plan view. Figure 12.3 illustrates the same staircase in 3-D.

ADVANCED TECHNIQUES IN AUTOCAD

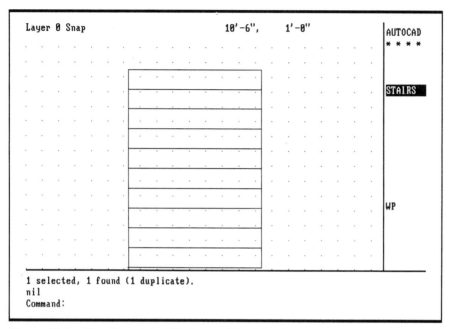

Figure 12.2 The Completed Staircase (Plan View)

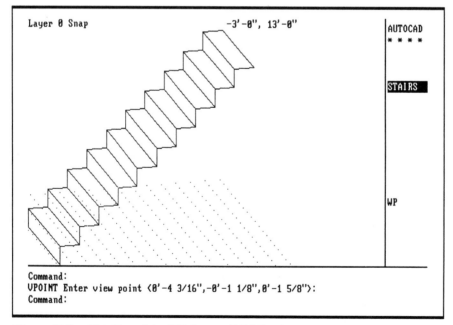

Figure 12.3 The Completed Staircase (3-D View)

The STAIRS.LSP Routine

Figure 12.4 contains the STAIRS.LSP routine. Its first function prompts the user for information in a manner similar to that of prompting functions you have seen before. The next function, STRCAL, begins by attempting to open the BLOCKS.MEM file:

```
(setq blkfil
  (open "blocks.mem" "r")
)
```

The file descriptor returned by the OPEN function is saved to the memory variable blkfil. If BLOCKS.MEM is not found on disk, the OPEN function returns nil, and blkfil also returns nil.

The next function checks to see if blkfil does not equal nil. If it doesn't, the file is read and the block name contained in the file is saved to the memory variable blk:

```
(if
  (not (equal blkfil nil))
  (setq blk
    (read-line blkfil)
  )
)
```

This is followed by a function that checks to see if blk is indeed nil. If it is, BLOCKS.MEM was never read. In such a case, blk is initialized to equal a starting block name, $$1:

```
(if
  (equal blk nil)
  (setq blk "$$1")
```

If BLOCKS.MEM was indeed read, the value of the memory variable blk must be updated. The following nested functions will do this:

```
(setq blk
  (strcat "$$"
    (itoa
      (1 +
        (atoi (substr blk 3))
      )
    )
  )
)
```

```
; * -- Get stair information
(DEFUN strinf ()
    (setq sp (getpoint "\nLower Left: "))
    (setq riser (getreal "\nRiser: "))
    (setq step (getreal "\nStep: "))
    (setq wide (getreal "\nWidth: "))
    (setq case (getint "\nNumber of Steps: "))
)
; * -- Calculate stairs
(DEFUN strcal ()
; * -- Open file containing block names
    (setq blkfil
        (open "blocks.mem" "r")
    )
; * -- If file exists, retrieve contents:
    (if
      (not (equal blkfil nil))
      (setq blk
            (read-line blkfil)
      )
    )
; * -- If file does not exist, initialize new block name:
    (if
      (equal blk nil)
      (setq blk "$$1")
; * -- Otherwise, update the block name by 1:
      (setq blk
            (strcat "$$"
                    (itoa
                        (1+
                            (atoi (substr blk 3))
                        )
                    )
            )
      )
    )
; * -- Initialize memory variables for points on first step:
    (setq pt4
        (polar sp 0 wide)
    )
    (setq uppt1
        (list (car sp)
              (cadr sp)
              riser
        )
    )
    (setq uppt2
        (list (car (polar uppt1 (dtr 90) step))
              (cadr (polar uppt1 (dtr 90) step))
              riser
        )
    )
    (setq uppt3
        (list (car (polar uppt2 0 wide))
              (cadr (polar uppt2 0 wide))
              riser
        )
    )
    (setq uppt4
        (list (car (polar uppt3 (dtr 270) step))
              (cadr (polar uppt3 (dtr 270) step))
              riser
        )
    )
```

Figure 12.4 The STAIRS.LSP Routine

```
        )
; * -- Initialize the step-count memory variable:
        (setq count 0)
; * -- Initialize the elevation memory variable:
        (setq el 0)
)
; * -- Draw the first step:
(DEFUN strdrw ()
        (command "3DFACE"
                sp
                uppt1
                uppt4
                pt4
                ""
        )
        (COMMAND "3DFACE"
                uppt1
                uppt2
                uppt3
                uppt4
                ""
        )
; * -- Make it a block:
        (COMMAND "BLOCK"
          blk
          sp
          "c"
          (polar sp (dtr 215) 0.01)
          (polar sp (dtr 45) 0.01)
          uppt3
          ""
        )
        (COMMAND "OOPS")
; * -- Update the current elevation:
        (setq el (+ el riser))
; * -- Update the current insertion point:
        (setq sp

                (list (car (polar sp (dtr 90) step))
                        (cadr (polar sp (dtr 90) step))
                        el
                )
        )
; * -- Update the step count:
        (setq count (1+ count))
) ; * -- End of STRDRW function
; * -- Build the staircase:
(DEFUN build ()
; * -- Insert the new block:
        (COMMAND "INSERT"
          blk
          sp
          1
          1
          0
        )
; * -- Update the current elevation:
        (setq el (+ el riser))
; * -- Update the current insertion point:
        (setq sp
                (list (car (polar sp (dtr 90) step))
                        (cadr (polar sp (dtr 90) step))
                        el
```

Figure 12.4 The STAIRS.LSP Routine (continued)

ADVANCED TECHNIQUES IN AUTOCAD

```
            )
        )
    ; * -- Update the step count:
        (setq count (1+ count))
    )
    ; * -- Define AutoCAD command Stairs:
    (DEFUN C:STAIRS ()
    ; * -- Get stair information:
        (strinf)
    ; * -- Set new screen values:
        (setq oldblp (getvar "BLIPMODE"))
        (setq oldech (getvar "CMDECHO"))
        (setq oldelv (getvar "ELEVATION"))
        (setvar "CMDECHO" 0)
        (setvar "BLIPMODE" 0)
        (setvar "ELEVATION" 0)
    ; * -- Calculate and draw:
        (strcal)
        (strdrw)
        (while
            (< count case)
            (build)
        )
    ; * -- Reset screen:
        (setvar "BLIPMODE" oldblp)
        (setvar "CMDECHO" oldech)
        (setvar "ELEVATION" oldelv)
    ; * -- If file was opened, close it now:
        (if
            (not (equal blkfil nil))
            (close blkfil)
        )
    ; * -- Reopen file as a write-file:
        (setq blkfil
            (open "blocks.mem" "w")
        )
    ; * -- Write last block name to file:
        (write-line blk blkfil)
    ; * -- close file again:
        (setq blkfil (close blkfil))
    ) ; End of C:STAIRS function
```

Figure 12.4   The STAIRS.LSP Routine (continued)

The deepest function returns part of the contents of memory variable blk, beginning at the third character, which is the part of the block name containing the number:

> (substr blk 3)

This string must be converted to an integer:

> (atoi (substr blk 3))

The integer must be incremented by 1:

> (1 +
>   (atoi (substr blk 3))
>)

The integer must be converted back to a string:

```
(itoa
  (1 +
    (atoi (substr blk 3))
  )
)
```

The string must then be added to the $$ symbol to form the unique block name:

```
(strcat "$$"
  (itoa
    (1 +
      (atoi (substr blk 3))
    )
  )
)
```

Finally, the new block name must be saved to the memory variable blk:

```
(setq blk
  (strcat "$$"
    (itoa
      (1 +
        (atoi (substr blk 3))
      )
    )
  )
)
); end if
```

The next function sets the lower-right point on the first step:

```
(setq pt4
  (polar sp 0 wide)
)
```

The nested functions that follow create a 3-D point based on the lower-left point entered by the user. The LIST function is used to create a list of three points: the x-coordinate of point sp, the y-coordinate of sp, and the height of the memory variable named riser, which can be used as the z-coordinate of the point. This list is saved to the memory variable uppt1:

```
(setq uppt1
```

```
(list (car sp)
  (cadr sp)
  riser
 )
)
```

Similar functions create three more 3-D points. When connected, they will form a horizontal 3-D plane representing the first step in the stair-case. These points are called uppt2, uppt3, and uppt4:

```
(setq uppt2
  (list (car (polar uppt1 (dtr 90) step))
    (cadr (polar uppt1 (dtr 90) step))
    riser
  )
)
(setq uppt3
  (list (car (polar uppt2 0 wide))
    (cadr (polar uppt2 0 wide))
    riser
  )
)
(setq uppt4
  (list (car (polar uppt3 (dtr 270) step))
    (cadr (polar uppt3 (dtr 270) step))
    riser
  )
)
```

The next two functions initialize memory variables that keep track of the number of steps inserted and the height of the staircase:

```
(setq count 0)
(setq el 0)
```

The STRDRW function begins by drawing two 3-D faces, using the points created:

```
(command "3DFACE"
  sp
  upsp
  uppt4
  pt4
  ""
)
```

```
(command "3DFACE"
  upsp
  uppt2
  uppt3
  uppt4
  ""
)
```

The faces are then saved as a block with the new block name. To be certain that both faces are found, the command references them by means of a crossing window. The corners of the crossing window are referenced in relation to the point sp. You need to use a window as the selection mechanism because the vertical face shares a common line with the horizontal face, and the window guarantees that both are selected:

```
(command "BLOCK"
  blk
  sp
  "c"
  (polar sp (dtr 215) 0.01)
  (polar sp (dtr 45) 0.01)
  uppt3
  ""
)
```

The step is erased when the block is created. The AutoCAD OOPS command returns it:

```
(command "OOPS")
```

Now that the block has been created, the value of the memory variable el is updated to reflect the current height of the staircase. The insertion point of the block is changed, and the step count is incremented by 1:

```
(setq el (+ el riser))
(setq sp
  (list (car (polar sp (dtr 90) step))
    (cadr (polar sp (dtr 90) step))
    el
  )
)

(setq count (1 + count))
```

The BUILD function inserts the block at the current insertion point, at the same scale and orientation. After insertion, the current insertion point, elevation, and step count are updated:

```
(command "INSERT"
  blk
  sp
  1
  1
  0
)
(setq el (+ el riser))
(setq sp
  (list (car (polar sp (dtr 90) step))
    (cadr (polar sp (dtr 90) step))
    el
  )
)
(setq count (1 + count))
```

The new AutoCAD STAIRS command is defined by using previously described techniques for changing the screen display and executing the new functions. A looping function builds the staircase:

```
(while
  (< count case)
  (build)
)
```

After the staircase is built, the following functions test to see if BLOCKS.MEM was opened. If the memory variable blkfil is not nil, then the file was opened as a read-only file and should now be closed:

```
(if
  (not (equal blkfil nil))
  (close blkfil)
)
```

Once the file has been closed (or if it was never opened), it can safely be opened as a write-only file, and the current generic block name can be written to it. Then the file will be closed. The value of the memory variable blkfil will be reset to nil, and the routine is complete:

```
(setq blkfil
  (open "blocks.mem" "w")
```

```
)
(write-line blk blkfil)
(setq blkfil (close blkfil))
```

Using the techniques demonstrated in this LISP routine, you can use files on disk to store any information you wish to save from drawing session to drawing session, allowing AutoCAD to "remember" information that otherwise would be lost. However, if you move around between different default subdirectories, you may create a situation in which AutoLISP cannot locate a requested file. This can be avoided by placing all such files in their own subdirectory. The OPEN function can call a file using its full path name, like this:

(setq blkfil (open "c:/acad/memfiles/blocks.mem" "r"))

This example calls BLOCKS.MEM from the subdirectory MEMFILES of the subdirectory ACAD. (Remember that the forward slash is used to separate subdirectory names in AutoLISP, since the backslash is reserved for control characters.)

A Version of STAIRS.LSP for AutoCAD 2.5 and Earlier

The version of STAIRS.LSP shown in Figure 12.5 will work in AutoCAD versions 2.18 and 2.5 +. In this version, the lower-left and lower-right points are given a thickness equal to the height of the riser; a horizontal plane is given a thickness of zero and an elevation equal to the height of the riser. These three entities are made into a block and copied. The block is elevated by repeatedly invoking the AutoCAD CHANGE command. Differences between this version and the 2.6 version are noted with the comment line "!! ver 2.18 + " in the figure.

Drawing a Spiral Staircase: SPIRAL.LSP

The LISP routine shown in Figure 12.6 draws a 3-D spiral staircase with a center pole and a handrail. It requires Version 2.6 or later. Because it uses functions you have seen before, this routine is presented with embedded comments only. Figures 12.7 through 12.10 illustrate the process of drawing a spiral staircase with SPIRAL.LSP.

While the functions in SPIRAL.LSP are interesting examples of AutoLISP's ability to read and write information from files, the technique shown in this routine has the potential for a more powerful application: you can use it to import and export entire ASCII text files to and from

```
(DEFUN strinf ()
   (setq sp (getpoint "\nLower Left: "))
   (setq riser (getreal "\nRiser: "))
   (setq step (getreal "\nStep: "))
   (setq wide (getreal "\nWidth: "))
   (setq case (getint "\nNumber of Steps: "))
   (setq blkfil
        (open "blocks.mem" "r")
   )
   (if
     (not (equal blkfil nil))
     (setq blk
          (read-line blkfil)
     )
   )
)
(DEFUN strcal ()
   (if
     (equal blk nil)
     (setq blk
          "$$1"
     )
     (setq blk
          (strcat "$$"
                   (itoa
                       (1+
                           (atoi (substr blk 3))
                       )
                   )
          )
     )
   )
   (setq uppt2 (polar sp (dtr 90) step))       ; !! Ver. 2.18+
   (setq uppt3 (polar uppt2 0 wide))           ; !! Ver. 2.18+
   (setq uppt4 (polar uppt3 (dtr 270) step))   ; !! Ver. 2.18+
   (setq pt4 (polar sp 0 wide))
   (setq count 0)
   (setq el 0)
)
(DEFUN strdrw ()
   (COMMAND "POINT"                             ; !! Ver. 2.18+
    sp
   )
   (COMMAND "POINT"                             ; !! Ver. 2.18+
    pt4
   )
   (COMMAND "CHANGE"                            ; !! Ver. 2.18+
     sp
     pt4
     ""
     "e"
     el
     riser
   )
   (COMMAND "PLINE"                             ; !! Ver. 2.18+
    sp
    uppt2
    uppt3
    uppt4
    "c"
   )
   (COMMAND "CHANGE"                            ; !! Ver. 2.18+
     "L"
     ""
```

Figure 12.5   The STAIRS.LSP Routine for AutoCAD 2.5 and Earlier

```
        "e"
        riser
        0
     )
     (COMMAND "BLOCK"
        blk
        sp
        "w"                              ; !! Ver. 2.18+
        sp
        uppt3
        ""
     )
     (COMMAND "OOPS")
     (setq el (+ el riser))
     (setq sp (polar sp (dtr 90) step))
     (setq count (1+ count))
)
(DEFUN build ()
     (COMMAND "INSERT"
        blk
        sp
        1
        1
        0
     )
     (command "CHANGE"                   ; !! Ver. 2.18+
        "L"
        ""
        "E"
        el
        0
     )
     (setq el (+ el riser))
     (setq sp (polar sp (dtr 90) step))  ; !! Ver. 2.18+
     (setq count (1+ count))
)
(DEFUN C:STAIRS ()
     (strinf)
     (setq oldblp (getvar "BLIPMODE"))
     (setq oldech (getvar "CMDECHO"))
     (setvar "CMDECHO" 0)
     (setvar "BLIPMODE" 0)
     (strcal)
     (strdrw)
     (while (< count case) (build))
     (setvar "BLIPMODE" oldblp)
     (setvar "CMDECHO" oldech)
     (if
        (not (equal blkfil nil))
        (close blkfil)
     )
     (setq blkfil
          (open "blocks.mem" "w")
     )
     (write-line blk blkfil)
     (close blkfil)
)
```

Figure 12.5   The STAIRS.LSP Routine for AutoCAD 2.5 and Earlier (continued)

AutoCAD. To accomplish such text exporting, you must first become acquainted with other data types used by AutoLISP: the entity name, association list, and selection set, as well as a few functions that are specifically predefined for them. These data types greatly expand the

```
(DEFUN spinfo ()
   (setq cp (getpoint "\nCenter of Spiral Staircase:"))
   (setq sp (getpoint "\nLower Left Corner of Staircase:"))
   (setq riser (getreal "\nRiser:"))
   (setq step (getreal "\nStep:"))
   (setq wide (getreal "\nWidth:"))
   (setq case (getint "\nNo. of Steps:"))
   (setq hrl (getreal "\nHeight of Handrail: "))
) ; End of SPINFO function
; * -- Open block name file or initialize block name, calculate
;       additional points needed for 3-D visualization, and
;       initialize counters for loop:
(DEFUN spcalc ()
   (setq blkfil
         (open "blocks.mem" "r")
   )
   (if
     (not (equal blkfil nil))
     (setq blk
           (read-line blkfil)
     )
   )
   (if
     (equal blk nil)
     (setq blk
           "$$1"
     )
     (setq blk
           (strcat "$$"
                   (itoa
                       (1+
                          (atoi (substr blk 3))
                       )
                   )
           )
     )
   )
   (setq pt4 (polar sp 0 wide))
   (setq uppt1 (list (car sp) (cadr sp) riser))
   (setq uppt4 (list (car pt4) (cadr pt4) riser))
   (setq count 0)
   (setq el riser)
; * -- Draw a scratch line and arc, which locate a point that will
;       determine the angle of back step line:
   (command "LINE"
     sp
     pt4
     ""
   )

   (command "ARC"
    (polar sp
          (angle sp pt4)
          (/ (distance sp pt4) 2.0)
    )
   "C"
   cp
   "l"
   step
   )
   (command "LINE"
   ""
   0
   ""
```

Figure 12.6 The SPIRAL.LSP Routine

```
  )
; * -- Obtain the critical reference point:
  (setq rp (getvar "LASTPOINT"))
; * -- Erase the scratch lines:
  (command "ERASE"
  rp
  ""
  )
  (command "ERASE"
    rp
    (polar sp
          (angle sp pt4)
          (/ (distance sp pt4) 3.0)
    )
    ""
  )
; * -- Obtain the angle of the back step line
  (setq diag (angle cp rp))
; * -- Initialize another counter variable, which will be used to
;      increment the succeeding angles at which additional steps
are drawn:
  (setq incr diag)
; * -- Obtain additional drawing points based on back step angle:
  (setq uppt3
      (list (car  (polar cp diag (distance cp pt4)))
            (cadr (polar cp diag (distance cp pt4)))
            riser
      )
  )
  (setq uppt2
      (list (car  (polar cp diag (distance cp sp)))
            (cadr (polar cp diag (distance cp sp)))
            riser
      )
  )

; * -- Obtain drawing points for a handrail section:
  (setq hrlpt3
      (list (car (polar uppt4
                        (angle uppt4 uppt1)
                        (/ (distance uppt4 uppt1) 10)
                  )
            )
            (cadr (polar uppt4
                        (angle uppt4 uppt1)
                        (/ (distance uppt4 uppt1) 10)
                  )
            )
            (+ riser hrl)
      )
  )
  (setq hrlpt4
      (list (car (polar uppt3
                        (angle uppt3 uppt2)
                        (/ (distance uppt3 uppt2) 10)
                  )
            )
            (cadr (polar uppt3
                        (angle uppt3 uppt2)
                        (/ (distance uppt3 uppt2) 10)
                  )
            )
```

Figure 12.6   The SPIRAL.LSP Routine (continued)

```
                        (+ riser riser hrl)
            )
        )
        (setq hrlpt1
            (list (car (polar hrlpt3
                            (angle hrlpt3 hrlpt4)
                            (/ (distance hrlpt3 hrlpt4) 2)
                        )
                  )
                  (cadr (polar hrlpt3
                            (angle hrlpt3 hrlpt4)
                            (/ (distance hrlpt3 hrlpt4) 2)
                        )
                  )
                  (+ riser (/ riser 2) hrl)
            )
        )
        (setq hrlpt2
            (list (car (polar hrlpt3
                            (angle hrlpt3 hrlpt4)
                            (/ (distance hrlpt3 hrlpt4) 2)
                        )
                  )
                  (cadr (polar hrlpt3
                            (angle hrlpt3 hrlpt4)
                            (/ (distance hrlpt3 hrlpt4) 2)
                        )
                  )
                  riser
            )
        )
; * -- Draw the step:
    (command "3DFACE"
      uppt1
      uppt2
      uppt3
      uppt4
      ""
    )
; * -- Draw the riser:
    (command "3DFACE"
      sp
      uppt1
      uppt4
      pt4
      ""
    )
; * -- Draw a handrail section:
    (command "3DLINE"
      hrlpt1
      hrlpt2
      ""
    )
    (command "3DLINE"
      hrlpt3
      hrlpt4
      ""
    )
; * -- Turn the step, riser, and handrail section into a block:
    (command "BLOCK"
      blk
      sp
      "c"
```

Figure 12.6   The SPIRAL.LSP Routine (continued)

```
            (polar sp (dtr 215) 0.1)
            (polar pt4 (dtr 90) (distance uppt4 uppt3))
        ""
        )
        (command "OOPS")
        (setq count (1+ count))
        (setq diag2
            (angle uppt1 uppt2)
        )
        (setq isd
            (distance uppt1 uppt2)
        )
        (setq sp
                (list
                        (car (polar sp diag2 isd))
                        (cadr (polar sp diag2 isd))
                        riser
                )
        )
; * -- Convert the value of diag to degrees -- to be used as the
;       insertion angle in the upcoming Insert command:
        (setq insang (* (/ diag pi) 180)
        )
; * -- Update the elevation of the staircase
        (setq riser (+ riser el))
) ; End of SPCALC function
; * -- Insert the block, update the insertion point, and
;       increment all counters:
(DEFUN sbuild ()
    (command "INSERT"
    blk
    sp
    ""
    ""
    insang
    )
    (setq diag2 (+ diag2 incr))
    (setq sp
            (list
                    (car (polar sp diag2 isd))
                    (cadr (polar sp diag2 isd))
                    riser
            )
    )
    (setq diag (+ diag incr))
    (setq insang (* (/ diag pi) 180))
    (setq count (1+ count))
    (setq riser (+ riser el))
) ; End of SBUILD function
; * -- Draw the centerpole:
(DEFUN pole ()
    (command "CIRCLE"
    cp
    (polar cp 0 (/ (distance cp sp) 10))
    )
    (command "CHANGE"
    "L"
    ""
    "p"
    "e"
    0
    "th"
    (+ riser 65)
```

Figure 12.6   The SPIRAL.LSP Routine (continued)

```
       " "
     )
) ; End of POLE function
; * -- New AutoCAD command SPIRAL:
(DEFUN C:SPIRAL ()
   (setq oldblp (getvar "BLIPMODE"))
   (setq oldech (getvar "CMDECHO"))
   (setq oldelv (getvar "ELEVATION"))
   (setvar "BLIPMODE" 0)
   (setvar "CMDECHO" 0)
   (setvar "ELEVATION" 0)
   (spinfo)
   (spcalc)
   (while (< count case) (sbuild))
   (pole)
   (setvar "BLIPMODE" oldblp)
   (setvar "CMDECHO" oldech)
   (setvar "ELEVATION" oldelv)
; * -- Close BLOCKS.MEM if necessary:
   (if
      (not (equal blkfil nil))
      (close blkfil)
   )
; * -- Write block name to BLOCKS.MEM and close it:
   (setq blkfil
      (open "blocks.mem" "w")
   )
   (write-line blk blkfil)
   (close blkfil)
) ; End of C:SPIRAL function
```

Figure 12.6   The SPIRAL.LSP Routine (continued)

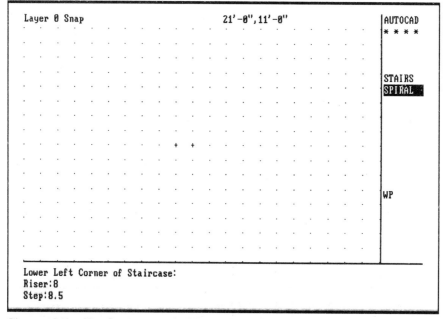

Figure 12.7   The Beginning of SPIRAL.LSP

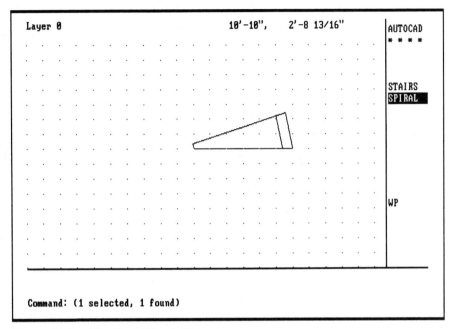

Figure 12.8 The First Step Is Drawn

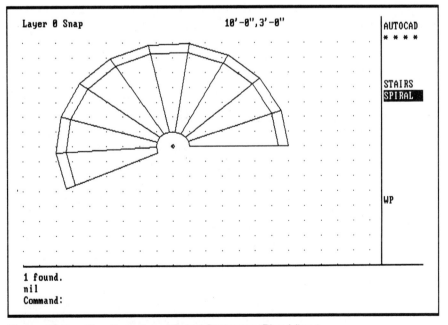

Figure 12.9 The Completed Spiral Staircase (Plan View)

ADVANCED TECHNIQUES IN AUTOCAD

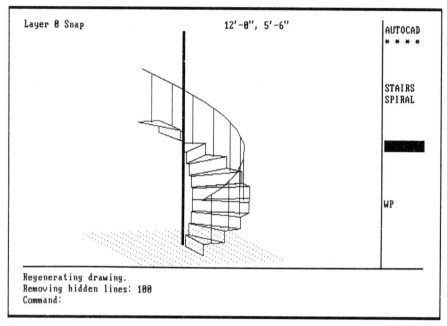

```
Layer 0 Snap                    12'-0",  5'-6"              AUTOCAD
                                                           * * * *


                                                           STAIRS
                                                           SPIRAL




                                                           WP




Regenerating drawing.
Removing hidden lines: 100
Command:
```

Figure 12.10   The Completed Spiral Staircase (3-D View)

power of AutoLISP, allowing you a variety of new ways to modify drawings and to create unique AutoCAD commands.

AUTOCAD'S ENTITY DATABASE

All the various AutoCAD drawing elements contained in an AutoCAD
drawing—lines, arcs, blocks, text, and so on—are stored in a specialized
database. They are called *entities*, so the database is referred to as the
entity database. AutoCAD Version 2.5 and later versions include powerful, specialized AutoLISP functions that allow you to directly access and
modify AutoCAD's entity database, selecting items to be modified
either individually or in groups. This can speed up your work by reducing
the time you spend in the selection process, or it can free you to do
other work while AutoCAD searches your drawing file and makes a
series of repetitive changes for you.

Entity Names

Each entity in the database is automatically assigned a unique *entity
name* at the time it is created. The entity name is actually an eight-digit

number in hexadecimal notation. The internal structure of entity names and their assignment to entities is completely transparent to the user.

Linked to each entity name is any information required to produce that entity on the screen or plotting device. For example, a new line drawn in AutoCAD would automatically be given a unique entity name. That name would be associated with the type of entity it is (LINE); the layer it is on; its line type (if not the default for the layer); its starting point; its endpoint; its elevation (if any); its thickness (if any); and its color (if not the default for the layer).

Association Lists

Special functions in AutoLISP allow each entity in the database to be extracted and returned in the form of an *association list*. An association list is a list of other lists, called *sublists*, which contain the data necessary to produce the entity. The first item in a sublist is a number, called a *group code*, that identifies a particular property of the entity. For example, the first sublist in any association list is the entity name itself. The entity name always has a group code of − 1. Given an entity name of 60000014, the sublist for the entity name would look like this:

(-1 . <Entity name: 60000014>)

The use of group codes allows AutoCAD to identify any particular sublist, regardless of the order in which it appears within the association list. Some group codes are common to all drawing-entity association lists. They are as follows:

−1 . *Entity name*
0 . *Entity type*
6 . *Entity line type (present when not default)*
8 . *Layer name*
38 . *Entity elevation*
39 . *Entity thickness*
62 . *Color number (present when not default)*

Most sublists contain only two items of information: the group code, and the specific item of drawing information associated with the group code. When sublists contain only two items, the two items are separated by a dot, the period that you see in each sublist above. Sublists that have this dot are called *dotted pairs*. Dotted pairs take up less space in memory than ordinary lists.

Some sublists contain coordinate-point information, and thus will contain three or four items of information: the group code, the x-coordinate, the y-coordinate, and perhaps the z-coordinate. A dotted pair will not work in this case, so these sublists appear as ordinary lists of data. The group codes for coordinate-point information are group codes 10 through 16. They look like the following example, which shows a starting point at 12.5,12.5:

(10 12.500000 12.500000)

By manipulating association lists and their sublists, it is possible to do a variety of useful things in AutoCAD. For example, you can do the following:

- Locate all entities on a given layer and move them to a new layer

- Change all entities with a given thickness or elevation to a new thickness or elevation

- Find entities with one common property and change a different property to a common value; that is, find all text and change its style

These global changes can be made without going through the complex selection processes at the AutoCAD command prompt.

Summary of Entity Association Lists

Table 12.1 summarizes the group codes and sublists found on individual AutoCAD entity association lists, in addition to the common group codes just listed. Not all sublists shown here will be returned for each entity name. AutoCAD maintains only the information used to produce a particular entity; if an individual group code is unnecessary or is assigned by default (for example, a default color that is assigned by the LAYER command), that sublist may not appear as part of the individual association list. Group codes that display as dotted pairs are shown with a "Yes" between the group code and its data.

The following example is an association list for a line that begins at point 1,1 and ends at point 240,240. The line is located on the Walls layer, has a thickness of 10 feet, and has an elevation of zero. It is the only green line on a white layer. Notice how nested parentheses are used to define each sublist within the single set of parentheses that define the association list.

```
(
    (–1 . <Entity name: 60000014>)
    ( 0 . "LINE")
```

Group Code	Dotted Pair	Sublist
0	Yes	"ARC"
10	No	Center point
40	Yes	Radius
50	Yes	Starting angle
51	Yes	Ending angle
0	Yes	"ATTDEF" (Block attribute definition)
1	Yes	Default value
2	Yes	Tag
3	Yes	Prompt
7	Yes	Text style
10	No	Text starting point
11	No	Text alignment point (if aligned)
40	Yes	Text height
41	Yes	Text width factor
50	Yes	Text rotation
51	Yes	Text oblique angle
70	Yes	Text attribute flags (1 = invisible, 2 = constant, 3 = verify)
71	Yes	Text generation flags (1 = mirror on, 4 = upside-down)
72	Yes	Text justification codes (0 = left, 1 = centered, 2 = right, 3 = aligned, 4 = "M" centered, 5 = "F" fit)
0	Yes	"ATTRIB" (Block attribute)
1	Yes	Attribute value
2	Yes	Tag
7	Yes	Text style
10	No	Text starting point
11	No	Text alignment point

Table 12.1   Group Codes and Sublists Found on Entity Association Lists

Group Code	Dotted Pair	Sublist
		"ATTRIB" continued
40	Yes	Text height
41	Yes	Text width factor
50	Yes	Text rotation
51	Yes	Text oblique angle
70	Yes	Text attribute flags (1 = invisible, 2 = constant, 3 = verify)
71	Yes	Text generation flags (1 = mirror on, 4 = upside-down)
72	Yes	Text justification codes (0 = left, 1 = centered, 2 = right, 3 = aligned, 4 = "M" centered, 5 = "F" fit)
0	Yes	"CIRCLE"
10	No	Center point
40	Yes	Radius
0	Yes	"DIMENSION"
1	Yes	Dimension text
2	Yes	Pseudo-block name
10	No	Starting point
11	No	Text middle point
12	No	Continue point
13	No	Line and angle point 1
14	No	Line and angle point 2
15	No	Diameter, radius, or angle point
16	No	Angle-dimension arc point
40	Yes	Leader length
50	Yes	Angle (in radians)
70	Yes	Dimension type (0 = horizontal or vertical, 1 = aligned, 2 = angular, 3 = diameter, 4 = radius)

Table 12.1   Group Codes and Sublists Found on Entity Association Lists (continued)

Group Code	Dotted Pair	Sublist
0	Yes	"INSERT" *(For blocks)*
2	Yes	*Block name*
10	No	*Insertion point*
41	Yes	*x-scale*
42	Yes	*y-scale*
44	Yes	*z-scale*
44	Yes	*Column spacing (Minsert)*
45	Yes	*Row spacing (Minsert)*
50	Yes	*Angle (In radians)*
66	Yes	*Block attributes present*
70	Yes	*Number of columns (Minsert)*
71	Yes	*Number of rows (Minsert)*
0	Yes	"LINE"
10	No	*Starting point*
11	No	*Endpoint*
0	Yes	"POINT"
10	No	*Point*
0	Yes	"POLYLINE"
10	No	*Starting point*
40	Yes	*Starting width*
41	Yes	*Ending width*
66	Yes	*Attributes (for example, vertices are present)*
70	Yes	*PLINE flags (1 = closed, 2 = fit curve added)*
0	Yes	"SOLID"
10	No	*First point*
11	No	*Second point*
12	No	*Third point*
13	No	*Fourth point (if any)*

Table 12.1 Group Codes and Sublists Found on Entity Association Lists (continued)

Group Code	Dotted Pair	Sublist
0	Yes	"TEXT"
1	Yes	Text string
10	No	Starting point
11	No	Align point (if aligned)
40	Yes	Height
41	Yes	Width factor
50	Yes	Rotation
51	Yes	Oblique angle
70	Yes	Attribute flags (1 = invisible, 2 = constant, 3 = verify)
71	Yes	Generation flags (1 = mirror on, 4 = upside-down)
72	Yes	Justification codes (0 = left, 1 = centered, 2 = right, 3 = aligned, 4 = "M" centered, 5 = "F" fit)
0	Yes	"VERTEX" (Used with "POLYLINE")
10	No	Vertex point
40	Yes	Starting width
41	Yes	Ending width
42	Yes	Bulge (if fit curve was applied)
50	Yes	Tangent (if fit curve was applied)
70	Yes	Vertex flags (1 = extra vertex created by fit curve, 2 = fit-curve tangent defined)

Table 12.1   Group Codes and Sublists Found on Entity Association Lists (continued)

```
( 8 . "WALLS")
(10 1.000000 1.000000)
(11 240.000000 240.000000)
(39 . 120.000000)
(62 . 3)
)
```

ENTITY ACCESS FUNCTIONS

Since association lists are structured as lists of data enclosed within matched sets of parentheses, they can be used and modified by Auto-LISP functions. Some functions have been predefined to act exclusively upon association lists. These functions begin with the letters ENT.

Retrieving and acting upon entity association lists is a three-step process. First, the entity name is retrieved from the drawing database. Second, sublists associated with the entity name are retrieved and modified by referencing the appropriate group code. Third, the entire association list is updated in the drawing database to include the changed entities. The functions that act upon entity association lists are presented in the following sections.

Entity Name Functions

The functions in this section provide you with a variety of ways to retrieve a single entity name, either by analyzing the drawing database and automatically selecting a specific entity, or by allowing the user to select a single entity from the screen while in the Drawing Editor.

ENTNEXT   The ENTNEXT function has the syntax

(entnext [*entity-name*])

It returns the name of the first entity following the entity name given as the argument of the function. By repeatedly selecting the next entity and storing its name to a memory variable, this function allows you to go through the drawing database sequentially, entity by entity.

ENTNEXT returns the first entity name in the database if it is called without arguments. For example, given three entities in a drawing database, you can call each one sequentially with the following series of functions:

(setq first-one (entnext))
(setq next-one (entnext first-one))
(setq next-one (entnext next-one))
(setq next-one (entnext next-one))

This sequence stores the entity name of the first entity found in the database to the memory variable first-one. The next three functions continually update the contents of next-one by binding it sequentially to the following entity names. It would be possible, therefore, to use other functions in between these to analyze and modify the entities, because next-one is bound to them.

ENTLAST has the syntax

(entlast)

It returns the entity name of the last entity in the drawing database. This has the same effect as selecting the Last option from AutoCAD's "Select objects:" prompt. ENTLAST is often used to select and store an entity that has just been created by a previous command or function. Usually, an entity name returned by this function has a memory variable bound to it, as in

(setq x (entlast))

Here, memory variable x would contain the entity name. This variable could be passed as an argument to other AutoLISP functions that expect object selection.

ENTSEL has the syntax

(entsel *prompt*)

It allows the interactive selection of an entity that is visible on the screen. You must select the entity by picking a point—window and crossing options are not allowed. The function displays the prompt argument if one is given, and pauses for the user to supply a single point.

When an entity is selected using this function, both the entity name and the coordinates of the selection point are saved as a list. For example, imagine a line drawn from point 0,0 to point 5,5. ENTSEL could be used to retrieve that entity at point 5,5 as follows:

(setq x (entsel "Please pick the endpoint of the line: "))

In response to the prompt, the user could either enter 5,5 as the point pick for selecting the line or use the OSNAP override ENDP to snap to the desired point. In either case, memory variable x would be bound to the following list:

(<Entity name: *nnnnnnnn*> (5.000000 5.000000))

Here, n represents the numbers that make up the entity name.

Once a memory variable is bound to a list of this type, the memory variable may be used as a response to any of AutoCAD's object selection prompts. AutoCAD will interpret the memory variable as an entity selection that was made by picking the coordinate points contained in the list. The first item on the list, the entity name, can be extracted from the list by means of the CAR function, and the entity name can be used in response to functions that require an entity name argument. The point information can also be extracted from the list by means of CADR. It can be operated upon like any other point, using AutoLISP functions, and it can be stored in a memory variable of its own.

Association List Functions

After entity names have been returned by the previous functions, the following functions will act upon them, either to extract their association lists, delete them altogether, or make changes to them.

ENTGET   has the syntax

(entget [*entity name*])

It is frequently used after an entity name has been selected and stored in a memory variable. This function returns a list of all the sublists in an entity's association list. For example, the following function will bind the memory variable x to the full association list of a screen entity selected by the user:

(setq x (entget (setq y (entsel "\nSelect an object: "))))

The following functions will then store the entity name to z and the selection point to y:

(setq z (car y))
(setq y (cadr y))

ENTDEL   has the syntax

(entdel [*entity name*])

It finds the entity name referenced as the function argument and deletes it from the database. If the entity was previously deleted, ENTDEL restores it to the drawing database. Thus, ENTDEL acts as a toggle between deleting and restoring an entity. This function restores only the entities that have been deleted during the current drawing session.

Certain entities (for example, polyline vertices and block attributes) are linked to main entities and cannot be deleted or restored with ENTDEL. Only the main entities (Polyline and Insert, for example) can be deleted and restored with this function.

ENTMOD   has the syntax

(entmod [*association list*])

It updates information in the drawing database. The function's argument must be an association list with an entity name that is present in the drawing database. ENTMOD will replace the entity data present in the drawing database with the entity data referenced as its argument. If ENTMOD is given an argument that is not a valid association list, or if the entity name found in the association list does not match an entity name in the drawing database, ENTMOD will return only nil.

Functions for Changing Sublists

The following functions are general AutoLISP functions that can be used at any time. However, you will find that they are especially useful for retrieving and modifying sublist information.

ASSOC   has the syntax

(assoc *item sublist*)

It searches an association list, examining the first item in each sublist until it finds an item that matches the item supplied as the first argument. It then returns the entire sublist. For example, consider the following association list:

```
(
    (-1 . <Entity name: 60000014>)
    ( 0 . "LINE")
    ( 8 . "WALLS")
    (10 1.000000 1.000000)
    (11 240.000000 240.000000)
    (39 . 120.000000)
    (62 . 3)
)
```

Assume that this association list is stored in a memory variable named x. The following function will return the sublist containing the starting point of the line:

(assoc 10 x)

This function returns

(10 1.000000 1.000000)

Since the coordinate information is the second item found in the sublist, you can use the CADR function to extract it, as in the following example:

(setq sp (cadr (assoc 10 x)))

Here, the ASSOC function is nested with the CADR function, extracting the starting point from the association list stored in memory variable x. Both of these functions are nested with a SETQ function, which automatically stores the starting point returned by CADR to the memory variable sp. This function returns

(1.000000 1.000000)

The technique of using ASSOC with CADR will extract the data information in any sublist of an association list.

CONS has the syntax

(cons [*first item*] [*second item*])

It can be used to construct dotted pairs. When used in this fashion, it requires two arguments, each an individual item of information. For example,

(cons 7 "STANDARD")

returns

(7 . "STANDARD")

CONS can also be used to construct lists by adding new items of information to the beginning of existing lists. For example, consider the following sequence of functions:

(setq x '(1.000000 1.000000))
(setq x (cons 10 x))

This sequence returns

(10 1.000000 1.000000)

LIST has the syntax

(list *items*)

It is similar to CONS, but it cannot be used to construct a dotted pair. In general, the LIST function takes individual items of information and returns them as a single list. For example,

(list 10 1.000000 1.000000)

returns

(10 1.000000 1.000000)

The items of information that LIST will use can be another list or lists, including dotted pairs. LIST will then return a list within a list. For example,

```
(list
    '(-1 . <Entity name: 60000014)
    '(0 . "POINT")
    '(10 1.000000 1.000000)
)
```

returns the following association list:

```
(
    (-1 . <Entity name: 60000014>)
    (0 . "POINT")
    (10 1.000000 1.000000)
)
```

SUBST has the syntax

(subst *'new 'old list*)

You have seen the SUBST function before as a function that can edit string information stored as a list. SUBST searches a list, referenced as its third argument, and replaces every occurrence of the second argument (*old*) with the first argument (*new*).

This is useful when you are modifying the data in an association list. For example, the following function will change the starting point of the previous association list from 1,1 to 2,2:

(subst '(2.0 2.0) '(1.0 1.0) (assoc 10 x))

Listing the contents of the association list will show how it has changed:

```
(
    (-1 . <Entity name: 60000014>)
    ( 0 . "LINE")
    ( 8 . "WALLS")
    (10 2.000000 2.000000)
    (11 240.000000 240.000000)
    (39 . 120.000000)
    (62 . 3)
)
```

Selection-Set Functions

A *selection set* is a group of entity names that is given a name of its own. Once they are given a group name, the entities can be acted upon as a whole. This process is similar to the windowing mechanism used in response to AutoCAD's "Select objects:" prompt. The functions presented here have been predefined to work specifically with selection sets.

SSGET   has the syntax

(ssget [*selection mode*] [*point*] [*point*])

It pauses and allows the user to select a group of one or more entities. If SSGET is called without arguments, AutoLISP uses AutoCAD's "Select objects:" prompt. The user is free to use windows, crossing, add, and remove options at will, as is the case whenever responding to this prompt.

If SSGET is called with an optional selection-mode argument, it is no longer interactive and will automatically select entities based on the particular mode used. The mode arguments are as follows:

- **(ssget "L")** selects the last entity in the database.

- **(ssget "P")** reselects the previously selected set.

- **(ssget '(*point*))** selects the entity that is passing through the quoted coordinate point. Do not use this except as a last resort. AutoLISP sometimes will select the incorrect object by quoting a coordinate point if other objects are close by.

- **(ssget "C" '(*point1*) '(*point2*))** selects entities crossing a window with opposite corners from *point1* to *point2*.

- **(ssget "W" '(*point1*) '(*point2*))** selects entities contained within a window with opposite corners of *point1* and *point2*.

AutoCAD commands that use the "Select objects:" selection mechanism will accept a memory variable that contains a selection set, if selection by the Last option (L) is also valid at the time. This is the same as individually selecting the entities in the selection set.

SSLENGTH   has the syntax

(sslength [*selection set*])

It returns an integer that is equal to the number of entities in the selection set. If the user has selected the same entity more than once, the selection set will contain only one reference to that entity.

SSNAME has the syntax

> (ssname [*selection set*] [*integer*])

It is used to retrieve specific entity names from the selection set. Once an entity name is retrieved, it can be acted upon like any other entity name.

Entity names in selection sets are numbered with integers, starting with integer zero. The first argument of SSNAME is the name of the selection set being sought. The second argument is the number of the entity within the selection set. If the number is out of range, this function returns nil.

SSADD has the syntax

> (ssadd [*entity name*] [*selection set*])

It adds an entity name to a selection set. This is the basic means of constructing and modifying selection sets.

SSADD can be called without the name of a selection set. In such a case, this function creates a new selection that contains the name of the single entity. If SSADD is called with no arguments, a new selection set is created, but it contains no entities. This selection set can have entities added to it with subsequent SSADD calls.

SSADD returns the name of the updated selection set. If a referenced entity is already contained in the selection set, SSADD does nothing.

SSDEL has the syntax

> (ssdel [*entity name*] [*selection set*])

It deletes an entity name from a selection set. If the entity is not a member of the selection set, SSDEL returns nil.

SSMEMB has the syntax

> (ssmemb [*entity name*] [*selection set*])

It is a logical function that determines if an entity name is a member of a specific selection set. If it is, the function returns the entity name. If not, the function returns nil.

Fundamental Entity Modification Routines

The following routine prompts the user to select a line and a new starting point, and changes the starting point of the line:

```
(defun C:NSP( )
  (setq oldech (getvar "CMDECHO"))
  (setvar "CMDECHO" 0)
  (setq obj (car (entsel "\nSelect a line: ")))
  (setq nsp (getpoint "\nSelect a new starting point: "))
  (setq alist
    (subst (list 10 (car nsp) (cadr nsp))
      (assoc 10 (entget obj))
      (entget obj)
    )
  )
  (entmod alist)
  (setvar "CMDECHO" oldech)
)
```

The first function in this routine defines a new AutoCAD command, NSP. The second function stores the current value of the command echo; the third turns it off. The fourth function prompts the user to select a line and, by means of the CAR function, stores the entity name in the memory variable obj. The fifth function prompts the user and stores a new starting point to the memory variable nsp.

SUBST is the key function in this routine. It substitutes the value of nsp for the starting point of the selected object. The first argument is the new data: the LIST function creates a list of the code 10 group, the x-coordinate of nsp (extracted by applying the CAR function to nsp), and the y-coordinate of nsp (extracted by applying the CADR function to nsp). The second argument is the old data. This argument uses the ENTGET function to extract the association list for the entity name stored in the memory variable obj. Next, it uses the ASSOC function to extract the starting-point sublist from the association list. This becomes the argument for the old data in the SUBST function.

The third argument of the SUBST function is simply the association list extracted from memory variable obj by means of the ENTGET function. Once the contents of the association list have been changed, the ENTMOD function, with memory variable obj as its argument, updates the drawing database and shows the line beginning at the new starting point.

ADVANCED TECHNIQUES IN AUTOCAD

The routine shown in Figure 12.11 changes all of the text in a drawing to a new text style. Comments have been added to explain new lines. If the user enters a nonexistent text style in response to the NEWSTYLE command, it will do nothing, because all ENTMOD calls will return nil.

```
(defun update()
; * -- This function uses the CONS function to update group code 7
;       of a particular association list. The memory variable newst
;       contains the value of the new style. Memory variable alist
;       contains the association list:
    (setq alist
            (subst (cons 7 newst)
                   (assoc 7 alist)
                   alist
            )
    )
; * -- The new association list replaces the old:
    (entmod alist)
; * -- The routine now extracts the next entity name in the drawing
;       database:
    (setq ename (entnext ename))
; * -- If the value of ename is nil, you are at the end of the
;       drawing database. Otherwise, extract the new association list
;       and store it to memory variable alist:
    (if (/= ename nil)
        (setq alist (entget ename))
    )
) ; end of UPDATE function
(defun next()
; * -- This function simply skips to the next entity name in the
;       drawing database and updates memory variable alist:
    (setq ename (entnext ename))
    (if (/= ename nil)
        (setq alist (entget ename))
    )
) ; End of NEXT function
(defun C:NEWSTYLE()
; * -- Store and turn off command echo:
    (setq oldech (getvar "CMDECHO"))
    (setvar "CMDECHO" 0)
; * -- Prompt for new style:
    (setq newst (getstring "\nNew Style for All Text: "))
; * -- Get first entity in the drawing database. Store the entity
;       name to ename and its association list to alist. This is done
;       with a single nested function:
    (setq alist (entget (setq ename (entnext))))
; * -- While memory variable ename is not nil, you are not at the
;       end of the drawing database. Loop until ename is nil,
;       meaning you've reached the end:
    (while (/= ename nil)
; * -- Check the value of group code zero. If "TEXT" is associated
;       with it, perform the change, otherwise skip to the next entity:
            (if (= "TEXT" (cdr (assoc 0 alist)))
                (update)
                (next)
            )
    ) ; end of WHILE function
; * -- Reset the command echo to original value:
    (setvar "CMDECHO" oldech)
) ; End of C:NEWSTYLE function
```

Figure 12.11   The NEWSTYLE.LSP Routine

AutoLISP Routines Using Selection Sets

Figure 12.12 shows a variation on the NEWSTYLE routine. In this variation, the user may select a portion of the drawing with windows, crossing, individual selection, and so on. All text entities within the window will then be changed to the new style, leaving any text outside the window, and any nontext entities, unchanged. Comments are added where this version differs from the earlier version.

The chief advantage in using LISP routines of this type is that they reduce the time spent selecting objects with common properties from a complex drawing. The user can simply window a group of objects and have only those with specific drawing properties changed.

By varying this LISP routine you can produce a variety of useful global edits, limited only by your imagination. For example, the routine shown in Figure 12.13 will take all entities found on a selected layer and move them to a new selected layer. If the new layer does not yet exist, the function will create a new layer with that name. Using this routine, you can create a layer and move specific objects to it with a single command. Beware, however, of misspelling the name of the target layer. As a safety device, you could place layer names on a custom screen menu or on your tablet and select them from there.

The variation shown in Figure 12.14 finds all entities of a selected thickness and changes them to a new thickness. This is very useful for raising and lowering walls. The same technique can be used for changing elevations.

In this variation, some thickness must be present for any entity to be changed with the NEWWALL command. Thus, it cannot be used to supply thicknesses to ordinary lines and polylines. However, the CHANGE command can be used to do this. C:NEWWALL will only change the thicknesses of lines that have thicknesses equal to the user-supplied "old" thickness.

Importing and Exporting ASCII Text Files

The routine shown in Figure 12.15 imports an ASCII text file into Auto-CAD. The routine in Figure 12.16 exports text from AutoCAD to an ASCII file. In this routine, the user is prompted for a file name. If the file name exists, the user is offered the choice of overwriting the file or aborting the process. Pressing Return will repeat the command.

Using these two AutoLISP routines, you can import from and export to any program that creates or reads ASCII files. An example is a spreadsheet program that prints out an ASCII file of spreadsheet data. (If you

```
(defun update()
    (setq alist
        (subst (cons 7 newst)
               (assoc 7 alist)
               alist
        )
    )
    (entmod alist)
; * -- This updating process uses a memory variable named test,
;       bound to an integer value. Test is now incremented by one:
    (setq test (1+ test))
; * -- The routine now extracts the next entity name in the selection
;       set by applying the value stored in a memory variable named
;       test to a memory variable containing the name of the selection
;       set, txtset:
    (setq ename (ssname txtset test))
; * -- If the previous function did not return nil, the association
;       list for the entity name stored in ename is stored in memory
;       variable alist:
    (if (/= ename nil)
        (setq alist (entget ename))
    )
)
(defun next()
; * -- Here the previous updating procedure is applied without any
;       changes, for cases where the selection set may contain nontext
;       entities:
    (setq test (1+ test))
    (setq ename (ssname txtset test))
    (if (/= ename nil)
        (setq alist (entget ename))
    )
)
(defun C:CHGSTYLE()
    (setq oldech (getvar "CMDECHO"))
    (setvar "CMDECHO" 0)
    (setq newst (getstring "\nNew Style for Selected Text: "))
; * -- The fully interactive selection mechanism used to obtain a
;       selection set. The selection-set name is stored in memory
;       variable tset:
    (setq txtset (ssget))
; * -- The number of elements in the selection set is stored in
;       memory variable total:
    (setq total (sslength txtset))
; * -- The memory variable test is bound to a value of integer zero:
    (setq test 0)
; * -- The first entity name in the selection set is extracted:
    (setq ename (ssname txtset 0))
; * -- If not nil, the association list for the entity name
;       is stored in memory variable alist:
    (if (/= ename nil)
        (setq alist (entget ename))
    )
; * -- This WHILE function checks the value of memory variable test.
;       As long as it is less than the total number of entities in
;       the selection set, either the UPDATE or NEXT function will be
;       called. (Both these functions increment the value of test.)
    (while (< test total)
        (if (= "TEXT" (cdr (assoc 0 alist)))
            (update)
            (next)
        )
    )
    (setvar "CMDECHO" oldech)
)
```

Figure 12.12   The CHGSTYLE.LSP Routine

```
(defun newlyr()
     (setq alist
; * -- Change to update to new layer:
             (subst (cons 8 newlr)
                    (assoc 8 alist)
                    alist
             )
     )
     (entmod alist)
     (setq test (1+ test))
     (setq ename (ssname tset test))
     (if (/= ename nil)
          (setq alist (entget ename))
     )
)
(defun next()
     (setq test (1+ test))
     (setq ename (ssname tset test))
     (if (/= ename nil)
          (setq alist (entget ename))
     )
)
(defun C:NEWLAYER()
   (setq oldech (getvar "CMDECHO"))
   (setvar "CMDECHO" 0)
; * -- Prompt for old and new layer names:
   (setq oldlr (getstring "\nOld Layer Name: "))
   (setq newlr (getstring "\nNew Layer Name: "))
   (setq tset (ssget))
   (setq total (sslength tset))
   (setq test 0)
   (setq ename (ssname tset 0))
   (if (/= ename nil)
       (setq alist (entget ename))
   )
   (while (< test total)
; * -- Test for layer equal to old:
          (if (= oldlr (cdr (assoc 8 alist)))
              (newlyr)
              (next)
          )
   )
   (setvar "CMDECHO" oldech)
)
```

Figure 12.13   The NEWLAYER.LSP Routine

are interested in importing from or exporting to a spreadsheet, check your spreadsheet documentation for details on whether it creates and reads ASCII files.) Once these files are created, they can easily be turned into AutoCAD text. If you have AutoCAD Version 2.6 or later, use Monotxt text font or a custom monospaced text font to import tables of data. Also, when exporting such tables to a spreadsheet, be sure that the column widths of your spreadsheet match the spacing between the columns of ASCII text in your file.

Most word processors will accept ASCII files. This means you can make changes to large amounts of text with a word processor and import the text into AutoCAD. If it needs substantial reediting, you can

ADVANCED TECHNIQUES IN AUTOCAD

```
(defun newlth()
; * -- Change to update to new thickness:
      (setq alist
          (subst (cons 39 newth)
                 (assoc 39 alist)
                 alist
          )
      )
      (entmod alist)
      (setq test (1+ test))
      (setq ename (ssname tset test))
      (if (/= ename nil)
          (setq alist (entget ename))
      )
)
(defun C:NEWWALL()
    (setq oldech (getvar "CMDECHO"))
    (setvar "CMDECHO" 0)
; * -- Prompt for old and new thicknesses:
    (setq oldth (getreal "\nOld Wall Height: "))
    (setq newth (getreal "\nNew Wall Height: "))
    (setq tset (ssget))
    (setq total (sslength tset))
    (setq test 0)
    (setq ename (ssname tset 0))
    (if (/= ename nil)
        (setq alist (entget ename))
    )
    (while (< test total)
; * -- Test for thickness equal to old thickness:
        (if (= oldth (cdr (assoc 39 alist)))
            (newlth)
            (next)
        )
    )
    (setvar "CMDECHO" oldech)
)
```

Figure 12.14   The NEWWALL.LSP Routine

```
      File name: TEXTIN.LSP:
  (defun import()
; * -- Prompt user for the starting point and the height of the text.
;       A rubber-band line will help visualize the height of the text:
    (setq sp (getpoint "\nStarting point: "))
    (setq th (rtos (getdist sp "\nText height: ")))
; * -- Prompt for the name of the text style:
    (setq style
        (getstring "\nEnter Text Style or ? <RETURN=Current style>: ")
    )
; * -- If user enters a "?", list the styles and continue:
    (while (= style "?")
      (command "STYLE" "?")
      (setq style
          (getstring "\nEnter Text Style or ? <RETURN=Current style>: ")
      )
    )
```

Figure 12.15   The TEXTIN.LSP Routine

```
;  * -- If you have Version 2.6+, you may use the following sequence
;        of functions to prompt for text style, instead of the above.
;        This sequence does the same thing, but displays the name of
;        the current text style as part of the prompt:
;             (setq ts (getvar "TEXTSTYLE"))
;             (setq style (getstring
;                              (strcat "\nEnter Text Style or ?: <" ts "> ")
;                         )
;             )
;             (while (= style "?")
;               (command "STYLE" "?")
;               (setq style (getstring
;                              (strcat "\nEnter Text Style or ?: <" ts "> ")
;                           )
;               )
;             )
;  * -- After prompting for the text style, read the first line of
;        the selected ASCII file:
   (setq tline (read-line tfile))
;  * -- Write the line as AutoCAD text, using starting point and height:
   (command "TEXT"
            "s"
            style
            sp
            th
            ""
            tline
   )
;  * -- While there are still lines remaining in the file, import each
;        one in succession. (When file is fully imported, tline will
;        equal nil):
   (while (/= tline nil)
          (setq tline (read-line tfile))
          (command "TEXT"
                       ""
                       tline
          )
   )
;  * -- Close the file:
   (close tfile)
)
;  * -- Define the AutoCAD command to execute these functions:
(defun C:TEXTIN()
   (setq oldech (getvar "CMDECHO"))
   (setq oldhlt (getvar "HIGHLIGHT"))
   (setvar "CMDECHO" 0)
   (setvar "HIGHLIGHT" 0)
;  * -- Get the name of the file:
   (setq tfile (getstring "\nName of file to import: "))
;  * -- If a file name was given (tfile will not be nil or an
;        empty Return), open the file for reading:
   (if (and (/= tfile nil) (/= tfile ""))
      (setq tfile (open tfile "r"))
   )
;  * -- If a file with the given name exists (tfile is not nil),
;        import it. Otherwise, prompt that no file was found and end
;        the command. (Pressing Return will repeat the command.):
   (if (and (/= tfile nil) (/= tfile ""))
      (import)
      (prompt "\nFile not found. Press Return to repeat command.\n")
   )
   (setvar "HIGHLIGHT" oldhlt)
   (setvar "CMDECHO" oldech)
) ; End of C:TEXTIN function
```

Figure 12.15   The TEXTIN.LSP Routine (continued)

```
            File name: TEXTOUT.LSP:
(defun export()
; * -- Use a selection set to gather text lines:
  (setq lines (ssget))
; * -- Tell the user that the file is being written. Sometimes it
;       takes a while - it's nice to have a message of reassurance
;       that something is happening:
  (prompt
      (strcat "\nWriting file "
               (strcase testfil)
               " -- One moment...\n"
      )
  )
; * -- Open the file for writing using the name supplied by the user:
  (setq fname (open testfil "w"))
; * -- In addition, get the number of entities in the selection set,
;       and initialize a memory variable for testing the end of the
;       selection set:
  (setq total (sslength lines)
        test 0)
; * -- While the value of test is less than the value of total, do
;       the following:
;       1) Each time through the following loop, print a hyphen in the
;          command prompt area, so that the user can see that something
;          is going on.
;       2) Get the first association list.
;       3) If it's text, write the text character string to a new
;          line in the open file.
;       4) Update the value of memory variable test.
  (while (< test total)
      (prin1 '-)
      (setq alist (entget (ssname lines test)))
      (if
          (= "TEXT" (cdr (assoc 0 alist)))
          (write-line (cdr (assoc 1 alist)) fname)
      )
      (setq test (1+ test))
  ) ; End of WHILE function
; * -- Close the file:
  (close fname)
; * -- Tell the user the process is complete:
  (prompt (strcat "\nFile " (strcase testfil) " written.\n"))
) ; End of EXPORT function
(defun oldfile()
; * -- This is an error trap if the user supplies a file name that
;       already exists. First, close the open file:
  (close fname)
; * -- Prompt the user either to abort or overwrite the file:
  (setq yn
     (getstring "File already exists. Do you want to overwrite it? <N> ")
  )

; * -- If the response is either Return or N, set a memory variable
;       named "go" to nil, aborting the function. Otherwise set go to 1,
;       allowing the file to be overwritten:
   (if (or (= yn "") (= (strcase yn) "N"))
       (setq go nil)
       (setq go 1)
   )
) ; End of OLDFILE function
(defun C:TEXTOUT()
   (setq oldech (getvar "CMDECHO"))
   (setq oldhlt (getvar "HIGHLIGHT"))
   (setvar "CMDECHO" 0)
```

Figure 12.16   The TEXTOUT.LSP Routine

```
    (setvar "HIGHLIGHT" 0)
; * -- Bind the memory variable go to a non-nil value:
    (setq go 1)
; * -- Prompt the user for a file name:
    (setq testfil (getstring "Name of ASCII file to create: "))
; * -- Attempt to open the file name for reading. If this function
;       returns nil, the file does not exist yet. If it returns a
;       non-nil value, the file exists:
    (setq fname (open testfil "r"))
; * -- If the file exists, call the OLDFILE function:
    (if (/= fname nil)
        (oldfile)
    )
; * -- If the file does not exist or the user has instructed that it
;       be overwritten, call the EXPORT function:
    (if (/= go nil)
        (export)
    )
  (setvar "HIGHLIGHT" oldhlt)
  (setvar "CMDECHO" oldech)
) ; End of C:TEXTOUT function
```

Figure 12.16   The TEXTOUT.LSP Routine (continued)

reedit it with the word processor, erase the AutoCAD text, and import the new version.

The *AutoLISP Programmer's Reference* offers a useful AutoLISP routine for making small changes to text while you are inside the Drawing Editor. This routine is called TXTCHG.LSP. You can find it, along with other useful routines, in the "Sample LISP Files" section of the reference manual.

An AutoLISP Routine for Bulge Arcs

If you are interested in creating shape files that contain arcs, the routine shown in Figure 12.17 will calculate the bulge factor for any arc drawn on the screen. (The use of bulge factors is explained in Chapter 4, "Shape and Text-Font Files.") Although this routine will not actually write out complete shape descriptions, it will help make the process of creating them a little easier.

The user is prompted to select an arc, and the bulge factor is displayed in the command prompt area. The user will have to make a note of the bulge factor displayed by this routine and add it to the shape description file using a word processor. Instead of requiring the user to make note of the bulge factor, you could, if you wish, modify this routine so that it would open a file on the hard disk and write the bulge factor to that file.

```
(defun C:BULGE()
; * -- Get the arc from the user:
  (setq uarc
    (entsel "\nSelect arc: ")
  )
; * -- Calculate bulge factor. Calculation is as follows:
;       If the starting angle of the arc is less than the ending angle,
;       then the arc angle is the difference between them. If the
;       starting angle is greater than the ending angle, the arc angle is
;       the value of the ending angle plus the difference between
;       360 degrees and the starting angle.
  (if
    (<
      (cdr
        (assoc 50 (entget (car uarc))
        )
      )
      (cdr
        (assoc 51 (entget (car uarc))
        )
      )
    )
    (setq ang1
      (-
        (cdr
          (assoc 51 (entget (car uarc))
          )
        )
        (cdr
          (assoc 50 (entget (car uarc))
          )
        )
      )
    )
    (setq ang1
      (+
        (cdr
          (assoc 51 (entget (car uarc))
          )
        )
        (-
          6.283185
          (cdr
            (assoc 50 (entget (car uarc))
            )
          )
        )
      )
    )
  )
; * -- Convert to degrees -- store in memory variable rtod:
  (setq rtod (dtr ang1))
; * -- Convert to bulge factor and store to memory variable bulge:
  (setq bulge
    (* 127 (/ rtod 180)
    )
  )
; * -- Display the results:
  (prompt
    (strcat "\nArc degrees are: " (rtos rtod 2 0) " "
    )
  )
  (if (< rtod 180)
```

Figure 12.17   The BULGE.LSP Routine

```
    (prompt
     (strcat "Bulge for this arc is: " (rtos bulge 2 0) "\n"
     )
    )
    (prompt "Arc too large for bulge. Break it first.\n"
     )
   )
  )
 )
```

Figure 12.17   The BULGE.LSP Routine (continued)

WHERE DO I GO FROM HERE?

In earlier chapters, you became acquainted with fundamental Auto-LISP functions and saw AutoLISP routines that demonstrate how these functions work together. You also worked with plain-English pseudocode, a tool for organizing your thoughts and the basis for assembling AutoLISP functions into working routines. In this chapter you have learned how to make changes to the drawing database by directly accessing its contents. You have also seen how you can use AutoLISP to import and export text files. These are fairly advanced uses of Auto-LISP. Where do you go from here?

- Practice. The only way to become fluent in a new language like AutoLISP is to use it. Think about what you would like AutoCAD to do for you. Break down the goal into a series of small steps that can be executed in sequence—this will be your pseudocode. Use this book and the *AutoCAD Programmer's Reference* to help you translate your pseudocode into AutoLISP. If you are worried about experimenting on important drawings, just make a backup of the drawing first, and work with the backup. Then, if something goes wrong, you can make another backup of the original and go on working until you have a successful AutoLISP routine. You'll find that the time you spend developing and debugging an effective AutoLISP routine will more than pay for itself in time saved later.

- Read the *AutoLISP Programmer's Reference*. Technical reference manuals are a chore to decipher if you are brand new to a topic. However, now that you have worked through this book, the *Auto-LISP Programmer's Reference* will make a lot more sense to you. Sit down and read through it. You will find some additional functions of interest, and additional examples to guide you.

- Pace yourself. Don't try to work out problems that are over your head at the outset—you'll just end up frustrated. Learning to use the more advanced tools in AutoCAD's toolbox can be very enjoyable if you pace yourself. Work at a comfortable level and develop a few simple routines at first. Indeed, you may find that as you gain more experience and develop increasingly complex routines, you'll return to the simple, small routines more frequently. The simplest AutoLISP routines are often the most valuable ones in the long run.

- Experiment to learn more. Get into the habit of asking "What if...?" and then sitting down at the AutoCAD command prompt and working with AutoCAD to find the answer. Most of the examples in this book were worked out in that manner. If you make it fun, you'll learn more than you ever thought possible.

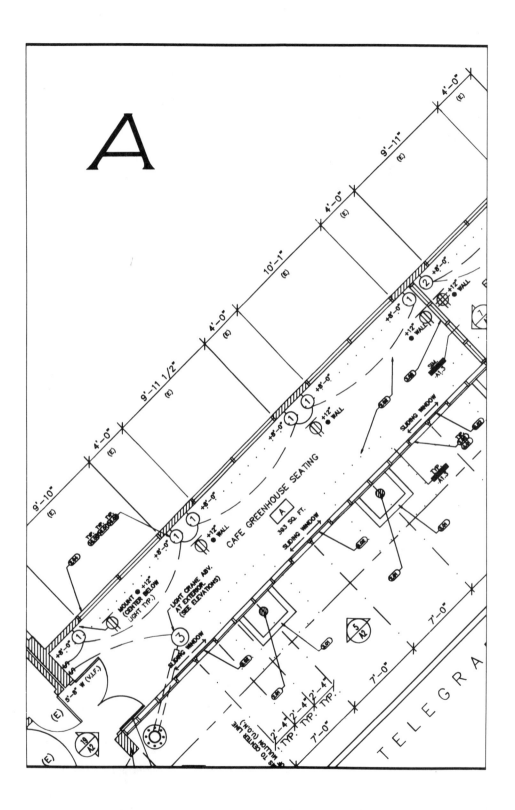

Appendix A
General-Purpose
LISP Routines

THIS APPENDIX INCLUDES ADDITIONAL AUTOLISP ROUTINES that you may type in "as is" or modify to suit your own needs. Commentary is minimal, since most of the functions used in these routines have been discussed in the body of this book or are explained fully in AutoCAD's documentation.

CALC.LSP

The CALC.LSP routine, shown in Figure A.1, requires Version 2.6 or later. It creates a function (not a command) called CALC, which interrupts AutoCAD commands to prompt for some simple math calculations. Then it passes the result of the calculation to the AutoCAD command. For example, the following sequence uses the CALC function to rotate the last drawn object a calculated amount (78.65 degrees minus 6.293):

> Command: ROTATE
> Select objects: L
> 1 found
> Select objects: [press Return]
> Base point: [pick point]
> <Rotation angle>/Reference: (CALC)
> (M)ultiply (D)ivide (A)dd (SU)btract (SQR)oot of (SQU)are of: SU Subtract:
> 6.293
> From: 78.65
> Result is: 72.357000 (Object is rotated this number of degrees)
> Command:

ADVANCED TECHNIQUES IN AUTOCAD

```
(defun calc()
    (Progn
; Prompt for which operation (modify this to include your own math):
        (Initget "Multiply Divide Add SUbtract SQRoot SQUare")
        (setq x
            (getxkword
                "\n(M)ultiply (D)ivide (A)dd (SU)btract (SQR)oot of (SQU)are of:"
            )
        ) ; end setq x
; Based on above response, do one of the following:
        (cond
; If subtraction
            ((= (strcase x) "SUBTRACT")
                (setq b (getdist "\nSubtract: "))
                (setq a (getdist "From: "))
                (setq res (- a b))
            )
; If squaring:
            ((= (strcase x) "SQUARE")
                (setq a (getdist "\nSquare of: "))
                (setq res (* a a))
            )
; If square root:
            ((= (strcase x) "SQROOT")
                (setq a (getdist "\nSquare Root of: "))
                (setq res (sqrt a))
            )
; If addition:
            ((= (strcase x) "ADD")
                (setq a (getdist "\nAdd: "))
                (setq b (getdist " To: "))
                (setq res (+ a b))
            )
; If division:
            ((= (strcase x) "DIVIDE")
                (setq a (getdist "\nDivide: "))
                (setq b (getdist " By: "))
                (setq res (/ a b))
            )
; If multiplication:
            ((= (strcase x) "MULTIPLY")
                (setq a (getdist "\nMultiply: "))
                (setq b (getdist " By: "))
                (setq res (* a b))
            )
; -- Your own math functions can be added here.
        ) ; End Cond
; Converts whole numbers to integers (uses different conversion for
; square-root math):
        (if (/= (strcase x) "SQROOT")
                (if (= (- res (fix res)) 0)
                        (setq res (fix res))
                )
                (if (< 0.0000009 (- res (fix res)))
                        (setq res (1+ (fix res)))
                )
        ) ; End if
; Displays the result of the math:
        (if (= (type res) 'REAL)
            (prompt (strcat "\nResult is: " (rtos res 2 6)))
            (prompt (strcat "\nResult is: " (itoa res))))
        )
; Returns the result to AutoCAD:
```

Figure A.1   The CALC.LSP Routine

```
        (eval res)
    ) ; End Progn
) ;   End Calc()
; EOF CALC.LSP
```

Figure A.1   The CALC.LSP Routine (continued)

You can modify CALC.LSP to include any form of math calculation. To do so, first include an appropriate keyword in the INITGET string, as in the following (the italics have been added for emphasis):

(initget
   "Multiply Divide Add SUbtract SQRoot SQUare *Yourmath*"
)

Then add you math sequence to the COND function, like this:

((= (strcase x) "YOURMATH")
   (<your prompting functions as required>)
   (<your math functions as required>)
); close sublist within "cond" function

CALC.LSP includes code that will convert whole numbers to integers, just in case you are using a command that requires an integer answer. If the result of the math is not a whole number and the command is expecting an integer, AutoCAD will present a message to that effect and repeat the prompt.

Square-root math can present some problems in rare cases. If the result of square-root math is a whole number (for example, the square root of 4 equals 2.0), AutoLISP won't accurately convert the whole number to an integer with the FIX function alone. Thus, the LISP file contains some extra code to account for those extremely rare cases in which a square root returns a whole number and AutoCAD wants an integer. Most of the time, this simply won't be the case, and the extra code will have no effect.

GETPROP.LSP

The GETPROP.LSP routine, shown in Figure A.2, requires Version 2.6 or later. It creates an AutoCAD command called GETPROP, which prompts the user to select an existing entity from the screen. When the user selects this entity, the settings for the current layer, color, line type,

```
(defun C:GETPROP()
  (setq oldcmd (getvar "CMDECHO"))
  (setvar "CMDECHO")
; Prompt for object:
  (setq obj (entsel "\Select object, or RETURN for current properties: "))
; If no object selected, inform user; otherwise, change settings:
  (if
      (= obj nil)
      (prompt "\nNo Object Selected.")
      (progn
; Get the association list for the selected object:
        (setq obj (entget (car obj))
; Establish additional memory variables for subsequent commands:
                c   (cdr (assoc 62 obj))
                lt  (cdr (assoc 6 obj))
                elv (cdr (assoc 38 obj))
                th  (cdr (assoc 39 obj))
        ) ; End Setq
; If the selected object was a block, get its name and inform the user:
        (if
            (equal (cdr (assoc 0 obj)) "INSERT")
            (prompt
              (strcat
                "\nBlock " (cdr (assoc 2 obj)) " selected.  "
                "Elevation and thickness will not be changed."
              ) ; End Strcat
            ) ; End prompt
        ) ; End If
; First, change the layer:
        (command "LAYER"
                 "s"
                 (cdr (assoc 8 obj))
                 ""
; Change the color setting. If the object's color is default, c will equal
; nil. In such a case, change the setting to "BYLAYER":
                 "COLOR"
                 (if
                    (/= c nil)
                    (eval c)
                    "BYLAYER"
                 )
; Change the line-type setting. This is similar to changing the color setting:
                 "LINETYPE"
                 "s"
                 (if
                    (/= lt nil)
                    (eval lt)
                    "BYLAYER"
                 )
                 ""
        ) ; End Command

; If the object is not a block, change the elevation and thickness:
; If the association list contains no settings for elevation and
; thickness, change the drawing settings to zero.
        (if
            (not (equal (cdr (assoc 0 obj)) "INSERT"))
            (progn
                (if
                    (/= elv nil)
                    (setvar "ELEVATION" elv)
                    (setvar "ELEVATION" 0.0)
                )
                (if
```

Figure A.2   The GETPROP.LSP Routine

```
                              (/= th nil)
                              (setvar "THICKNESS" th)
                              (setvar "THICKNESS" 0.0)
                          )
                  ) ; End ProgN (inner)
              ) ; End If (inner)
          ) ; End ProgN (outer)
      ) ; End If (outer)
    ; Display the settings, whether an object was selected or not:
      (prompt
              (strcat
                      "\nCurrent Color: " (getvar "CECOLOR")
                      "     Layer: " (getvar "CLAYER")
                      "  Linetype: " (getvar "CELTYPE")
                      "         "
              )
      )
    ; If selected object was not a block, or no object selected,
    ; display settings for elevation and thickness:
      (if
          (not (equal (cdr (assoc 0 obj)) "INSERT"))
          (prompt
              (strcat
                      "\n          Elevation: " (rtos (getvar "ELEVATION"))
                      "  Thickness: " (rtos (getvar "THICKNESS"))
                      "      "
              ) ; End Strcat
          ) ; End Prompt
      ) ; End If
) ; End Defun
; EOF GETPROP.LSP
```

Figure A.2   The GETPROP.LSP Routine (continued)

elevation, and thickness are set to match. If no entity is selected or if the user presses Return, the current drawing settings are displayed.

Because blocks are defined in relatively complex ways, the settings for elevation and thickness are *not* changed if the user selects a block. A message indicates the name of the block and the new setting for layer, color, and line type only. If the selected entity's properties are defined by the layer it is on (for example, the color is BYLAYER), the drawing settings are also changed (in this example, to BYLAYER).

INSWALL.LSP

The INSWALL.LSP routing, shown in Figure A.3, requires Version 2.5 or later. It is a variation on the parallel line generator presented earlier in this book. A few functions are added to PRLINF and PRLDRW, and two new functions are defined for this routine: INSDRW, which scales the texture patter placed between the lines, and C:INSWALL, which is the new AutoCAD command to execute.

```
(defun prlinf()
; Prompt for distance between lines:
  (if
    (<= init 0)
    (while
      (<= init 0)
      (setq init (getreal "\nPlease Specify Distance Between Lines: "))
    )
    (setq init
      (getdist
        (strcat "\nPlease Specify Distance Between Lines <"
                (rtos init)
                ">: "
        )
      )
    )
  )
  (if
    (<= init 0)
    (setq init dist)
    (setq dist init)
  )
;   (Multiple-pattern prompts can be added here.)
  (setvar "BLIPMODE" 1)
  (setq sp
    (getpoint "\nEnter starting point: ")
  )
  (setq ep
    (getpoint sp "\nEnter endpoint: ")
  )
  (setvar "BLIPMODE" 0)
)
(defun prldrw()
; Save the starting point and endpoint for additional fillets later.
  (setq sqx sp)
; Draw the lines, save info to variables
  (command "LINE"
        (setq osp1
            (polar sp
                  (+ (angle sp ep) 1.570796)
                  (/ dist 2)
            )
        )
        (setq oep1
            (polar ep
                  (+ (angle sp ep) 1.570796)
                  (/ dist 2)
            )
        )
        ""
  )
  (command "LINE")
        (setq osp2
            (polar sp
                  (- (angle sp ep) 1.570796)
                  (/ dist 2)
            )
        )
        (setq oep2
            (polar ep
                  (- (angle sp ep) 1.570796)
                  (/ dist 2)
            )
```

Figure A.3   The INSWALL.LSP Routine

```
            )
            " "
      )
(setq isp1 osp1
      iep1 oep1
      isp2 osp2
      osp4 osp2
      iep2 oep2
      oep4 oep2
)
) ; End Prldrw
(defun getmor()
;   Temporarily set the blips to their original value:
    (setvar "BLIPMODE" oldblip)
;   Prompt the user for the next endpoint and store it to ep2:
    (initget "C")
    (setq ep2
      (getpoint ep "\nTo Point: ")
    )
;   Turn the blips back off:
    (setvar "BLIPMODE" 0)
;   Check the value of ep2.  If ep2 is NOT nil or the original starting
;   point, spx, draw and fillet the lines.  If it IS spx, close the
;   polygon.  If ep2 is NIL, do nothing:
    (if
      (and
        (not (equal ep2 nil))
        (not (equal ep2 "c"))
        (not (equal ep2 "C"))
        (not (equal ep2 spx))
      )
      (drw1)
      (if
        (or
          (equal ep2 spx)
          (equal ep2 "C")
          (equal ep2 "c")
        )
        (closer
      )
    )
) ; End Getmor
(defun drw1()
;   Define the new memory variable osp3 as the offset START point of
;   one of the parallel lines:
    (setq osp3
      (polar ep
            (+ (angle ep ep2) 1.570796)
            (/ dist 2)
      )
    )
;   Define memory variable osp4 as its counterpart:
    (setq osp4
      (polar ep
            (- (angle ep ep2) 1.570796)
            (/ dist 2)
      )
    )
;   Define the new memory variable oep3 as the offset END point of
;   the first parallel line:
    (setq oep3
      (polar ep2
            (+ (angle ep ep2) 1.570796)
```

Figure A.3   The INSWALL.LSP Routine (continued)

```
                        (/ dist 2)
                )
        )
;    Define memory variable oep4 as its counterpart:
        (setq oep4
            (polar ep2
                    (- (angle ep ep2) 1.570796)
                    (/ dist 2)
            )
        )
; Define memory variable int13 as the point of intersection between
; lines 1 and 3:
        (setq int13 (inters osp1 oep1 osp3 oep3 nil))
; Define memory variable int24 as the point of intersection between
; lines 2 and 4:
        (setq int24 (inters osp2 oep2 osp4 oep4 nil))
; If the memory variables fint13 and fint24 are nil, initialize
; them with the current values of int13 and int24:
        (if (= fint13 nil)
            (setq fint13 int13
                  fint24 int24
            )
        )
; Erase the original lines:
        (command "ERASE"
            oep1
            " "
        )
        (command "ERASE"
            oep2
            " "
        )
; Draw new lines using the new intersection points:
        (command "LINE"
            osp1
            int13
            " "
        )
        (command "LINE"
            osp2
            int24
            " "
        )
        (command "LINE"
            int13
            oep3
            " "
        )
        (command "LINE"
            int24
            oep4
            " "
        )
; Reinitialize new memory variables, updating the start and end points of
; the centerline; the starting points of the offset lines (as the intersection
; points) and the endpoints of the offset lines:
        (setq sp ep
              ep ep2
              osp1 int13
              osp2 int24
              oep1 oep3
              oep2 oep4
        )
```

Figure A.3   The INSWALL.LSP Routine (continued)

```
) ; End Drw1
(defun closer()
;    Define the new osp3 as the offset START point of the first
;    parallel line, using the unchanged ep as the reference point
;    this time, and also referencing the ORIGINAL start point, spx, in
;    order to determine the angle of the final centerline:
     (setq osp3
        (polar ep
                (+ (angle ep spx) 1.570796)
                (/ dist 2)
        )
     )
;    Define memory variable osp4 as its counterpart:
     (setq osp4
        (polar ep
                (- (angle ep spx) 1.570796)
                (/ dist 2)
        )
     )
;    Define the new memory variable oep3 as the offset END point of one of the
;    final parallel lines.  Use the original starting point:
     (setq oep3
        (polar spx
                (+ (angle ep spx) 1.570796)
                (/ dist 2)
        )
     )
;    Define memory variable oep2 as its counterpart:
     (setq oep4
        (polar spx
                (- angle ep spx) 1.570796)
                (/ dist 2)
        )
     )
; Erase the lines on either end of the final lines:
     (command "ERASE"
        oep1
        " "
     )
     (command "ERASE"
        oep2
        " "
     )
     (command "ERASE"
        isp1
        " "
     )
     (command "ERASE"
        isp2
        " "
     )
; Draw new lines from the most recent intersection, to the starting point of
; the final lines (an intersection point), to the endpoint of the final
; lines (also an intersection point), to the initial intersection point,
; intx13:
     (command "LINE"
        int13
        (inters osp1 oep1 osp3 oep3 nil)
        (inters osp3 oep3 isp1 iep1 nil)
        fint13
        " "
     )
; Do the same for the parallel mate:
```

Figure A.3   The INSWALL.LSP Routine (continued)

ADVANCED TECHNIQUES IN AUTOCAD

```
          (command "LINE"
              int24
              (inters osp2 oep2 osp4 oep4 nil)
              (inters osp4 oep4 isp2 iep2 nil)
              fint24
              ""
          )
      ) ; End Closer
      ; Create the insulation pattern. (Substitute variable symbol for "insul"
      ; when using multiple patterns):
      (defun insdrw()
        (command "SHAPE"
      ; Substitute the variable pat for "insul" if earlier you prompted
      ; for a shape name:
            "insul"
            osp4
            dist
            (rtd (angle osp4 oep4))
        )
      : Change the snap angle to properly locate the array:
        (setvar "SNAPANG" (angle osp4 oep4))
      ; Array the shape:
        (command "ARRAY"
          "L"
          ""
          "r"
          "l"
          (fix (/ (distance osp4 oep4) dist))
          dist
        )
      ) ; End Insdrw
      (defun C:INSWALL()
        (setq oldblip
          (getvar "BLIPMODE")
        )
        (setq oldcmd
          (getvar "CMDECHO")
        )
        (setq oldsnap)
          (getvar "SNAPANG")
        )
        (setq oldreg)
          (getvar "REGENMODE")
        )
        (setq oldpb
          (getvar "PICKBOX")
        )
        (setvar "CMDECHO" 0)
        (setvar "REGENMODE" 0)
        (setvar "PICKBOX" 0)
      ; Reset the values of ep2, intx13, and intx24 to their starting values:
        (setq ep2 '0,0)
        (setq fint13 nil
              fint24 nil
        )
        (prlinf)
        (setvar "BLIPMODE" 0)
        (prldrw)
        (insdrw)
      ; Check the value of ep2.  If ep2 is NOT nil or spx,
      ; prompt for the next endpoint.  If ep2 IS nil or spx,
      ; end the function:
        (while
```

Figure A.3   The INSWALL.LSP Routine (continued)

```
      (and
        (not (equal ep2 nil))
        (not (equal ep2 spx))
        (not (equal ep2 "C"))
        (not (equal ep2 "c"))
      )
      (getmore)
      (if
        (not (equal ep2 nil))
        (insdrw)
      )
    )
    (setvar "BLIPMODE" oldblip)
    (setvar "CMDECHO" oldcmd)
    (setvar "REGENMODE" oldreg)
    (setvar "SNAPANG" oldsnap)
    (setvar "PICKBOX" oldpb)
) ; End C:INSWALL
; EOF INSWALL.LSP
```

Figure A.3   The INSWALL.LSP Routine (continued)

After each set of parallel lines have been drawn and the corners have been cleaned up, a shape named Insul is set between the lines and arrayed at the same angle as the lines, until the lines are filled with the pattern. The result is a textured wall. The Insul shape definition must have been previously compiled and loaded into the drawing for this routine to work. (Refer to Chapter 4, "Shape Files and Text-Font Files," for details on this process.) The shape definition is as follows:

*1,15,INSUL
003,4,002,024,001,014,00A,(1,-044),02C,00A,(1,044)014,0

This shape may be placed in its own file or added to an existing shape file. If you added it to an existing file, be sure to change its shape number to a number not already in use.

A library of wall-texture patterns can be used with this code—just put them together in a shape file, compile and load the file, and add a prompt for the desired pattern at the location indicated in Figure A.3. One possible prompt sequence is as follows:

(initget 1 "<your texture shape names>")
(setq pat
    (getkword "\nTexture Pattern <your texture shape names>: ")
)

When the pat symbol is bound to a texture shape name in this way, substitute the symbol name where the shape name "insul" currently appears in the INSDRW function:

(command "SHAPE"\

```
pat                    ; used to be: "insul"
osp4
dist
(rtd (angle osp4 oep4))
)
```

Any shape used in this routine must be scaled to overall dimensions of one-by-one drawing unit. Otherwise, the memory variables used in the SHAPE and ARRAY commands may not work. The shape insertion point is currently set as the starting point of the second parallel line. When defining the shape, this point could be changed to a different point if you prefer. The important thing to remember is that the dimensions and the insertion point of the shape must work together to size and position the shape between the lines correctly. Study the Insul shape description to see how the current settings work.

Notice that this routine calls the DTR and RTD function to convert angles between radians and degrees, so both of these functions must be previously defined. (See Chapter 8 for definitions of these functions.)

LISTBLK.LSP

The LISP routine shown in Figure A.4 requires AutoCAD Version 2.6 or later. When loaded, LISTBLK.LSP creates a new AutoCAD command called LISTBLK, which will list all of a drawing's blocks in the screen menu area of the Drawing Editor and allow the user to select a block by picking it with the mouse or digitizing device. After the block name is selected, the original menu display is restored and the INSERT command is invoked by using the selected block name.

A word of warning, however: do not attempt to repeat this command by pressing the Return button on your mouse or digitizing device. If you do, chances are that the routine will display a long series of nested Auto-LISP functions followed by an error message. Using the Return button on your mouse or digitizer causes the GRREAD function to interpret the Return as a response to the "Pick block name" prompt. It will not pick up the keyboard input in this way. However, you can repeat the command by pressing Return on your keyboard.

If you forget and get the error message, you will not hurt your drawing. Simply enter this function at the AutoCAD command prompt:

(grtext)

Everything will be restored to normal.

```
(defun blk()
; 1. Create a list of the block names. Find the next block in the database
;      and add it to the list started in function C:LISTBLK:
      (prompt "\nExtracting block names. One moment...")
      (setq blst
            (list
                   (cdr (assoc 2 (tblnext "BLOCK"))
                   )
                   blst
            )
      )
; 2. Continue searching. As long as another block is found, add the name to
;      the list:
      (while
            (setq nb (tblnext "BLOCK"))
            (setq blst
                   (cons
                          (cdr (assoc 2 nb))
                          blst
                   )
            )
      ) ; End While
;  3. Copy the list:
      (setq alst blst)
;  4. Do the following routine while names remain on blst and no block is
;      selected:
      (prompt "\nDisplaying block names...")
      (while (and
                   (/= blst nil)
                   (= x_blk nil)
            )
;      4a. Set the value of num to zero:
            (setq num 0)
;      4b. While num is less than 19 and block names are still on blst,
            (while (and
                          (<= num 19)
                          (/= blst nil)
                   )
;           do the following:
;           4b-1. If num doesn't equal 19 yet, blank out the line in the
;                 screen menu area at the line corresponding to the current
;                 value of num plus 1, and display the block name there:
                   (progn
                          (if (/= num 19)
                                 (grtext (1+ num) "            ")
                          )
                          (grtext num (car blst))
;           4b-2. Add one to the value of num:
                          (setq num (1+ num))
;           4b-3. Remove the block name from blst:
                          (setq blst (cdr blst))
                   ) ; End Progn
            ) ; End While (4b)
;      4c. If names still remain on blst,
            (if (/= blst nil)
;           display "--MORE--" on the next screen menu line:
                   (grtext num "--MORE--")
            ) ; End If
;      4d. Prompt for input:
            (if (/= blst nil)
                   (progn
                          (prompt "\nPick block name (or select <--MORE-->): ")
;      4e. User selects a screen menu line; stored to x:
                          (setq x_blk (nth 1 (grread)))
```

Figure A.4   The LISTBLK.LSP Routine

```
;       4f. If x doesn't equal num, find the corresponding block name
;           from alst:
                            (if (/= x_blk num)
                               (setq x_blk (nth x_blk alst))
;           Otherwise, set x to nil:
                               (setq x_blk nil)
                            ) ; End If
;       4g. Set the value of alst equal to the remaining names on blst:
                            (setq alst blst)
                         ) ; End Progn
;       4h. Otherwise (if no more names on blst), prompt to select a
;           block name from display:
                         (progn
                            (prompt "\nPick block name: ")
;       4i. Read as before:
                            (setq x_blk (nth 1 (grread)))
                            (setq x_blk (nth x_blk alst))
;       4j. Update list as before:
                            (setq alst blst)
                         ) ; End Progn
                  ) ; End If
;       4k. If a block name was supplied, insert it and restore menu:
             (if (/= x_blk nil)
                (progn
                   (command "INSERT" x_blk )
                   (grtext)
                )
             ) ; End If
      ) ; End While (4a-k)
) ; End Defun BLK()
(defun C:LISTBLK()
; Reset critical variables:
   (setq alst nil
         blst nil
         x_blk nil
   )
; 1. Find first block name in symbol table
   (setq blst
         (cdr (assoc 2 (tblnext "BLOCK" 1))
         )
   )
; 2. If found, start building list and running screen display routine:
   (if (/= blst nil)
          (blk)
;     Otherwise, prompt that no blocks exist:
          (prompt "n\ ** NO BLOCK FOUND **")
   ) ; End If
; 3. Restore the screen menu when finished:
   (grtext)
) ; End C:LISTBLK
; EOF LISTBLK.LSP
```

Figure A.4   The LISTBLK.LSP Routine (continued)

LISTLYR.LSP

The LISTLYR.LSP routine, shown in Figure A.5, does the same thing as LISTBLK.LSP, except that LISTLYR.LSP creates a command called LISTLYR, which lists layer names on the screen instead of block names.

```
(defun lyr()
; 1. Create a list of the layer names. Find the next layer in the
;     database and add it to the list started in function C:LISTBLK:
      (prompt "\nExtracting layer names. One moment...")
      (setq blst
            (list
                  (cdr (assoc 2 (tblnext "LAYER")))
                  )
                  blst
            )
      )
; 2. Continue searching. As long as another layer is found, add the name to
;     the list:
      (while
            (setq nb (tblnext "LAYER"))
            (setq blst
                  (cons
                     (cdr (assoc 2 nb))
                     blst
                  )
            )
      ) ; End While
; 3. Copy the list:
      (setq alst blst)
; 4. Do the following routine while names remain on blst and no layer is
;     selected:
      (prompt "\nDisplaying layer names...")
      (while (and
                  (/= blst nil)
                  (= x_lyr nil)
             )
; 4a. Set the value of num to zero:
            (setq num 0)
; 4b. While num is less than 19 and layer names are still on blst,
            (while (and
                        (<= num 19)
                        (/= blst nil)
                   )
; do the following:
; 4b-1. If num doesn't equal 19 yet, blank out the line in the
;       screen menu area at the line corresponding to the current
;       value of num plus 1, and display the layer name there:
                  (progn
                     (if (/= num 19)
                        (grtext (1+ num) "           ")
                     )
                     (grtext num (car blst))
; 4b-2. Add one to the value of num:
                     (setq num (1+ num))
; 4b-3. Remove the layer name from blst:
                     (setq blst (cdr blst))
                  ) ; End Progn
            ) ; End While (4b)
; 4c. If names still remain on blst,
            (if (/= blst nil)
; display "--MORE--" on the next screen menu line:
               (grtext num "--MORE--")
            ) ; End If
; 4d. Prompt for input:
            (if (/= blst nil)
                  (progn
                     (prompt "\nPick layer name (or select <--MORE-->): ")
; 4e. User selects a screen menu line; stored to x:
```

Figure A.5　　The LISTLYR.LSP Routine

```
                                (setq x_lyr (nth 1 (grread)))
;       4f. If x doesn't equal num, find the corresponding layer name
;           from alst:
                            (if (/= x_lyr num)
                                (setq x_lyr (nth x_lyr alst))
;           otherwise, set x to nil:
                                (setq x_lyr nil)
                            ) ; End If
;       4g. Set the value of alst equal to the remaining names on blst:
                            (setq alst blst)
                        ) ; End Progn
;       4h. Otherwise (if no more names on blst), prompt to select a
;           layer name from display:
                        (progn
                            (prompt "\nPick layer name: ")
;       4i. Read as before:
                                (setq x_lyr (nth 1 (grread)))
                                (setq x_lyr (nth x_lyr alst))
;       4j. Update list as before:
                                (setq alst blst)
                        ) ; End Progn
                ) ; End If
;       4k. If a layer name was supplied, set it and restore menu:
                (if (/= x_lyr nil)
                    (progn
                        (command "LAYER" "S" x_lyr "")
                        (grtext)
                    )
                ) ; End If
        ) ; End While (4a-k)
) ; End Defun LYR()
(defun) C:LISTLYR()
; Reset critical variables:
    (setq alst nil
          blst nil
          x_lyr nil
    )
; 1. Find first layer name in symbol table:
    (setq blst
        (cdr (assoc 2 (tblnext "LAYER" 1)))
    )
; 2. If found, start building list and running screen display routine:
    (if (/= blst nil)
        (lyr)
    ) ; End If
; 3. Restore the screen menu when finished:
    (grtext)
) ; End C:LISTLYR
; EOF LISTLYR.LSP
```

Figure A.5   The LISTLYR.LSP Routine (continued)

The syntax is virtually the same, and the same warning applies regarding the Return button on a mouse or digitizing device.

REFS.LSP

REFS.LSP, shown in Figure A.6, contains 2-D and 3-D reference-point functions that prompt the user for an arbitrary reference point, and an angle and distance from that reference point. It can be used when the exact x-y

```
;    2-D reference-point function:
 (defun ref ( / x)
 ;    Reset "lastpoint" with user pick:
     (setvar "LASTPOINT" (setq x (getpoint "Reference point: ")))
 ;    Prompt for distance and angle,
 ;    convert both to "@XX<XX" string, and return it to ACAD:
     (strcat
             "@"
             (rtos (getdist x "\nDistance: "))
             "<"
             (rtos (rtd (getangle x "\nAngle:     ")))
     )
 ) ; End Defun REF()
 ;    A variation of the REF function, called 3DREF, can be used
 ;    to identify 3-D points in AutoCAD Version 2.6 and later, as follows:
 (defun 3Dref ( / x r_pt oldel newel)
     (setq x (getpoint "Reference point: "))
     (setq r_pt
             (strcat
                     "@"
                     (rtos (getdist x "\nDistance: "))
                     "<"
                     (rtos (rtd (getangle x "\nAngle:     ")))
             )
     )
     (setq oldel (getvar "ELEVATION"))
     (setq newel
             (getdist (strcat "\nNew elevation <"
                             (rtos (getvar "ELEVATION"))
                             ">: "
             )
     )
     )
     (setvar "LASTPT3D" (list
                             (car x)
                             (cadr x)
                             (if (= newel nil)
                                 (eval oldel)
                                 (setvar "ELEVATION" newel)
                             )
                     )
     )
     (eval r_pt)
 ) ; End Defun 3DREF()
```

Figure A.6   The REFS.LSP Routine, Version 1

coordinates are difficult to pinpoint and when OSNAP cannot help because no current-entity Osnap point is available. The 2-D reference-point function will work with AutoCAD 2.18 or later. The 3-D reference-point functions require AutoCAD 2.6 or later. Here is an example command sequence:

Command: LINE
From point: (ref)
Reference Point: <select>
Distance: <input distance - keyboard or two points>
Angle: <input angle - keyboard or two points>
To point: <continue with command>

ADVANCED TECHNIQUES IN AUTOCAD

The 3DREF function in Figure A.6 changes the value of the ELEVATION system variable each time it is used. The following version of 3DREF sets the elevation of the requested 3-D point only, without changing the value of the ELEVATION system variable:

```
(defun 3Dref ( / x r_pt oldel newel)
  (setq x (getpoint "Reference point: "))
  (setq r_pt
    (strcat
      "@"
      (rtos (getdist x "\nDistance: "))
      "<"
      (rtos (rtd (getangle x "\nAngle: ")))
    )
  )
  (setq oldel (getvar "ELEVATION"))
  (setq newel
    (getdist (strcat "\nTemporary elevation <"
        (rtos oldel)
        ">: "
      )
    )
  )
  (setvar "LASTPT3D" (list
      (car x)
      (cadr x)
      (if ( = newel nil)
        (eval oldel)
        (eval newel)
      )
    )
  )
  (eval r_pt)
) ; End Defun 3DREF( )
```

If a temporary elevation of one point only is useful to you, this function will provide such an elevation in response to any AutoCAD command that requests a point.

```
(defun el( / tempel x)
  (setq tempel (getdist "\nElevation for this point: "))
  (setq x (getpoint "\nPoint: "))
  (setq x (list (car x) (cadr x) eval tempel)))
```

) ; End Defun EL( )
; EOF REFS.LSP

The following command sequence illustrates how it works:

Command: 3DLINE From point: (el)
Elevation for this point: < enter elevation >
Point: < enter point >
To point: < continue command at original elevation >

TUBE.LSP

The routine shown in Figure A.7 is most useful with AutoCAD Version 2.18, although it can be used with later versions as well. TUBE.LSP creates two commands, TUBE and TUBE2. TUBE draws a series of alternating parallel lines and arcs, with a visible centerline on a separate layer, called Center. This layer (or another layer of your choice) must be defined as part of the current drawing, or the centerline will be drawn on the current layer.

TUBE2 takes up where TUBE leaves off, and continues drawing alternating parallel lines and arcs. The resultant image forms a "highway" shape on the screen. It was originally created to represent bent aluminum tubing; hence, the routine's name.

```
(DEFUN draw1 ()
  (if
    (<= init 0)
    (while
      (<= init 0)
      (setq init (getreal "\nPlease Specify Tube Diameter: "))
    )
    (setq init
      (getdist
        (strcat "\nPlease Specify Tube Diameter <"
                (rtos init)
                ">: "
        )
      )
    )
  )
  (if
    (<= init 0)
    (setq init dist)
    (setq dist init)
  )
  (setq sp (getpoint "\nLine Segment - Starting Point: "))
  (setq ep (getpoint "\nEndpoint: "))
  (setq dist2 (/ dist2))
```

Figure A.7   The TUBE.LSP Routine

```
    (setq ang1 (+ 1.570796 (angle sp ep)))
    (setq ang2 (- (angle sp ep) 1.570796))
      (command "LAYER"
      "s"
      "center"
      ""
      )
      (command "LINE"
      sp
      ep
      ""
      )
      (command "LAYER"
      "s"
      "0"
      ""
      )
      (command "LINE"
      (polar sp ang1 dist2)
      (setq bsp (polar ep ang1 dist2))
      ""
      )
      (command "LINE"
      (polar sp ang2 dist2)

      (setq bsp (polar ep ang2 dist 2))
       ""
       )
   )
(defun draw2 ()
    (setq tp (getpoint "\nBend in Which Direction? "))
    (setq tnum (- (angle sp tp) (angle sp ep)))
    (if (< tnum 0) (setq tnum (+ tnum (* 2 pi))))
    (if (< tnum pl)
        (setq center (polar ep ang1 dist))
        (setq center (polar ep ang2 dist))
    )
    (setq ang5 (getreal "\nIncluded Angle of Bend: "))
    (if (> tnum pi) (setq ang5 (- 0.0000 ang5)))
    (command "LAYER"
    "s"
    "center"
    ""
    )
    (command "ARC"
    ep
    "c"
    center
    "a"
    ang5
    )
)
(defun draw3 ()
    (setq sp2
          (polar center
                 (+ (* pi (/ ang5 180.00)) (angle center ep))
                 (distance center ep)
          )
    )
    (setq len (getdist "\nLength of Straight Segment: " sp2))
    (command "LINE"
    ""
    len
    ""
    )
```

Figure A.7   The TUBE.LSP Routine (continued)

```
)
(defun draw4 ()
   (setq ep2 (getvar "LASTPOINT"))
   (setq angA1 (+ 1.57077 (angle sp2 ep2)))
   (setq angA2 (= (angle sp2 ep2) 1.57707))
   (setq csp (polar sp2 angA1 dist2))
   (setq npa (polar ep2 angA1 dist2))
   (setq dsp (polar sp2 angA2 dist2))
   (setq npb (polar ep2 angA2 dist2))
   (if (< ang5 0) (setq x asp) (setq x csp))

   (if (< ang5 0) (setq w csp) (setq w asp))
   (if (< ang5 0) (setq y dsp) (setq y bsp))
   (if (< ang5 0) (setq z bsp) (setq z dsp))
   (command "LAYER"
   "s"
   "0"
   " "
   )
   (command "LINE"
   csp
   npa
   " "
   )
   (command "LINE"
   dsp
   npb
   " "
   )
   (command "ARC"
   w
   "c"
   "cent"
   ep
   x
   )
   (command "ARC"
   y
   "c"
   "cent"
   ep
   z
   )
)
(defun draw6 ()
   (setq ang1 (+ 1.570796 (angle sp2 ep2)))
   (setq ang2 (- (angle sp2 ep2) 1.570796))
   (setq tp (getpoint "\nBend in Which Direction? "))
   (setq tnum (- (angle sp2 tp) (angle sp2 ep2)))
   (if (< tnum 0) (setq tnum (+ tnum (* 2 pi))))
   (if (< tnum pi)
       (setq center (polar ep2 ang1 dist))
       (setq center (polar ep2 ang2 dist))
   )
   (setq ang5 (getreal "\nIncluded Angle of Bend: "))
   (if (> tnum pi) (setq ang5 (- 0.0000 ang5)))
   (command "LAYER"
   "s"
   "center"
   " "
   )
   (command "ARC"
   ep2
   "c"
```

Figure A.7   The TUBE.LSP Routine (continued)

ADVANCED TECHNIQUES IN AUTOCAD

```
            center
            "a"
            ang5
            )
    )
    (defun draw7 ()
        (setq sp2
                (polar center
                        (+ (* pi (/ ang5 180.00)) (angle center ep2))
                        (distance center ep2)
                )
        )
        (setq len (getdist "\nLength of Straight Segment: " sp2))
        (command "LINE"
        ""
        len
        ""
        )
    )
    (defun draw8 ()
        (setq ep2 (getvar "LASTPOINT"))
        (setq angA1 (+ 1.57077 (angle sp2 ep2)))
        (setq angA2 (- (angle sp2 ep2) 1.57707))
        (setq csp (polar sp2 angA1 dist2))
        (setq dsp (polar sp2 angA2 dist2))
        (if (< ang5 0) (setq w dsp) (setq w npb))
        (if (< ang5 0) (setq x npa) (setq x dsp))
        (if (< ang5 0) (setq y csp) (setq y npa))
        (if (< ang5 0) (setq z npb) (setq z csp))
        (setq npa (polar ep2 angA1 dist2))
        (setq npb (polar ep2 angA2 dist2))
    (command "LAYER"
    "s"
    "0"
    ""
    )
    (command "LINE"
    csp
    npa
    ""
    )
    (command "LINE"
    dsp
    npb
    ""
    )
    (command "ARC"
    w
    "c"
    "cent"
    sp2
    x
    )
    (command "ARC"
    y
    "c"
    "cent"
    sp2
    z
    )
    )
    (defun C:TUBE ()
        (setq oldblp (getvar "BLIPMODE"))
        (setq oldech (getvar "CMDECHO"))
```

Figure A.7   The TUBE.LSP Routine (continued)

```
        (setvar "CMDECHO" 0)
        (draw1)
        (setvar "BLIPMODE" 0)
        (draw2)
        (draw3)
        (draw4)
        (setvar "BLIPMODE" oldblp)
        (setvar "CMDECHO" oldech)
)
(defun C:TUBE2 ()
        (setq oldblp (getvar "BLIPMODE"))
        (setq oldech (getvar "CMDECHO"))
        (setvar "CMDECHO" 0)
        (setvar "BLIPMODE" 0)
        (draw6)
        (draw7)
        (draw8)
        (setvar "BLIPMODE" oldblp)
        (setvar "CMDECHO" oldech)
)
;    EOF TUBE.LSP
```

Figure A.7   The TUBE.LSP Routine (continued)

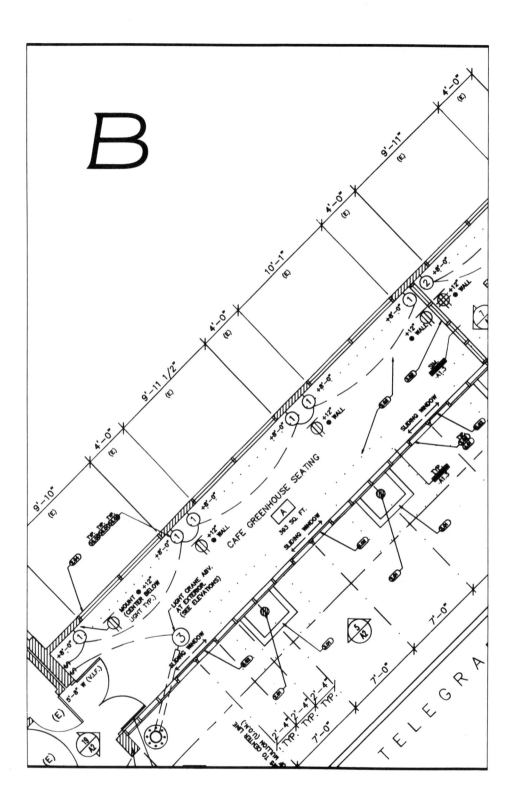

Appendix B
Third-Party Products
and Vendors

THE FOLLOWING LIST of products and vendors may be of interest to users who customize AutoCAD. Inclusion on this list is neither a guarantee nor an endorsement of the described products. You should direct all inquiries to the vendor at the address given.

ACAD Partner

ACAD Partner is a complex, multifeatured menu system for digitizers. It supports a variety of template overlays for various drawing disciplines. The product is available from

Chase Systems
623 Park Meadow Road, Suite M
Westerville, OH 43081
(614) 899-0400

Ausfont and Soltex

Ausfont includes 18 font styles for AutoCAD. Soltex produces large text characters and supports kerning via AutoLISP. These products are available from

Graphic Computer Services Pty. Ltd.
2 Second Avenue, Mt. Lawley
Western Australia 6050
(619) 271-8022

AutoCAD BBS

This is a semiprivate, 24-hour on-line bulletin board dealing exclusively with AutoCAD. Board services include messages, information exchange, answers to questions, and LISP files. A subscriber fee is required for one year of uploading and downloading files. AutoCAD BBS is available from

Off-Broadway Business Systems
316 38th Street
Oakland, CA 94609
(415) 547-8801 (Voice)
(415) 547-5264 (Modem)

AutoScheduler

This product generates bills of material, and custom schedules, in AutoCAD DWG file format directly from an AutoCAD drawing. It is available from

SSC Softsystems, Inc.
5645 Poplar Avenue
Memphis, TN 38119
(901) 767-1330

AutoShapes

This utility program generates SHP files based on AutoCAD DXF files. The product includes special drawing templates and custom menus. It is available from

CAD Systems Unlimited, Inc.
5201 Great America Parkway, Suite 443
Santa Clara, CA 95054
(408) 562-5762

AutoWord

AutoWord helps insert text into AutoCAD drawings. Extra features include table grid-line generation and column alignment help. This product is available from

Technical Software
28790 Chagrin Boulevard, Suite 300
Cleveland, OH 44122
(216) 765-1133

CADfont

This product builds font sets using Hershey Database typesetting characters mapped into AutoCAD SHP files. It is available from

ADSI
190 East Fifth Avenue
Naperville, IL 60540
(312) 355-4666

AutoLISP consulting and training services are also offered by this company.

IsoCad

IsoCAD converts plan drawings to named isometric views using Auto-LISP. A demonstration disk, as well as the product, is available from

Looking Glass Microproducts
4233 W. Eisenhower Boulevard
Loveland, CO 80537
(303) 669-2681

Letter Ease

With Letter Ease, fonts and symbols are inserted into a drawing as blocks instead of as shapes, and they can be enlarged to any size. A special AutoLISP program allows insertion of letter blocks in a manner similar to text. This product supports kerning. It is available from

CAD Lettering Systems
P.O. Box 850
Oldsmar, FL 33557
(813) 855-7823

Letter Sets

This product offers several predefined fonts for AutoCAD in SHX format only. It is available from

Symbol Graphics, Inc.
1047 W. 6th Street, Box 27
Corona, CA 91720
(714) 735-1622

Pretty-Printer

This product formats, indents, and counts parentheses in AutoLISP code. It is available from

M. Slinn Engineering
3158 W. 32nd Avenue
Vancouver, B.C. CANADA V6L 2C1
(604) 266-5380

Turbo Keyboard

This product condenses AutoCAD commands and macros into one or two keyboard keystrokes. It is available from

Digital Dynamics
24301 Elise Court
Los Altos Hills, CA 94022

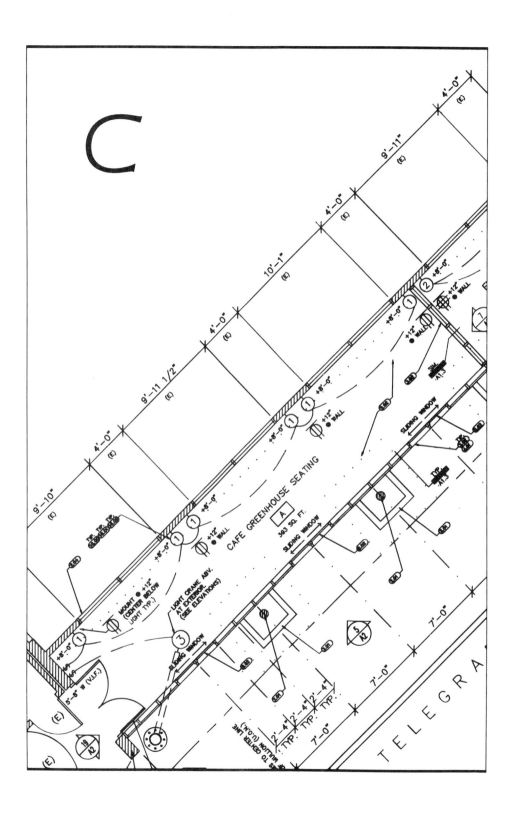

Appendix C
AutoCAD Release 9:
New Features

ON SEPTEMBER 17, 1987, Autodesk announced the surprise release of a new version of AutoCAD, AutoCAD Release 9. Among the features included in this new release are several command options that offer improved speed and flexibility, the ability to move drawing files between different operating systems without file-format conversion, 20 new text-font files (in SHX format only, therefore not customizable), and a few enhancements to AutoLISP.

A new feature of Release 9 that will undoubtedly be of great interest to customizers is a feature called the *Advanced User Interface* (or AUI for short). At the time of this writing, the new interface is available for users of CGA, VGA, EGA, and Hercules graphics cards. The Advanced User Interface will also be available for users who have installed the Autodesk Device Interface (ADI) driver. Autodesk will certainly be adding more graphics drivers to this list in the near future; check with your dealer if your card is not one of these.

The Advanced User Interface includes a new menu bar that appears across the top of the screen whenever the user moves the screen crosshairs to the status-line area. As many as ten user-definable *keywords* can appear in this menu bar; selecting one will activate a pull-down menu containing AutoCAD commands, options, and features.

In addition, pop-up *icon menus* are available. These permit the user to review as many as 16 slide files of graphic input options before selecting one. The pull-down menus and pop-up icon menus are fully customizable, and they can be "swapped" to allow the display of additional commands and options that may not fit on a single screen.

In addition to the features of the Advanced User Interface, Release 9 offers customizers the ability to redefine or modify standard AutoCAD commands by substituting, for the standard command, an AutoLISP routine of their choice. This appendix will discuss techniques for customizing the new pull-down menus and icon menus and redefining standard AutoCAD commands. Noncustomizable features are fully explained in the Release 9 documentation.

CREATING PULL-DOWN MENUS

Figure C.1 illustrates the standard menu bar as it is supplied by Autodesk. In this illustration, the user has moved the crosshairs into the upper-left corner of the screen, activating the horizontal menu bar. The user then highlighted the Draw keyword. When the user pushed the Select button, the pull-down menu below the keyword appeared on the screen.

The pull-down menu remains in place until the user takes one of four possible actions:

1. Selects a command or option from those displayed on the screen in any menu area

2. Selects any point on the graphics screen

3. Types anything at the keyboard

4. Moves the pointing device into the original screen menu area

Although the appearance and behavior of the pull-down menu is different from that of the AutoCAD standard screen menu, the techniques for creating or modifying it are similar to those for standard AutoCAD screen menus and menu macros.

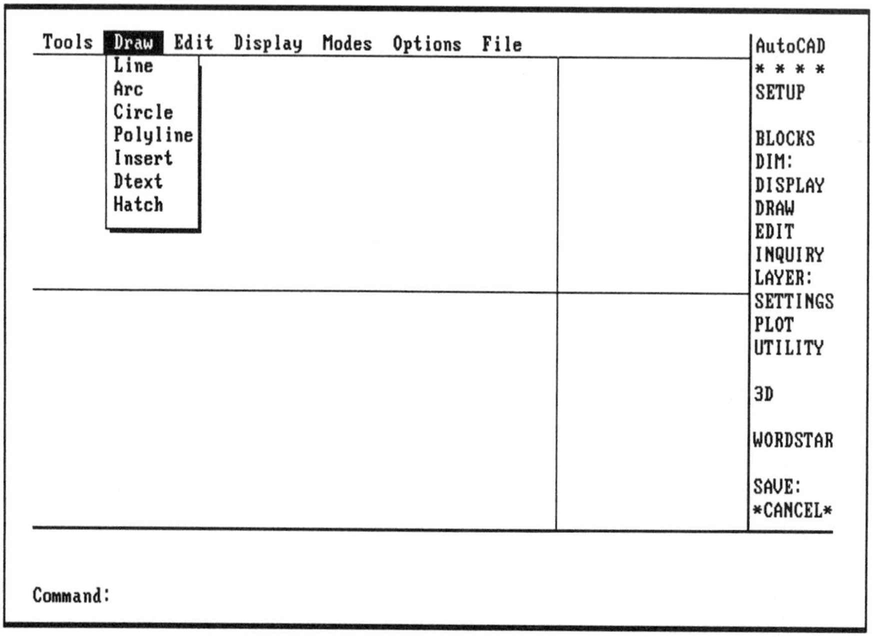

```
Tools  Draw  Edit  Display  Modes  Options  File        AutoCAD
       Line                                              * * * *
       Arc                                               SETUP
       Circle
       Polyline                                          BLOCKS
       Insert                                            DIM:
       Dtext                                             DISPLAY
       Hatch                                             DRAW
                                                         EDIT
                                                         INQUIRY
                                                         LAYER:
                                                         SETTINGS
                                                         PLOT
                                                         UTILITY

                                                         3D

                                                         WORDSTAR

                                                         SAVE:
                                                         *CANCEL*



       Command:
```

Figure C.1   AutoCAD's Pull-Down Menu Bar

The Structure of Pull-Down Menus

Pull-down menus are adjusted so that they are as wide as the longest word they contain. All words in a pull-down menu are left-justified within the display. They appear just below the selected keyword in the horizontal menu bar.

You can create pull-down menus that are as wide as your screen, but as you add pull-down menus and the number of keywords increases, you will be forced to use ever-narrowing menu displays. If you use all ten pull-down menu keywords in your horizontal menu bar, the keywords should average no more than eight letters each so that they will fit the display. If the keywords cannot fit, the rightmost ones will be ignored and will therefore be inaccessible.

Pull-down menu syntax is added to AutoCAD's ASCII menu file, ACAD.MNU. The pull-down menu command sequences are contained in as many as ten new menu sections that can be added to the ACAD.MNU file; they are given menu-section labels Pop1 through Pop10. In the Release 9 version of ACAD.MNU supplied by Autodesk, the new sections can be found immediately after the Buttons menu section. The following list contains the menu items found in Pop2, the Draw section:

```
***POP2
[Draw]
[Line]* ^C^C$S=X  $s=line line
[Arc]* ^C^C$S=X  $s=poparc arc
[Circle]* ^C^C$S=X  $s=popcircl circle
[Polyline]* ^C^C$S=X  $s=pline pline
[Insert] ^C^Csetvar attdia 1  $s=insert insert
[Dtext]* ^C^C$S=X  $s=Dtext Dtext
[Hatch] ^C^C$i=hatch1  $i=*
```

Notice the first line after the Pop2 menu-section label. This line contains the Draw keyword enclosed in brackets. The first line in any Pop menu section always contains only the single keyword in brackets. It is not followed by a command sequence. AutoCAD places the keyword into the horizontal menu bar. When that word is selected by the user, the commands following it in the menu section are displayed in the form of a pull-down menu on the screen. If no menu commands follow a keyword, the word will still appear, but the user will not be able to highlight or select it.

In ACAD.MNU, the command sequences in pull-down menus are structured like commands in the original AutoCAD screen menu. When the user moves the crosshairs to highlight the display of one of these commands and then selects it, the command sequence following the brackets will be executed by AutoCAD as if it had been typed at the keyboard. The command sequence can include changes in the display of the original screen menu.

A few new menu features are included in the example just shown. The asterisk that immediately follows the brackets is one new feature. In AutoCAD Release 9 only, if an asterisk follows the brackets in any menu command sequence, the selected command will repeat continuously until the user either selects a new command or presses Ctrl-C to cancel the command. This special Release 9 syntax can be used within the original screen menu as well as in the new pull-down menus.

If your pointing device does not have a Cancel button, you may want to add a Cancel sequence in a convenient location on your screen menu or pull-down menu. Then you can cancel repeating commands without selecting another command or typing Ctrl-C at the keyboard. One possibility is to add the following Cancel sequence to the last line of the root menu:

```
[*CANCEL*]^C^C
```

In this position, the Cancel sequence will remain active and visible through many screen menu changes. It will disappear if a menu subsection takes up all the lines available in the screen menu area, but it will reappear each time the root menu is referenced.

Another possibility is to change the command sequence following the asterisks below "AutoCAD" on the main menu. In a standard menu, this command sequence displays the Osnapb menu subsection. It can be changed as follows:

```
***SCREEN
**S
[AutoCAD]^C^C$S=S  $P4=P4A
[* * * *]^C^C
```

The display of the Osnapb menu subsection is duplicated in the Tools section of the pull-down menus, and can be accessed just as easily from there. These asterisks also remain in the screen menu area through most menu changes, so a handy Cancel sequence is available at almost any time. However, this approach may take some time to get used to.

Finally, you can edit the Tools pull-down menu, moving the Cancel sequence from the bottom of the menu to the top. This will make it a little easier to reach in a hurry.

Controlling the Pull-Down Menu Display

You do not necessarily have to select the word displayed in the horizontal menu bar in order to make a pull-down menu appear. A special menu command syntax can be used to cause the appearance of a pull-down menu:

$Pn=*

When you use this syntax, substitute the number of the desired Pop menu-section label for *n*. For example, to cause the appearance of the Pop3 menu, use this syntax:

P3=*

The syntax for the pull-down menu display can also be used from Auto-CAD's original screen menu if you wish. However, you must be certain that you move the crosshairs away from the original screen menu area quickly, or the pull-down menu will appear and quickly disappear again!

You can also create submenus within a pull-down menu. The syntax for displaying these submenus is similar to that for the subsection display used in the original screen menu. For example, here is the Pop4 section of ACAD.MNU, Display:

```
***POP4
[Display]
[Window]'zoom w
[Previous]'zoom p
[Dynamic]'zoom d
[Pan]'pan
```

In the next example, the pull-down menu has been revised to include some additional display commands:

```
***POP4
[Display]
[Attdisp:]^C^CATTDISP;
[Pan:]'PAN;
[Redraw:]'REDRAW;
[Regen:]^C^CREGEN;
[Rgenauto:]^C^CREGENAUTO;
[View:]'VIEW;
[Viewres:]'VIEWRES;
[Zoom:]'ZOOM;
```

This will work fine, but if the user selects Zoom from the pull-down menu, the options for the ZOOM command (Window, Dynamic, Previous, All, and so on) will have to be entered manually. You could, if you wish, include all the various Zoom options on the same pull-down menu, but a more attractive screen can be built by using a pull-down submenu.

In the following example, syntax lines have been added to the pull-down menu:

```
***POP4
**P4A
[Display]
[Attdisp:]^C^CATTDISP;
[Pan:]'PAN;
[Redraw:]'REDRAW;
[Regen:]^C^CREGEN;
[Rgenauto:]^C^CREGENAUTO;
[View:]'VIEW;
[Viewres:]^C^CVIEWRES;
[Zoom:]$P4=P4B  $P4=*

**P4B
[Zoom]
[Window]$P4=P4A 'zoom w;
[Previous]$P4=P4A 'zoom p;
[Dynamic]$P4=P4A 'zoom d;
[All]$P4=P4A 'zoom a;
[--]

[Display]$P4=P4A  $P4=*
```

Two new subsections, labeled P4A and P4B, have been created for this pull-down menu. The new subsection labels are preceded by two asterisks to differentiate them from the Pop4 menu-section label, which is preceded by three asterisks. The first subsection, P4A, will appear on the screen when the word Display is selected from the menu bar. Figure C.2 illustrates how the new Display menu appears on the screen.

Notice the command following [Zoom] in the syntax lines. This sequence changes the default subsection from P4A to P4B:

```
$P4=P4B
```

In order for the new subsection to appear immediately on the screen, this syntax is followed by

```
$P4=*
```

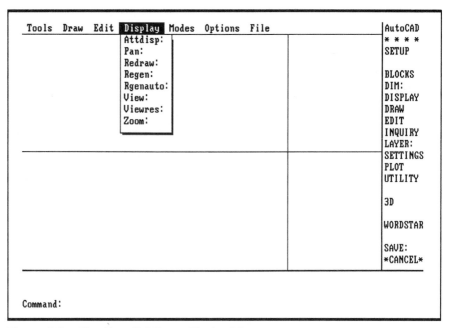

Figure C.2 The New Pull-Down Display Menu

Figure C.3 illustrates the appearance of the second menu subsection after the Zoom option has been selected. This new menu subsection—including the word Zoom displayed in the horizontal menu bar—will remain active during subsequent accessing of the horizontal menu bar, until the drawing session has been ended or the original menu subsection has been made active again.

In this example, the menu-subsection syntax is repeated when the user selects one of the options found on the new subsection P4B. This time, the syntax references the original subsection, P4A:

$P4=P4A

It is not necessary at this point to force the immediate display of the P4A subsection. It will appear when the user next highlights the horizontal menu bar. However, in case the user has selected the Zoom option (and hence, the ZOOM command) by accident, or in case the Zoom menu subsection is left active, the following command sequence is added to the P4B menu subsection:

[Display]$P4=P4A $P4=*

This sequence ensures that the user will be able to return to the original default menu subsection. As you build more complex menu structures,

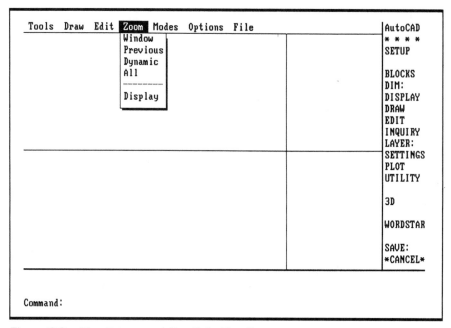

Figure C.3   The Submenu After Selecting Zoom

be certain that you always leave an "escape hatch" like this for the user.

You can have as many pull-down menu subsections as you like. Pull-down menus are always referenced by number, and you can change the display of any pull-down menu subsection from within any other menu subsection simply by referencing the correct menu-section number. Therefore, when you are building complex menu displays, be careful that you display only what you intend to display at any given time. Also keep in mind that only one pull-down menu can appear on the screen at any one time.

Other Pull-Down Menu Features

Two minor features can help you with the appearance of your pull-down menus. The first is a symbol composed of two hyphens surrounded by brackets:

[--]

When this symbol occupies a line in a pull-down menu, it causes a line separating the items in the pull-down menu to appear. You can choose to include a command sequence following this special symbol if you wish. In such a case, the command sequence will execute if the line itself is highlighted and selected by the user. If no command sequence follows this symbol, selecting the line will cause the pull-down menu to disappear from the screen.

Another pull-down menu feature allows you to adjust the display of words within brackets. When any bracketed item is preceded by a tilde (~), the item appears at a lower intensity than does a normal bracketed item. You can use this feature to identify short prompts or symbols that are not intended to represent commands, or for any other display purpose you wish. Except for their appearance on the screen, bracketed items preceded by a tilde will function like any other pull-down menu item. In the previous customized version of the pull-down Display menu, the syntax for creating a menu line is preceded by a tilde in order to slightly change its screen appearance.

CREATING ICON MENUS

Icon menus are likely to please the experienced user of AutoCAD because they represent a significant improvement for selecting blocks, shapes, text styles, or other forms of graphic input. After all, it is sometimes difficult to remember the exact difference between blocks with names like Part51A3 and Part52A3.

An *icon menu* offers a means for previewing graphic input selections before actually inserting them into a drawing. When an icon menu is displayed on the screen, up to 16 graphic options can be presented to the user, along with a special arrow character that moves to select the desired option. In addition, icon menus can reference other icon menus, making it possible to review any number of options in sequence. Figure C.4 illustrates an icon menu created using the standard ES shape file supplied with AutoCAD.

Creating an icon menu can be done in three simple steps:

1. Create an AutoCAD slide file for each option to be displayed in the icon menu. (You create a slide file by invoking AutoCAD's MSLIDE command followed by a file name of your choosing. The resulting slide file will contain a "snapshot" of whatever is displayed in the Drawing Editor when the command is invoked. Slide files are automatically given the file extension SLD.)

2. Use AutoCAD's SLIDELIB.EXE utility to combine the slides into a slide library file on the hard disk. (This step is optional.)

3. Add the syntax for displaying the icon menu to ACAD.MNU.

ADVANCED TECHNIQUES IN AUTOCAD

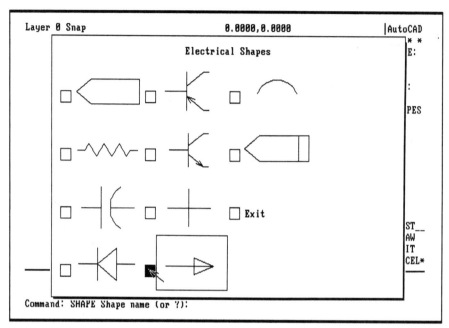

Figure C.4   ES Shapes Displayed in an Icon Menu

Each of these three steps is discussed in detail in the next sections. Once the slides have been created and ACAD.MNU has been changed, the display of the icon menu is handled automatically by AutoCAD. Fortunately, the icon menu syntax that must be added to ACAD.MNU is easy to learn; in most respects it follows conventions similar to other custom menu displays.

Creating the AutoCAD Slide Files

Slides to be used in icon menus are created in the same way you create any other AutoCAD slide, using the MSLIDE command and giving the slide file a unique name. Here are two tips to keep in mind:

- Keep the drawings as simple as you can. Don't use filled lines, solids, or complicated drawings. The display of your icon slide will be very small, and tiny details will be lost anyway. The simpler the slides, the faster the display of the icon menu.

- When making the slide, enlarge the graphic image to fill the entire Drawing Editor. If the image cannot fill the Editor, center the drawing in the Editor as well as you can.

To create the example icon menu shown in Figure C.4, slides were made of each shape in the AutoCAD standard slide file, ES.SHX. Each slide was given the same name as the shape it represented.

Once your slide files are created, you are ready to incorporate them into an icon menu. However, in order for your menu to work, all the slides must be on disk and available to AutoCAD. If you create a lot of icon menus, the dozens (or even hundreds) of slides will take up space on the hard disk and be quite cumbersome. Unfortunately, the disk-space problem is impossible to overcome at this time.

You can make it easier to manage groups of related slide files by combining them into a single disk file, called a *slide library*, by using a special utility provided with AutoCAD Release 9, SLIDELIB.EXE. A slide library file is not necessary for creating a working icon menu; however, it will speed up the display of icon menus and is therefore highly recommended.

Creating a Slide Library File

To create a slide library file, first use your word processor or text editor to create an ASCII file that contains a single-spaced list of the slide file names you intend to combine into the library file.

To create the library file used in the example ES icon file, the following list of slide file names was entered into an ASCII file named ESNAMES. You can name your own ASCII file anything you like.

```
c:\acad\CON1
c:\acad\RES
c:\acad\CAP
c:\acad\DIODE
c:\acad\PNP
c:\acad\NPN
c:\acad\MARK
c:\acad\ARROW
c:\acad\JUMP
c:\acad\CON2
```

The file extension SLD is assumed for each of these slide file names. The subdirectory path name for each slide (in this example, C:\ACAD) is included, although the path name will not be saved in the library file.

You can, if you wish, combine slides from several subdirectories into a single slide library file. Also, if you know that slides will be contained on the default subdirectory when you create the library file, you can safely omit the path name.

Once the ESNAMES file is created, be sure that it is copied onto the same subdirectory as the SLIDELIB.EXE file. Log onto that subdirectory and enter the following command:

SLIDELIB ES < ESNAMES

The first word in this line is, of course, the command to execute SLIDELIB.EXE. The next word is the name of the library file to be created. In this case, that file will be named ES and will be given a file extension of SLB automatically. (You may name your library files anything you like, but keeping the names short will simplify subsequent typing.) You need not specify the file extension in the command line. The third word on the line is the name of the ASCII list of slide names to be combined into the library file. It is preceded by the < symbol, indicating to DOS that the ESNAMES file should be used as input by SLIDELIB.EXE.

Once SLIDELIB.EXE has completed execution, the library file ES.SLB will be created, containing all the slides in the list. You can then copy the original slide files and the list of slide names onto a backup disk and erase them from the hard disk. This will open up some hard-disk space for you. Do not erase the slide files without backing them up first.

If you wish to add slides to the library, the only way to do so is to create a brand-new slide library to replace the old one. Thus, you may need to use the original slide files and the list of names again. There is no procedure for simply adding slides to an existing library file, nor is there a procedure for deleting individual slides from the library file.

You can view the library slides by responding to AutoCAD's VSLIDE prompt. Simply reference the library as part of the slide name, as in the following example:

ES(CON1)

The library name is followed by the slide name, which is contained in parentheses. No spaces are used to separate the names. A path name can be included as well in response to the VSLIDE prompt:

C:\ACAD\SLIDES\ES(CON1)

Any slide that is part of a library can be referenced with this syntax.

Creating the Icon Menu in ACAD.MNU

When you have created your slides and placed them in a library file, you are ready to modify ACAD.MNU so that it will include a reference to the new icon menu. All icon menus are contained within a new menu section labeled Icon. Each icon menu is a unique menu subsection within the

Icon menu section. In the Release 9 version of ACAD.MNU supplied by Autodesk, the Icon menu section follows the Pop menu sections.

To add the ES menu icon to ACAD.MNU, first locate the Icon menu section. The first few lines may look like this:

```
***icon
**as
[Select Ashade Command]
[acad(camera)]^C^C$S=X  $S=CAMERA camera \\\$i=as  $i=*
[acad(point)]^C^C$S=X  $S=LIGHTS LIGHT \p \$i=as  $i=*
[acad(directed)]^C^C$S=X  $S=LIGHTS LIGHT \d \\$i=as  $i=*
[acad(scene)]^C^C$S=X  $S=ACTION scene
[acad(filmroll)]^C^C$S=X  $S=ACTION filmroll
[ Exit]^c^c
```

You need to insert a new subsection label, ES, just underneath the Icon menu label as follows:

```
***icon
**ES
```

Again, the subsection label is preceded by two asterisks to distinguish it from the menu-section label. Your next step is to add the title of the icon menu in brackets, on the line just below the ES menu-subsection label as follows:

```
***icon
**ES
[Electrical Shapes]
```

Each line that follows this title line begins with the name of a slide in brackets. Following the slide names, you can type in any command sequence that you want executed, when that particular slide is picked from the icon menu. The following example illustrates this: here, the command sequence is the SHAPE command, followed by the selected shape name:

```
***icon
**ES
[Electrical Shapes]
[es(con1)]^C^CSHAPE;CON1;
[es(res)]^C^CSHAPE;RES;
[es(cap)]^C^CSHAPE;CAP;
[es(diode)]^C^CSHAPE;DIODE;
[es(pnp)]^C^CSHAPE;PNP;
```

```
[es(npn)]^C^CSHAPE;NPN;
[es(mark)]^C^CSHAPE;MARK;
[es(arrow)]^C^CSHAPE;ARROW;
[es(jump)]^C^CSHAPE;JUMP;
[es(con2)]^C^CSHAPE;CON2;
[#Exit]^C^C
```

The last line of this icon menu contains the word Exit in brackets, followed by a Cancel sequence. This removes the display of the icon menu from the screen if the user selected it by accident. This line does not mean there is an Exit slide. The first character within the brackets is a space; when AutoCAD reads the initial space inside the brackets, it understands that there is no slide to be displayed, and that the word within the brackets should be displayed on the icon menu instead.

Icon menus are flexible. You can combine different libraries of slides in the same icon menu. You can also combine slides that are not in library files with slides that are in library files. In addition, you can reference slide names by including a full path name if you choose, as in the following example:

```
[res2]^C^CINSERT;RES2;
[c:\acad\slides\insul2]^C^CINSERT;INSUL2;
[es(con1)]^C^CSHAPE;CON1;
[es(res)]^C^CSHAPE;RES;
```

Here, slide files named RES2 (on the default subdirectory) and INSUL2 (on the C:\ACAD\SLIDES subdirectory) have been referenced along with slides that are part of the ES.SLB library file (also on the default subdirectory).

Remember that the command sequences following the slide names must be valid AutoCAD menu command sequences, and they are subject to all of the rules that pertain to custom menu commands and macros. You can include up to 16 individual command sequences on a single icon menu. A technique for using more than one icon menu to handle larger numbers of command sequences is discussed in the following section.

Displaying the Icon Menu on the Screen

Once the icon menu has been set up in ACAD.MNU, the only step that remains is to include a reference to it in another command sequence of your choosing. The reference can be placed in a pull-down menu section, an original screen menu section, or both.

The following is a typical icon menu reference for the ES icon menu:

```
[ESHAPES]$i=es $i=*
```

Notice the similarities to pull-down menu references. In this case, the first reference causes the icon menu subsection ES to become active:

$i=es

The letter i follows the dollar sign; a number is not used because there can be only one icon menu section. An equal sign follows the letter i, followed by the name of the icon menu subsection. This syntax lets Auto-CAD know that icon menu subsection ES is now *active*, or capable of being displayed.

With icon menus, when a menu subsection has been referenced, you will almost always want to display it on the screen immediately. The reference that does this is similar to the pull-down menu's display reference:

$i = *

When AutoCAD reads this syntax, the active icon menu subsection is displayed immediately, and the user is free to choose one of its options.

You can also include icon menu references in icon menus. For example, if you had more than 16 options and needed two or more icon menus for them, you could include the following command sequence as one of the options in the first icon menu:

[Next]$i=es2 $i = *

The icon menu would then display the Next label (because of the leading space). Selecting this label would display another icon menu subsection, labeled ES2. The icon menu ES2 could also contain an option, as in the following example:

[Previous]$i=es $i = *

This would allow the user to return to the first icon menu. Both menus should contain an exit sequence as well, to allow the option of not selecting anything:

[Exit] ^c ^c

Pressing Ctrl-C at the keyboard also causes the icon menu to disappear from the screen.

You will find that you can display complex series of icon menus if you wish. The standard version of the Release 9 ACAD.MNU file includes a series of three icon menu subsections for hatch patterns. These subsections are useful for study; the slide files used for them are contained in the file ACAD.SLB. Unfortunately, the individual slides contained in this library are not included on the AutoCAD program diskettes, so this library file cannot be modified. If you wish to add to or modify the standard AutoCAD icon menus, you can do so by using your own slide files or library files in combination with ACAD.SLB.

REDEFINING AUTOCAD COMMANDS

Release 9 offers you the opportunity to safely change the standard AutoCAD commands. This is a two-step process:

1. Invoke AutoCAD's new UNDEFINE command, followed by the name of the command you wish to undefine. This will disable the standard AutoCAD command for the remainder of the editing session.

2. Load an AutoLISP routine that defines a new AutoCAD command with the same name.

When this process has been completed, invoking the newly defined AutoCAD command will execute the AutoLISP routine instead.

You can always execute the standard AutoCAD command simply by preceding the command with a period (as in .END or .DRAW). You can also restore the standard command by using AutoCAD's REDEFINE command followed by the name of the standard command.

This feature can be used to add special prompts or additional functions to standard AutoCAD commands. For example, using the LOG.LSP routine shown in Figure C.5, you could create a new AutoCAD command called LOG. The LOG command will prompt for the user's name, then redefine the END command so that, in addition to ending the session, END will create a listing of pertinent editing information. Also, the redefined END command will append the listing to an ASCII file of listings from previous sessions, thus maintaining a simple diary of AutoCAD edits. LOG.LSP can be added to ACAD.LSP, and it will load automatically at the start of each drawing session.

The LOG.LSP routine stores the total amount of time in the Drawing Editor to a memory variable named stime. Next, it creates a new AutoCAD command named LOG. When the user invokes LOG, AutoCAD prompts for the user's name. After receiving the user's name, AutoCAD undefines the standard END command. It then redefines the command so that when END is invoked, it calculates the time spent editing the current drawing and then appends the user's name, the date, the drawing's name, and the editing time to a file named DIARY on the ACAD subdirectory. This file can be used as an ongoing record of all AutoCAD edits.

```
(setq stime
      (getvar "TDINDWG")
)
(defun C:LOG()
  (setq oldcmd (getvar "CMDECHO"))
  (setvar "CMDECHO" 0)
  (if (/= uname nil)
      (progn
          (setq temp uname)
          (setq uname
                (getstring t (strcat "\nYour Name? <" uname ">: "))
          )
          (if (or
                (= uname nile)
                (= uname "")
              )
              (setq uname temp)
          )
      )
  )
  (while (or
            (= uname nil)
            (= uname "")
         )
         (setq uname
                (getstring t "\nYour Name? ")
         )
  )
)
(command "UNDEFINE"
         "END"
)
(defun C:END()
  (setq uname (strcat uname "
  (setq x (getvar "DWGNAME"))
  (setq etime
      (* (- (getvar "TDINDWG") stime) 24.0)
  )
  (setq month
      (substr (rtos (getvar "CDATE")) 5 2)
  )
  (setq day
      (substr (rtos (getvar "CDATE")) 7 2)
  )
  (setq year
      (substr (rtos (getvar "CDATE")) 3 2)
  )
  (setq diary (open "c:/acad/diary" "a")) ; You may, if you choose,
                                          ; substitute a path and
                                          ; file name of your own
                                          ; for "c:/acad/diary"


  (write-line (strcat "User: "
                      (substr uname 1 25)
                      " -- Date: "
                       month "/" day "/" year
              )
              diary
  )
  (write-line (strcat "Drawing: " x) diary)
  (write-line (strcat "Editing time: "
                      (itoa (fix etime))
                      " hours, "
                      (itoa (fix (setq mins
```

Figure C.5   The LOG.LSP Routine

```
                                             (* (- etime (fix etime)) 60.0)
                                       )
                                 )
                           )
                           " minutes, "
                           (itoa (fix (* (- mins (fix mins)) 60.0)))
                           " seconds."
                     )
                     diary
            )
      (write-line "* * * * * * *" diary)
      (close diary)
      (command ".END")
   )
   (setvar "CMDECHO" oldcmd)
   (princ)
)
```

Figure C.5   The LOG.LSP Routine (continued)

Here are some points worth noting in this routine:

- Within the redefined END command, the COMMAND function includes the AutoCAD standard END command preceded by a period (.END). This ensures that the correct END command is invoked at the proper time. If you choose to redefine AutoCAD commands, it is a safe practice to precede all standard commands called from within LISP routines with periods. Then a standard command will be invoked whenever you want.

- Do not use AutoCAD's UNDEFINE command in ACAD.LSP unless it is nested within a DEFUN function, as in this routine. Otherwise, UNDEFINE will cause problems.

- Beware of using such interactive functions as GETSTRING in ACAD.LSP, unless these functions are also nested within DEFUN. Problems may arise, especially if you attempt to use GETSTRING with the optional argument that allows spaces.

INDEX

D

M

Character Set (00–7F) Quick Reference

DECIMAL VALUE	➡	0	16	32	48	64	80	96	112
⬇	HEXA DECIMAL VALUE	0	1	2	3	4	5	6	7
0	0	BLANK (NULL)	►	BLANK (SPACE)	0	@	P	`	p
1	1	☺	◄	!	1	A	Q	a	q
2	2	☻	↕	"	2	B	R	b	r
3	3	♥	‼	#	3	C	S	c	s
4	4	♦	¶	$	4	D	T	d	t
5	5	♣	§	%	5	E	U	e	u
6	6	♠	▬	&	6	F	V	f	v
7	7	•	↨	'	7	G	W	g	w
8	8	◘	↑	(	8	H	X	h	x
9	9	○	↓	)	9	I	Y	i	y
10	A	◎	→	*	:	J	Z	j	z
11	B	♂	←	+	;	K	[	k	{
12	C	♀	∟	,	<	L	\	l	¦
13	D	♪	↔	—	=	M	]	m	}
14	E	♫	▲	.	>	N	∧	n	~
15	F	☼	▼	/	?	O	_	o	△

Character Set (88–FF) Quick Reference

DECIMAL VALUE ➡	HEXA DECIMAL VALUE ⬇	128 / 8	144 / 9	160 / A	176 / B	192 / C	208 / D	224 / E	240 / F
0	0	Ç	É	á	░	└	╨	∝	≡
1	1	ü	æ	í	▒	┴	╤	β	±
2	2	é	Æ	ó	▓	┬	╥	Γ	≥
3	3	â	ô	ú	│	├	╙	π	≤
4	4	ä	ö	ñ	┤	─	╘	Σ	∫
5	5	à	ò	Ñ	╡	┼	╒	σ	∫
6	6	å	û	ª	╢	╞	╓	µ	÷
7	7	ç	ù	º	╖	╟	╫	τ	≈
8	8	ê	ÿ	¿	╕	╚	╪	Φ	°
9	9	ë	Ö	⌐	╣	╔	┘	θ	•
10	A	è	Ü	¬	║	╩	┌	Ω	·
11	B	ï	¢	½	╗	╦	█	δ	√
12	C	î	£	¼	╝	╠	▄	∞	ⁿ
13	D	ì	¥	¡	╜	═	▌	φ	²
14	E	Ä	₧	«	╛	╬	▐	∈	■
15	F	Å	ƒ	»	┐	╧	▀	∩	BLANK 'FF'

Technical Reference Manual, pp.7-12–7-13, © 1984 International Business Machines Corporation

DISKETTE ORDER FORM

If you would like to use the examples shown in this book, but do not want to type them out yourself, you may obtain a copy of them on a 5¼" disk. If your version of AutoCAD is 2.5 or later, the disk includes both SHP and SHX files for an outline-bold text font. Please fill out the order form below and return it with a check or money order for $15.00 (plus applicable city and county sales taxes, California residents only). Allow three weeks for delivery.

Mail the completed form to

Thomas Enterprises, ltd.
628 Clement Street
San Francisco, CA 94118

Please send _____ LISP File Diskette(s) to:

Name: _____

Company: _____

Address: _____

_____

City: _____

State: _____ Zip Code: _____

AutoCAD Version (specify):

(Font not available for Version 2.18)

2.18 _____   2.5 _____   2.6 _____

Release 9 _____

_____ disks @ $15.00 ea.: $ _____

Sales Tax (CA residents only): $ _____

Total: $ _____

Enclose check or money order payable to: Thomas Enterprises

Thomas Enterprises, ltd. makes no representation or warranties with respect to the contents of the above referenced software and specifically disclaims any implied warranties of merchantability or fitness for any particular purpose. By the act of ordering, purchaser agrees that in any event the sole liability of Thomas Enterprises, ltd. is limited to replacement of the original diskettes should they prove defective within 30 days of shipment.

TO JOIN THE SYBEX MAILING LIST OR ORDER BOOKS

PLEASE COMPLETE THIS FORM

1 _____

NAME_____

COMPANY_____

STREET_____

CITY_____STATE___ZIP_____

___Please mail me more details of SYBEX titles.

2 _____

ORDER FORM   (There is no obligation to order)

PLEASE SEND ME THE FOLLOWING:

TITLE   QTY   PRICE

_____

_____

_____

_____

TOTAL BOOK ORDER   _____ $ _____

SHIPPING AND HANDLING PLEASE ADD
$2.00 PER BOOK VIA UPS

FOR OVERSEAS REGISTERED MAIL
ADD $15.00 PLUS $3.25 REGISTRATION   _____
FEE

CALIFORNIA RESIDENTS PLEASE ADD
6.5% SALES TAX.   _____

TOTAL AMOUNT PAYABLE

( )CHECK ENCLOSED   ( )VISA   _____

( )MASTERCARD   ( )AMERICAN EX-
PRESS

ACCOUNT NUMBER_____

EXPIRY DATE_____DAYTIME PHONE_____

CUSTOMER SIGNATURE

_____

HELP US PUBLISH THE BOOKS THAT YOU NEED BY CHECKING BOXES 3-7

3 _____

CHECK AREA OF COMPUTER INTEREST

1___BUSINESS SOFTWARE

2___TECHNICAL PROGRAMMING

3___OTHER:_____

4 _____

THE FACTOR THAT WAS MOST IMPORTANT IN YOUR SELECTION:

1___THE SYBEX NAME   2___QUALITY

3___PRICE 4___EXTRA FEATURES

5___COMPREHENSIVENESS6___STYLE/APPEARANCE

7___CLEAR WRITING STYLE

8___OTHER_____

5 _____

OTHER COMPUTER TITLES YOU WOULD LIKE TO SEE IN PRINT

_____

_____

_____

6 _____

___OCCUPATION

1___PROGRAMMER 2___SENIOR EXECUTIVE

3___COMPUTER CONSULTANT

4___MIDDLE MANAGEMENT

5___ENGINEER/TECHNICAL 6___CLERICAL/SERVICE

7___BUSINESS OWNER/SELF EMPL 8___TEACHER

9___HOMEMAKER 10___RETIRED

11___STUDENT 12___OTHER:_____

7 _____

CHECK YOUR LEVEL OF COMPUTER USE

1___NEW TO COMPUTERS

2___INFREQUENT COMPUTER USER

3___FREQUENT USER OF ONE SOFTWARE PACKAGE:

NAME_____

4___FREQUENT USER OF MANY SOFTWARE PACKAGES

5___"POWER USER"

6___PROFESSIONAL PROGRAMMER

FOR U.K. ORDERS, PLEASE MAIL TO
LONGMANS U.K. FOR OTHER COUNTRIES,
PLEASE MAIL TO YOUR DISTRIBUTOR..

Please fold, seal, and mail to SYBEX _____

8 _____

OTHER COMMENTS: